Safavid Iran

Safavid Iran

Rebirth of a Persian Empire

ANDREW J. NEWMAN

I.B. TAURIS

LONDON · NEW YORK

Preface and Acknowledgements

I have been interested in Safavid Iran since 1977 when, as a first-year graduate student at the University of California, Los Angeles, searching for a PhD topic, I read Laurence Lockhart's 1958 description of the well-known Twelver Shi'i scholar Muhammad Baqir Majlisi (d. 1699) as 'an extremely bigoted *mujtahid*', 'a rigid and fanatical formalist', an opponent of all philosophical inquiry and a persecutor of Jews and Armenians. Echoing the decades' old judgement of E. G. Browne (d. 1926), Lockhart stated that Majlisi's influence was such as to render Safavid Iran unable to respond to the attacks which culminated in the fall of the capital of Isfahan to the Afghans in 1722. Although alone the 1982–3 Beirut edition of *Bihar al-Anwar*, Majlisi's massive, Arabic-language collection of the *hadith*s of the twelve imams, runs to some 110 volumes, Lockhart's source for such sweeping characterisations was a single, rather short, essay of Majlisi composed in Persian.[1]

My 1980 oral examinations, the passing of which allowed me to commence my dissertation research, were partly predicated on a proposal to examine Majlisi's life and works. In the process of that research I discovered a dearth of secondary-source works on Twelver Shi'ism and the 1986 PhD became, instead, an examination of developments in Shi'i jurisprudence from the disappearance of the twelfth Imam in 873–4 to the years immediately following the establishment of Twelver Shi'ism as the realm's official faith following the 1501 capture of Tabriz by the first Safavid shah, Ismail. Several subsequent articles on Shi'ism in the Safavid period did not immediately relate to Majlisi. When I returned to Majlisi, while preparing a paper for the Third International Round Table on Safavid Persia, which I convened in 1998 in Edinburgh, I discovered that although Western scholars had yet to commence any systematic examination of his many, mostly Arabic-language, works the aforementioned sweeping characterisations of the man and his legacy had, in fact, assumed the status of 'received wisdom' in the field.

In 2000, in the aftermath of sending in the proofs for my first book, on Twelver doctrine and practice in the late ninth and early tenth centuries,[2] I.B.Tauris asked me to write a new general history of the

Safavid period. Given the logarithmic expansion in the scholarly interest in the period since the Iranian revolution, as discussed below, this was a daunting challenge for someone whose research interests in the period had to date involved research into apparently arcane aspects of Shi'i religious discourse.

In attempting to rise to this challenge I owe much to the comments, criticisms and assistance of such well-respected figures in Iranian and Safavid history as Iraj Afshar, Sussan Babaie, Kathryn Babayan, Stephen Blake, Sheila Canby, Ehsan Eshraqi, Willem Floor, Gene Garthwaite, Edmund Herzig, Robert Hillenbrand, Rasul Jafariyan, Paul Luft, Rudi Matthee, Sandy Morton, Sholeh Quinn, Mansur Sefatgol and Maria Szuppe. These, along with many others, may well not recognise their own contributions to, and in any case are to be absolved of responsibility for any aspect of, the present volume, let alone my failure to adhere to the original deadline for its submission. The latter has been met only with the utmost patience and forbearance of I.B.Tauris's Publisher and Managing Editor Mr Iradj Bagherzade, my patient editor Dr Lester Crook and his assistant Ms Clare Dubois.

I would also like to thank Dr Ian Revie, Head of the School of Languages, Literatures and Cultures of the University of Edinburgh for his help in securing the support of the School's Research Fund to assist with the reproduction of the dustjacket.

I must also thank my wife and, especially, my daughter, to whom this volume is dedicated, for their constant patience and encouragement over the last four-plus years.

Upon my graduation from Dartmouth College in New Hampshire in 1974, having never been West of Harrisburg, Pennsylvania, let alone outside the US, with the encouragement of Dartmouth Professor Gene Garthwaite I journeyed to, and spent two years in Iran. There, teaching English and travelling throughout the country, I became acquainted with something of Persian language, culture and history. As many travellers in 'the East', my sojourn was also an occasion for introspection and, when I commenced my graduate studies in California in 1977, with the encouragement of Afaf Marsot, Peter Gran, Amin Banani and Nikki Keddie and such colleagues as Yahya Sadowski, Fred Lawson, Ken Cuno, Halah Fattah and others, I became as interested in the study of the study of the history of Iran and the region as a whole as in the memorisation of legions of names and dates.

In the years since and, especially, in the aftermath of the Iranian revolution, the Safavid period has taken on meanings for Iranians different to those it has in the West. The present volume is directed primarily to the Western-language audience, including the growing number of specialists in the various sub-disciplines of Safavid Studies and those in other branches of Middle Eastern Studies but also, and in particular, the non-specialist interested in Iran and the region generally. Hence any 'scientific' effort to reconcile the all-too many efforts to transliterate Arabic and Persian words into English by recourse to a complicated system of diacritical marks is eschewed in favour of somewhat idiosyncratic system of transliteration based loosely on that used in the *International Journal of Middle Eastern Studies* (*IJMES*). Dates also are generally given only in their 'AD' version, except for occasional dates of publication; where this makes for flagrant inaccuracy, two Christian years may be given as, for example, in AD 873–4, corresponding to the Hijri 260, the year of the disappearance of the twelfth Shi'i Imam. Moreover, while footnotes do refer to Persian and Arabic sources, care is also taken to refer to available translations of primary sources as well as secondary works by specialists available in English and other Western languages. The bibliographical convention of omitting names of publishers is followed throughout.

Edinburgh
July 2005

available to earlier researchers. Some two dozen Persian-language 'court' chronicles produced over the period are now available, most in published form (see Appendix II). These and such other Persian-language sources as, for example, court/diplomatic correspondence and religious endowment (*vaqf*) documents vie for attention with the accounts of contemporary Western travellers and residents in to Iran, written variously in English, French, German, Italian, Latin, Russian and Polish. There are also the records of contemporary Western commercial and political interests, composed in Dutch, English, French, German, Portuguese and Spanish, and a substantial body of Armenian-language material. Although Safavid-period religious figures composed some of their works, especially those of a 'popular' nature, in Persian, most Shi'i clerics of the day, whether resident in Iran or abroad, composed their scholarly works in Arabic. The contemporary biographical dictionaries of the period's clerics, nearly all of which are now available in published form, were produced in both languages. Given the interaction between the Ottomans and the Safavids, there are also Turkish-language political/military, commercial and religious sources, for the most part still stunningly under-utilised. Important 'non-textual' sources include, for example, buildings, monument inscriptions, coins, pottery, carpets, paintings, metalwork and manuscript and single-page illustrations.

The post-Revolution growth in scholarly interest in the period, in both the West and Iran, together with the growth of available source materials has in fact encouraged the appearance of sub-disciplines within the field. Where before 1978 study of the period focused mainly on the period's political history, the field's scholarly output now includes studies on the Safavid economy and military, on the political relations between Safavid Iran and its neighbours as well as of Safavid socio-cultural history. The latter, construed broadly, encompasses research on the family and women, tribal life and customs, religious life and discourse, religious minorities, science and medicine, art and architecture, painting, metalwork, ceramics, carpets, history-writing and court-sponsored and popular literary expression. If several of these sub-disciplines are at present somewhat sparsely populated others are sufficiently well-developed as to have generated a series of lively internal 'debates'.

Despite the recent enormous growth in scholars and sources and notwithstanding the efforts of the Round Tables' organisers to encourage discussions between scholars of the field's different sub-disciplines, Safavid studies nevertheless remains bifurcated between studies of the socio-economic and political realms and those of the cultural: the contributions of the one group of scholars still generally do not figure in the analyses, and often not even the footnotes and bibliographies, of the other.

More importantly, regardless of their specific areas of research, most authors continue to subscribe to the conventional understanding of the period which is outlined above and whose origins date, at least, to the early years of the last century. Thus, for example, the political boundaries of the period are still accepted as demarcated by the twin politico-military events of Tabriz' capture and Isfahan's fall. Implicitly identifying the geographical boundaries of the modern Iranian state as 'normal', scholars project these back to the Safavid period and label variations therein over the period as 'territorial gain' or 'loss'. Indeed, in reference to the Safavids the continued use of the term 'state' itself, connoting, for example, fixed, internationally recognised borders, a common language and a monopoly at the centre of the use of force, is itself particularly problematic. In fact, to take but one example, Qizilbash tribal elements and the early shahs especially were more comfortable in dialects of Turkish, native Iranians (Tajiks) spoke Persian and the primary language of the established faith was Arabic.

Perhaps most strikingly, post-1980 works on particular aspects of Safavid history – socio-economic, political or 'cultural' – continue to refer to the period in terms of the inherent and continuous conflict between Qizilbash and Tajik, of the repeated, largely vain, efforts of various shahs to curb the political/military and spiritual influence of Qizilbash leaders and levies and, particularly beginning in the seventeenth century, the growing imbalance between *khassa* and *mamalik* lands, the rise of a 'shadow' government based in the haram, the growing intolerance of Safavid Shi'ism and the presence of 'strong' or 'weak' rulers. The second Safavid century in particular continues to be portrayed as having begun with a burst of cultural and intellectual achievement, in an atmosphere of military, political, and economic stability – ascribed solely to the presence of Abbas I, a 'strong' ruler – only to end in the darkness of fanatical religious orthodoxy amid military, political, and economic chaos and 'weak' leadership at the centre. Whatever their specific sub-discipline, scholars of the period continue to take as given the inevitable decline and fall of the Safavid 'state', as represented by the 1722 Afghan capture of Isfahan.[9]

Preoccupation with the Safavid 'fall' and, especially, dating the onset of Safavid 'decline' ever earlier in the period, is reinforced by recourse to the critiques of the Safavid system on offer in both Persian-language historical chronicles and a variety of Western-language sources.

However, of the Persian-language sources on which Western writers have relied to explain the 'decline' of the 'state', especially during the reigns of Shah Sulayman (reg. 1666/68–94) and Sultan Husayn (reg. 1694–1722), most were composed well after the 1722 capture of Isfahan[10] and the varied agendas of their authors have yet to be acknowledged and explored as Quinn has done with earlier court chronicles.[11]

Western scholars of the period have also relied heavily on the accounts of various Western residents in, and travellers to, Iran over the period. Absent from these Western-language studies is any critical discussion of the information and 'analyses' on offer therein even though, as the few examples to be cited herein suggest, the authors of these accounts frequently contradict each other on trends, events, facts and figures, present as historical 'fact' information gathered well after the occurrence of the events in question, or in such detail – about life and politics at court, for example, including life in and the influence of the haram – as to beg credulity, and write from vantage points or possess political, religious and/or commercial agendas which render their contributions less than 'objective'.[12] Similarly, the recent focus on Western economic data for the period, if long overdue, has, nevertheless facilitated according a key, if not determinist, role in Safavid 'decline' to such purely economic trends and events as the movement of specie and the trade in silk on a par with that which gripped Ottoman Studies from the late 1970s as it explored the roots of Ottoman 'decline' under the influence of I. Wallerstein's 1974 *The Modern World System* and the subsequent emergence of 'world system theory'.[13]

If Ottoman studies, which for so long laboured under the burden of 'decline studies', has begun to move on,[14] the suggestion that the end of Safavid dynasty was the inevitable result of an increasingly dysfunctional society's inability to respond to an increasingly severe series of internal and external challenges remains well accepted. Indeed, within the larger Western-language field of Middle Eastern Studies general histories of the region reproduce the paradigm without reference to secondary, let alone primary, sources.[15]

An alternative synthesis

A study of the period which simply 'updated' Savory's volume by adding the detail available in, and references to, all of the many primary and secondary sources on the period which have appeared since 1980 would only reinforce, in overlong form, the teleological framework of analysis which continues to dominate the West's study of the period. On the other hand, a study whose primary goal was to challenge individual aspects of the conventional approach to the period or render a 'verdict' on one or more of the 'debates' within the field's many sub-disciplines risks both being arcane and overly negative, particularly for the non-specialist reader for whom the present work is at least partly intended.

Taking the lead from the avowed goals of the several Round Tables to date, here the Safavid story is told, first, by adopting a multi-disciplinary approach to address trends and events in and across the socio-economic, political and 'cultural' realms and, secondly, by rejecting the conventional preoccupation with Safavid 'decline' to ask, instead, why the Safavids endured as long as they did. Indeed, if the 1501–1722 dates are accepted, the Safavid was the longest-lasting of Islamic Iran's various polities, outlasting such of its Western contemporaries as the Tudors, the

Stewarts and the Republic in England or, in France, the Valois and their successors the Bourbons.[16]

Dispensing also with the term 'state', given the problems therewith cited above, such terms as 'project', 'polity' and 'realm' appear frequently herein in relation to the Safavid enterprise. These are intended to underline the manner in which from the very first different, and potentially mutually conflicting, interests and agendas were intertwined with each other and with the fortunes of the Safavid house, itself embodied in, and led by, the shah. The distinctly heterogeneous 'discourse' of the shah – that discourse itself comprising both statements and actions – reflected and thereby legitimised the individual discourses of each of the polity's constituent elements and facilitated both the recognition and incorporation of 'new' constituencies into the project, even as extant 'members' retained prominence therein, and the transcendence and thus the subordination of each.[17] The Safavid story is the story of the growth of its composite constituencies: where from well prior to the capture of Tabriz throughout most of the sixteenth century allied Turk political-military and Tajik administrative interests dominated the project's political centre, Sultan Husayn commanded the recognition of an array of foreign commercial, political and religious interests as well as Turk and non-Turk tribal, Tajik, and *ghulam* military, political and administrative and other court elements, and indigenous Muslim, Christian and foreign artisanal and commercial-political classes.

Over the period fealty to the person of the sitting shah bespoke acceptance of both the presence of others of the realm's constituencies and the hierarchical manner of their arrangement around his mediating and transcendent headship which obtained over his reign and the resulting broader project itself, even if the occasionally incompatible interests of some of these constituencies caused intermittent outbreak of internal discord.

Only disloyalty to the authority and legitimate rule of the sitting shah constituted treason, not only to himself and to the Safavid house but also, and more importantly, to the very configuration of constituencies whose precise ordering around the head of the house underlay the rule of the shah in question. Those who put forth such challenges therefore paid the ultimate price. Indeed loyalty was as valued as competence if not more so; loyal incompetents, generally, were only replaced. If they suffered worse, the consequence of their transgressions were seldom visited upon their progeny. Otherwise, considerable political autonomy at the central and provincial level was the norm and individual discourse, especially of the broadly construed 'cultural' nature – artistic and religious, for example – however discordant, was tolerated. Indeed, as will be seen, the centre frequently strove to identify simultaneously with the more contradictory of those of the realm's independent discourses which did not overtly challenge its authority and thus rise above, and transcend, the mêlée.

As to the above-mentioned outbreaks of internal discord, in the first Safavid century especially the death of the sitting ruler, which removed the single individual around whose inclusive and transcendent discourse the realm's constituencies had achieved an arrangement, was most often the cause thereof. Indeed, perhaps the greatest challenges to the polity came with the deaths of Ismail and Tahmasp, the consequent breakdown of the precise configuration of the realm's constituencies, especially among and between the Qizilbash tribes, and a consequent political and military disorder which encouraged the Ottoman and/or Uzbek incursions. In these two instances especially, the support of the core Turk–Tajik alliance for the overall project remained solid, however. In fact over the longer term this alliance oversaw and acquiesced both in changes in the core constituencies over the period to endow an ever larger number of elements with an interest in the Safavid project and in the steady institutionalisation of the realm's political processes which underlay increasingly peaceful successions over the period. Such developments, in the context of the economic benefits accruing to the realm with the 1555 Amasya treaty with the Ottomans and, especially, the nearly century-long peace with the Ottomans which commenced in 1639, underpinned the increasing domestic political stability which marked the second Safavid century.

A myriad of discourses, one ruler to unite them

The inclusivity at the heart of the longevity of the Safavid project was hardly unknown in Islamic history. In the early ninth century, for example, the Abbasid caliphs included in their personal retinues scholars of different religious backgrounds including, famously, non-Muslim medical practitioners, and sponsored the translation into Arabic of a myriad of non-Arabic philosophical and scientific texts.

Given its status as a geographical cross-roads, pre-Islamic and, in the Islamic period, pre-Safavid Iran had its own history of ethnic, religious and cultural diversity and inclusivity. Most recently, in the aftermath of both the Mongol conquests of the thirteenth century and those of Timur (d. 1405) both sets of 'foreign' rulers adopted Islam as the dominant spiritual discourse and sponsored various projects which attested to their regard for the faith. Cognisant of the region's historical religious diversity, they also patronised discussions between spokesmen for the various indigenous religious traditions, thereby acknowledging the legitimacy of each and their own transcendent authority over all.[18] These rulers also employed skilled members of the native Iranian Tajik class to administer their empire and adopted, and patronised, the latter's distinctive cultural discourse, especially the 'traditional' Tajik literary arts and crafts.

The Qaraquyunlu and Aqquyunlu tribal entities which succeeded the Timurids on the region's political scene pursued a similarly inclusive 'project': Islam was their religion, their tribal military levies were Turks, their administrators were Tajiks and their cultural discourse was Persian. Such inclusivity was especially a feature of the reign of Uzun Hasan (d. 1478), ruler of the Aqquyunlu (White Sheep) tribal confederation who, in the face of opposition from the Ottomans, Mamluks and the Qaraquyunlu (Black Sheep) Turkish tribal confederacy, held sway over a territory stretching from the Euphrates in the West to Kirman in the East and from Transcaucausia in the North to the Persian Gulf in the South. In the tradition of both Timur and the Qaraquyunlu ruler Jahan Shah (d. 1467), during whose thirty-year reign the Qaraquyunlu had amassed considerable territory, Uzun Hasan's spiritual discourse paid homage to urban and rural, and especially tribal, spiritual discourse, even while it underlined his own claims to 'universal leadership' over them all. Uzun Hasan patronised religious structures, encouraged religious endowments and students, including Tajik sayyids, descendants of the Prophet Muhammad (d. 632), and patronised the arts and sciences. He also claimed his victories were foretold in the Qur'an and was even hailed by the theologian and philosopher Jalal al-Din Davani (d. 1503) as 'the envoy of the ninth [i.e. fifteenth] century' – in reference to the Prophet's statement that in every century Allah would send someone to 'renew' the faith – an upholder of secular justice and Islamic law, 'the shadow (*zill*) of Allah, the caliph of Allah and the deputy (*naib*) of the Prophet' and 'holy warrior (*ghazi*) in the path of Allah'. The great Persian Sunni Naqshbandi Sufi poet Jami (d. 1492), invoking an earlier religio-political legitimacy associated with holy war and raids on the infidel, described Uzun Hasan, known to have worn darvish dress at public audiences, as 'Sultan of the *ghazis*'. In mosque inscriptions Uzun Hasan was also described as 'the just sultan' and 'the just Imam', terms which in Twelver Shi'i discourse could be construed as identifying Uzun Hasan as the returned twelfth Imam himself. Uzun Hasan even also paid homage to the Mongol legacy.[19]

Uzun Hasan's 'universalist' discourse was advanced in the midst of the various discourses of a mass of both quietist and militantly pantheistic, messianic and egalitarian Sufi orders and other spiritual movements whose polemics often exhibited a distinctly Shi'i, anti-establishment tinge and all of which were swirling throughout the region, especially in the aftermath of the political fragmentation following Timur's death.[20] In the context of continued Qaraquyunlu politico-military setbacks, such discourse facilitated the re-alignment of both Qaraquyunlu member tribes and Tajik administrators under his leadership.[21]

In his struggle for the 'hearts and minds' of Turk and Tajik Uzun Hasan undertook also to identify with such discourse as was espoused by various of these Sufi orders. Among these the Safavids, based at Ardabil, were deemed of sufficient importance to merit two marriage alliances. In *c.* 1456–9, Uzun Hasan married his sister to the order's leader Junayd (d. 1460), a direct descendant of its founder Shaykh Safi al-Din. He also supported Junayd's claim to rule the order over that of an uncle who enjoyed Qaraquyunlu support. In *c.* 1471–2, Uzun Hasan married his daughter, herself the daughter of the last Christian emperor of Trabzond and thus of noble Greek descent, to Junayd's twelve- or thirteen-year-old son, and leader of the order, Haydar (d. 1488); the later, by the previous marriage, was already Uzun Hasan's nephew. Haydar's three sons from this marriage included his third son Ismail, born in 1487.[22]

Ismail's grandfather and father led an order which, based on its growing association with a number of the region's Turkish tribes, was indeed both propounding a more radical, messianic discourse and undertaking a pro-active military strategy. Indeed both men were killed in battle: Junayd fighting Shirvanshah associates of Jahan Shah Qaraquyunlu, and Haydar also against the Shirvanshah, as Uzun Hasan's sons' and grandsons' struggle for succession in the aftermath of his death so fractured the Aqquyunlu polity as to pave the way for the rise of the Safavids. At Haydar's death Ismail was hidden by supporters first at Ardabil and then for some years in Lahijan under the protection the local governor Mirza Ali Karkiya, a Zaydi Shi'ite whose sayyid family had ruled the area since the late 1360s.

Thus was Ismail by birth descended on both sides from princely families of differing faiths, by upbringing associated with well-established Tajik sayyid practitioners of a distinct body of Shi'i doctrine and practice and, at his father's death, the spirituo-political leader (*shaykh, pir, qutb, murshid-i kamil*) of a Sufi-style movement comprised of the region's Turkish tribal levies, some with Aqquyunlu associations, whose spirituality was informed by similarly Shi'i-tinged radical messianism circulating in the region of what is now Northern Syria and Iraq, Eastern Turkey and Northwestern Iran. Unsurprisingly, Ismail's own words and actions – his 'discourse' – reflected each of his own several personalities, each aspect of which – Christian and Shi'i Muslim, Tajik and Turk – was recognised and thereby legitimised and subordinated.

In 1499, as rival Aqquyunlu princes and their tribal supporters continued their internecine fighting, Ismail and his supporters left Lahijan for Syria and Asia Minor where, near Irzinjan, he was met by more followers. In 1500, near Shamakhi, Ismail met in battle and defeated elements of the same Shirvanshah who had killed his grandfather and father. In 1501, a century after the death of Timur, having defeated a rump Aqquyunlu contingent at Shurur, near Nakhchivan, Ismail entered Tabriz, the capital of the Ilkhanids, Jahan Shah Qaraquyunlu and his own grandfather the Aqquyunlu Uzun Hasan. In 1503 Ismail defeated another Aqquyunlu force near Hamadan and secured control over Central and Southern Iran. Mazandaran and Gurgan, along the Caspian Sea, fell as did Yazd. Diyar Bakr, Uzun Hasan's homeland where his son-in-law and Ismail's father Haydar had spent his formative years, was also taken. Baghdad fell in 1508. Shirvan and Khurasan fell, the latter after a decisive battle at Marv in December of 1510 with the Uzbeks who had taken the area in 1507 after the death of the last Timurid, Husayn Bayqara, in 1506. Several days later Ismail entered Herat and soon thereafter the rest of Khurasan also came under Safavid control.

Between the capture of Tabriz and Herat, that is, in less than a decade, Safavid forces secured territories previously ruled by eight different rulers.[23]

1

Laying the Foundations
Ismail I (1488–1524)

Ismail as Turk and Tajik

Haydar's son Ismail, to whom fell the leadership of the Safavid Sufi order at his father's death in battle in 1488, was but fourteen at the capture of Tabriz.

Although a contemporary, overt opponent of the Safavids linked both Ismail's grandfather Junayd and his father Haydar with overtly extremist spiritual polemics,[1] Ismail's own *divan* of poetry reveals rather a distinctly heterogeneous, multi-confessional messianic dimension as lying at the heart of his spiritual discourse.

Using the pen-name 'The Sinner (*Khatai*)', in one poem Ismail wrote of himself,

1   Today I have come to the world as a Master. Know truly that I am Haydar's son.
2   I am Faridun, Khusraw, Jamshid, and Zohak. I am Zal's son (Rustam) and Alexander.
3   The mystery of Anal-Haqq [lit. 'I am The Truth'] is hidden in this my heart. I am the Absolute Truth [or 'Allah'] and what I say is Truth.
4   I belong to the religion of the 'Adherent of the Vali [Ali]' and on the Shah's path I am a guide to every one who says: 'I am a Muslim.'
5   My sign is the 'Crown of Happiness'. I am the signet-ring on Sulayman's finger.
6   Muhammad is made of light, Ali of Mystery. I am a pearl in the sea of Absolute Reality.
7   I am Khatai, the Shah's slave full of shortcomings. At thy gate I am the smallest and the last [servant].

Elsewhere he wrote:

1   My name is Shah Ismail. I am God's mystery. I am the leader of all these *ghazi*s.
2   My mother is Fatima, my father is Ali; and I am the *Pir* of the Twelve Imams.

3   I have recovered my father's blood from Yazid. Be sure that I am of Haydarian essence.
4   I am the living Khidr and Jesus, son of Mary. I am the Alexander of [my] contemporaries.

In still other poems Ismail, using terms which echoed those circulating in the discourses of the various militant, mystical and messianic movements abroad in the region at the time, addressed his followers as *ghazi*, Sufi, and 'brother (*akhi*)' and, employing mystical terminology, 'men of recognition (*ahl-i iqrar*)' and 'men of truth (*ahl-i haqq*)' – the latter being the name of a contemporary movement linked to the Biktashis – as well as *qizilbash*, after his followers' distinctive twelve-pleated *taj* which denoted the same veneration for the Imams found in the discourses of other contemporary messianic discourses and was said to have been adopted during Haydar's time.[2]

The manner of Ismail's identification with Twelver Shi'ism, proclaimed as the new realm's faith at Tabriz' capture in 1501, added further dimensions to this messianic discourse. He and his immediate retinue were in fact relatively unacquainted with the intricacies of Twelver Shi'i doctrines and practices.[3] However, his long-term residence in Zaydi Shi'i Lahijan endowed Ismail with some familiarity with Shi'i discourse, for example, awareness that references to himself as 'the perfect, the just Imam (*al-imam al-adil al-kamil*)' or 'the just sultan (*al-sultan al-adil*)' would allude both to his status as secular successor to his grandfather Uzun Hasan, to whom similar terms had been applied, but also, in Twelver tradition, to himself as the now-returned twelfth Imam.[4]

The Safavids also advanced claims to their status as sayyids. Such claims, if not also further substantiating Ismail's identification with the Hidden Imam himself, also put the Safavids on a par with the sayyid founders of such other of the region's contemporary millenarian movements as the Hurufis, the Kubravis, the Nimatallahis and the Mushasha.[5]

Contemporary 'popular' tales also identified Ismail as Abu Muslim, the leader of the Khurasan-based Arab armies which defeated the Umayyads in 765 to establish the pro-Shi'i Abbasid state and who was believed to have gone into hiding to return to establish justice in this world.[6]

Taken together, the discourse surrounding Ismail in this period projected both his abject status – 'the Sinner' – in relation to and as the transcendent embodiment of the spirituo-cultural traditions of the region's key discourses. The young shah was thus simultaneously one with the chief figures of the Tajik Persian cultural legacy – Faridun, Khusraw, Jamshid, Rustam, Alexander; of Shi'ism – Khidr, Ali and Ali's 'adherent', the twelve Imams and their *pir*, the now returned Hidden Imam, if not also Allah himself; of key figures in the Christian religious and historical tradition;[7] and the *pir* of the region's numerous messianic, egalitarian Sufi movements – *ghazi*, *akhi*, Abu Muslim. Ismail, being 'the universal-simultaneous ruler who is both transcendent and dominant', stood at once as both the servant of, and the paramount figure above, all. He spoke to, embodied and thus surpassed each of these traditions as each existed on both the urban scene and among the region's rural and especially tribal elements likely in more commingled, than distinct, forms.[8]

In the midst of continued post-Uzun Hasan intra-Aqquyunlu clashes such complex discourse certainly facilitated the realignment of Aqquyunlu tribal contingents with Ismail, all the more so as the *divan* was composed in a Turkish dialect peculiar to the region comprising parts of modern-day northeastern Iraq, northwestern Iran, Eastern Turkey and the Southern Caucasus from whence these elements were drawn and similar discourses flourished.[9]

Turk and Tajik at the heart of the realm

Ismail's heterodox spiritual discourse, especially appealing to both Turk and Tajik, was matched by practical recognition of the importance of these two key constituencies to the life of the emerging Safavid polity, further facilitating the moves of elements of each from the Aqquyunlu to Ismail and the Safavid 'camp' and intertwining their fortunes with, and thus furthering their acceptance of and loyalty to, each other, Ismail and the Safavid enterprise itself.

At the political-military heart of the Safavid project in this period stood the various Turkish tribes of the Qizilbash confederation, the loyalty of whose chiefs and levies guaranteed Ismail's early military victories. Marriage alliances between the Safavid house, even before Tabriz, and grants of territory later allocated to, the Ustajlu and Shamlu tribes – the latter with Aqquyunlu connections – attest to the pre-eminence of these two within the confederation over these years. Leading members of both married sisters of Ismail, for example.[10] Like the Shamlu, the Mawsillu had been an important member of the Aqquyunlu confederation but elements thereof had paid fealty to Ismail after the capture of Diyar Bakr from another Mawsillu chief. In a testament of their importance to the polity, and certainly to encourage further loyalty, Ismail himself twice married into the tribe; a Mawsillu was the mother of Tahmasp, Ismail's oldest son, and a key figure at her son's court.[11] A prominent figure of the Qaramanlu, another former Aqquyunlu confederate, married one of Ismail's sisters and, sometime before 1510, a Kurdish chieftain married yet another sister.[12] The presence of tribal chiefs from the Dhul-Qadr and Afshar, both also former associates of the Aqquyunlu, and of Talish and Rumlu chiefs in secondary posts affirms the relative importance of these tribes in the Qizilbash confederation.[13]

Given their prominence it is not surprising that later Safavid chroniclers identified these tribes – and some of the above-mentioned individuals in particular – as among Ismail's companions when he departed Lahijan in

1499[14] and accorded them pride of place in their accounts of Safavid forces at key battles between 1500 and 1514[15] even if the genuine origins of some – including the Mawsillu, Afshar, Qajar and other associates of the Aqquyunlu tribal confederation – cannot be identified with any accuracy.[16]

Not all of the lands which came under Ismail's authority were secured by Qizilbash levies in battle, however. Indeed, a number of local, sitting rulers acknowledged Safavid authority and consequently retained their positions and relative autonomy. These included rulers in Gharjistan, North of Khurasan, Khuzistan – the latter after Ismail fought and killed the local Mushasha ruler – Kurdistan, one of whose princes, as noted, married a sister of Ismail, Luristan and Sistan.[17]

Local Iranian elements also had another, perhaps more important role to play. Administering the vast territory which so quickly came under Safavid hegemony required the input of a constituency different to the Qizilbash tribal levies. Thus, just as some Aqquyunlu tribal elements 'defected' to the Safavids over this period, so former Aqquyunlu administrators, native Iranians, took up administrative positions at both the central and provincial levels. Their acceptance of these posts signalled Tajik acceptance of, and lent further legitimacy to, both the assumption of power in the region by the Safavids under Ismail and the larger Safavid project and, as part and parcel thereof, the key role of the Turkish constituency in that project. The Turks, in both encouraging and working with these Tajik elements, thereby acknowledged the importance of the Tajik contribution to the life of the polity.

Among the more prominent of these Tajik administrators was Muhammad Zakariya Kujuji (d. 1512–13), an Aqquyunlu *vizier* whose family had served Timur and who himself, prior to Tabriz, had advised Ismail on the confused state of affairs among, and urged an ultimately successful attack on, the Aqquyunlu. He was subsequently appointed Ismail's first *vizier*.[18] The Savji family had served Uzun Hasan and his avowedly anti-Shi'i and anti-Safavid son and successor Yaqub, but now one, a judge in Iraq, served as Ismail's envoy to the Uzbeks in 1510 and later became judge of all of Khurasan. Another was chief judge in Tabriz.[19] At its conquest in 1503–4, a member of Isfahan's Jabiri family, which had also served the Aqquyunlu, was appointed *vizier* of Fars, under a Dhul-Qadr governor; the family remained prominent in Isfahan over the Safavid period and in the Fars administration until the eighteenth century.[20]

That none of these figures hailed from families with any history of any profound commitment to, or themselves had any detailed knowledge of, the newly established faith of Twelver Shi'ism[21] was clearly no barrier to employment.

Nevertheless, special efforts were also made to reach out to native Iranian sayyids, descendants of the Prophet himself. The Sunni Sayyid Nur al-Din Abd al-Vahhab, a descendant of the third Shi'i imam, Husayn, had been *Shaykh al-Islam* of Tabriz under Uzun Hasan and was related by marriage to the Aqquyunlu house while other family members had also served, and were related to, the Qaraquyunlu. At the capture of Herat Ismail received the Sayyid with honour and, after Chaldiran, appointed him ambassador to the Ottoman Sultan Selim I (reg. 1512–20).[22] Following the capture of Khurasan gifts were distributed among, and accepted by, the descendants of Imam Riza, the eighth Shi'i Imam, who administered the shrine at the Imam's tomb in Mashhad.[23] A judge from the Qazvin branch of the Marashi sayyids, administrators of the shrine in the city which housed the mausoleum of a son of the same Imam, was an envoy to the Uzbeks.[24]

The identities of key office holders over these early years, insofar as these can be charted, suggest an effort to balance the interests of Turk and Tajik at the polity's centre.[25] Thus, for example, the post of *amir al-umara*, a pre-Saljuk office which now amounted to commander-in-chief of the Qizilbash forces, was, perhaps naturally, held by tribal amirs; signalling their paramount influence within the tribal confederation, the Ustajlu and Shamlu dominated the post.[26] Another military post, the office of *qurchibashi*, dating from the Mongol period and referring to the head of the mounted cavalry or royal guards, was held by Ustajlu, Dhul-Qadr and Takkalu amirs.[27] By contrast, the 'civilian' position of *sadr*, a Timurid-period post related to the religious institution, was held throughout this period by Tajiks, including many sayyids. Like the tribal elite and the other Tajik administrators named above, however, neither these holders of the post or their families possessed any demonstrable Twelver Shi'i links; indeed, the first *sadr*, appointed in 1501, the year of Tabriz' occupation, had been Ismail's religious tutor in Lahijan and so was probably a Zaydi Shi'ite. The *vizier*s were also all Tajiks in this period as were the holders of the post of *mustawfi al-mamalik*, the comptroller-general.[28]

In at least one instance prior to Chaldiran in 1514 the effort to accommodate Tajik interests at the administrative level entailed some Turkish compromise. As with many of the realm's top posts, that of *vakil*, the vice-regent in charge of mainly non-military matters, including some religious issues, was already in existence under the Aqquyunlu. Husayn Bek Shamlu, from another branch of the Shamlu to that of Ismail's brother-in-law Abdi Be, was made *vakil* in the year of Ismail's entrance into Tabriz, when Ismail was fourteen years of age, but was replaced in 1510 by the Gilani goldsmith Najm al-Din, a native Iranian. Abdi Beg was compensated with the post of governor of Herat, however.[29]

The culture of politics, the politics of culture

The centre's contributions to 'culture', broadly construed, during Ismail's reign recall the somewhat limited scale of those of his Aqquyunlu and especially Qaraquyunlu predecessors.

While these pale in comparison with Mongol and Timurid, let alone later Safavid, patronage, the Safavids' early-projected association with a distinctly Persian cultural discourse at once cast the project as a successor to the region's earlier polities in this regard and bespoke Qizilbash recognition of the cultural legacy of their Tajik associates whose skills were so essential to the administration of the realm. Other Tajiks were thereby reassured as to the legitimacy of their presence in, and the importance of their involvement to, the Safavid project.

The young ruler personally was, in fact, no doubt familiar with the Persian cultural legacy at least from his several years' residence in Lahijan; indeed, in 1493–4, the year Ismail arrived in Lahijan, its ruler had taken delivery of a *Shahnama* with over 300 illustrations.[30]

After Tabriz the elaborate centres of book production – which included calligraphers, illuminators, miniaturists and binders, each requiring a plethora of specialist materials – which had flourished at Tabriz, Shiraz and Herat under the patronage of previous political establishments continued to produce works in their distinctive styles. The occasional Safavid 'twist' soon became observable, however. Thus, early in the period Ismail's workshop at Tabriz a manuscript of the *Khamsa* of Nizami (d. 1202) originally commissioned by the Timurid Babur (reg. 1483–1530) and continued under Uzun Hasan's anti-Shi'i anti-Safavid son Yaqub, was now embellished with additional illustrations featuring the distinct Safavid twelve-pleated *taj*.[31] In Fars the newly ensconced Dhul-Qadr tribal elite maintained Shiraz's reputation as a centre of book and miniature production: the city's workshop produced manuscripts of some classical Persian texts which featured illustrations clearly informed by the city's earlier styles as well as others which utilised both Herati and earlier Turkish styles, and featured a distinctly Shirazi-style *taj*.[32] Herat, whose artisans remained in the city after its 1510 capture by the Safavids, also continued as a metalworking centre. The Timurid style of small, tight arabesques and interlocking lobed cartouches continued on into the early Safavid period although inscribed invocations to Ali begin appear after 1510,[33] paralleling the appearance of the Safavid *taj* in contemporary manuscript illustrations.

Persian itself had been the region's literary language following the Persianisation of Rum/Asia Minor from at least the thirteenth century when Persian men of letters fled West in the face, especially, of Mongol incursions in the East. Jahan Shah Qaraquyunlu had composed poetry in Persian and patronised large numbers of poets and prose writers; even Ottoman rulers composed poetry in Persian.[34] Herat under the last Timurid ruler, Husayn Bayqara, was a noted centre of traditional Persian culture. Both Sultan Husayn and his *vizier* Mir Ali Shir Navai (d. 1501) were accomplished poets in Persian and Turkish, and the city was a focal point for artists, poets, historians and musicians. Nur al-Din Abd al-Rahman Jami (d. 1492), the leader of the Sunni Naqshbandi Sufi order, was based in Herat and the style of his *masnavi*s recalled those of Sadi and Hafiz (d. 1391) and his *ghazal*s those of Iraqi-*qasida* writers.

Ismail, although he had composed his own *divan* in Chagatai Turkish, demonstrated his desire to associate himself with Persian literary traditions and his continuing pragmatic attitude toward employing non-Shi'ites, and requested Jami's nephew Hatifi (d. 1520–1), who had served Husayn Bayqara, to undertake an historical epic on the lines of his earlier *Zafarnama*, written in celebration of Timur.[35] Many other poets who had served the Timurid and Aqquyunlu court also now served at the pleasure of Ismail.[36]

If Persian was now the cultural discourse of choice, the newly established Turk-Tajik centre also undertook to solidify its identification with Islam itself and Shi'i Islam in particular, in the pattern of preceding of the region's political establishments. Nevertheless, the identification with Shi'ism was not exclusive, given continuing widespread Sunni tendencies in the realm.

Ismail personally is identified with refurbishment of Imam Riza's shrine in Mashhad, though this stands as a relatively minor project compared, for example, with the mosque built there by Shah Rukh's wife Gawhar Shad in 1418–19.[37]

Others at the centre, however, also participated in such projects. In 1512 in Isfahan, where Ismail and his retinue frequently wintered, the architect Mirza Shah Husayn Isfahani, the Tajik *vizier* to Durmish Khan Shamlu – whose mother was Ismail's sister and who was Isfahan's governor from 1503, built the Harun-i Vilayat tomb for a son of one of the Imams on the square (maydan) of the same name which was then the focal point of the city's life. Some of the inscriptions thereon recall the distinctly messianic Shi'i, if not especially Twelver, dimensions of the region's spiritual discourse and Ismail's own identification therewith in his poetry: a *hadith* on the portal facade mentions Harun, associates Ismail with Ali as his ancestor and endows Ismail with such titles as *ghazi* and *mujahid* (holy warrior), the first of which was used by Ismail in his poetry. Other inscriptions, such the Prophet's statement 'I am the city of knowledge and Ali is its gate', recall conventional, if not distinctly messianic, Shi'i references.[38] Indeed, the names Ali, Muhammad and Allah appear in a Kufic cartouche at the apex of the entrance arch of the Eastern door. Chinese clouds appear in a panel below, and beneath that panel is the name Ismail, such that all four individuals are clearly linked. Interestingly, the traditional style of the building itself evokes continuity, not radical change,[39] suggesting an intention to portray the Safavids as successors to the region's earlier polities. Moreover, as a joint Turk-Tajik project, the undertaking also attested to the loyalty of each constituency to, and their identification with, each other and the larger polity which their alliance underpinned, this but a decade after Tabriz.

Ismail's continued attention to Ardabil, as well as contributions to the family tombs at and near the city, bespeak simultaneous concern to enhance further the place of the Safavid house itself, the role of Safavid Sufi order and himself as head of both.[40]

Taken together these undertakings affirm the centre's care to continue to project a heterodox spiritual discourse to identify with the individual discourses of elements key to the life of the newly established polity.

Messianic discourse focusing on alternative personages was by definition, however, illegitimate. Thus, although the Mushasha of Southern Iraq pledged fealty to Ismail following the 1508 conquest of Baghdad, the joint rulers of the confederation were killed later the same year by the new Safavid governor of Shushtar, likely on Ismail's orders and probably owing to their continuing efforts to claim association with the Twelver faith.[41] When, in 1511–12, in the aftermath of a failed millenarian uprising in Ottoman territory, surviving Takkalu tribal elements fled to Safavid territory and plundered a caravan of merchants along the way, Ismail had their leaders executed.[42] Ismail also turned on the Nizari Ismaili Shi'a, based at Andijan, near Arak, as their activities became increasingly open following the Safavids' appearance; the shah ordered the execution of Shah Tahir, the thirty-first imam of the Muhammad-Shahi branch of the Nizari Ismailis, who fled to India in 1520.[43] Ismail also moved against popular equation of himself and the Safavid rising with the return of Abu Muslim.[44]

Spokesmen for other competing spiritual discourses signalled a desire for a *modus vivendi*. As already noted Jami's nephew Hatifi, the leader of the Naqshbandi order who had served Husayn Bayqara in Herat, accepted a commission from Ismail. The Yazdi notable Sayyid Abd al-Baqi, a descendant of the founder of the Nimatallahi Sufi order, Shah Nimatallah Vali (d. 1413), was both *sadr* and, from 1512, *vakil*. Some Nurbakhshis accepted land grants from Ismail.[45]

Internal and external challenges: Chaldiran and after

Over Ismail's reign the Safavid polity faced, and survived, several internal and one important external challenge. Within its first decade the militarily incompetent and quarrelsome Khuzani *vakil* Najm-i Thani was put in charge of a multi-tribal force sent to restore to the Timurid Babur those of his Khurasani territories taken by the Uzbeks. The Uzbeks defeated the Safavid force in 1512. In that defeat both Husayn Bek Shamlu, Herat's governor, and a Talish commander fled the field, the *vakil* Najm-i Thani was caught and beheaded and, ultimately, the Uzbeks took the city.

Nevertheless, when Ismail, whose son Tahmasp has just been born, arrived from Isfahan with another force the Safavids retook the city. *Realpolitik* dicated the shah's exercise of a 'light touch' vis-à-vis the Qizilbash amirs who had fled the field.[46]

With Ismail occupied in the East, his half-brother Sulayman challenged the shah's authority by entering the Safavid capital Tabriz at the head of a large procession in a clear effort to recreate and eclipse Ismail's entrance into the city more than a decade before. Neither the local population nor, more importantly, the local Ustajlu commander, whose brother was the future *vakil* Muhammad Bek Ustajlu, were impressed, however, and for advancing such a direct challenge the rebel was killed.[47]

A far greater, external, threat emerged from the West. For the Ottomans the rise of the Safavids had presented an important internal challenge in Eastern Anatolia, the home of many Qizilbash and other tribal elements with overtly pro-Safavid sympathies, as witnessed by the 1511–12 Takkalu rising. Following an intra-Ottoman conflict over succession to Bayazid, proponent of a non-military approach to the 'Eastern question', his successor Selim I, joining with a former Aqquyunlu notable and a Dhul-Qadr chief loyal to Egypt's Mamluks, engaged and defeated Safavid forces at Chaldiran, 80 miles northwest of Tabriz, in August 1514. Although soon thereafter Selim himself entered Tabriz, apparently without a fight, he did not press his advantage and instead turned southwest. In 1515 the Ottomans captured a fort near Irzinjan and, in 1516, took both Diyar Bakr and Kurdistan. Eventually, Selim moved against the Mamluks and entered Cairo in 1517.[48]

Tabriz was, therefore, reoccupied a month after its capture. However, the Safavids lost the former Aqquyunlu capital Diyar Bakr and Irzinjan, where Ismail had rallied his tribal supporters troops some twenty years before. The following year, 1515, Ismail was also unable to prevent Portuguese consolidation of control over the Persian Gulf island of Hormuz and signed a treaty ceding control to Portugal and in return for a military-commercial anti-Ottoman alliance.

Despite the deaths of a number of key Qizilbash and Tajik figures, Ismail's wives and, with the fall of Tabriz, loss of the centre's treasury and key artisans,[49] the Turk-Tajik alliance underpinning Ismail's reign held, allowing the shah to continue active in defence of the realm. Selim's movements having offered the Safavids a moment of respite, Ismail dispatched a large Qizilbash force to support Mamluk resistance as the Ottomans moved South. After a warning from the Mawsillu and Rumlu governors of Qayin and Balkh of a severe famine, the Shamlu governor of Herat and Khurasan was replaced with the same Mawsillu *amir* who was sent to Herat with the three-year old Tahmasp as his charge.[50] Three years later, in 1520, Shamlu and Takkalu forces were sent to check a move by Sultan Selim toward Baghdad which, however, collapsed with the Sultan's death that year.[51] When the Mawsillu governor of Herat was suspected of rebellion, following the Uzbeks' 1521 crossing of the Oxus and seizure of parts of Herat, he and his charge accepted recall to court and replacement by Ismail's new-born son Sam Mirza, son of a Georgian woman, in the care of Durmish Khan Shamlu. The latter's mother was Ismail's sister. The Shamlu checked the Uzbek incursion and new Shamlu, Takkalu, Rumlu and Afshar sub-governors were appointed. Qizilbash forces also checked a series of local risings in

Damghan, Mazandaran, Rasht in 1518 and in 1521–2 in Georgia, all no doubt encouraged by the Safavid defeat.[52] Too, in this period Ismail also entered into profuse correspondence with European powers seeking aid against the Ottomans.[53]

The continuing loyalty of the Ustajlu and Shamlu, whose links to Ismail and pre-eminence within the Qizilbash confederation pre-dated the capture of Tabriz, certainly encouraged continuing overall Qizilbash loyalty and intra-Qizilbash stability following Chaldiran. The Shamlu held Herat and, with the death at Chaldiran of the Tajik *vakil* Najm-i Thani, Muhammad Bek Ustajlu jointly held the posts of military *vakil* and *amir al-umara* from 1514–5 until his death in 1523–4. He was succeeded by his son who was, in turn, succeeded by a Rumlu. The Ustajlu also held the post of *qurchibashi* from 1514 to 1518.[54]

Tajik support for the project also remained demonstrably firm. For the remainder of Ismail's reign Tajiks accepted the post of *vizier*, for example. The longest-serving was Mirza Shah Husayni, the architect-*vizier* of Durmish Khan Shamlu in Isfahan, who was appointed to the post in 1514 and was also the non-military *vakil*. A grating personality, Husayni held the post for ten years until his assassination in 1523, with issues of personal finance providing the final straw. He was succeeded by another Tajik, Jalal al-Din Muhammad Tabrizi, who was of the same Kujuji family as the above-mentioned Amir Zakariya.[55] The post of *sadr* also remained in Tajik hands after Chaldiran; none of its holders, as before, was known for any profound, overtly Twelver Shi'i sympathies,[56] attesting to efforts to retain the loyalities of the Sunni population.

Before Chaldiran marriage alliances had both recognised the importance of, and apparently succeeded in, binding the fortunes of the Safavid house to those of key Qizilbash tribal elements. Following Chaldiran Ismail contracted marriage alliances with important local Northern dynasties, clearly in hopes of obviating the need for military action to secure his Northern borders, and with little regard for their religious preferences. Following Durmish Khan Shamlu's suppression of the revolt by the governor of Rasht in 1518, the governor himself attended the court at Tabriz, was given a new title and, in 1521–2, a daughter of Ismail in marriage.[57] In 1519–20 Ismail married another daughter to Sultan Khalil Shirvanshah, whose grandfather had in fact killed Ismail's father; Ismail later married Khalil's sister.[58]

Such practical efforts to insure the allegiance of the Turk-Tajik alliance in the aftermath of Chaldiran were complemented by a discourse which further expanded on the person and position of the shah as the apex of the spirituo-political and cultural discourses of the polity's key constituencies. Among the region's rural and tribal elements especially, for example, Qizilbash tribal elements, the messianic discourse surrounding Ismail continued to be both promoted and accepted.[59]

Post-Chaldiran religious discourse was marked also by an increasingly overt Safavid identification with Twelver Shi'ism, particularly its messianic dimensions. A 1519 inscription on a wooden panel of a box at the grave of Imam Musa referred to the command to build the box as having been issued by 'the just, the perfect sultan . . . Shah Ismail . . . the Husaynid'.[60] Such titles, as before, echoed similar terms as applied both to such of Ismail's predecessors as Uzun Hasan, as well as claims to sayyid status and identity as the returned twelfth Imam. Isfahan's 1522 *Masjid-i Ali*, in whose construction the same Tajik Mirza Shah Husayni – Isfahan's *vizier* now appointed administrative *vakil* after Chaldiran – was involved, contains inscriptions citing the name Ismail as appearing twelve times in the Qur'an, as many as the number of the Imams, including the, very implicitly, now-returned twelfth Imam. The chronogram 'He has come, the opener of Gates' clearly implied Ismail's supra-mortal status.[61]

Ismail's Mawsillu wife, Tajlu Khanum (d. 1540), also participated in this increasingly overt identification with the faith. In 1522 she endowed the farms, gardens and villages she owned around Varamin, Qum and Qazvin to the shrine of Fatima, the sister of the eighth Imam, in Qum and she encouraged the establishment of other pious foundations. She financed the repair of a bridge in Eastern Azerbaijan and, promoting her husband's simultaneous status as head of the Safavid Sufi order, Tajlu Khanum also financed substantial portions of Ismail's projected tomb at Ardabil.[62] Ismail himself also undertook improvements to various religious shrines and buildings in this period.[63]

Ismail's identification with, and promotion of, the traditional discourse of the Safavid's Tajik constituency, also continued apace after Chaldiran. In 1522, eight years after the battle, Ismail recalled his son Tahmasp to Tabriz from Herat. The latter had been studying under the great Timurid painter Bihzad whose own acceptance of Safavid rule was demonstrated by his painting of the poet Hatifi, the descendant of the Naqshbandi Jami who had earlier accepted a commission from the shah, wearing the Safavid *taj*. Bihzad, and possibly other Herati painters in the Timurid style, accompanied Tahmasp and soon thereafter, following Bihzad's apparent appointment as head of Ismail's workshop, the Tabrizi Sultan Muhammad, the previous head, ceased work on the *Shahnama* previously commissioned by Ismail and commenced a new one.

In this manuscript the Tabrizi style of painting was adapted to the Herati style to suit the heir apparent and thereby inaugurated the union of the Eastern and Western Iranian traditions of painting which distinguished the Tabrizi school for the next three decades.[64] Substantively, those of this manuscript's illustrations completed before Ismail's death in 1524 highlight such 'historical' Iranian victories as that of over the forces of Turan. As such the project appears to have been intended as a reaffirmation both of the legitimacy of the distinctly Tajik interest, and role, in the Safavid project as well as, especially, in the aftermath of Chaldiran, Ismail's identification with Persian heritage – perhaps, especially, the divine right of the king to rule and his subjects' corresponding imperative to follow – and a suggestion as to the eventual triumph of

Persian forces over more contemporary enemies. Ismail also commissioned other works in the Persian tradition, including a 1524–5 *Nizami*, to make up for the depletion of Tabriz' manuscript collection during the Ottomans' brief occupation of the city.[65]

The Shiʿi clerical response

Although there was some interest in orthodox Twelver Shiʿism in the Iranian heartland in the late fourteenth and early fifteenth centuries, and the Tajik Shiʿi sayyids in Qazvin and Mashhad, at least, had accepted Ismail's gifts and, therefore, at least ostensibly, his claims,[66] the region's major Shiʿi centres were located in Arabic-speaking lands, particularly the Lebanon, the Iraqi shrine cities of Najaf and Karbala and the Eastern Arabian coastland known as Bahrayn. The heterodoxy of Safavid religious expression and practice, especially as embellished by such critics as Khunji and Pakaraji, the Safavid military and administrative elite's at best cursory interest in and commitment to the faith and the Chaldiran defeat less than fifteen years after Tabriz can only have suggested to these clerics both the problematic, and transient, nature of the Safavid project.

Indeed, over this period only one Arab Twelver Shiʿi cleric is known to have journeyed East specifically to associate himself with Safavid Shiʿism. From at least 1504, three years after Tabriz, the very junior Lebanese Ali Karaki (d. 1534) was both associated with the court and in receipt of considerable remuneration therefrom. By 1510, Karaki held some administrative authority in the newly conquered areas of Arab Iraq, an annual stipend and had endorsed the Safavid use of such terms as 'the just sultan' and 'the just Imam' as references to Ismail, intimating the latter's identification as the now-returned Twelfth Imam. Karaki subsequently modified this understanding, to justify his relationship with the shah by portraying himself as 'the general deputy (*naib amm*)' of the Imam to the community until the latter's return who, according to the perhaps-majority interpretation by this time, was authorised in the interim to interact with the established political authority.[67]

Karaki was welcomed by Tajik sayyids based at Imam Riza's shrine in Mashhad and subsequently contracted a marriage alliance with a prominent Astarabadi sayyid family. However, both junior and senior Arab clerical contemporaries abroad both directly and indirectly condemned Karaki's association with Ismail and, implicitly therefore, the legitimacy of the Safavid project itself. One prominent Arab scholar, having journeyed to Safavid territory and having seen Ismail for himself, returned to the Lebanon.[68]

Summary and conclusion

Although it has been suggested that only in the establishment of Twelver Shiʿism did the Safavid differ from the Aqquyunlu dynasty,[69] the limited manner of Twelver Shi'ism's establishment in these years could hardly have sustained the Safavid project through such a crisis as Chaldiran. In fact, it was Ismail's very heterodox spiritual discourse coupled with very practical actions – marriages, allotments of land and appointments to important posts – which publicly recognised, legitimated and further encouraged the participation of Turk and Tajik in support of, and their identification with, a Safavid project larger than each which sustained the enterprise. Certainly aided by the Ottomans' fortuitous move to the southwest after the battle, the continuation of Ismail as the transcendent head of this project clearly remained sufficiently consequential to these constituents to warrant their continued allegiance after Chaldiran.[70]

However, the earlier Aqquyunlu formation – many of whose Turk and Tajik elements now served the Safavids – had not survived the combination of both a major military defeat – in 1473 defeat by the Ottomans at Bashkent – and the death of a ruler – five years later, in 1478, of Uzun Hasan. It remained to be seen whether the Safavid project and the Turk-Tajik alliance which had to date underpinned it could survive the passing of Ismail himself in Tabriz in May 1524, ten years after Chaldiran, following a fever.

2

Reconfiguration and Consolidation
The Reign of Tahmasp (1524–1576)

Ismail both stood simultaneously at the apex of the Safavid project's component spirituo-religious and cultural traditions and, as the universal ruler, was the sole spokesman for their transcendent sum total. His spiritual discourse, reinforced by 'practical' measures, linked the interests of the polity's two key constituencies – Turk and Tajik – to each other and to himself sufficiently strongly to withstand the challenge of Chaldiran. The civil war which raged for more than a decade after Ismail's passing did not reflect serious questioning of the legitimacy and authority of the Safavid house itself but was in the main a struggle between and among Qizilbash tribal elements and their Tajik associates to construct a new hierarchical alignment of those interests around Ismail's eldest son, the ten-year old Tahmasp.[1]

Civil war, and its aftermath . . .

Ismail's death initially encouraged a Rumlu challenge, in alliance with the Takkalu and Dhul-Qadr, to the existing Ustajlu-Shamlu dominance of the Qizilbash confederation. From this challenge arose a tripartite alliance of Rumlu, Takkalu and Ustajlu elements. The Ustajlu were quickly excluded from this grouping, stripped of their territorial holdings, and, in 1526–7, defeated in battle by the Takkalu. The Takkalu, having then defeated the Rumlu, assumed *de facto* regency from 1527–31 and even withheld assistance to the Shamlu governor of Herat in the face of Uzbek attacks.[2] A 1531 Shamlu march against the royal camp in Isfahan sparked an attack on, and 'massacre' of, Takkalu elements by a combined force including Ustajlu, Rumlu, Dhul-Qadr and Afshar elements. A Shamlu regency ensued, from 1530–1 to 1533–4. The Shamlu took both the best lands and the key posts but the Ustajlu, as related to the Safavid house by marriage as were the Shamlu, were important junior partners and held key provincial appointments.[3] Takkalu and some Dhul-Qadr elements then implicated the Shamlu chief in a plot to poison his cousin the shah in favour of Sam Mirza, Tahmasp's half-brother by a Georgian woman. Most other factions of the Takkalu and some Dhul-Qadr remained loyal to Tahmasp, however, such that Tahmasp was able to order the Shamlu leader's execution. Sam Mirza himself chose to wait in the wings and besiege Mughal Qandahar. At his defeat by the Mughals in 1536, Sam returned to court. Tahmasp received his half-brother but the subsequent execution of Sam Mirza's Shamlu supporters marked the effective end of Shamlu dominance and the civil war, and left the Ustajlu at the head of the Qizilbash confederation.[4]

At the centre itself the fortunes of key Tajik associates of the different tribal factions varied according to those of their tribal patrons. Jalal al-Din Muhammad Tabrizi, of the Tabrizi Kujuji family, had, for example, been appointed *vizier* just prior to Ismail's death. An associate of the Ustajlu-Shamlu alliance which underlay Ismail's reign, at Ismail's death Tabrizi was killed by the insurgent Rumlu. The Rumlu then exiled his Ustajlu-nominated replacement, the Tajik sayyid Qadi Jahan Qazvini (d. 1552–3), whose life was twice saved by the intervention of Tahmasp's Mawsillu wife. Jafar Savji, previously governor of Isfahan, was appointed *vizier* in 1524–5 and served through the Takkalu regency. He was dismissed at their fall in 1531 and eventually executed. With the rise of the Shamlu, the pro-Shamlu *vizier* in Khurasan, the Tajik Nur Kamal Isfahani, replaced Savji. As the Shamlu fell in 1533–4 Nur Kamal's property was seized. He was tortured and, although freed, replaced jointly by the same Qadi Jahan and a member of the prominent Khuzani family of Isfahan which had furnished Ismail's *vizier* Najm-i Thani. The latter was executed in 1535. With the Ustajlu resuming their position of pre-eminence at the centre from the following year, their protégé Qadi Jahan retained the post until his retirement *c.* 1550–1.

This pattern applied in the provincial level as well: as the Ustajlu–Shamlu alliance emerged, for example, another Khuzani was appointed *vizier* for Mashhad and the affairs of Imam Riza's shrine.[5]

. . . and external threats

Both the Uzbeks and Ottomans seized the advantage offered by this period of prolonged internal disorder to launch full-scale invasions of Safavid territory. The Uzbeks launched five attacks on Khurasan between 1524 and 1540. During the fourth, lasting from 1531 to 1534 – in the aftermath of the Takkalu 'massacre', an Ottoman invasion eastward and the Qizilbash counter-move – the Uzbeks advanced as far as Rayy, South of present-day Tehran.[6]

The Ottomans represented the greater threat. In the aftermath of the above-mentioned Takkalu massacre some surviving Takkalu elements urged the Ottomans to intervene. In early 1532, following a European peace treaty which settled challenges on their Western borders, the Ottomans commenced two decades of invasions into Safavid territory.

During their 1532–3 to 1535 incursion the Ottomans seized Tabriz, Kurdistan and attracted support in Gilan. In 1534, the year of the plot to poison Tahmasp, the Ottomans accepted the peaceful surrender of Baghdad and all of Arab Iraq, including the Shiʿi shrine cities of Najaf and Karbala. Basra surrendered in 1538. During their 1546 to 1548 invasion the Ottomans entered Safavid territory in support of Alqas (d. 1548), Ismail's son by another Mawsillu woman, who had risen against Tahmasp in 1536 while governor of Shirvan. Pardoned by Tahmasp, Alqas rose again and finally sought refuge with the Ottomans. When his attacks on Hamadan, Qum, Kashan, Isfahan and Fars failed to attract domestic support Alqas surrendered to Tahmasp who had him jailed.

In *c.* 1553, in response to Safavid counter-moves in Kurdistan, Irzirum and Van the Ottomans launched another series of incursions. The Safavids sued for peace. The resulting treaty of Amasya, concluded in 1555 and remaining in force until after Tahmasp's death,[7] recognised Ottoman sovereignty over Arab Iraq/Mesopotamia, including Baghdad, and Kurdistan.[8] In the aftermath of this treaty – which, given the losses in Anatolia and Arab Iraq shifted the Safavid geographical centre eastwards – Qazvin replaced Tabriz as the Safavid capital.[9]

The Turkish response

While detailed contemporary information on the changing influence of the different Qizilbash tribes during the civil war period is scanty,[10] the tribal origins of the holders of the centre's key offices over the entire period, especially during the civil war, mainly reflected the fractioning of the Qizilbash confederation at Ismail's death and their jostling for position around his very young son and successor Tahmasp as they had around Ismail himself.[11] If they were paramount tribe at the end of the civil war, by Tahmasp's death in 1576 the Ustajlu occupied fifteen such key posts, including such influential positions as the guardians to various royal princes as well as the governorship of Khurasan. The latter entailed the post of guardian to the future Abbas I (b. 1571), second son of Tahmasp's eldest son Muhammad Khudabanda (d. 1595).[12] The Ustajlu also held the governorships of Sarakhs, Sistan, Shushtar and Dizful. Other Qizilbash tribes were allotted posts in the post-civil war period according to their, decidedly secondary, hierarchical importance at the polity's political-military centre of the polity.[13]

Military, and therefore political, power continued to lie with the tribes at both the central and provincial levels such that once lands were allocated among tribal elements, the centre exercised a light touch over provincial affairs.[14] Although provincial political-administrative structures apparently replicated those of the centre, tribes treated the lands they were allocated in the provinces – as *tuyul*s, *iqta* or land grants – as personal property. Revenues therefrom were, in effect, wages over which the centre exercised very little control. Local authorities also appointed their own judges and enjoyed autonomy in the organisation of local religious affairs.[15]

As they had during the time of Ismail, marriage alliances were used to bolster further support for the Safavid house and Tahmasp himself. Tahmasp's mother was a Mawsillu and his principal wife, whom he likely married right around Ismail's death, was the Mawsillu Sultanum Bekum (d. 1593–4). She gave Tahmasp two sons, including Muhammad Khudabanda who was born in 1532, during the early years of the Shamlu-Ustajlu regency, when Tahmasp himself was only eighteen years old, and Ismail II, born in 1537.[16]

Several of Tahmasp's eight daughters were given in marriage to others within the Safavid house itself, no doubt to stave off any further risings such as those associated with Tahmasp's two brothers. One daughter married Ibrahim (d. 1577), son of Tahmasp's full brother Bahram (d. 1549), when the latter was governor of Mashhad. Another daughter was promised to another son of Bahram who, however, died in 1576.[17]

Key posts were also allocated to family members. Before his rebellion Alqas, Tahmasp's brother by another Mawsillu woman, had been Shirvan's governor. He was replaced by Tahmasp's son Ismail. Bahram's son Ibrahim was sent to Khurasan – a posting mainly allotted to a high-ranking family member, usually the oldest son.[18] Masum Bek Safavi (d. 1569), whose great-grandfather was a brother of Haydar, Tahmasp's grandfather, was the administrator of the Ardabil shrine *c.* 1536–7 and governor of Ardabil *c.* 1544–5. His loyalty, and presumably his competence, not found wanting, he rose high over the later years of Tahmasp's reign. With the support of others of the ruling house and key Mawsillu, Rumlu, Afshar and Ustajlu chiefs he played a key role in the 1565 crushing of a Takkalu revolt.[19] Masum Bek was involved in the arrest of Tahmasp's son Ismail in 1556 shortly after the latter's arrival in Herat as Khurasan's governor, following Ismail's commission of 'certain acts displeasing to his father' for which he was jailed until 1576.[20]

The continuation of Tajik support

The continued Tajik presence at the central and provincial levels of administration after the civil war signalled both the Turks' need for Tajik administrative support and the latter's continuing acceptance of their role alongside the Turks in the larger Safavid project.[21] Some of these elements had served the political centre during Ismail's reign, but there were also some new faces in the administration, especially at the provincial level. These included many sayyids,[22] a number of whom served in the provinces,[23] some, especially in the case of Khurasan, as direct appointees of the centre.[24]

The period's court chronicles, authored by Tajiks, also attest to Tajik acceptance of, and continued Safavid claims to, sayyid status and a special relationship with Shi'ism; in return for such overt acceptance of these claims as these betokened, the centre remained tolerant of continued Tajik sympathies for Sunni Islam. In his *Habib al-Siyar*, completed in 1524, the sayyid Ghiyas al-Din Khvandamir (d. 1535–7), who had described his earlier patron the Timurid Sultan Husayn Bayqara as 'Allah's shadow on earth' and retained pro-Sunni tendencies, accepted Ismail's claims to descent from the seventh Imam, Musa, and praised the Imams themselves as repositories of divine knowledge and miraculous powers.[25] Khvandamir's son Amir Mahmud voiced similar sentiments in his 1550 *Zayl Habib al-Siyar*, composed in Herat.[26] In his 1542 *Lubb al-Tavarikh*, completed for Tahmasp's full-brother Bahram, Yahya Qazvini (d. 1555), who remained in Qazvin after its capture by Ismail and throughout the civil war, described the Imams as infallible and Ali as 'the rightful Imam' and possessor of 'prophetic knowledge'. Qazvini praised both his patron and the Safavid house as a whole and, himself a Husayni sayyid, accepted Safavid claims to being descendants of Imam Musa, although he retained some sympathies for the Sunni perspective on key historical events in Islamic history.[27] In the same year Mir Abul-Fath, another Husayni sayyid, also affirmed the Safavids' status as sayyids in his revision to the chief work on Safavid genealogy, *Safvat al-Safa*.[28] Another Qazvini, Ahmad b. Muhammad Ghaffari (d. 1567), from a family of local Sunni judges, in his 1552 *Nigaristan* and his 1563–4 *Nusakh-i Jahan-Ara* traced the Safavid family line back through Imam Musa and referred to Tahmasp's accession as 'the end of time' and to the shah himself as 'the shadow of Allah on earth' – a title bestowed by Davani on the Safavids's Sunni forebearer Uzun Hasan less than a century before – even as, like Sayyid Yahya, his perspective on Islamic history bespeaks Sunni sympathies.[29]

Local elements also signalled their acceptance of the continued legitimacy of the Safavids, and Tahmasp in particular, in other, more public, ways. In 1543, after the end of the civil war, Qutb al-Din, an Isfahani notable, built a mosque whose founding inscription dates the building to the reign of 'the most just, the most noble, the shadow of Allah to the Faithful . . . Sultan Shah Tahmasp, the Husaynid'. The same year one Shaykh Muhammad Safi built the Dhul-Fiqar mosque, a nearby school and bathhouse in Isfahan's bazaar. The inscription dates the building to 'the days of the caliphate of the most just Sultan . . . Shah Tahmasp, the Husaynid'.[30]

The centre utilised a combination of efforts to further encourage security in potentially troublesome areas in this period. On the one hand, following the consolidation of the new Ustajlu-dominated Qizilbash hierarchy around the shah, the centre moved to limit the independence of territories which had previously enjoyed considerable autonomy. In *c.* 1537–8, much of Sistan came under a tribal governor and from *c.* 1558 until 1598–9 the province was ruled by a Safavid prince with a Qizilbash *amir* as his guardian. In 1538 and 1551 respectively, direct control was secured over Shirvan and Shakki. Baku also came under central control in this period.[31] Between 1540 and 1554 the Safavids also launched a series of attacks in the Caucasus,[32] and Georgian districts were brought under control with local governors being appointed from, and taxes being paid to, the centre.[33]

Other less problematic areas continued to enjoy some degree of autonomy.[34]

The house continued to utilise marriages to cement alliances with local notables,[35] still with little regard for the extent of new relatives' religious commitments. In *c.* 1549, Tahmasp himself married a Shirvani woman who had been married to his brother Bahram at the latter's death. In *c.* 1567–8 Jamshid Khan (d. 1580–1), governor of Western Gilan and himself grandson of the marriage between a daughter of Ismail and Amira Dubbaj of Rasht, married a daughter of Tahmasp. As these daughters were the products of intermarriages with various Circassian and Georgian houses, these marriages linked these notables both to Tahmasp himself and the Safavid house and also to each other.[36] Indeed, *c.* 1549, Tahmasp's son Khudabanda, son of a Mawsillu, married the daughter of the marriage of a Gilani notable to the daughter of the sayyid Qadi Jahan Qazvini, the Tajik *vizier* whose life Khudabanda's Mawsillu mother had saved during the civil war. In 1565–6 Khudabanda took a second wife, Khayr al-Nisa, of the Marashi sayyid family which had ruled in Mazandaran since the fourteenth century; this union produced Abbas I.[37]

With selected Tajiks even being granted the right to wear the distinctive Safavid *taj*,[38] the fortunes of Turks, Tajiks and the Safavid house itself were thus ever more firmly linked.

Safavid heterodoxy reasserted

The widespread reappearance of the Abu Muslim traditions at Ismail's death and over the civil war period[39] further attests that Ismail's death removed the single individual who had projected himself also as the transcendent spokesman of the region's various messianic spiritual polemics. In response, the post-civil war political realignment of Turk and Tajik around Tahmasp's leadership was further encouraged by the reaffirmation of the same inclusive and transcendent spirituo-cultural discourse which had obtained under, and focused on, Ismail.

Just as his father had, in addition to projecting his divine status, simultaneously styled himself 'the Sinner', Tahmasp's several experiences of personal repentance (*tawba*) also publicly projected his status as an individual, and very human, believer. Not coincidentally, these repentances occurred at particularly problematic points in his reign. Tahmasp's first repentance came during the civil war, for example, as he rushed back from engaging the Uzbeks in Khurasan to face the Ottomans and in the aftermath of the Shamlu plot to poison him and to put his half-brother Sam Mirza on the throne, and resulted in Tahmasp's decree (*firman*), issued *c.* 1533–4, banning such non-Islamic practices as gambling, prostitution, music and drinking. Following a second *tawba*, *c.* 1555–6, in the aftermath of the humiliating Amasya 1555 treaty with the Ottomans and perhaps also the subsequent decision to move the capital from Tabriz to Qazvin, Tahmasp ordered the country's 'amirs and notables' to 'repent of all their sins'.[40] The next year, 1556–7, he also charged his nephew Ibrahim, sent to replace Khurasan's Qizilbash governor, to enforce religious edicts there.[41] In 1563–4, following a dream in which he saw the Imam, Tahmasp issued decrees forbidding the *tamgha* – a trades' tax dating at least to the Mongol period – certain guild taxes, gambling and drinking houses all as contrary to Islamic law,[42] such an edict clearly pointing to the failure of earlier prohibitions.[43] In *c.* 1571–2 Tahmasp is said to have taken action against musicians and singers at court.[44]

If such actions projected Tahmasp's mortality they also, implicitly and simultaneously, projected a superior image of the shah as defender of the faith, thus reinforcing his spiritual legitimacy and authority at precisely such times as his political and military fortunes were being severely tested.

Indeed, further simultaneous public proclamation of Tahmasp's superior, messianic and implicitly divine status, in addition to that on offer in the Tajik-authored court chronicles cited above, is attested during and in the aftermath of the civil war.[45] A 1531–2 inscription at the Isfahan Congregational Mosque, during the Takkalu regency, described the shah as 'the leader of the army of the Mahdi, the Lord of the Age (*sahib al-zaman*) . . . Shah Tahmasp the Safavid, the Husaynid'.[46] After the civil war Tahmasp continued to be identified as a Husayni sayyid, *sahib al-zaman* and 'the just sultan', the latter terms referring both to his secular authority and lending themselves, as during his father's life, to being identified as the now-returned twelfth Imam.[47] As late as 1571, five years before his death, a Venetian report noted that Tahmasp's subjects regarded him as 'not a king, but as a god, on account of his descent from the line of Ali'.[48]

Tahmasp also remained attentive to the status of the Safavid Sufi order and his own position as its head. Between 1536 and 1542, after the civil war, Tahmasp constructed a new building at the Ardabil shrine, the very large Jannat Sarai, to encourage, and accommodate an overflow of, visitors for devotions if not also religious/spiritual performances, at the shrine or even his own tomb.[49]

This reaffirmed Safavid messianism remained as exclusive in this period as it had during Ismail's reign. Between 1526 and 1531, at the height of the intra-Qizilbash struggle, and coincident with the decline in Ustajlu influence in particular, the above-mentioned resurfacing of legends attesting to the imminent reappearance of Abu Muslim generated an uncompromising response from the centre.[50] The Nimatallahi Sufi order as well remained the particular focus of efforts to link its fortunes to those of the Safavids and, thereby, effectively limit, if not neutralise, the independence of its discourse. The head of the order Nur al-Din Baqi (d. 1564), the son of the Yazdi notable Mir Abd al-Baqi Yazdi, Ismail's *sadr* and *vakil*, was confirmed as *naqib* and governor of Yazd when Tahmasp acceded to the throne and, *c.* 1535–6, married a sister of Tahmasp, following the 1521–2 death of the latter's first husband, another Tajik, Amira Dabbaj Rashti.[51] In 1554–5, the daughter of this union married Tahmasp's son, the future Ismail II who, the next year, was sent to Khurasan as its governor.[52] Court chronicles of the period similarly downplayed any independent Nimatallahi Sufi discourse, likely reflecting the official denigration of any alternative to the Safavid hegemony over Sufi discourse.[53]

The Nurbakhshi were not so accommodating. In *c.* 1537 the successor to Shah Qasim Nurbakhsh, who had himself been well treated, refused the hand of a sister of Tahmasp, bespeaking an effort to maintain Nurbakhshi independence. He was subsequently executed.[54]

As for other potentially alternative Shi'i discourses, the already-mentioned intermarriages between the Safavid house and prominent Gilanis, some of whom were Zaydi Shi'a, bespeak efforts to guarantee their loyalty.[55] The son of Shah Tahir, the imam of Muhammad-Shahi branch of the Nizari Ismailis, attended Tahmasp, thereby according him some degree of obeisance, before he returned to the Deccan. The Andijan-based Qasim-Shahi Ismailis were persecuted *c.* 1573, however, and their Imam was jailed and executed.[56] The Shi'i discourse of the Khuzistan-based Mushasha sayyids was deemed sufficiently problematic that Qizilbash governors were sent to Shushtar in 1539–40 and Dizful in 1541–2.[57]

Tahmasp and the Tajiks

Continued Tajik loyalty to the Safavid project was encouraged by the centre's continued efforts to identify with, and patronise, traditional Persian cultural discourse. Special veneration for the early Safavids and Ismail, as in the various Tajik-authored histories mentioned above, for example, reflected well in turn on Ismail's son and successor Tahmasp. Such veneration is evident also in the *Shahnamah-yi Ismail*, a work commenced by Jami's nephew Hatifi, who had served both the Timurid Sultan Husayn Bayqara and Ismail, but which was completed in 1533, during the Shamlu–Ustajlu regency, by the latter's student, the Tajik poet Qasimi Gunabadi (d. 1574). Writing in the midst of internal strife and external challenges Gunabadi drew on, and sometimes contrived, parallels between the careers, and military successes, of Ismail and Timur and their respective houses, and thereby bestowed special attention on Tahmasp as his father's successor.[58]

Perhaps the centre's best-known cultural contribution during Tahmasp's reign was the continuing patronage by the shah, himself well versed in the Persian 'arts of the book' from the time of his residence in

Herat, of the *Shahnama* project commenced during his father's reign in the aftermath of Chaldiran in 1514 but completed between 1535 and 1537,[59] when Tahmasp was aged about twenty-six, as Shamlu-Ustajlu dominance gave way to Ustajlu domination and the civil war came to an end. That, in the midst of intra-tribal struggles and repeated foreign incursions from both the East and West, successive Turk-Tajik factions at the centre continued to devote the necessary, and substantial, resources to this most Persian of undertakings,[60] with its distinctly militarist overtones and its special emphasis on such themes as the divine right of kings, together with the already-noted contribution of Qasimi, attests to different ruling factions' united dedication to the paramount position of the Safavid house. It further suggests that the civil war was less about replacing Ismail's first-born son and, hence, natural successor Tahmasp or overturning the rule of the house itself than about assuming paramount influence over both.

The same homage to the Tajik cultural legacy is evident in the illustrations of a *Khamsa* completed between 1539 and 1543, after the end of the civil war. The *Khamsa*'s now appropriately unwarlike themes hearken back to a more traditional dynasty ruling in Iran – Timurid or Turk – and a relative absence, at least, of internal unrest, even if foreign dangers continued to threaten.[61]

Later years saw no diminishment in the centre's interest in and patronage of Persian as the dominant cultural discourse. In the new capital of Qazvin, for example, Tahmasp commissioned new palaces, a whole complex known as the Sa'adatabad Garden, with bathhouses, four markets, and the Iram gardens.[62] The former garden was divided by two avenues at the intersection of which stood the Chihil Sutun palace. The latter, completed c. 1556, was replete with paintings with strongly Persian lyrical themes, including images of hunts and picnics, games of polo and women promenading with friends in a garden. Some were apparently designed by Tahmasp and others by Muzaffar Ali, a relative of the famous Bihzad. In 1558–9 and 1561–2 *ghazals*, some by Hafiz, were added to its walls.[63]

The same interest in the Persian was also in evidence in the provinces. Thus, Tahmasp's nephew Ibrahim, governor of Mashhad since 1556–7, commissioned an illustrated edition of Jami's *Haft Awrang*. The work was apportioned among the skilled illuminators, calligraphers and illustrators based in Mashhad, Herat and Qazvin. The project took nine years to complete, exhibits a variety of stylistic differences, helped establish a number of younger artists including Shaykh Muhammad of Sabzavar and Ali Asghar and influenced others based as far away as Shiraz.[64] Herat's artists also produced single-page illustrations of dancing Sufis, hunts and picnics and male and female figures for the non-court market[65] although its poets did drift to Uzbek or other Safavid centres. Tabriz, despite losing its status as capital, continued to be a centre of the arts of the book as did Shiraz.[66]

These same distinctly Persian themes were visible in manuscript illustrations, textiles and a fine silk carpet produced in Kashan which features dragons, *simurgh*s, flowers and pheasants. The latter two appear also on the inside of a period lacquer bookbinding.[67]

Nevertheless, the traditional artisnal styles in all these areas of expression also experienced modifications over the period. Thus, where the style of candlesticks featuring in the illustrations for the above-mentioned *Shahnama* and *Khamsa*, with their wide conical bases and cylindrical shafts, suggests little change from the thirteenth century, a 1539 candlestick produced in Lahore exhibited a distinctly Persian style of arabesques.[68] The illustrations for Tahmasp's *Shahnama* feature the continued juxtaposition of Turkish and Timurid styles.[69]

Tahmasp himself was also known for his patronage of Persian poetry. Prominent poets of note in this period included the Nimatallahi Vahshi (d. 1583–4) of Bafq, in Kirman, who wrote *qasida*s in praise of the shah, Sayyid Ali b. Khvaja Mir Ahmad known as Muhtasham, of Kashan (d. 1587–8 or 1592), a writer of elegies, *qasida*s and *ghazal*s and Urfi Shirazi (1556–6 to 1590–1). Poets such as the *vakil*'s son Sharaf Jahan (d. 1560), the satirist Hayrat (d. 1553), Damiri (d. after 1578) and Abdi Bek Shirazi (d. 1580) were also associates of Tahmasp's court.[70] Although Muhtasham's panegyric poetry at one point earned Tahmasp's disapproval and some poets, including Muhtasham himself, subsequently turned to religious poetry, praising the Imams in particular,[71] Tahmasp continued to patronise non-religious verse and to compose such poetry himself.[72] The provincial courts, including those of Tahmasp's own relatives, continued their active support of 'traditional' Persian poetry throughout period.[73]

Female members of the household were also well-known patrons of the traditional Persian arts. Tahmasp's full sister Mahin Banu, known as Shahzada Sultanum (d. 1562), a close counsellor of her brother, studied Persian and the Qur'an with Tajik teachers, studied with the librarian, great calligrapher and manuscript illuminator and painter Dust Muhammad, and was a patroness of Persian literature and religious writings.[74] Tahmasp's daughter Gawhar Sultan Khanum (d. 1577), whose mother is not known and who married Tahmasp's nephew Ibrahim, was also a patron of the arts and known for her piety and learning[75] as was Pari Khan Khanum (d. 1578), Tahmasp's daughter by a Circassian.[76]

Tribal elements were also both patrons, and practitioners, of the traditional Persian arts, thus signalling their acceptance of the cultural discourse of their Tajik associates as the realm's prevailing cultural discourse. Musayyib Khan Takkalu (d. 1590), for example, a relative of the Safavid house via a marriage alliance with the Mawsillu, was a notable patron of the arts, a musician and a calligrapher.[77]

Tahmasp and the faith

Tahmasp had been solicitous of Shi'ism during in his early years. During his several campaigns against the Uzbeks between 1528 and 1533 Tahmasp made several pilgrimages to Imam Riza's shrine in Mashhad.[78] In *c.* 1531, Tahmasp's Mawsillu mother Tajlu Khanum (d. 1540) endowed property to Qazvin shrine as did the son of his *vizier* Qadi Jahan Husayni and in 1531 Tahmasp himself issued a *firman* confirming the Marashi family's guardianship of the shrine.[79]

Just as Ismail after Chaldiran so in the aftermath of the civil war the centre was increasingly attentive to its identification with the faith. Tahmasp was a prominent patron of Ashura ceremonies and was said to have left a sister of his unmarried for the Imam and a horse saddled and ready for the latter's return.[80] In 1537 he further confirmed the Marashi's trusteeship of the shrine in Qazvin, two years later he forgave the taxes of two members of the family and, following the relocation of the capital to Qazvin, he ordered the shrine's refurbishment and enlargement.[81] Tahmasp also repaired and/or embellished a number of religious sites, including for example, *c.* 1559–60, the great mosque at Kirman, and, *c.* 1565–6, that in Sabzavar.[82]

In a clear effort to link Turk and Tajik with Shi'i discourse in art as in life an illustration in the court-sponsored *Shahnama* associated with an early passage describing a journey on a ship whose passengers are the Prophet, Ali and the latter's sons Hasan and Husayn, depicts all of them wearing the Safavid *taj*. Shi'i invocations also feature in some of the manuscript's architectural panels.[83] A similarly Shi'i agenda is also in evidence in other works of the period.[84]

Others at the Safavid centre, including members of both the Safavid household, Turk and Tajik, also publicly affirmed their adherence to the faith. The Qazvin shrine was the burial place of choice for a number of prominent figures, including the *vizier* Qadi Jahan, Tahmasp's sister Shahzada Sultanum, and a son of Tahmasp's Tajik *sadr* Amir Muhammad Yusuf (d. 1570).[85] The same Shahzada Sultanum made important donations to the Iraqi shrine cities and at her death in 1564 another sister, Khanish Khanum, was buried in Karbala.[86] In Isfahan in 1566–7, an Afshar chieftain built a canal from the nearby Zayanda Rud to the Masjid-i Ali and appointed the city's *Shaykh al-Islam*, the Arab Ali Minshar Karaki, as supervisor of its *vaqf*,[87] suggesting the presence of a working relationship between elements of the Twelver clergy, including non-Tajiks, and the tribal military/political elite. Too, as attested by an Isfahani grain merchant's 1539–40 dedication of the revenues of a group of fruit trees to the Imamzada of Harun-i Vilayat,[88] in the civil war's aftermath local elements also moved to declare publicly their allegiance to the new faith.

Nevertheless, as already noted, over Tahmasp's reign the centre's spiritual discourse remained as heterodox as it was under Ismail. Turk and

Tajik elites, in the early years of Tahmasp's reign especially, preoccupied with the very fate of the Safavid project itself, generally evinced limited interest in any of the details of Twelver Shi'i doctrine and practice per se: none of the polity's chief officers, Turk or Tajik, were known for any decidedly, or specifically, Twelver Shi'i tendencies.

Ali Karaki, one of the few Arab Twelver clerics known for certain to have relocated from the Arab West in this period to Safavid Iran to participate in the faith's establishment, suffered the same fate as the various Tajik protégés of the contending Qizilbash tribes during the civil war.[89] Karaki, whose rising fortunes during Ismail's reign had coincided with Shamlu-Ustajlu pre-eminence, faced a particular challenge during the 1527–31 Takkalu regency. A network composed of the joint-*sadr*s Sayyid Mansur Dashtaki – a native of Shiraz and, although like the sixth *sadr*, Astarabadi, a student of the Sunni philosopher Davani, at least a nominal Twelver, and Sayyid Nimatallah Hilli, a genuine Twelver, their court-based allies and Sulayman Qatifi, under whom Hilli had studied, and whose opposition to Karaki dated at least to 1510, mounted a series of challenges to Karaki, who as yet held no official court position. Hilli, echoing his teacher's ruling, challenged Karaki's postulation that the cleric, as deputy (*naib*) of the Hidden Imam, was permitted to lead the Friday prayer during the Imam's absence.[90] In the event, in 1529, as the Takkalu struggled to maintain their position, Hilli was dismissed and banished. Two years later, in 1531–2, as the Shamlu-Ustajlu alliance, during whose pre-eminence in Ismail's reign Karaki had prospered, achieved power, Dashtaki was dismissed and replaced as *sadr* by a student of Karaki.

Coincident with the return of the Shamlu-Ustajlu alliance, during whose earlier pre-eminence in Ismail's reign his fortunes had flourished, Karaki participated in the centre's move against the Abu Muslim legends which had surfaced at Ismail's death and flourished during the regency of, and were perhaps encouraged by heterodox elements among, the Takkalu.[91] In 1533, with Karaki's loyalty to the Shamlu-Ustajlu centre thus attested, Tahmasp issued a *firman* ceding authority over the realm's religious affairs to Karaki and ordering all officials and elites to give 'obedience and submission . . . in all affairs' to Karaki, who was therein styled the 'seal of the *mujtahids*'. The *firman*'s distinctive religious terminology, in which the shah declared Karaki 'deputy of the Twelfth Imam (*naib al-imam*)', suggests its composition by Karaki himself as the newly re-emerged Shamlu-Ustajlu ruling coalition, struggling to assert its pre-eminence internally and externally, ceded responsibility for details of the faith's doctrines and practices to an individual of proven loyalty. If so, his allowing the temporal ruler to identify the Imam's representative in the document permitted the identification of the shah as the *imam* himself; indeed, during the reign of Tahmasp's father Karaki had initially similarly fostered the possibility of identifying Ismail as the returned Imam.[92]

Karaki subsequently moved to exercise his new-found authority to further establish both the faith and that authority. He ordered changes in the prayer direction of mosques throughout Safavid territory, an issue on which he and Dashtaki had clashed, and also changes in the levying of the land tax. He also ordered the appointment of a prayer leader in every village to instruct the people in the tenets of Twelver Shi'ism. The latter especially suggests the limited extent of the faith's appeal throughout the realm some three decades after Tabriz. Indeed the Friday prayers which Karaki had argued the clergy were entitled to perform during the absence of the Hidden Imam were discontinued soon after Karaki's own death in 1534, as the Shamlu focused on the Ottoman incursions which culminated in the loss, in the same year, of Baghdad and the shrine cities, in the aftermath of which Shamlu domination collapsed and the Ustajlu commenced their ascendancy.[93]

Most contemporary Arab clerics remained sufficiently sceptical of Safavid Shi'ism, perhaps all the more so given Karaki's continued associations therewith and the loss of its Western territories, as to avoid Safavid territory over the civil war period, even after Karaki's death. The Lebanese Husayn b. Abd al-Samad Amili and his associate Shaykh Zayn al-Din Amili in particular offered criticisms of Karaki's legacy and his Safavid connections.[94] Even Zayn al-Din's sudden execution by the Ottomans in 1557, two years after the Amasya treaty, and Shaykh Husayn's subsequent flight to Iran, failed to spark any mass exodus of Arab Shi'i clerics to Safavid territory.[95]

Subsequently, however, the Ustajlu-dominated centre, clearly mindful of Karaki's loyalty, was attentive to other members of his family. Karaki's son, for example, was honoured at court. Special attention was reserved for the son of one of Karaki's daughters, Sayyid Husayn (d. 1592–3), who came to Iran *c.* 1552, nearly twenty years after the death of his grandfather and five decades after Tabriz. Sayyid Husayn, as a clear mark of particular favour, was appointed Ardabil's Shaykh al-Islam. After a 1559 essay for Tahmasp in which he argued for the legitimacy of the clergy's performance of Friday prayer during the absence of the Hidden Imam – the position for which his grandfather had been roundly criticised – Sayyid Husayn was invited to the newly designated capital of Qazvin where, *c.* 1563, he was appointed the capital's *Shaykh al-Islam*, replacing Shaykh Husayn, who, as his teacher Zayn al-Din, had opposed Ali Karaki's position on this issue. Like his grandfather Sayyid Husayn was later accorded the title 'seal of the *mujtahids*'.[96]

Summary and conclusion

Although it has been suggested that soon after the 1555 Amasya treaty Tahmasp scarcely left his Qazvin palace until his death in 1576,[97] in fact the shah was continually active over this period in the face of a variety of internal and external challenges. In 1556, mindful of his half-brother

Alqas' treachery with the Ottomans, Tahmasp organised the arrest and jailing of his own son, the future Ismail II, in Herat. In 1557 Tahmasp sent troops to recover Astarabad. In 1558 he attacked and retook Qandahar from the Mughals and received the Ottoman prince Bayazid who had fled East after rebelling against Sulayman. In 1560 he received an Ottoman delegation and the following year he sent Bayazid back to the Sultan. In 1563 he parried another Uzbek attack and sent Masum Bek to take Mazandaran. In 1564 the same Masum Bek and a number of tribal amirs put down a rebellion in Herat and the next year this column moved North to check a potential threat. In 1566, raids were launched against Khurasan from Bukhara and the next year Tiflis was threatened and the governor of Gilan revolted. Masum Bek and a number of amirs checked this latter threat and Gilan was given to an Ustajlu governor.

In 1567 Tahmasp dispatched his own *Shahnama* with a large delegation to the recently ascended Ottoman Sultan Selim II (reg. 1566–74). Although perhaps intended to attest to continued good relations with the new sultan, the gift of this lavishly illustrated, very Persian text simultaneously spoke to the continued prominence of Persian culture at the Ottoman court, promoted Safavid superiority therein and, perhaps most importantly, as per our earlier discussion of the work, affirmed to the new Ottoman ruler the unity of the forces behind the Safavid project;[98] implicit too therein was the eventual 'Persian' triumph over more contemporary adversaries. In 1569 an Afshar tribal figure was sent to remove a recalcitrant governor near Bandar Abbas. In 1571 forces in Gilan rose and were put down and, in 1573 over-taxation of local guilds sparked a rising in Tabriz.[99]

The deaths of Jihan Shah Qaraquyunlu and of both Uzun Hasan, the latter in the aftermath of the 1473 Ottoman rout of Bashkent, and Yaqub of the Aqquyunlu, had inaugurated intra-confederation struggles from which neither the Qaraquyunlu or Aqquyunlu polities recovered. Indeed, the political fragmentation among the Aqquyunlu at Yaqub's death certainly contributed to an upturn in Safavid fortunes, especially as key tribal elements detached themselves from the Aqquyunlu system and aligned with the Safavid project.[100]

By contrast, in the face of both Chaldiran and Ismail's death ten years later, the Safavid project survived. The fractioning of the Qizilbash confederation at Ismail's death did not betoken any efforts to identify alternate successors to Ismail – Tahmasp's brothers Sam Mirza and Alqas Mirza attracted Turk or Tajik support – or to overturn the project itself, but rather stemmed from clashes for positions of influence around his very young successor. Arguably, once again, good fortune smoothed the success of the reconstitution of a new Turk-Tajik alliance around a new shah as both the realm's traditional enemies, the Uzbeks and the Ottomans, were unable, or simply failed, to press home the obvious advantages which each, the Ottomans in particular, enjoyed in this period as they had following Chaldiran.

At the same time, however, the realm's key constituents did not pass up the opportunities afforded them, especially following the Amasya treaty. Over Tahmasp's reign the Ustajlu, prominent under Ismail, only further consolidated the position of pre-eminence they achieved at the Safavid centre at the end of the civil war. As under Ismail, the other Qizilbash tribes came to be arrayed hierarchically below. Land grants, marriages and allocations of key posts, as before, secured the loyalty of both key members of these tribes and key members of the family itself to the reconstituted centre. Encouraged by the ongoing, and in this period perhaps necessary, Safavid acceptance of nominal Tajik conversions to Shi'ism and together with tolerance of continued widespread Sunni tendencies, Tajik elites also stood by the project. Judiciously applied sticks and carrots encouraged the loyalty of notables along the realm's Northern marches. Paralleling and further cementing these practical efforts to insure the support of its chief constituencies was the continued promulgation of the heterodox but exclusive spiritual discourse familiar from Ismail's reign coupled with the continued patronage, by tribal and family members in particular, of traditional Tajik cultural markers.

Over the longer term Tahmasp's reign thus less witnessed the establishment of any system of relations among and between the realm's core constituencies radically different to that which had obtained during Ismail's reign than it did the reconfiguration of those constituencies' arrangement. In both instances the Ustajlu were a key force at the centre. At the apex of the project's component parts stood the shah himself, whose discourse, as that of his father, both gave voice to, and mediated between, the potentially conflicting interests, agendas and cultural traditions, of these constituencies and in the process transcended them all.

3

The Second Civil War
Ismail II (1576–1577) and
Khudabanda (1578–1587)

As during Ismail's lifetime so over the nearly fifty-year reign of his son Tahmasp the Safavid project came to turn fundamentally on the person of Tahmasp as simultaneously the spokesman for, mediator between and transcendent figure above, the interests and agendas of the polity's core constituencies arranged hierarchically around him. Thus, as at Ismail's death five decades before, the configuration of constituencies which established itself at the centre over Tahmasp's reign was voided with his death in 1576, but with results which were both familiar – prolonged internal disorder – and unfamiliar – the formation of alliances both between and among traditional and newer members of the project's key constituencies and the pre-emptive murder of potential contenders for the throne and their supporters.

Alliances and antagonisms

Tahmasp's mother was a Mawsillu and his own Mawsillu wife was the mother of both Muhammad Khudabanda (b. 1532) and the future Ismail II (b. 1537). Of Tahmasp's other known wives four were Georgian, one each was a Circassian and Daghistani, and two others were concubines.[1] In 1556, nearly two decades after Ismail's birth, one of Tahmasp's Georgian wives bore him a son, Haydar.[2]

The succession of Haydar, twenty years old at his father's death, was supported by a complex coalition which consisted of Ustajlu, some Talish, Takkalu and Georgian elements at court, the supporters of Masum Bek Safavi and his son, called the Shaykhavandis, some *qurchi* elements and Tahmasp's nephew Ibrahim.[3]

This coalition was opposed by a similarly complex grouping of Rumlu, Afshar, Qajar, Bayat and Varsaq elements, Kurds, Pari Khan, Tahmasp's daughter by a Circassian wife, and Pari Khan's Circassian uncle Shamkhal Sultan. In short order this latter group captured and killed Haydar and freed his older half-brother Ismail who had been imprisoned since 1556. Members of Haydar's party having fled the capital, Ismail was brought thence and declared shah in August 1576. Later accounts embellish the accession ceremony itself[4] but the subsequent disposition of key positions of state and key provinces reveals that in addition to those mentioned above, elements of the Dhul-Qadr, Shamlu, Takkalu and, even some Ustajlu, were also among key supporters.[5]

The latter, no doubt mindful of the earlier threats posed to Tahmasp by his half-brothers Alqas and Sam, quickly moved against potential contenders for the throne and their supporters. Leading Ustajlus were killed as were a number of Ismail II's half-brothers, Ibrahim – Tahmasp's nephew – and other supporters of both Haydar and his father Tahmasp. Masum Bek's son, likewise a family member, was also jailed.[6] Pari Khan also soon fell out of favour and her wealth was seized. In 1577, that is within a year, however, Ismail was dead, possibly of an accidental overdose of opium.[7]

Although Pari Khan quickly resurfaced, other Qizilbash, including Shamlu, Dhul-Qadr, Ustajlu and Afshar elements, now settled on Muhammad Khudabanda, Ismail II's older uterine brother by Sultanum Bekum Mawsillu. Khudabanda, then aged about forty-six, was Tahmasp's oldest son, but his blindness owing to an eye affliction had caused him to be passed over at his father's death. Now, however, his Qizilbash supporters brought him to Qazvin from Shiraz and gradually withdrew their support of Pari Khan. Soon after Khudabanda's coronation Pari Khan and her Circassian uncle were killed, she by her own Afshar guardian. Ismail II's infant son was also killed.[8]

Khudabanda's second wife was Khayr al-Nisa, of the Mazandarani Marashi sayyids. She was, like Pari Khan, a non-Qizilbash who enjoyed Qizilbash support – in Khayr al-Nisa's case, especially from the Shamlu. Khayr al-Nisa now initiated an effort to have her first-born son, twelve-year-old Hamza (b. 1566–7), recognised as her husband's successor.[9] When, however, she moved against a number of key Qizilbash elements, and especially when she attempted to bypass key figures among the Afshar, Dhul-Qadr, Shamlu, Ustajlu – one of whom was in command of Ardabil and who shared control of Khurasan with the Shamlu – and Turkman tribes, all of whom had previously supported her against Pari Khan, they complained vigorously to Khudabanda. In 1579, less than two years after her husband had been declared shah with their support, these same amirs therefore sanctioned her murder. At this widespread disorder broke out both in the capital and the provinces among Qizilbash levies; some of Khayr al-Nisa's Mazandarani associates were targeted and even the Afshar *qurchibashi* and a Dhul-Qadr official sought the protection of their fellow amirs.[10]

A Takkalu-Mawsillu-Turkman tribal alliance now declared Khayr al-Nisa's first son Hamza crown prince. In response, a Shamlu-Ustajlu alliance rose in Khurasan in 1581 to assert the claim of their protégé,

Khayr al-Nisa's second son Abbas (b. 1571), whom both Ismail II and Khayr al-Nisa had tried to have killed. A march eastward against this alliance by Khudabanda, Hamza and their allies the next year turned back when faced with Ottoman incursions in the West. The following year, 1586, Hamza was killed in camp in Azerbaijan.[11]

At Hamza's death some Shamlu and Ustajlu elements supported the designation of the young Abu Talib Mirza (b. 1574–5), Khudabanda's third son by Khayr al-Nisa, as crown prince. In Khurasan other Shamlu had lost control of Abbas to Murshid Quli Khan Ustajlu who, with the support of elements of the Turkman – to whom he was related by marriage – Afshars and Qajars, brought Abbas toward Qazvin, picking up additional support along the way from the Dhul-Qadr. Abbas' formal accession, in 1587, with Khudabanda handing his crown to his sixteen-year-old son some ten years after his own enthronement and then himself being jailed in Rayy, signalled the return of the Ustajlu as the pre-eminent tribal force within the Qizilbash confederation.[12]

As during the years following Ismail I's death, foreign enemies took advantage of the internal struggles which followed Tahmasp's death. An Uzbek attack, launched in 1578, was repulsed by the Turkman governor of Mashhad. More importantly, however, just as a peace treaty with the European powers had permitted the Ottomans to launch the series of invasions of Safavid territory which began in 1532, so now the defeat which the Ottomans suffered at Lepanto in 1571 together with Hapsburg acknowledgement of Ottoman power freed Sultan Murad III (reg. 1574–95) to launch a series of incursions into Safavid territory between 1578 and 1590. Parts of Azerbaijan, Georgia, Shirvan, Kurdistan and Luristan fell, as did, in 1585, Tabriz. The internal disorder also encouraged risings in Kurdistan and Shirvan and feuding among Georgian princes in the North.[13]

The internal dynamic: Turk and Tajik in the second civil war

Over this period key Qizilbash elites dominated the polity's key central and provincial political-military posts, if commensurate with shifting political alignments. At the centre, Khudabanda made his son Hamza his *vakil* and, at his death in 1586, Abu Talib, Hamza's full brother by Khayr al-Nisa, assumed the position. However Murshid Quli Khan, the Ustajlu chief who put his protégé, Khayr al-Nisa's second son Abbas, on the throne, made himself *vakil*, thus signalling the resumption of the tribal domination of the post.[14] The Afshar held the post of *qurchibashi* in this period, as they had since 1534.[15]

Provincial governorships were held by tribal elites appointed from the centre or, as a sign of the inability of the coalition controlling the capital to enforce its writ throughout the realm, retained by tribes out of favour at the centre. In either case provincial authorities continued to retain considerable local autonomy.[16] Indeed Khayr al-Nisa's attempt to remove Kashan from the Turkman and otherwise undermine the role of other key tribal amirs had marked the beginning of her end.

Tajiks continued as administrators at both the central and provincial levels. Mirza Salman, of Isfahan's Jabiri family which had served the Aqquyunlu and, at the 1503–4 Safavid conquest of Fars, provided a *vizier* for the province under the Dhul-Qadr, was assistant to the *vizier* of Azerbaijan and then became supervisor of the royal workshops. Having changed allegiances several times immediately after Tahmasp's death, he was appointed *vizier* in 1577 during Ismail II's short reign and remained in post into Khudabanda's reign. Although at the murder of Khayr al-Nisa he was surrendered by Khudabanda and Hamza as part of the price for continued support of the Turkman-Takkalu alliance which controlled Qazvin and was murdered, the family maintained its hold over the *vizierate* of Fars until the eighteenth century.[17]

In another contrast with the first civil war, during this period there was a greater degree of continuity of service among the Tajiks in the central and provincial administration, irrespective of religious affiliations or association with changing tribal ruling fractions. Tajiks, and sayyids especially, continued to hold the post of *sadr*, for example.[18] Tahmasp's chief accountants were all Tajiks and most remained in post throughout the civil war. Mirza Shukrallah Isfahani, Tahmasp's last comptroller-general, was Ismail II's *vizier* and, at Khudabanda's succession, became *vizier* of Khurasan and warden of the Mashhad shrine. A Khuzani also served the Ustajlu Murshid Quli Khan in Khurasan under Khudabanda.[19] A member of the Tabrizi Kujuji family was Ismail II's chief scribe, comptroller near Hamadan and then comptroller-general. He served Hamza and Abbas I made him *vizier*.[20] At the provincial level also there was continuity in the Tajik domination of junior and senior administrative posts.[21] Khudabanda was especially respectful of the Tajik sayyid class, in 1578 confirming the Marashi sayyids as custodians of the shrine in Qazvin[22] and receiving at court Mir Damad (d. 1630–1), Ali Karaki's grandson through marriage to a prominent Astarabadi sayyid family, when he left Mashhad.[23]

Although Turk and Tajik remained pre-eminent at the centre, as will have been seen from the descriptions of the key actors at the centre in these years, newly incorporated Georgian and Circassian elements now began to appear on the scene, attesting to their rising influence within the polity. Pari Khan's uncle, Shamkhal Sultan, was sealkeeper during Ismail II's short reign, when the Ustajlu were out of power and a Qizilbash-Circassian alliance dominated the centre.[24] In 1585 Farhad Bek, a *ghulam* and chief administrator of the imperial household during Tahmasp's later years, became chief agent to Khudabanda's son Hamza. He built himself a huge mansion in Isfahan's Naqsh-i Jahan garden, away from the Harun-i Vilayat district, the city's traditional centre, using materials from a palace of Ismail I.[25]

Elite-level marriages contracted in this period, as earlier, point to efforts to win the support of, or at least placate, certain key constituents. Although under Ismail II many pro-Haydar Ustajlus were killed and he himself was son of a Mawsillu, he married an Ustajlu woman and in 1576, the same year as his father's death, he married a woman from the Khunuslu, apparently an Ustajlu sub-clan. He also seems to have married one of his own daughters to Salman Khan Ustajlu, whose father was Ismail I's grandson. In a clear attempt to strengthen his hand with newer members of the polity as well Ismail, also in 1576, married the daughter of his sister Pari Khan's Circassian uncle Shamkhal Sultan. His new wife's sister was Tahmasp's Circassian wife and remained Pari Khan's close advisor during this period and was killed with her.[26]

Khudabanda also used marriages to trawl for Tajik support. In 1555 Ismail II had married the daughter of the 1535–6 marriage between a sister of Tahmasp and the Nimatallahi Nur al-Din Yazdi (d. 1564), son of Ismail's *sadr* and *vakil*. In 1578–9, Khudabanda married a daughter of his brother Ismail II to Khalilallah b. Mir Miran Yazdi (d. 1607–8), the son of the same Nur al-Din.[27]

Marriages of others of Tahmasp's daughters in this period reflect similar political acumen. In 1577–8, i.e. after Tahmasp's death, another of Tahmasp's daughters – Maryam Bekum (d. 1608–9) – married Khan Ahmad Khan Lahiji, of a family long associated with the Safavids.[28] Ismail II promised another of Tahmasp's daughters, Zaynab Bekum, full sister of Maryam, to Ali Quli Khan, the Shamlu guardian of Abbas I and governor of Khurasan in 1576–7; the latter died before the marriage could take place, and she never married.[29] In 1580 another, the daughter of a concubine promised to a son of Tahmasp's full brother Bahram, then governor of Qandahar, was, at the latter's death in 1576, instead married to the Mawsillu-Turkman governor of Tabriz.[30] Another daughter, by a Daghistani princess, was promised to Musayyib Khan Takkalu, a cousin, but in 1580–2 married the same Salman Khan Ustajlu who married a daughter of Ismail II.[31] As for Khudabanda, in 1586, his first son by Khayr al-Nisa, Hamza (d. 1586), married into the family of the Tajik Salman Jabiri, whose career spanned the reigns of Tahmasp, Ismail II and Khudabanda, and whose family had served the Aqquyunlu.[32]

A Sunni interlude

As during the reigns of Ismail and Tahmasp so in this period, as typified by references in contemporary court chronicles, few of the realm's non-clerical elites – Turk, Tajik or northerner – were especially well versed in the details of the doctrines and practices distinctive to the established faith.[33] As earlier in the century many Tajiks, as already noted, retained discernible Sunni proclivities. Nominal profession of Twelver Shiʻism remained sufficient to secure employment at the central or provincial level over this period for those elites whose families, or who themselves, had served the region's earlier non-Shi'i political establishments. Such profession signified an expression of fealty to the person of the shah which, for the Tajiks especially, included acknowledgement of the Safavids' sayyid status, and amounted to a profession of loyalty to the larger Safavid project and their own part therein.

The widespread reappearance of the Abu Muslim traditions in the realm at Ismail's death and the risings among Nuqtavi elements in Kashan and Ismaili elements in Andijan during Tahmasp's 1574 illness[34] had demonstrated the clear continued potential for challenges to the dominant Safavid spiritual discourse at times of uncertainty at the centre. These were only aggravated by the struggles between the supporters of Haydar and Ismail II over the succession.

The case of Mirza Makhdum Sharifi (1544/5–1587) illustrates the relative weighting which the centre continued to accord loyalty and faith, especially at such times. Although his family could trace its lineage back to Sharif Jurjani, the famous theologian who had served Timur himself, Mirza Makhdum was descended from Sayyid Sharif al-Din Ali who, though not known for any especially long-standing Shi'i proclivities, became *sadr* in 1512, and the Sunni Husayni sayyid Qadi Jahan Qazvini. The latter, supported by the Ustajlu, was *vizier* during the latter years of Ismail I's reign and the early years of Tahmasp's, was dismissed during the first civil war only to be reappointed as the Ustajlu reasserted their predominance; his granddaughter married Khudabanda *c.* 1549.

Mirza Makhdum, appointed chief judge in Fars, where the family had extensive land holdings, came to the capital Qazvin later in Tahmasp's reign. He did not, according to Munshi's later account, enjoy the shah's immediate favour. He was allowed to preach in the city, however, and the large crowds he drew attested to his own prominence as a Sunni, to the continued presence of Sunni sentiments at the very political heart of the polity and to the centre's continuing tolerance of Sunnism.[35]

At Tahmasp's death, Pari Khan chose Mirza Makhdum to read the *khutba* at her brother Ismail II's accession and he was appointed co-*sadr*, sharing the post with Shah Inayatallah Isfahani. With such support Mirza Makhdum subsequently made even less effort to conceal his Sunni sympathies.[36]

The tolerance shown Mirza Makhdum and his overtly Sunni tendencies by Ismail II, Pari Khan and their Qizilbash and, apparently also, their Circassian allies coincided with efforts to moderate Safavid Shi'ism's exclusionist tendencies.[37] This was itself in accord with the terms of the 1555 Amasya treaty with the Ottomans which had required the Safavids to end the ritual cursing of the first three caliphs. Such moves would thereby obviate any Ottoman excuse for breaking the treaty and, more importantly, could only have encouraged greater loyalty among the realm's many at best nominally-Shi'i Tajiks[38] and, thereby, bolster Ismail II's own internal political position.

In the event, some Qizilbash amirs in alliance with prominent Iranian

Shi'i clerics rejected Ismail II's Sunni flirtation, bespeaking the extent to which Shi'ism, if not the detailed body of Twelver Shi'i doctrine and practice, continued to be the centre's faith of choice even, or perhaps especially, in these times of political, and concomitant spiritual, uncertainty. At Ismail II's perhaps timely death Mirza Makhdum, narrowly missing being killed by Qizilbash elements, fled to Ottoman territory.[39] However brief, the Sunni flirtation together with the political disorder which marked the period further can only have further deterred key Twelver Shi'i clerics based outside the realm from association with the Safavid project.[40]

The aftermath of the Mirza Makhdum episode and Ismail II's death witnessed a renewal in the realm's spiritual uncertainty: in the first four or five years after Ismail II's death contemporary sources record the rising of several pseudo-Ismails, described as darvishes (*qalandar*s) unattached to any recognised Sufi order. These were said to have enjoyed widespread support, among Tajiks especially in Luristan, Fars, Khuzistan, Hamadan, Gilan and Khurasan; one originated in the Ardabil area, the spiritual home of the Safavid Sufi order. The widespread, apparently non-Qizilbash, tribal support these risings also enjoyed, among Kurds and Lurs especially, suggests interest in the primacy of the militant Sufi dimension characteristic of early Safavid spiritual discourse.[41]

Not surprisingly, therefore, Khudabanda's subsequent ten-year rule witnessed a resumption in the identification of Twelver Shi'ism as the realm's established faith and the person of the shah with, as chief spokesman for and defender of, the faith. An inscription in Isfahan's Congregational Mosque dated to 1578, the year of his accession, refers to Khudabanda as 'the most just ... Sultan' and 'the Shadow of Allah'. Isfahan's Shah Zayd *Imamzada* dates to 1586 and mosque repairs were carried in Shiraz in the same year.[42] As well, a number of prominent court figures were buried at the Qazvin shrine, including Ismail II himself.[43]

The arts in the second civil war

Patronage of the traditional Persian discourse by the different factions in control of the centre did not suffer as much in this period of political disorder and spiritual contention as might be thought. Perhaps precisely in the midst of such challenges, the strengthening of bridges to the Tajik class, whose active support was indispensable to the realm's daily life, was all the more crucial. Indeed, as with members of that administrative class itself over this period, there was little turnover in the court-based artists between the reign of Tahmasp and that of his immediate successors.

Ismail II, himself a calligrapher, poet and painter, was pointedly interested in the arts of the book. Such painters as the Afshar Sadiqi Bek, Zayn al-Abidin, Siyavush, and Ali Asghar, who had served both Tahmasp and his nephew Ibrahim – killed following Ismail II's accession

– at the latter's court in Herat, all entered Ismail II's service and were
involved in the lavish illustration of a *Shahnama* which Ismail commissioned but which, likely because of his early death, was never completed.
If some of these artists' works were less detailed and perhaps less interesting than the works they had produced for Tahmasp, such artists as
Shaykh Muhammad, who had also worked for Ibrahim, continued to
produce works in the style reminiscent of the pre-civil war period. The
Husayni sayyid and calligrapher Mir Sayyid Ahmad of Mashhad served
both Tahmasp and Ismail II.[44] Khudabanda's son Hamza supported the
work of Siyavush, a student of Muzaffar Ali who had contributed to
Tahmasp's *Garshaspnama* and Ismail II's *Shahnama*.[45]

The arts also flourished in the provinces. Based in Herat Muhammadi
enjoyed the special patronage of Ali Quli Khan Shamlu, Abbas' relative
and guardian, in the years prior to Abbas' accession. Trained at the court
of Tahmasp, Muhammadi both contributed to a *Gulistan* dated to 1582
and produced single-page works, drawn and painted, for inclusion in
albums, suggesting that artists were as mindful of the need to seek support among individual patrons as that of the court whose patronage
could, especially in this period, vary with the taste of the ruler, let alone
the ruler himself.[46]

In Mashhad Abdallah Shirazi served Ibrahim for twenty years and
then entered Ismail II's service before returning East. In the early 1580s
Shirazi illustrated and illuminated collections of Ibrahim's poetry, perhaps with the patronage of Ibrahim's daughter Gawhar Shad (d. 1587).
His colleagues are identified with a page from a *divan* of Hafiz dated to
1581–2. The latter was produced under the patronage of the Turkman
governor of Tun and Tabas whose sister was married to Murshid Quli
Khan Ustajlu, the governor of Mashhad and prime supporter of Abbas
I's candidacy.[47] Kashan also continued as such a centre; the painter
Ali Asghar returned to his native city after Ismail II's death but continued
to produce works in a distinctly Qazvini style. The centre's scribes also
appear to have found work in the shrine cities of Mashhad and Qum
copying Qur'ans and other religious materials. Motifs found in bookbinding and illumination also continued to feature in carpet and metalwork and ceramics in this period and to attest to developments in each of
these crafts and their continued cross-fertilisation.[48]

Among prose writers also there was also some continuity of employment over the period. The Husayni sayyid Qadi Ahmad Qummi, whose
father had served Tahmasp and Tahmasp's nephew Ibrahim in Herat
and died in 1582, held employment throughout the reigns of both
Ismail II – who entrusted Qadi Ahmad with the project which, when
completed in 1590, two years after 'Abbas' enthronement, was the
chronicle *Khulasat al-Tavarikh* – and Khudabanda.[49]

Summary and conclusion

The conventional wisdom on the events of this period stresses the inherent dichotomy between Qizilbash and Tajik interests, with the recently arrived Georgian and Circassian elements allying themselves with the Tajiks.[50] In fact, however, contemporary political events are more usefully explained as the result of the break-up of the Qizilbash confederation between and among its tribal components and the forging of alliances between these and such newly emerging, and incorporated, elites as the Georgians and Circassians, while links were maintained with Tajik elements whose support for the project in fact remained consistent over the period. Too, political murder first features prominently on the Safavid scene following Tahmasp's death.

If times of crisis provide better evidence of mettle than do times of peace, then the struggles in this period in particular attest to the ongoing, if not yet final, breakdown of any remaining parochialisms which separated Turks both from each other but especially from Tajiks together with the beginnings of the integration of new constituencies into the Safavid project less than a century after the capture of Tabriz. So well developed were the ties between and among these constituencies and the Safavid house itself that all supported the perpetuation of the Safavid project – if not always on their own ranking within the centre's hierarchy and, therefore, on its leader. Safavid elites also agreed on the continued establishment of Twelver Shi'ism, at least and especially as it distinguished their project from both domestic and external alternatives, even if most were still unfamiliar with its finer points.

4

Monumental Challenges and Monumental Responses
The Reign of Abbas I (1587–1629)

Abbas' 1587 enthronement in Qazvin was supported by, and represented the reassertion of the military and political pre-eminence of,
elements among the Ustajlu. Other Qizilbash elements arrayed themselves around the Ustajlu-dominated centre:[1] soon after the formal
accession, various provincial amirs – including Afshar from Kirman,
Dhul-Qadr from Fars and Qum, Talish from Astara and Turkman from
Ardabil – arrived to pay homage to the new ruler. Under Murshid Quli
Khan Ustajlu's supervision, these received letters confirming their provincial holdings and listing the number of troops to be provided for an
expedition to break the Uzbek siege of Herat. The expedition was commanded by the same Shamlu *amir* whom Ismail II had ordered to kill
Abbas.

   In this same time frame, two royal marriages were arranged, one
between Abbas and the daughter of one of Tahmasp's sons killed by
Ismail II and another with the widow of Khudabanda's son Hamza,
herself the granddaughter of Tahmasp's full brother, Bahram.[2] Thus was
Abbas' position within, and as the head of, the house further bolstered.

The challenges

The situation was not stable, however. Murshid Quli Khan was soon
challenged by rival Ustajlu and Shamlu elements and their Tajik associates. Murshid Quli Khan's subsequent, and likely calculated, failure to
relieve his Shamlu rival in Herat which permitted the city's capture by
the Uzbeks,[3] can only have hastened his own murder, sanctioned by an
alliance of Qizilbash, including rival Ustajlu, and Tajik administrative
elements. The victorious Ustajlu faction soon dispatched those who had
served Khudabanda and his son Hamza and some non-Ustajlu amirs,
including some Shamlu and Turkman. Abbas freed his father from jail in
Rayy, where he had been consigned by Murshid Quli Khan.[4]

   The writ of this new configuration of forces and, by extension, that of

Abbas himself, did not extend very far, however. In Khurasan other amirs and troops, including Qajars and other Ustajlu, deserted to other Safavid princes, including the grandsons of Ismail I through his son Bahram. In Isfahan still other amirs supported Abbas' full brothers, Abu Talib, at thirteen three years younger than Abbas, and the younger Tahmasp (b. 1576). The feuding spilled over into Fars, Kirman and Yazd during the third year after Abbas' accession.[5] The Tajik associates of the various Qizilbash factions played roles in these machinations.[6]

The ongoing disarray after Abbas' accession allowed the Ottomans, who had commenced a series of invasions of Iran in 1578 and captured Tabriz in 1585, to continue their incursions. In the East, the Uzbeks, having seized Herat, moved against Mashhad.

The internal politico-military challenges to Abbas authority coincided with, and no doubt encouraged and were encouraged by, spiritual challenges. Between 1587 and 1589–90, certain Sufi elements openly questioned Abbas I about the identity of their *pir*, implying that the still-living Khudabanda remained the order's head. The reaction of the young Abbas, and his tribal backers, to such overt disloyalty to the person of the shah was absolute: the Sufis were executed. So, too, in 1592–3, was the leader of a group of Sufis in Lahijan which had supported Ismail I when he was in hiding in Gilan but who, in this period, also questioned the identity of Abbas as the present *pir*.[7]

Spiritual challenges were also offered by Nuqtavi elements. These, whose discourse focused on the cyclical renewal of prophecy, bespeaking associations with Hurufi and Ismaili doctrine as well as other millenarian discourses, had risen in villages around Kashan when Tahmasp fell ill two years before his death in 1576.[8] In 1590, several years after Abbas' enthronement, a rising by a Shiraz-based Nuqtavi poet whom Tahmasp had blinded in 1565, was foiled by local clerics. Two years later, however, the Nuqtavi Darvish Khusraw rose up in Qazvin. The darvish, from a family of refuse collectors and well-diggers, had been active and popular in the city, as well as in Sava, Kashan, Isfahan, Nain and Shiraz, late in Tahmasp's reign. Tahmasp himself had examined the darvish's polemic and had banned him from public speaking. After his accession both Abbas and other officials visited the darvish's lodge, in a clear effort, in the midst of the disorder recounted above, to derive credibility from associating themselves with such an evidently popular preacher. On the basis of numerology, Nuqtavi elements forecast 1593 as the year in which a Nuqtavi who had achieved true unity with Allah would assume power. In the context of the ongoing disorder this preaching is said to have attracted significant support among both 'Turk [i.e. Qizilbash] and Tajik'. The movement was also put down, with the shah's personal intervention,[9] but boiled up in Kashan, Mashhad and Fars. An Ustajlu *amir* and other Qizilbash elements associated with it were executed.[10]

Twice in the years after 1590, when Abbas was occupied with Uzbek challenges in Khurasan, the Mushasha Arabs of lower Iraq, known for their Twelver associations, moved to assert their independence; on the second occasion, they occupied Dizful. Safavid forces checked both moves.[11]

Although all these challenges came to nought, they reflected clear, ongoing disquiet among both Turk – even some Qizilbash – and Tajik, rural and urban elements, with the new shah's spiritual credentials, especially in the context of ongoing political strife.

Political and military responses: creation, consolidation and expansion

Once again, political pragmatism prevailed. A 1590 peace treaty with the Porte recognised Safavid losses of territory to the Ottomans, including parts of Azerbaijan, Georgia and Qarabagh, Khuzistan and Shirvan and parts of Luristan and Kurdistan and Tabriz itself, and included a clause requiring the Safavids cease cursing the first three caliphs.[12] With peace secured in the West, albeit in as humiliating a fashion as the Amasya treaty decades before, in the same year Abbas moved against and defeated the *ghulam* governor of Isfahan, and blinded and jailed his own two brothers. In 1590 also Abbas defeated Yaqub Khan Dhul-Qadr, governor of Shiraz, effectively marking the end of the realm's second civil war.[13]

Organisation for and the retaking of territories seized by the Uzbeks and Ottomans over the two decades since Tahmasp's death soon commenced and, in 1598–9, Eastern Khurasan, including Herat, Mashhad, Balkh, Marv and Astarabad, were retaken although Balkh, and much artillery, was lost to a Uzbek reinvasion in 1602–3. Turning West, Safavid forces took Azerbaijan, Nakhchivan and Irivan. An Ottoman counterattack on Tabriz was crushed, and Shirvan was retaken in 1607–8. Although a 1612 peace treaty recognised the 1555 Amasya boundaries, a further Ottoman effort to recover their lost territories, focusing on the Caucasus, followed. Despite a 1619–20 treaty, in 1623–4 the Safavids retook parts of Kurdistan, Baghdad and the shrine cities and occupied Diyar Bakr. A series of campaigns over the period brought parts of rebellious Georgia into Safavid territory. Qandahar, lost to the Mughals in 1594, was retaken in 1622.

Abbas' own court chronicler Munshi credits these military successes to Abbas' divinely inspired creation of the *ghulam* or *qullar* corps – small forces composed mainly of non-Qizilbash Arab and Persian tribal volunteers and captured Georgian, Circassian and Armenian youth, converted to Islam and trained in the military arts.

In fact, the formation of such a force pre-dated Abbas,[14] and the *ghulam*s served both as military levies and commanders, joining with tribal elements at the military-political centre and, alongside Tajiks, as administrators; there were even *ghulam* artisans in the royal workshops. In this period, moreover, the military *ghulam*s in particular were neither an independent, or especially large, body of troops or group of commanders, let alone the most prominent military force, or political power.[15]

By Munshi's own accounts, the Safavid forces involved in the minor and major campaigns against the centre's internal and external opponents over Abbas' reign comprised combinations of military forces – Qizilbash tribal contingents, *qurchi*s, *ghulam*s, non-*qurchi* Qizilbash, and even corps of musketeers. These forces were led, individually or sometimes jointly, by commanders drawn from various backgrounds. These included, for example, the Qaramanlu commander Farhad Khan (d. *c.* 1598–9), who was *amir al-umara* of Azerbaijan and governor, variously, of Astarabad, Fars, Gilan, Herat and Shiraz, and warden of the Ardabil shrine[16]; the Armenian *ghulam* Allahvirdi Khan (d. *c.* 1613), chief of the *qullar* corps (*qullaraqasi*) and governor of Fars; and the Kurdish commander Ganj Ali Khan (d. 1624–5), later governor of Kirman.[17]

Overall, if the *ghulam*s did supply both commanders and levies the balance of military and, hence, political, power over Abbas' reign remained with tribal forces, organised in their traditional tribal contingents or as unified cross-tribal, *qurchi* forces.[18]

Two other important developments further strengthened tribal military-political pre-eminence. First, certain members of the Qizilbash confederation including, especially, a number of Takkalu and Dhul-Qadr elements whose loyalty and reliability was suspect, were eliminated.[19]

Perhaps more importantly, however, the period witnessed the gradual incorporation into the Qizilbash confederation of a number of previously non-Qizilbash tribal elements. Thus, in his list of Qizilbash amirs holding the realm's key posts at the end of Abbas' reign,[20] Munshi identified as Qizilbash subclans or as 'tribes subordinate to them' many formerly non-Qizilbash tribal elements which had existed on the fringes of the Safavid project. The latter included, especially, substantial Kurdish, Luri and Chagatai elements.[21] Attesting to their important, but clearly secondary, position within the realm, only after listing all the Qizilbash amirs did Munshi then name those *ghulam*s who had been raised to '*amir*' status. The latter designation, he explained, occurred 'when a Qizilbash *amir* or governor died and there was no one in his tribe suitable for promotion to the rank'. By this gradual, somewhat casual process, by 1629 – the year of Abbas' death – *ghulam*s came to comprise only one-fifth of the realm's amirs.[22]

Similarly, although by Abbas' death *ghulam*s held eight of the fourteen key provincial governorships,[23] over the course of Abbas' reign, both the key posts at the centre and key provincial governorships remained in tribal hands; over the course of Abbas' reign the Shamlu and Dhul-Qadr emerge as especially prominent in these posts as they did in the number of *amir*-ships.[24] Over this period, as before, for example, tribal leaders mainly held the posts of *qurchibashi*[25] and *divanbeki*; the latter, although ostensibly a judicial post, was first and foremost a military position.[26]

Marriages contracted over the period further attest to the continued primary importance of non-*ghulam* elements. Immediately following his accession, as already noted, Abbas himself contracted two marriages within the household, further securing his position of prominence therein. One of Abbas' daughters married Isa Khan Safavi, grandson of Masum Bek, the *qurchibashi* from 1612–13 into Shah Safi's reign. Such was the importance of this particular family line that the first tribe in Munshi's 1629 list of the Qizilbash tribes was the 'Shaykhavand' – not a real 'tribe' at all but simply members of the Masum Bek line of the Safavid house – who were thereby accorded Qizilbash status.[27]

The prominence of the Ustajlu early in Abbas' reign was attested by the marriage, soon after Abbas' accession, of the daughter of Haydar, the son of Khudabanda's son Hamza, to the Ustajlu governor in Hamadan, Hasan Khan Ustajlu (d. 1624–5), who led the 1603 campaign against the Ottomans.[28]

Abbas, in the manner of his predecessors, also used marriages to cement further ties with local notables, especially those of potentially troublesome regions. In 1591, Abbas' eldest son Muhammad Baqir, known as Safi, was betrothed to the Gilani Yakhan Bekum (d. *c.* 1602), the daughter of the 1577–8 marriage of Khan Ahmad Khan Gilani (d. 1577–8) to Tahmasp's daughter Maryam Bekum (d. 1608–9).[29] In fact the marriage did not take place and in 1602, in the midst of an Uzbek reinvasion of Khurasan, Abbas himself married Yakhan Bekum. In *c.* 1590–1, in the midst of the Sufi and Nuqtavi unrest, Tahmasp's daughter Maryam Bekum, after the death of her husband in 1577–8, married Shah Nimatallah III, son of Mir Miran Yazdi, of the Nimatallahi Sufi order, with whom the Safavid house had been allied by marriage since early in Tahmasp's reign. An Afshar married a daughter of Mir Miran,[30] further signalling the degree of interaction between Turk and Tajik not common in the region prior to the rise of the Safavids.

Mir Miran's was a sayyid family and in this period, in fact, five of Abbas' six daughters were married into prominent Tajik sayyid families. One daughter was married to Mirza Razi, of Isfahan's Shahristani sayyids, who was Abbas' *sadr c.* 1607, succeeding his own uncle in the post. Mirza Razi's nephew Mirza Rafi al-Din, who married the same daughter of Abbas at Mirza Razi's death in 1617, succeeded Mirza Razi as *sadr*. The Shahristanis had served Ismail and Tahmasp and a member of the family was Isfahan's *vizier* during Abbas' reign.[31] The Shahristani sayyids intermarried with Isfahan's Khalifa sayyids, originally from Mazandaran, one of whom was *sadr* in this period. Mirza Rafi al-Din himself contracted a marriage with the family of the Khalifa *sadr*; the son of the latter, Khalifa Sultan (d. 1654), also known as Sultan al-Ulama, was *vizier* between from 1624 to 1632, into Safi's reign, and again in the reign of Abbas II. Through his mother Khalifa Sultan was also related to Abbas' own Marashi sayyid mother, Khayr al-Nisa, and he himself married one of Abbas' daughters.[32]

If, although Christian blood flowed in Safavid veins, members of the house never formally contracted marriages with originally Christian *ghulam*s, the *ghulam*s' 'special' status was nevertheless recognised. Thus, the presence of particularly prominent Caucasian *ghulam* at Abbas I's court bespoke an effort to associate with local elites[33] and *ghulam*s who were Christian by birth. Too, despite their conversions, Christian *ghulam*s were permitted to continue to observe their pre-conversion, non-Islamic practices.[34] As will be noted below, that Abbas II and Sulayman were the product of marriages with Circassians was never an issue.

Tajik elements, including many sayyids, also continued to be prominent in the central and provincial 'civilian' administration. All the period's *vizier*s were Tajiks, for example: together the Tajik Hatim Bek Urdubadi and his son, descendants of Nasir al-Din al-Tusi (d. 1274), served as *vizier*s to Abbas for three decades as earlier members of the family had served the early Safavids. Abbas' last two *vizier*s, including the above-mentioned Khalifa Sultan, were members, by marriage, of the household itself.[35] All those who held the post of *sadr* were Tajik sayyids; most, as we have seen, also related by marriage to the house itself.[36] Tajiks were comptrollers of the realm's finances.[37]

Outside the capital Abbas confirmed the Qazvini branch of the Marashi sayyid family as guardians of the city's shrine, various *suyurghal* grants as hereditary in nature and the management of the shrine's affairs as independent of the centre.[38]

Spiritual responses: reinvigorating Abbas' credentials

The centre not only oversaw the incorporation of new tribal and *ghulam* elements as 'members' of the project's key constituencies and the consolidation of the house's connections with Tajik sayyids and other notables, as described above, but also the reinforcement of the legitimacy of Abbas' political and spiritual authority in the realm. This process included reinvigorating the projection of the shah as simultaneous representative of the agendas and discourses of each of the realm's component constituencies, and thus sole arbiter among and between them and universal, transcendent ruler of, and over, their sum total.

The vast scale of this reinvigoration process itself attests to the perceived vast scale of both the internal and external challenges to Abbas' rule.

The greatest of the manifestations of this effort and its complex nature are to be found in Isfahan following its designation as the realm's capital – its central location making it relatively safer than Qazvin from Ottoman and Uzbek incursions – perhaps as early as *c.* 1590, concomitant with the effective end of the second civil war.[39]

In *c.* 1595, in the aftermath of that designation, Abbas repaired and renovated the area of Maydan-i Harun-i Vilayat, the city's traditional centre, and soon thereafter commenced work on the Chahar Bagh (Four

Garden) avenue and plans for the construction of great buildings for the Naqsh-i Jahan garden. A 1592–3 flood had destroyed many bridges across Isfahan's Zayanda Rud and in 1597–8 Abbas commenced a new bridge which was completed three years later. In 1602–3, following the 1598 recapture of Mashhad and Herat from the Uzbeks and with work on the Chahar Bagh avenue completed, and bowing to local residents' opposition to any further expansion of the city's traditional centre, the Harun-i Vilayat square,[40] work commenced on a new square based at the Naqsh-i Jahan garden retreat. This was the Maydan-i Naqsh-i Jahan. The Qaysariyya Bazaar (the Imperial Market) was also laid out so as to connect the newer with the older *maydan*.[41] On the new square construction also began on the Ali Qapu palace, whose gateway, perhaps functioning as an entryway into the Chahar Bagh Avenue gardens, so pushed its way into the new square as to break the symmetry of the facade itself, all the more projecting power and authority.[42] Although between 1602 and 1611 the court hardly visited the city,[43] construction on these projects and planning for others continued apace. Abbas also established the Abbasabad suburb, on the banks of the Zayanda Rud, for refugees from Tabriz. Although, thereafter preoccupied with a retreat in Mazandaran, Abbas made only five more visits to the capital before his 1629 death,[44] these 'secular' building projects insured that the new square, itself based on a traditional Iranian courtyard,[45] advanced the claim of Abbas and his retinue to authority in the politico-military sphere on a scale which dwarfed all other Safavid building projects to date.

The same image of the shah's authority was also promoted in similar fashion outside Isfahan. Thus, possibly prior to the relocation of the capital to Isfahan, Abbas made additions to the palace complex at Qazvin. In 1611, in the aftermath of victories against the Ottomans and as work on Isfahan's Shah Mosque began, work commenced also on the Farahabad (Place of Happiness) Palace on the banks of a local river in Mazandaran. Recalling Isfahan, the site included an arcaded square with a mosque at the South and palace buildings to the North; a separate palace was built for official receptions and administration. In 1612–13, another palace was established in Astarabad, complete with workshops and bathhouses, gardens and parks, the latter with intricate water-features. Abbas also commenced a further palace-garden complex in Kashan.[46]

The number and scale of religious edifices which appeared in the same time frame alongside, and all around, the above 'political' structures point to an especial effort to reassert Safavid spiritual legitimacy commensurate with political authority in response to the domestic political-spiritual challenges thereto discussed above. Reassertion of the centre's spiritual legitimacy was all the more important given the various internal challenges to Abbas' spiritual authority recounted above. Promotion of the association with Twelver Shi'ism in particular was all the more important in light of the Safavids' continued loss of control over the Shi'i shrine cities to the West.

The best-known of the capital's religious buildings, in fact, date from early in Abbas' reign. These included, most famously, the Mulla Abdallah Shushtari school, dated to 1599,[47] and the Lutfallah Maysi (1602 to 1618–19) and the Royal Mosques (1611 to 1630–1), the latter two both on the new *maydan*, as well as other mosques located elsewhere in the city.[48]

That there was a distinctive 'authority' dimension to these 'spiritual' projects is clear. The Lutfallah Mosque, still standing on Abbas' new square, for example, contained a inscription, executed in 1603–4 – even as Balkh had just been retaken by the Uzbeks – by Ali Riza Abbasi, in which the shah is pointedly referred to as 'the greatest and most dignified sultan . . . the reviver of the customs of his forefathers, the propagator of the faith of the infallible Imams . . . Abbas, the Husaynid, the Musavid'.[49]

On the new *maydan*'s Southern side work on the Shah, or Royal, Mosque was commenced in 1611, in the aftermath of victories against the Ottoman campaigns, Tabriz' recapture and as work commenced on the Qaysariyya Gateway on the opposite side of the new square. Completed two decades later, and nearly a decade after the recapture of Iraq, the new mosque eclipsed the older Congregational Mosque located in the city's traditional spiritual-commercial Harun-i Vilayat square, portions of which structure dated to the Saljuk period. The new mosque's traditional four-*ayvan* plan, like the new *maydan* itself, recalled the classical tradition of Iran's Islamic architecture. With its huge footprint and multiple functions, the new structure also recalled the huge mosques of the early Islamic period: the East and West *ayvan*s lead into domed chambers, the sanctuary features long eight-domed winter prayer halls, and the four minarets are located two each at the gateway and the *qibla ayvan*, with the gateway *ayvan* enlarged by wings projecting from each side.

As important for the shah's position as propagator of the faith, the new mosque also contained two schools, at the Eastern and Western corners of the courtyard, with underground rooms so that teaching could be continued in the hot summer and cold winter months.[50]

Further projecting power and authority, a unique double-dome structure was utilised in the mosque with the outer dome rising some 52 metres so as to be visible from four different places on the road from Kashan.[51] The 1616 mosque inscription, completed by Ali Riza Abbasi, stated that the command to build the mosque had been issued by Abbas, 'the Husaynid, the Musavid', and recalled the memory of Tahmasp, Abbas' grandfather. Other inscriptions, such as the Prophet's statement 'I am the city of knowledge and Ali is its gate', attested to the distinctly Alid nature of the project and, hence, the very Alid commitments of its patron.[52]

Outside the capital from early on in his reign Abbas was an especial patron of Mashhad, site of the shrine of the eighth Imam. Abbas visited the shrine some twelve times, often in the course of military campaigns. He also ordered much restoration work undertaken, and made numerous endowments, to the shrine[53] and commanded that the bodies of Ismail II and his own Mazandarani mother Khayr al-Nisa Marashi be moved to Mashhad.[54] The former capital Qazvin and, especially, its shrine, also merited the centre's attention and patronage over Abbas' reign.[55] In the environs of Kashan and Natanz also, much attention was lavished on religious buildings.[56] Too, the shah immediately visited the Iraqi shrine cities when these were retaken, along with Baghdad, in 1624, and also two years later, after an Ottoman effort to retake Baghdad was repulsed. He also reached out to the Shi'a of the Hijaz dedicating, c. 1605, a substantial portion of the income of the new *maydan*'s royal sarai, the city's chief sarai built in 1603, to the male and female sayyids in Najaf and Madina.[57]

The centre also openly associated itself with key Arab and Iranian Twelver clerics of the period. In addition to the buildings for Lutfallah Maysi and Abdallah Shushtari who had emigrated from Arab centres of the faith, Mir Damad, the Tajik sayyid descendant of Ali Karaki who came to court from Mashhad during the reign of Khudabanda, was another close associate of Abbas' court. Mir Damad's own marriage to Shushtari's daughter further solidified the alliance between Tajik sayyids and immigrant Arab clerics which dated to the Karaki-Astarabadi marriage of which Mir Damad himself was a product. The marriage of Sayyid Husayn Karaki's son Habiballah to a daughter of Maysi certainly solidified the latter's position among the realm's clerical elite.[58]

Mir Damad himself was a student of Shaykh Husayn Amili. As in other instances, neither Mir Damad's prospects nor those of the Shaykh Husayn's son Shaykh Bahai were diminished by Shaykh Husayn's demotion by Tahmasp in favour of Sayyid Husayn Karaki and Shaykh Husayn's subsequent departure from Iran. Indeed, Bahai succeeded his father as Herat's *Shaykh al-Islam*, was appointed to same post in Isfahan, took an active role in the capital's building programme and undertook domestic political missions for Abbas. He also managed the constitution as *vaqf* of the Qaysariyya bazaar and all the bazaars of the new square, including a sarai and bath, and the *vaqf* transactions relating to the Shah Mosque. Like Ali Karaki, Bahai also accompanied the shah on military campaigns.[59] He was also said to have cited a *hadith* from his father foretelling the rise of Ismail in Ardabil.[60]

The centre was simultaneously mindful of various, more 'popular' challenges to the shah's spiritual authority and took care to associate itself with such spiritual expression as a means of mitigating, if not also directing, the discourse and influence thereof. In 1596–7 Abbas removed Tahmasp's body from Mashhad, when his grandfather's tomb had been defiled by the Uzbeks at their seizure of the city, and buried it in Isfahan's

Imamzada Darb-i Imam, itself the final resting place of two descendants of the Imams. Abbas also endowed a *vaqf* of three hundred *tumans* to the shrine.[61] He also commenced work on a tomb for a grandson of the second Imam, Hasan, itself part of a complex of a mosque and school[62] and on a tomb for the mystic Baba Rukn al-Din (d. 1367–8), on the South bank of the Zayanda Rud.[63] In Kashan, where Abbas had also commenced a palace and ordered repairs to various religious buildings, the thirteenth-century *imamzada* of a descendant of the sixth Imam, Jafar al-Sadiq (d. 765), received special attention in this period. Indeed, obviously taken with the city and the shrine, Abbas himself would be buried inside the *imamzada*, metres from the tomb of the Imam's descendant Habib b. Musa.[64]

Abbas also encouraged Muharram ceremonies and the commemoration of the martyrdom of Imam Ali and sponsored display-clashes between the Nimati and Haydari factions – the traditional factional groups into which Iran's urban population were divided. The shah also revived the practice of illuminations on major and minor occasions, as sponsored either by the court or by sympathetic merchants, although, when such occasions fell during Muharram, they occurred even the disapproval of such court-associated clerics as Shaykh Bahai. Abbas also promoted both the celebration of the traditional Iranian New Year based on the solar calendar, where the Islamic calendar is lunar-based, and the celebration of *ayd-i qurban*, at least part of which, the procession of a camel chosen for ritual slaughter, was the subject of great popular celebration.[65]

At the same time the centre was also attentive to its distinctly Sufi associations, all the more important in the face of the already-noted challenges to the exclusivity of this link. Abbas' thirteen visits to the family shrine at Ardabil, as with his Mashhad visits, often at pivotal times, reminded the faithful – especially tribal elements whose politico-military support was so badly needed but whose spiritual allegiance was in question – of his status as the head of the Safavid Sufi order.[66] The continued importance of Sufi discourse to the Safavid project was further attested by the prominence accorded the traditional Sufi *tawhidkhana* at the Ali Qapu palace and other rituals and practices associated with the Safavid Sufi order itself – including the granting of the *taj* – which also projected Abbas' exclusive leadership thereof. Sufi elements were conspicuously present both at Abbas' accession and his funeral.[67]

Indicative of continuing regard for Tajik interests, traditional Persian cultural discourse was also encouraged. In the aftermath of Abbas' accession, the reign's chief manuscript-illustrators, including the Afshar Sadiqi Bek, appointed director of the royal artists' workshops, Zayn al-Abidin, Ali Asghar and his son Riza Abbasi, Shaykh Muhammad and Siyavush – all of whom had served earlier shahs and had spent time in Herat – commenced work on an illustrated *Shahnama*. What was completed of the project attests to a greater attention to detail and expression

as well as such motifs as jutting rock formations and various Qazvini-
style elements which had featured in Sadiqi Bek's contributions to Ismail
II's *Shahnama* and highlight the involvement of Shaykh Muhammad,
Riza Abbasi and Sadiqi Bek in developing a new style of painting within
the familiar tradition of the illustrated *Shahnama*.[68]

Other manuscripts from the period reveal these artists' simultaneously
increasing familiarity with and receptivity to European styles of expression, thanks to Shaykh Muhammad's introduction of such styles of
painting into Iran. A greater naturalism became visible and European
figures appeared in paintings otherwise dominated by distinctly Iranian
images and literary allusions.[69]

Economic responses

The rapid development of Isfahan, in line with the centre's effort to
project its military, political and spiritual authority, had concrete economic dimensions. By 1599, just a decade into Abbas' reign, the sub-
urban sectors of Isfahan were said to have 600 sarais, many serving as
centres for specific professions or for merchants from a particular region,
and the owners of many of which, like other urban sarais, constituted the
revenues therefrom as *vaqf* to schools, mosques and hospices.[70]

At the North end of the new *maydan* the Qaysariyya (Imperial) gate,
completed *c.* 1617–8, opened into the Qaysariyya Bazaar, built in 1603
at the same time as the royal sarai itself. The new bazaar's shops gradually spread northwards to link the new *maydan* with the old city centre.
Over the century the latter gradually became the socio-economic centre
for the common people and a place for religious festivals while the new
square to the South was increasingly dominated by, and the centre of, the
economic and politico-cultural activities of the court; the latter included,
for example, polo and horse-racing as well as ambassadorial receptions,
celebrations of the New Year in March and coronations.[71]

As part of its projection of military and political authority, but also
with profound economic implications, the centre paid great attention to
restoring the road security which had deteriorated during the second
civil war period. A network of caravansarais came to dot the major trade
routes which criss-crossed the realm, with the effect of boosting both
local/internal and long-distance trade. Abbas himself was associated
with a system of sarais connecting Kashan, an obvious favourite of the
shah, with Isfahan and many other sarais, most no longer extant.[72]

The realm was thus in perfect position to take advantage of other
economic developments of the time.

Just as the *ghulam* were added to the realm's constituencies to bolster
the projection of Safavid military-political fortunes, the addition of
Armenians, wealthy Armenian long-distance merchants in particular,
enhanced the economy. In *c.* 1604, and at least partly because of the
Safavid scorched-earth policy adopted in the Ottoman wars, between

5,000 and 10,000 Armenians were forcibly moved from Julfa, in Eastern Anatolia, into Iran's own heartland, to New Julfa in Isfahan. If a decidedly violent process,[73] on the road to Isfahan the wealthier Armenian merchants were treated better than others of their coreligionist deportees,[74] attesting to awareness of the position of these as the key middle men in the international system of trade passing West through Iran to the Eastern Mediterranean ports and Southern Europe, North to the Black Sea and Russia, and East to Afghanistan, India, China and the Philippines.[75]

By the mid-fifteenth century Iranian silk, known in the West from the thirteenth century, was one of the most profitable items in this Armenian-dominated long-distance trade.[76] Since 1543 the Portuguese had been using Hormuz, which they had seized in 1515 in the aftermath of Chaldiran, to tranship that silk to their possessions in India. The great Western European merchant trading companies, particularly the English and Dutch companies, were established in the late sixteenth and early seventeenth centuries precisely to seek out trading routes and monopolies in such items in the East independent of the Italian, Ottoman and Iberian trading systems.[77]

In the face of rising European demand for Iranian silk, as part of a general, renewed Western European economic expansion eastwards, Iran's silk output and trade and the overland route generally had suffered through Ottoman interference with trade and repeated wars over the century and, especially, Ottoman domination of the silk-producing areas in Gilan from 1585 to 1603.[78]

The Safavid centre, struggling to consolidate Abbas' authority against enemies foreign and domestic, was as much in need of allies as Ismail after Chaldiran and of specie with which to raise armies and fund other initiatives.[79] Thus, a redirection of trade away from the Ottoman-dominated Levant ports through the newly arrived Gulf-based English East India Company (EIC) and Dutch East Indian Company (VOC) portended a cut in Ottoman Customs revenues and a corresponding rise in Safavid economic, if not also politico-military, fortunes. Abbas therefore left few stones unturned in an effort to establish a variety of links – economic, political and cultural – by which to strengthen ties to the West, welcoming merchant delegations, political envoys, travellers and even missionaries. He sent the Englishman Anthony Sherley, who had arrived in Qazvin in 1598 with a request from England for an anti-Ottoman alliance, back to Europe with an Iranian envoy. From 1607 Abbas attempted to divert the silk trade to Portuguese-controlled Goa in India from which silk might be shipped direct to Europe. In an atmosphere of renewed tensions with the Ottomans *c.* 1615, Abbas sent Sherley back to Europe to explore further possibilities for alliances. Abbas also linked up with English forces to retake Hormuz from the Portuguese in 1622, accepted gifts from the EIC and VOC, and signed treaties with each in 1617 and 1627 respectively.[80]

While the joint military operation to take Hormuz succeeded, the companies' interest in and trade with Iran, in silk especially, fluctuated in accord with and depended on broader, world-wide trading patterns in goods. The companies, in fact, increasingly hoped to sell enough of their goods locally to finance purchases of Iranian silk,[81] and so company representatives sought full rights to organise their trade inside Iran commensurate with their own requirements. By contrast, the court wanted immediate payment for goods purchased, silk especially, in specie.[82]

The Armenian merchants, newly arrived in Isfahan, gradually re-established their pre-eminent position in the region's overland trade to the direct financial benefit of the Safavid court: in 1619 Armenian merchants outbid the EIC to take delivery of the shah's recently monopolised silk.[83] The Ottomans, despite, and in the midst of, Ottoman-Safavid hostilities, were mindful of the revenues to be made from the transit trade and were consequently increasingly reluctant to hinder movement of goods, including silk, through their territory. The companies gradually realised that the Gulf trade promised little consistent profit and much expense, and directed their interests elsewhere, mainly further East, while for Iran the overland route to the West, organised by the New Julfan Armenians, was consistently more profitable than the Gulf.[84]

The Safavid centre was in fact especially pro-active in its efforts to assist the recently arrived Armenian newcomers to establish themselves in Isfahan, just as it had been for the refugees from Tabriz. Abbas allocated the Armenian community land and seed and a 1604 decree exempted its clerics from a series of taxes. Just as Christian *ghulams* were permitted to continue their religious practices, so the Safavid court encouraged the Armenians to do the same. Trade clearly being good, the first churches soon appeared; the famous Church of Mary was built by a prominent silk merchant in 1613. A 1614 *firman* encouraged the building of large churches and by 1618–19 the community boasted ten. A later *firman* allowed the building of a cathedral and later still royal land was granted the Armenians along the Zayanda Rud.[85]

The centre was not lax, however, in simultaneously seeking out other economic opportunities. The court greatly expanded the range and depth of court-based workshops beyond the production of luxury items to include workshops for other, more mundane, 'domestic' activities and 'state-owned manufactories', both to maintain an independent source of labour and to make money by selling workshop-produced items locally and abroad at advantageous prices. The centre also moved to tax both imports and exports, to institute royal trading monopolies – including, from 1619, a monopoly on domestic silk – to sell concessions, to force local sales of royally imported and requisitioned, domestically produced goods at prices advantageous to the centre, and to employ royal merchants to handle all such commercial operations undertaken by the court. Such measures had been practised during the reigns of Ismail and

Tahmasp but not on the scale now adopted. Concomitant with Safavid pragmatism, in all these operations the centre benefitted from the services of Jews, the newly arrived Armenians of New Julfa, resident Indian merchants, called Banyans, and Muslims.[86]

The centre also moved to address its need for gold and silver. Both were used for brocading and gilding but specie was, as the basis of Iran's coinage, used also to finance military expeditions and to purchase such key imports as steel, textiles, indigo and sugar. The latter all came from the Indian subcontinent which was, in fact, Iran's most important trading partner over the period. With no gold and silver mines of its own, Iran depended on the bullion which flowed into the realm, mainly via the overland routes from Russia and especially the Ottoman empire, to finance the purchase of such items as silk. To curb the outflow of specie, in 1593 Abbas initiated currency reform and in 1618, the year before the promulgation of the silk monopoly, he banned the export of specie by both foreign companies and local merchants. The need for specie was at the root of the court's insistence that the foreign trading companies pay for silk in specie.[87]

Throughout these processes, the centre remained especially attentive also to the economic concerns of key local interests and the populace in general. In Isfahan's Shah Mosque are inscribed a 1625 *firman* reducing taxes for rope-makers and a 1628 *firman* lowering taxes for various named guilds.[88] *Firman*s dated to 1590 and 1613 in Kashan's Imadi Mosque attest to several tax reductions in the city.[89] Repeated popular protests led to the repeal of a 1606 tax levied on Yazd's weavers guild, the weavers being immensely powerful in the country, to maintain the local military garrison.[90] Likewise the centre was also responsive to complaints about the conduct of its officials, even if these were prominent Qizilbash figures, in financial and other matters.[91]

The centre was mindful of the need for good centre-provincial relations, especially in times of crisis, and was aware that local officials along the routes to and at the Gulf ports derived their own incomes based on the autonomy they enjoyed in the trading process, including the right to impose their own tax schemes on the foreign traders. Hence it continued to allow local administrators considerable autonomy and undertook only limited reorganisation of provincial administration. As a result, in addition to those already so classified prior to Abbas' accession only a few additional provinces, especially silk-producing provinces, were made crown land in this period.[92]

Declarations of loyalty (and wealth)

In the previous century key figures from among the realm's two chief constituencies, Turk and Tajik, had utilised a variety of means – from the acceptance of key administrative posts to the writing of chronicles – to signify their acceptance of the politico-military and spiritual dimensions of the Safavid project. During Abbas' reign, similar undertakings bespoke similar intentions although, commensurate both with the expansion in the number of core constituencies and growing wealth, the scope and scale of such projects dwarfed those undertaken during the reigns of Abbas' predecessors.

Isfahan, as this centre's first and main, if not sole, 'capital' was perhaps naturally was the chief focus of this attention, as such declarations there spoke especially loudly. Among court associates, for example, in 1605–6, the Sufrachi, the head of the royal table, built a mosque at the Northwest corner of the imperial palace area; the language employed to describe Abbas in the building's inscriptions echoed that in the earlier, court-sponsored Lutfallah Maysi and Shah Mosques.[93] In 1609–10, the chief of the imperial heralds (*jarchibashi*) Malik Ali Sultan, an Isfahani with a *nisba* suggesting affiliation with the Taji-buyuk tribe, built a mosque in the Southern portion of the Imperial Bazaar which bears a similar inscription.[94] The *ghulam* Muhibb Ali Bek, who organised the *vaqf* for the Shah Mosque in 1614, also contributed to that *vaqf*.[95]

Tajik elements made similar declarations. In 1601–2, a member of Isfahan's Shahristani sayyid family, itself affiliated with the Safavid house by marriage and members of which had served Ismail and Tahmasp and now Abbas himself, tiled the dome of Isfahan's Imamzada Darb-i Imam; an accompanying inscription acknowledged the Safavids' lineage, describing Abbas as 'the Husaynid, the Musavid'.[96] In 1610, near the older Congregational Mosque on the Maydan-i Harun-i Vilayat, Nur al-Din Muhammad Jabiri Ansari, of the prominent Tajik Isfahani family whose members had served the political establishment since the time of the Aqquyunlu, and who himself had effected repairs to that older Congregational Mosque in 1587–8, built a school with some twenty-two rooms, and constituted the revenues of various villages and shops as *vaqf* to support the school. As Abbas I himself had done with revenues of the Imperial Bazaar, so Jabiri directed revenues to be spent on the Hijazi and Iraqi shrines.[97] In *c.* 1623, a member of the Farahani family of sayyids, one of whom had served as *vizier* of Shirvan during Tahmasp's reign, built a small mosque.[98] Maqsud Bek, a local artisan who rose to become superintendent of the royal workshops in this period, built a mosque just Northeast of the new *maydan* in 1601–2; the *mihrab* inscription was completed by the same Ali Riza Abbasi who would later embellish the Lutfallah Maysi and Shah Mosques. A *takiyya* stood nearby.[99]

Similar contributions by non-court elements similarly acknowledged authority and, also, suggest growing wealth. In 1609–10 one Mulla Aqa Hawaijdar – the name perhaps suggesting connections with the cloth trade – built a mosque in the Imperial Bazaar to replace a Buyid mosque of the same name and adorned it with familiar inscriptions of loyalty to the Safavid project.[100] One Nur al-Din Muhammad Isfahani commenced construction of the main mosque in the Dardasht area of the city,

Northwest of the old *maydan*, completing it in 1629–30, the first year of the reign of Shah Safi, Abbas' successor; inscriptions therein attested to fealty to both.[101]

Outside the capital both familiar elements and members of the more recently incorporated constituencies used similar means to demonstrate allegiance to the faith and, thereby, the multi-constitutional nature of the Safavid project as a whole. In Kirman Ganj Ali Khan, the Kurdish military commander and governor of the province from 1596, commenced a mosque, school and sarai complex.[102] In 1590, a prominent Mawsillu figure was buried in the Qazvin shrine.[103] In *c.* 1612 Allahvirdi Khan, the Armenian convert, general and governor of Fars, sponsored work at Imam Riza's shrine in Mashhad. At his death in 1613 Allahvirdi Khan, a *ghulam*, was himself buried in Mashhad, near the shrine of Imam Riza. In Shiraz, Allahvirdi Khan's son Imam Quli Khan, who succeeded his father as governor of Fars at the latter's death in 1613 and was himself an accomplished military commander, oversaw the building of the Khan school for the city's own Mulla Sadra, on whom see further below, in 1615. The school exhibited a style which was reminiscent both of earlier schools and of those in Isfahan and demonstrated the continuing vitality of provincial architectural styles.[104] The projects of Ganj Ali Khan and Allahvirdi Khan in particular point to the successful integration of the *ghulam* into the political-spiritual discourse of the larger Safavid project, and to the wealth being accumulated at the provincial level.

'Secular' buildings also attested to growing wealth and confidence. Thus, the commander of the musketeers and the court jester built large mansions in the capital. Provincial elements also asserted their presence, and allegiance, on the national scene in the same manner. Ganj Ali Khan had a grand mansion on the South bank of the Zayanda River and Imam Quli Khan also built a grand mansion next to the mosque of Lutfallah Maysi in Isfahan.[105] Rustam Khan Qaramanlu, a local governor in the Shirvan region, also built one of Isfahan's largest mansions, complete with a bathhouse and mosque.[106]

Court elements also actively participated in the realm's economic projects, thereby both declaring their loyalty to the larger project itself and, doubtless also, enhancing their own economic position in the prevailing healthy economic climate. Beginning in 1597–8 Allahvirdi Khan oversaw construction of a bridge in Isfahan commenced by Abbas I. When completed in 1607 later the still-visible forty-vaulted bridge linked the garden retreat of the Naqsh-i Jahan area and the Abbasabad garden retreat known as Hizar (one thousand) Jarib. Upstream from the latter, the Marnan Bridge connecting the New Julfa area with the Western sectors of the Abbasabad suburb was built by an Armenian merchant at Abbas' request.[107] When Malik Ali, chief head of the imperial heralds, built his mosque in 1610, he probably also built the nearby sarai which bears his name and housed the city's Jewish merchants.[108] The *ghulam*

Muhibb Ali Bek, who organised and contributed to, the *vaqf* for the Shah Mosque in 1614, also built a sarai for the Indian cloth merchants who traded in brocaded cloth, robes and turban cloth with silver and gold thread.[109]

Local merchants also undertook such projects. In Isfahan, for example, Abbas also approached a rich perfume-seller, one Maqsud, and convinced him to build a sarai. The latter obliged, of course, and made over the structure to Abbas himself. The shah, in turn, gave it to his sister. A coffee merchant built an inn for merchants from Natanz who sold raisins, linen and fruit.[110]

Outside the capital, familiar and recently incorporated elements contributed also to the development of both the polity's economic infrastructure and general security. Zaynab Bekum (d. 1641–2), Abbas' aunt by a Georgian woman, used her own income from the polltax (*jizya*) of Yazd's Zoroastrian community to complete one of the sarais on the road to Mashhad, together with a water tank and pond. The same Muhibb Ali Bek completed this work using income from both crown estates and those of Zaynab Bekum.[111] In Natanz a court minister who was a Husayni sayyid built a fortified rest house (*ribat*) *c.* 1619.[112] In Kirman the Kurdish general Ganj Ali Khan built a sarai as part of a mosque and school complex. The wife of the khan of Lar is said to have built a sarai on the road to Gombroon (Bandar Abbas).[113]

The growing production of single-page illustrations over this period further attests to the growing wealth of middle-ranking associates of the central and provincial courts, commercial and merchant elements, and certainly the newly incorporated constituencies, clearly eager to patronise the same artists who enjoyed the favour of the courts' elites. Where illustrations of young courtly figures had been popular in the previous century, in this period single-page paintings of older men, as darvishes and labourers, for example, were popularised by Riza Abbasi, Sadiqi Bek Afshar, Muhammadi and Siyavush. Indeed, during his period away from the court, between 1603 and 1610, when he frequented the company of wrestlers and engaged in other 'popular' pursuits, Riza devoted himself entirely to the such illustrations. After his return to court Riza made direct use of the paintings and drawings of Bihzad and later still his work exhibited aspects both of earlier styles – especially in use of slender, elongated torsos – and new styles – a 'new' face with thick eyebrows, round cheeks and full lips. His legacy set the stage for a whole school of later Safavid artists.[114]

Such innovative combinations of the traditional and the new are also found in other areas of material culture. Early in Abbas' reign the metalworking schools of Khurasan and Western Iran exhibited development of traditional styles within familiar forms of expression, as attested by candlesticks dated 1588–9 and 1598–9; the latter, an early example of enamelling in metalwork, features an image of Layla and Majnun and youths pouring wine. The appearance of a new form of ewer as early as

1602–3, perhaps deriving from an earlier Indian example, attests to a vitality of style and, in this case, a taste for the exotic – not unusual in the increasingly cosmopolitan, and increasingly wealthy setting of both the new capital and the realm itself.[115]

Similarly, domestic demand for ceramics, produced throughout the realm and both beholden to Chinese styles and exhibiting awareness of such other forms of expression as painting, grew so fast in this period that Abbas settled some 300 Chinese potters in Iran to boost domestic production. The growth in demand for such pottery products as hookah bases and ceramic water pipes was certainly boosted by the introduction of tobacco in the 1610s, as attested by the appearance of both items in a 1630 painting of Riza Abbasi. Iranian potters' output was of such quality that the VOC mixed the best Kirmani ceramics with Chinese items for export to Europe.[116] Similarly, early in the period carpet production in Kashan, Kirman and Herat continued apace but utilised designs similar to those of the previous century. The growth of Isfahan and the need for carpets to cover the floors of the capital's growing number of mosques and schools encouraged production of carpets using more silk and gold than had been seen before, another sign of growing wealth which also increased domestic demand for specie. The finest examples of these 'Polonaise' carpets, of silk warps and wefts, were produced both for domestic elites and also for export.[117]

History as politics

Like court chronicles composed during the previous century, so the chronicles of Abbas's reign also demonstrated the loyalty of their authors and, implicitly in turn, the constituencies of which they were members, to the Safavid project. Where, however, the sixteenth century's chronicles recalled Turko-Mongol claims to universal rule and rooted that present in the events of prehistory, the historians of Abbas' reign, reflecting a growing sense of self-assurance, generally reached back only to the distinctly Safavid past and such earlier Safavid chronicles as Khvandamir's *Habib al-Siyar*, whose roots lay in *Rawzat al-Safa* of his grandfather Mir Khvand, to project, to highlight and thereby to legitimate Abbas' position as the latest head of the family.

Within this common framework the historians of the period nevertheless pursued distinctly individual agendas. Qadi Ahmad Qummi (d. after 1606), the Tajik Husayni sayyid who completed his *Khulasat al-Tavarikh* in 1590–1, began his history with the life and times of Shaykh Safi al-Din whose line he traced back to the seventh of the twelve imams, Imam Musa, thus demonstrating Tajik sayyids' continuing acceptance of the Safavids as one of their own. In his *Tarikh-i Abbasi*, completed *c.* 1611–12, the court astrologer Jalal al-Din Yazdi offered an accounting of astrological bases underpinning the reign of Abbas before offering a detailed genealogy of Abbas' forebears which also included Imam Musa.

The court scribe Iskandar Bek Munshi (d. 1633) began his *Tarikh-i Alam Ara-yi Abbasi*, volume one of which dates to 1616 and which was completed in 1629, with an account of the life of the Prophet and the Imams.[118]

These chroniclers' embellishment of certain aspects of the Safavid past furthered its legitimacy in the present. Both Qadi Ahmad and Munshi emphasised associations between the Safavid house and Timur, the former with Shaykh Safi al-Din's son Sadr al-Din Musa (d. 1391), and the latter with Musa's son Khvaja Ali (d. 1427).[119] Qadi Ahmad retained the version of the distinctly Twelver Shi'i preparations for the funeral of Shaykh Zahid, Safi al-Din's mentor and spiritual guide, found in Amir Mahmud's 1550 *Zayl-i Habib al-siyar*, bespeaking Tajik sayyid acceptance of the longevity of Safavid claims to association with the faith.[120] In his *Afzal al-Tavarikh*, a three-volume history of the Safavids to the death of Abbas I begun in 1616–17, and the second volume of which was being revised in India in 1639, a decade after Abbas' death[121] Fazli Khuzani, whose forbears had served the Safavid court, embellished accounts of Ismail I's early years to emphasise the Sufi and Qizilbash dimensions to his career.[122]

Varying accounts of Abbas' victory over Yaqub Khan Dhul-Qadr and his 1590 execution, arguably marking the end of the second civil war, further highlight the preoccupations of the centre and its historians in this period. With his Timurid sympathies Qadi Ahmad notes Yaqub Khan built a fort with the stones from a Timurid-period religious school and orphanage which he ordered destroyed. In his 1598 *Nuqavat al-Asar fi zikr al-akhyar*, Mahmud Afushta Natanzi (b. 1531–2), of whom little is known, portrayed Yaqub Khan as an oppressor of tribes and commoners who failed to acknowledge Abbas' authority. Yazdi highlighted Yaqub Khan's destruction of the Timurid school but also the plundering of other schools, domes, arches and other buildings to build a castle and garden for himself, his killing of a cleric and plundering of Yazd. Munshi, the court secretary, focused on Yaqub's refusal of various summons to court and his claim to the province of Fars as his own.[123] Yaqub Khan emerges as the antithesis of key traditions of leadership – Sufi, Shi'i, Qizilbash/tribal and Tajik/administrative – with which the polity's various components were identified, and he thus comes to personify all the realm's enemies and all the challenges which Abbas, and the larger project which he embodied, faced over his reign.

The 'popular' dimension: spiritual disquiet on the urban scene

The physical expansion of Isfahan, if not of other cities as well, and especially the growth of urban 'popular' classes over the period, encouraged the expansion of links between urban artisans and craftsmen and urban-based messianic Sufi discourse already visible early in Abbas' reign with the urban appeal of the Nuqtavi and Darvish Khusraw. The growing presence of these elements, and these connections, are well attested. The painter Riza Abbasi, during his 1603–10 self-imposed removal from court, consorted with the urban 'lower orders'; many of his works from this period are replete with images of older men as the darvishes and labourers he saw in the city.[124] Mir Damad's student Mir Findiriski (d. 1640), a philosopher, poet and teacher of both mathematics and medicine, also spent much time among these elements.[125] In his 1617–18 *Kasr Asnam*, Sadr al-Din Muhammad Shirazi, known as Mulla Sadra (d. 1640), a Shirazi aristocrat and student of both Mir Damad and Shaykh Bahai, lamented the fact that artisans and craftsmen were abandoning their professions to associate themselves with popular Sufi movements.[126] An anonymous essay written between 1626 and 1629 attacking the messianic veneration of Abu Muslim points to the reappearance on the urban scene of this tradition, of which the centre had been wary since early in the previous century.[127]

Such sightings, as in the previous century, occurred especially at times when messianic fervour was abroad elsewhere in the realm. Indeed, *c.* 1614–16, coinciding with the apparent involvement of the shah's eldest son Muhammad Baqir in a plot which resulted in the prince's murder by a *ghulam* who was later freed for his act of loyalty, another group of Lahijani Sufis were executed, condemned as 'not being Sufis'[128], i.e. for disloyalty to the person of the ruling shah/*pir*. In 1619–20, coincident with the appearance of a 'pestilence' which struck down large numbers of courtiers and commoners and which was attributed to the appearance of a comet the year before and which rendered Abbas himself extremely ill, a rising incited by Gilani sayyids, one of whom proclaimed himself the deputy of the Hidden Imam, attracted a wide following.[129]

Concerned with the oppositional discourse on offer in some of the capital's coffee houses, patronised as they were by artists, poets, musicians, storytellers and Sufis, Abbas delegated clerical associates of the court to monitor the activities of these venues and to preach sermons or lead prayers along more acceptable lines.[130] The appearance of many Persian-language religious primers on various, basic aspects of Twelver doctrine and practice written by clerical associates of the court, including Shaykh Bahai, Mir Damad and such of their students and associates as Muhammad Taqi Majlisi (d. 1659),[131] represented efforts by the centre and its clerical associates to influence 'popular' spiritual discourse in the period, if not to insure its 'orthodoxy'.

Although Mir Damad and Bahai served the court, in their scholarly writings both were active in their pursuit of philosophical inquiry and, particularly, its reconciliation with Twelver Shi'ism. The former built on the illuminationist interpretations of Suhravardi (d. 1191) and Davani to transform the metaphysics of Ibn Sina (d. 1037) from a purely rational, abstract system of thought into a spiritual reality within a distinctly Twelver Shi'i framework.[132] Mulla Sadra was active in the reconciliation of philosophy with gnosis (*irfan*), based on many of the basic principles of gnosis as formulated by Ibn al-Arabi (d. 1240) and other prominent Muslim thinkers from the twelfth to the sixteenth century, but firmly grounded his reconciliation of these two traditions in the revelation of Twelver Shi῾ism.[133]

These same clerics also actively supported expanding the role of the senior clerics trained in the rationalist religious sciences, the *mujtahid* or *faqih*, in both the formulation of doctrine and practice and the clerics' assumption of many of the Imam's practical responsibilities of daily import to the life of the community during the Imam's absence, thus building on the principle of 'general deputyship' enunciated by Mir Damad's forbear Ali Karaki. Bahai argued for greater clerical control over the collection and distribution of both *zakat* and *khums* during the occultation. Mir Damad argued the *faqih* was permitted to lead the Friday congregational prayer service while the Imam was absent.[134]

To be sure, the audience for these clerics' Arabic-language philosophical, theological and jurisprudential writings, and their disputations, was likely restricted to the clergy itself.[135] However, the combination of recourse to rationalist philosophical thought and these clerics' consequent and exclusive claim to exercise many of the Imam's rights and prerogatives aroused lower-ranking, less well-connected clerics. The latter objected, in particular, first, to the claim to exercise authority over issues of doctrine and, especially, over affairs of daily, very public, import to the life of the community during the Imam's continued absence and second, to the court backing which these clerics, and their claims, enjoyed. The former's overt and wide-ranging interest in seemingly obscurantist philosophical inquiry, together with the tendencies of some to frequent the popular quarters, allowed their critics to challenge their authority by equating this sort of inquiry with the doctrines and practices of 'popular' Sufism itself. The strident denunciations of Shaykh Bahai's alleged Sufi tendencies, apparently visible in the supposed mystical dimensions of his poetry and the darvish dress he is said to have worn, as well as his preferences for an expanded role for the clergy, eventually forced him to resign as Isfahan's *Shaykh al-Islam*. Mulla Sadra was also denounced for his 'popular' Sufi tendencies and, despite repeated efforts to distance himself therefrom, finally abandoned the capital for a prolonged residence in Kahak, near Qum.[136] Taqi Majlisi who, like Mir Damad and his own teacher Shaykh Bahai, was descended from Arab émigrés and was interested in philosophical discourse, was himself publicly linked to the Abu Muslim revival.[137]

Debates over the extent of clerical authority during the Imam's absence continued as they had during the reigns of Ismail and Tahmasp and, indeed, since early in the faith's history. Muhammad Amin Astarabadi (d. 1640) criticised earlier Shi῾i scholarship, and such Safavid-period clerics as Ali Karaki, Shaykh Zayn al-Din and Bahai – Bahai's father having been a student of the Shaykh – for failing to ground their theological and jurisprudential analyses in the revealed texts of the faith, particularly the *hadiths*, or *akhbar*, of the Imams; hence the name Akhbari, for the 'school' of thought with which Astarabadi came to be identified. Related arguments surfaced questioning the textual basis for the *mujtahid*'s assumption of the Imam's responsibilities for issuing legal rulings, collecting and distributing believers' alms and leading of Friday prayer as the Imam's deputy (*naib*) during his absence. The court's clerical associates, including moderates of opposing persuasions, favoured the prayer. However, in that the prayer would have mentioned the shah's name and thereby legitimised his rule, its permissibility during the Imam's absence was as much a touchstone in the continuing debate over clerical authority and the clergy's association with, and its legitimisation of, the centre in this period as it had been in the previous century.[138]

Summary and conclusion

The great political-military, economic and cultural achievements with which Abbas' reign has been so often, and so often solely, identified – from the rise of the *ghulam* to the architectural embellishment of Isfahan, the flowering of philosophical inquiry, the legacy of the arts and even the rise of the Armenian community in Isfahan – as well as those achievements, such as the expansion of the Qizilbash, which have received less attention to date – were part and parcel of, and followed directly from, the questioning of the authority and legitimacy of Abbas and the Safavid project as a whole on all these levels.

The vast scale and multi-layered nature of these achievements over Abbas' reign followed from, and attests to, the range and perceived scale of these challenges.

The composition of Abbas' 'cabinet' at his death in particular reflects the success of the incorporation into the Safavid project, over the more than four decades since his 1587 accession, of new constituencies into the larger project without dislodging established ones and the importance of close family ties particular. In 1629, of the top thirteen members of the cabinet by office, five were Tajiks (including the *vizier* and the *sadr*, both of whom were sayyids), five were *ghulam*s and three had tribal connections (including a Shamlu *vakil* and the Shaykhavand *qurchibashi*). The *ghulam*, as soldiers and administrators, straddled the roles of both the traditional constituencies; eight of the fourteen key provincial governorships and about a quarter of the realm's *amir*s were *ghulam*s at Abbas' death.

Nevertheless, tribal elements still dominated the polity's political and military spheres, as represented by the gradually expanded Qizilbash confederation, with the Shamlu, especially, and Dhul-Qadr apparently replacing the Ustajlu as the pre-eminent tribes therein by Abbas' death: the balance of the realm's governorships were held by tribal elements who also constituted three-quarters of the total number of the realm's *amir*s.[139] Tajiks continued to play a key role outside the administrative sphere as well, and alliances with Northern notables were more firmly established in this period.

In addition to the *ghulam* as a new constituency, Twelver clerics, from home and abroad, now also appeared at the centre in numbers sufficient to constitute a distinct, loyal, interest group, their loyalty and integration into Iranian society further encouraged by key marriages and appointments. Armenians, and especially the great long-distance trading elements, also now figured as a constituency important to the life of the realm, that importance further attested by the centre's efforts to smooth their settlement in Isfahan and the freedom of religious expression accorded them there. In response, the Armenians, and Jews, returned loyalty (and financial support) to the shah and the project itself.[140] Even the foreign trading companies, official and unofficial political delegations, missionaries and other foreign travellers may be said to have constituted further constituencies of potential political and economic allies clustered about, if further away from, the court.

One by one these elements openly professed their loyalty to the larger Safavid project as headed by the shah, and together they participated in the demarcation of a politically stable, physically larger and economically more vibrant polity whose makeup was significantly more complex than it had been when Ismail I entered Tabriz over a century before.

That the *vizier, sadr* and *qurchibashi* were related to the house via connections to Abbas himself, demonstrates the perceived importance in this turbulent period of the loyalty of those related by blood ties. Their loyalty was seen as increasingly indispensable to the good fortunes of the polity and to the manner in which the family, as a constituent of and like the centre itself, continued to expand in Abbas' reign. This expansion, as before, was to secure the project's fortunes by linking the realm's constituencies both to itself and, thereby, to each other. In the midst of turmoil personal loyalty was the key to promotion to and longevity in these offices. Although both the latter might also turn on competence and popularity, loyalty to the person of the shah bespoke loyalty to the larger polity itself and, it followed, to the multi-constitutional project which underlay it.[141]

Could the configuration of both familiar and newer constituencies, all of whose traditions and discourses were recognised and encouraged over the period and which underpinned Abbas' rule, outlast the single figure around whom it had coalesced where, earlier in the dynasty's history, less complex configurations had failed to do so?

5

Shifts at the Centre and a Peace Dividend
Shah Safi (1629–1642)

A smoother accession? Turmoil at the centre

Abbas died in January 1629, at his summer palace in Mazandaran. The key officials present, several related to the house itself by marriage,[1] with no immediate alternatives available and to forestall potential problems caused by any delay in the succession, quickly agreed on the son of Abbas' eldest son, the eighteen-year-old Sam Mirza, whom Abbas had in fact designated his heir just days before his death.[2] These officials sent news of Abbas' death and his grandson's succession to senior court officials in Isfahan who, also forseeing possible trouble if the accession was delayed, acceded to the move. In February 1629, just weeks after Abbas' death, Sam Mirza was elevated to the throne as Shah Safi at a ceremony at Isfahan's Ali Qapu palace.[3]

Even with several new appointments the coterie of those at the political centre following Safi's accession was essentially that which had represented the coalition of the traditional and newer of the polity's key constituencies whose allegiance underpinned Abbas' reign and whose presence at the centre now attested to their support for the new ruler.[4] These individuals oversaw Safi's accession ceremonies. These both followed distinctly traditional Sufi customs and included as participants key clerical associates of Abbas' court, and thereby attested to recognition of the continued key role of both Sufi and Shi'i discourse in the Safavid project.[5] Financial inducements secured the support of other key palace and provincial elements.[6]

Despite such measures external and internal challenges were perhaps a foregone conclusion at such a juncture. Indeed, within six months of Safi's accession, the Ottomans under Murad IV (reg. 1623–40), their own Western borders secured by a treaty, moved East and occupied Hamadan in 1630. An Ottoman attack on Baghdad was repulsed,[7] but Irivan was lost and, in 1635, Tabriz was plundered. The former was retaken but, in 1638, the same year the Mughals seized Qandahar, the

Ottomans took Baghdad and the shrine cities. To the East Safi's reign also witnessed some eleven Uzbek incursions into Iran, some involving large numbers of Uzbek troops, although none resulted in significant territorial gains or losses. In the Gulf, the Portuguese attacked and plundered the town of Qishm on the Gulf island of the same name.[8] Internally, Abbas' death also occasioned minor risings among Arab tribes near Baghdad and Khurasan.

The centre also faced a series of domestic challenges to Safi's accession which focused on other members of the Safavid house and were encouraged by the lack of a clear father-to-son succession. Abbas' son Imam Quli, blinded by his father in 1626–7, and the eldest son of Isa Khan, whose wife was a daughter of Abbas, were associated with such claims, although Isa Khan himself had supported Safi's succession.[9] Imam Quli was executed in June 1630 and a month later Zaynal Khan Shamlu was murdered and Abul-Qasim Evughlu lost his post as chief officer of the haram, both now clearly suspect in a series of plots against Safi. When Safi fell ill the following summer, 1631, rumours spread as to possible successors.

In February 1632, the remaining figures at the centre who owed their positions to Safi's grandfather and whose loyalties were therefore apparently suspect, were violently displaced. All further potential claimants to the throne were eliminated,[10] retainers and associates at court were deposed,[11] and a new 'centre' – dominated by a different configuration of Abbasid loyalists drawn from the Turk, Tajik and *ghulam* constituencies – was briefly established.[12]

This configuration itself quickly gave way to a new alliance dominated by Mazandaran's *vizier*, Saru Taqi, who in August 1634, with Safi now aged twenty-two, was appointed grand *vizier*. Although the personnel which made up the configuration of Turks, Tajiks and *ghulam* in his vizierate differed only slightly from that which had immediately preceded it,[13] its rise sealed the fate of the immediate alliance of family members, tribal, *ghulam* and Tajik alliance – known as the Shaykhavand – which had dominated the centre during Abbas' later years but whose commitment to the young Safi had become problematic.[14]

The renewal of spiritual unrest

At Abbas' death the realm did not, therefore, descend into civil war on the scale which followed the deaths of Ismail and Tahmasp. The political machinations which eventually brought Saru Taqi to the fore were largely confined to the centre itself and mainly involved, as during Tahmasp's reign, manoeuvring for control of the centre.

If the transition between Abbas I and Safi was relatively smoother than earlier transitions, marked spiritual tensions did surface at Abbas' death. These continued apace, and were no doubt encouraged by, both the political tensions arising from the lack of a direct father-to-son accession and foreign invasions.

In the immediate aftermath of Abbas' death, Gilan witnessed a messianic rising by one Gharib Shah which attracted thousands of followers. Gharib, a descendant of the former ruling family, was proclaimed Gilan's ruler and led the plundering of Rasht and Lahijan which caused a fall in silk production and, hence, in government revenues. The revolt was crushed, with the help of Saru Taqi, then *vizier* of Mazandaran. Although Gharib himself was executed with some 2,000 followers in Isfahan's new square in June 1629, a follower who claimed to be Gharib's brother led another rising in Mazandaran.[15]

Two years later, in July 1631, a year after the Ottoman occupation of Hamadan and in the same month as the murders of Isa Khan Safavi's children and a number of Safavid princes, occurred the rising of one Darvish Riza in the former capital of Qazvin. The Darvish, an Afshar married to the daughter of a Safavid general, proclaimed himself 'Lord of the Age (Sahib al-Zaman)', a distinctly Shi'i reference to himself as the Hidden Imam which, combined with a overtly Sufi discourse, recalled and revived aspects of the messianic millenarianism prevalent during the reigns of Ismail I and Tahmasp. The local governor rejected the Darvish's claims and the rebels retreated to the city's famous shrine where the predicted imminent revival of a dead Marashi sayyid guardian of the shrine by the self-proclaimed '*mahdi*' drew considerable crowds. Although this rising was quickly crushed – the Darvish's head was displayed in Isfahan's main square – it attracted the support of a cross-section of Safavid society, including a prominent *ghulam* and the son of a provincial governor. Indeed, some eight years later a follower rose proclaiming himself the reincarnated Darvish, suggesting, as with the discourse of such earlier Nuqtavis as Darvish Khusraw, a degree of acceptance of the transmigration of souls, a heresy among orthodox Shi'a.[16]

Darvish Riza's rising occurred against the background of the continued resurgence of the messianic veneration of Abu Muslim, dating at least to 1629, particularly among Isfahan's artisnal and merchant classes and kept alive by 'popular' storytellers based in the city's growing number of coffee houses. This Sufi millenarianism was also evident in the provinces.[17]

Changing responses of changing centres: searching for legitimacy

The political configurations underpinning Safi's rule – identified here by reference to their respective *vizier*s Khalifa Sultan and Saru Taqi – adopted a variety of responses to these internal and external challenges.

Khalifa Sultan and those who promoted Safi's accession strove to solidify the support of the same configuration of Turk, Tajik and *ghulam* elements, and their clerical associates, which had achieved pre-eminence at the centre during Abbas' later years. In the face of the internal and external challenges described above, with the messianic challenges in particular attesting to rising spiritual disquiet, the centre, following a familiar pattern, promoted the new shah's close association with both the faith[18] and such of its chief practitioners, including Mir Damad, as had been among Abbas' clerical associates.[19]

At the same time, the impact of Safi's payments to central and provincial elites, the Ottoman wars and Gharib Shah's rebellion and the resultant respective reduction in overland trade and silk production forced a financial rethink. Cancelled were Safi's grandfather's very expensive effort to divert the waters of the Karun river to Isfahan as well as the court's silk export monopoly, the latter likely in return for a large, needed, financial gift from Isfahan's Armenians.[20] Indeed, enough Caspian silk continued to move overland to the Levant ports that the centre remained more interested in its ties with those Armenian merchants who oversaw that trade than in cultivating the foreign trading companies.[21]

Following his promotion to the vizierate, the efforts of Saru Taqi's alliance to maintain its pre-eminence were given added urgency both by the continued Sufi messianism at home and the continued territorial losses to the Ottomans, including the plundering of Tabriz in 1635, following which the court vainly sued for peace,[22] and the 1638 loss of Baghdad and the Shi'i shrine cities. Saru Taqi was even more interested than the Khalifa Sultan alliance in pursuing further cost-cutting and revenue-raising measures. The *vizier* is credited with having persuaded Safi to convert Fars to crown land following Imam Quli Khan's execution. He also imposed heavy taxes throughout the realm, including on Isfahan's Armenians, and investigated revenue flows of the previous governor of Gilan.[23] Such measures were coupled with, and made all the more necessary by, a series of tax concessions to various elements throughout the realm in an obvious effort to garner domestic support.[24]

With two brothers and one of their sons serving as consecutive governors of Mazandaran, Saru Taqi, himself formerly that province's *vizier*, was able to keep especially close touch with the state of the realm's silk production and trade. To the centre's advantage the *vizier* also continued to play off the foreign trading companies against each other and against the Armenian masters of the overland trade.[25] Ultimately, however, an oversupply of silk in Europe in the 1630s caused the Dutch to seek cheaper Bengali and Chinese silk and, later in the decade, to explore the possibility of exporting Iranian specie to Surat in place of silk to facilitate the company's purchase of items in India which would bring higher prices in Holland.[26]

Perhaps most importantly, both for the enhancement of Safi's authority and the well-being of the realm for the decades to come, in May, 1639, three years before Safi's death in 1642, the peace treaty of Zuhab was signed, bringing an end to the wars with the Ottomans.

The price of the treaty, as with previous such treaties with the Ottomans, was heavy. Zuhab acknowledged loss to the Ottomans of Eastern Iraq, including Baghdad and the shrines.

Also as with previous Ottoman-Safavid treaties, however, the domestic benefits of Zuhab were soon apparent.

Following the treaty the overland route to the Levant ports, briefly reopened in 1636 and porous even in wartime, was formally reopened for business. Export of silk by that, now more reliable, route, and controlled by Isfahan's rich Armenian merchants, had been and continued to be more profitable than the Persian Gulf route. As a result, just as the Dutch were reducing their purchases of Iranian silk for export via the Gulf the Julfans were sending out more silk via the Levant.[27] Not co-incidentally, as the fortunes of the Armenian merchants reached a high point in Safi's reign their taxes were, as mentioned above, increased,[28] although otherwise the centre continued extremely attentive to Armenian interests.[29] The continuing importance of India as Iran's major trading partner in the period and the overland route via Qandahar, not transhipping via the companies' ships in the Gulf, as the key transit route for this trade[30] further reduced the importance of the Gulf trade.

The Saru Taqi alliance adopted a complex response to the period's messianic Sufi challenges. The 1631 death of Mir Damad and the 1632 fall of Khalifa Sultan left in place the *sadr*, Habiballah Karaki, son of Sayyid Husayn Karaki and son-in-law of Lutfallah Maysi, who remained in the post to his death in 1653, eleven years after Safi 's own death in 1642.[31] Karaki's overt hostility toward Sufism was well known, as was that of Mir Damad's son-in-law Ahmad Alavi, the Shirazi *qadi* Alinaqi Kamrai (d. 1650), and even Abdallah Shushtari's son Hasan Ali, himself a student of Abbas I's close associate Shaykh Bahai.

This hostility checked Safi's initial interest, during the earlier Khalifa Sultan *vizier*ate, in enhancing his spiritual legitimacy by rekindling the alliance between the court and the philosophically minded scholar-clerics who had served his grandfather and only further encouraged the anti-Sufi diatribe which had emerged during the latter years of Abbas' reign. Indeed, in the two decades beginning in 1633–4, coincident with the rising fortunes of Karaki and Saru Taqi's accession to the *vizier*ate, some twenty essays appeared refuting the messianism of the Abu Muslim tradition, attacking the urban-based story-tellers for promoting the tradition and singling out Taqi Majlisi and defending the Tajik sayyid Muhammad Sabzavari (d. after 1672), known as Mir Lawhi, who had attacked Majlisi in the latter years of Abbas' reign for Majlisi's public association with the Abu Muslim tradition and who claimed he had been physically assaulted in the streets by Majlisi's supporters.[32]

This religious polemic was the vehicle by which the clerical associates of the Saru Taqi configuration moved to challenge the religious legitimacy which Abbas' court had derived from its own clerical associates, displayed their own spiritual credentials and, given that the messianism of the revived Abu Muslim discourse bespoke a challenge to the position of Safi himself, declared their loyalty to the realm's legitimate ruler.

Nevertheless, the Saru Taqi alliance simultaneously remained attentive to the Safavid project's own, very Sufi roots. Thus, in September 1633, following the fall of the Khalifa Sultan alliance and as a new wave of anti-Sufi polemics was getting underway, Safi visited the family shrine at Ardabil. Following Saru Taqi's 1634 appointment as *vizier*, Safi visited the shrine again in 1635, the year Irivan and Tabriz fell to the Ottomans, and in 1636, the year the former was retaken.[33] A 1641 manual listing various Qizilbash offices included, for example and in particular, the post of *khalifa al-khulafa* whose holder, as the deputy of the order's leader, i.e. the shah himself, could, for example, forgive sins and perform executions. In the latter capacity the *khalifa* was called upon especially to dispatch such tribal elements whose behaviour, sometimes described in the sources as 'un-Sufi', in fact comprised any expression of disloyalty to the shah as head of the order, and, by extension, to the broader Safavid project. Decrees were in fact issued over this period attesting to the importance of the *khalifa* within the Safavid order.[34]

Various 'popular' religious practices were also officially encouraged, as they had been under Abbas. Olearius, secretary to a mission sent by Frederick II Duke of Holstein which arrived in Iran in 1637 seeking to reroute the silk trade through Russia, recorded the funerary processions and the self-mutilations marking Ashura in Ardabil. Members of the mission were also invited to watch the illuminations staged on the last day of the month of Muharram. In Isfahan, at least from this period, separate mourning ceremonies for the notables and the common people were organised on the new *maydan*: the notables, including Safi himself, were accommodated at the Ali Qapu and the common people at the main gate to the bazaar. On the urban scene also Safi continued to encourage the ritualistic clashes between the Nimati and Haydari factions.[35]

In the context of the gradually improving economic situation which obtained after Zuhab the centre also gradually recommenced material efforts to strengthen the links between Safi and the faith. In 1639, the year the treaty was signed and some six years after Darvish Riza's revolt in Qazvin, Safi visited the former capital city and ordered improvements to the shrine.[36] In Isfahan Saru Taqi himself, clearly keen to associate himself with both the faith and the shah after such a bloody path to power, commenced work on a mosque which was completed in 1643–4, just after Safi's death. Saru Taqi commenced work on a second mosque, along with an adjacent sarai and bath, which was unfinished at his death in 1644–5.[37]

Indeed, like key personalities associated with Abbas, members of the Saru Taqi configuration established palatial residences for themselves in the capital itself, thereby projecting their power and authority, and growing wealth, as associates of the court. Saru Taqi himself worked for nearly two decades to complete a mansion in the Hasanabad section of the city, near the Shah Mosque; attached to it were a bazaar and a small mosque. Having given that mansion to Safi, Saru Taqi then built himself another mansion in the Abbasabad quarter, on the no-longer-extant Imperial Canal, and surrounded it with a bathhouse and a bazaar.[38] The Georgian Rustam Khan, made head of the *ghulam*s at Safi's accession and *vali* of Georgia in 1632, built himself perhaps the largest of the city's mansions.[39] Safi's Tajik physician is associated with a garden on the Chahar Bagh and the son of the governor of Qandahar who surrendered that city to the Mughals in 1638 also built himself a mansion in the city.[40]

The continuing patronage of Persian cultural discourse over this period bespeaks an effort to maintain Tajik support of the Safavid project in the context of the above internal and external challenges. The court painter Riza Abbasi was active until his death in 1635 and some of his work, and that of his student Muin Musavvir, points to a commission of Nizami's *Khusraw and Shirin* between 1632 and 1636, a period of considerable political disorder at the centre when Tajik loyalties would have been at a premium. Too, attesting to growing disposable wealth among non-elites, Muin and others continued to produce the single-page illustrations which had been popular for some years, Muin in the style of his master but with a tall, narrow-page format and fewer large-scale figures. The works of Muhammad Shafi – dubbed Shafi Abbasi in the reign of Safi's successor – especially his flower painting, some perhaps associated with textile production but others done for an album owned by Safi himself, reveal European, Persian and apparently Mughal influences, as does the work of Bahram Sufrakish, dated to 1640–1.[41]

Non-Iranian influences are also visible in the pottery of this period, as potters combined Indian, especially North Indian, style shapes with Chinese-style decoration. This process was encouraged by the demand of Iran-based Indian merchants and money-lenders if not also the wider local growth in the taste for Indian styles stemming from the influx of Indian goods into Iran. Chinese motifs clearly inspired the continuing production of blue and white ware although domestic styles, with floral patterns associated with both Kirman and Mashhad, were still popular. In the 1630s, although very fine glass products, including water pipes used for smoking tobacco, were imported from Venice in the 1630s, perhaps by Armenian merchants, Shiraz also possessed several locations for the making of glass. As with the production of single-page illustrations, production of these items suggests a strong, non-court/non-elite demand for the relatively cheaper domestically produced items.[42]

Provincial capitals also furnished patronage for artists of Safi's reign: Manuchir Khan, the governor of Mashhad, was likely the commissioner of a Persian translation of the Arabic-language *Suvvar al-Kawakib*, a project dated to between 1630 and 1632, to which the father of the above-named Muhammad Ali contributed. The involvement of the Khan, son of the Armenian *ghulam* Qarachaqay Khan, and previously governor and one of the realm's twenty-one *ghulam amir*s at Abbas' death, in such an undertaking yet again affirms the successful integration of the *ghulam* into the broader Safavid project whose predominant cultural discourse was Persian.[43]

Summary and conclusion

Almost without exception Western writers have accepted Chardin's verdict, which opens the present volume, to adjudge Abbas I's successors as failures.[44]

In fact, however, the policies pursued by the Khalifa Sultan and Saru Taqi alliances at the realm's centre over Safi's reign secured the project in the face of the external and internal challenges which arose with Abbas' death. Notably also, while the external challenges were severe, the realm experienced far less widespread domestic disorder both at Safi's accession and over his reign than had obtained during transitions between earlier rulers.

On balance, the Saru Taqi alliance may have been the more 'successful' of the two configurations, in particular maintaining sufficient domestic support to acquiesce to the terms of the Zuhab treaty with the Ottomans which acknowledged the loss of Eastern Iraq and to project the court's identification with each of, and thus to transcend, the realm's conflicting spiritual tendencies. The growing prosperity resulting from the treaty – attested by the gradual resumption of court-sponsored building projects and the growing purchasing power of non-court elements – can only have further assisted the Saru Taqi alliance in retaining its influence at the centre, its own quite representative composition relatively intact, through Safi's death in May 1642.[45]

6

The Peace Dividend
Consolidated
Shah Abbas II (1642–1666)

A smoother accession and a 'new' vizier

Muhammad Mirza – Abbas I' great-grandson by Safi and the Circassian Anna Khanum – was about nine years old when he ascended the throne as Abbas II in May 1642. Members of the Saru Taqi alliance, pre-eminent at the centre since 1634, presided over the accession process, attended the coronation ceremony itself[1] and, as at Safi's accession, arranged distribution of significant largesse among key sectors of the population.[2] The alliance remained intact and in control throughout the process.[3]

As at Abbas' death the widespread civil wars which marked the fragmentation of the ruling configuration, between and among key constituencies, which occurred with the deaths of Ismail I and his son and successor Tahmasp, did not obtain at Safi's death.

What internal disorder did occur following the accession was, as in the years immediately following Safi's accession, confined mainly to the court and involved struggles for control of the centre. The young shah's mixed blood apparently presented no problem to any of the centre's major constituents.

In early 1643, in alliance with a woman at court, Saru Taqi secured a decree to execute his personal rival the *ghulam sipahsalar* Rustam Bek, who was in Mashhad to organise an effort to retake Qandahar from the Mughals, for having refused to obey a direct command from the centre. Rustam was executed and his brother, the *divanbeki* Ali Quli, was dismissed from his post. The move was supported by Jani Khan Shamlu, *qurchibashi* since 1638, and the Shamlu *ishikaqasibashi*.

A marriage between Jani Khan's daughter and Saru Taqi's nephew, i.e. between Turk and Tajik, failed to secure a permanent alliance between the two, however.[4] The *vizier* was then implicated in a plot to replace the sitting shah with another relative. In 1645, supported by the elements of the military – whose financial situation had deteriorated following the

Zuhab treaty as Saru Taqi sought to maximise the centre's finances – Jani Khan and Shamlu, Shaykhavand and Ustajlu supporters, with the young shah's approval, killed the *vizier*. Several days later the Shamlu *divanbeki*, two *ghulam*s and several Chagatai amirs, in turn, murdered Jani Khan and his Shamlu and Ustajlu accomplices and their retainers, including a Qajar, on the grounds that they had plotted to do away with the shah's grandmother. Other associates of both Saru Taqi and Jani Khan Shamlu were beheaded in the days that followed.

By November 1645, a new coalition was in place at the centre: Abbas II bestowed large gifts on a new Shamlu *qurchibashi*, the *ghulam qullaraqasi* Siyavush Bek and the head of the musketeers, the latter two having held their posts under Saru Taqi.[5] Khalifa Sultan, the Tajik sayyid son-in-law of Abbas I, the young shah's great-grandfather and hence a relative of the young shah, was now appointed *vizier*, the post he had held from 1624 to 1632.[6] Although the balance of power between the realm's core constituencies – Qizilbash, Tajik and *ghulam* – was little different to that which had obtained under Saru Taqi,[7] just as during Abbas I's reign so now family connections would seem to have portended greater reliability.

Silk and specie

Perhaps especially because the realm did not descend into widespread internecine strife at Safi's death its Eastern and Western borders remained generally quiet. There were, nevertheless, other 'foreign policy' issues which demanded, and received, attention.

Over Saru Taqi's vizierate, the interest of the European trading companies in Iranian silk seems to have diminished. The Safavid centre, with the overland route through Ottoman territory to the Levant ports secured by the still-intact 1639 Zuhab treaty and aware of the fluctuating nature of the companies' interests in trade with Iran, adopted a firmer attitude toward the granting of concessions and privileges to the companies and the exploitation of their remaining interests in the Iranian market. The Dutch, therefore, continued frustrated with being required to pay for Iran's silk in cash, at prices higher than non-Iranian silk.[8] The team negotiating Iran's terms of trade initially remained unchanged after Abbas II's accession, and Saru Taqi remained adamant on the terms of trade. Unable to agree a lower price the VOC, conscious of the price differentials between the Gulf and Levant routes, decreed Iranian silk was to be purchased in the Levant, specie was not to be sent to Iran and cheaper Chinese silk was to be purchased to fill any excess demand. The specie profits of any trade in Iran were to be sent to India, a process calculated to generate greater profit than using the cash to buy the more expensive Iranian silk. The VOC's direct export of Iran's specie commenced *c.* 1643, the year after Abbas II's accession, with the Indian merchants resident in Iran, the Banyans, playing an increasingly prominent role in this trade. In

1644, a year before his death, Saru Taqi – clearly conscious of this turn of events – formally banned the export of all specie to India.[9]

Continued Dutch frustration with the terms of trade was a prime reason for the 1645 Dutch bombardment of the Gulf port of Bandar Abbas and the occupation of the island of Qishm. Saru Taqi responded with a softened Iranian position but, although his murder in late 1645 was much welcomed by the VOC, economic realities prevailed: the company purchased no silk from Iran from 1645 to 1651 while its export of specie continued apace.[10]

The EIC, whose purchases of Iranian silk had, except for 1630, been comparatively minimal and inconsistent, purchased no silk at all after 1642 preferring, as the Dutch, to export profits from trade in Iran trade as specie.[11]

With local Armenian, and Banyan and Jewish merchants heavily, and prominently, involved in the continuing export of specie, Khalifa Sultan, a month after his return as *vizier*, moved to force their conversions to Islam. In the same year, 1645, and again *c.* 1648, he also devalued the coinage. The new *vizier* also maintained his predecessor's tough bargaining position toward the Dutch.[12]

With the Zuhab treaty still in force on Iran's Western borders, the centre now attempted to retake Qandahar, a key city on the overland trade route to India, Iran's main trading partner. Qandahar had been taken by the Mughals in 1638 and its recapture portended increased customs revenue and a further chance to inspect caravans moving East for hidden specie. Spearheaded by a force as mixed as those under Abbas I, the cost of the short and successful venture (February 1649) was apparently so high[13] that in its aftermath the centre moderated its attitude toward the VOC's trade demands. Nevertheless, in 1652, the first year of the two-year First Anglo-Dutch War, VOC directors resolved to suspend all purchases of Iranian silk. Thus despite a new treaty agreed in 1652, which continued curbs on specie export, the Dutch generally so minimised their silk purchases – increasingly meeting the demand with Bengali silk while exporting greater amounts of specie earned in to India – that the court never pressured the VOC to buy the agreed silk quota.[14]

A balanced approach to spiritual turmoil

The large number of essays attacking Abu Muslim which appeared during Khalifa Sultan's second *vizier*-ship attests to the continued messianic veneration of Abu Muslim and interest in Sufi doctrine and practice at the 'popular' level. This was most likely especially prevalent among urban lower orders least able to stave off the combined effects of specie outflow, currency devaluations and price inflation especially in the context of continued wrangling at the political centre.[15] Indeed, that Khalifa Sultan's above-mentioned campaign against minority merchants included the closing-down of taverns and the banning of certain forms of coffee house entertainment points to the continued role of, and the centre's concern with, these as focal points for the capital's ongoing 'popular' spiritual movements over the period.[16]

The anti-Abu Muslim and anti-Sufi sections inserted in *Hadiqat al-Shi'a*, a work attributed to Ahmad Ardabili (d. 1585) – himself well known for his critique of the Safavid political institution, but in fact the work was written in the 1640s in the Deccan – suggest sympathy for these doctrines and practices among distressed urban elements. 'Ardabili' denounced some twenty-one named Sufi groups for such heretical beliefs as ascribing partnership to Allah (*musharika*), abandoning prayer and fasting, dancing (*raqs*), singing (*ghina*), and listening to poetry or music (*sama*),[17] suggesting these elements were forsaking the intercessory and interpretative authority claimed by orthodox elements to seek solace and meaning in a more direct, immanent and intimate relationship with the divine. Muhammad Tahir (d. 1687), a native of Shiraz who spent his formative years in Najaf and, newly arrived therefrom, may well have composed the anti-Sufi sections of *Hadiqa*. In any case under his own name Muhammad Tahir attacked both the Abu Muslim tradition and the heretical practices attributed to both contemporary and past Sufi groups in his Persian-language treatise *Radd-i Sufiyya*,[18] as part of an exchange with Taqi Majlisi, and thereby made common cause with the Iran-based critics of these 'radical' discourses such as the sayyids Mir Lawhi and Ahmad Alavi. The continued high profile of such open opponents of Sufism as Habiballah Karaki, who remained *sadr* until his death in 1652–3, and Alinaqi Kamrai, appointed the capital's Shaykh al-Islam in this period and also a known opponent of singing,[19] no doubt further encouraged this anti-Abu Muslim, anti-Sufi discourse.

Khalifa Sultan, if at least publicly critical of 'popular' religious practices,[20] nevertheless strove, as had Saru Taqi, to achieve a balance in the identification of the court with these conflicting spiritual polemics, and thereby transcend, and maintain the centre's legitimacy in the face of, them all. With the hostile Karaki and Kamrai remaining in post, the *vizier* appointed Muhammad Baqir Sabzavari (d. 1679) to a teaching post at the capital's Abdallah Shushtari School, replacing Abdallah's own son Hasan Ali (d. 1664–5). Hasan Ali was a well-known opponent of Friday prayer during the Imam's occultation, in contrast with his own father and such clerical associates of the court in Abbas I's later years as Mir Damad, Shaykh Bahai and their students Taqi Majlisi, Fayz Kashani, Sabzavari and Khalifa Sultan himself. At the deaths of the capital's *Shaykh al-Islam* Kamrai in 1650 and the *sadr* Habiballah Karaki in 1653, Sabzavari was appointed Isfahan's *Shaykh al-Islam* and *Imam Juma*, in charge of the capital's Friday prayer. However, in balance Karaki's son Mirza Muhammad (d. 1671), whose mother was Lutfallah Maysi's daughter, was appointed *sadr*.[21]

The vizierates of Muhammad Bek and Muhammad Mahdi Karaki: familiar centres and familiar policies

Khalifa Sultan died in 1654, during a harsh winter marked by severe famine and price inflation. The new *vizier* was an Armenian *ghulam*, Muhammad Bek. Having worked his way up through the ranks as Saru Taqi and other elites had done in the seventeenth century,[22] Muhammad Bek now 'presided' over a centre whose composition continued to recognise and reflect the importance of the allegiance of the polity's three key constituencies to the ruling shah and the larger Safavid project.[23] With the new *vizier* an experienced trade negotiator, in 1657 an additional Ottoman-Safavid trade agreement was reached which, building on the Zuhab treaty of 1639, further assured the importance of the Anatolian trade routes and the Armenians' role in the overland silk trade. As the volume of Iranian silk on the Anatolian routes rose markedly, the VOC, the only company still exporting Iran's silk to Europe via the Gulf, further reduced its Gulf silk exports.[24]

Nevertheless, the twin, and associated, problems of continued specie outflow and urban spiritual unrest continued as did the centre's complex response thereto. In 1655, the winter in which Khalifa Sultan died and Muhammad Bek was appointed his successor, was marked by famine and inflation. The new *vizier* dismissed Isfahan's Georgian *darugha* whose unpopularity had sparked demonstrations spearheaded by the city's guilds. Two years later, in 1657, the Qajar *divanbeki*, who had held the post since 1645, was dismissed, also at the behest of the city's guilds.[25] The same year, 1657, Abbas II also issued a decree forbidding the export of gold coins and bullion. In 1657 also Muhammad Bek, an Armenian by birth and formerly the *darugha* of the Julfan Armenians, launched a campaign against local Jews and Armenians – to convert the former and expel the latter from Isfahan proper – thus singling out both as prominent participants in the country's economic life and, especially, the continued export of specie, as 'scapegoats' for the hardships being suffered by Iran's population, especially the lower-ranking urban elements, as Khalifa Sultan had done during his second *vizier*-ship.[26] Notwithstanding these measures, the next year the VOC spirited record amounts of specie out of the country. In 1659, some five years after Muhammad Bek's appointment, the centre undertook a survey of taxable income, including that of the trading companies, and brought additional lands into the *khassa* system.[27] The *vizier* also sought to raise revenue by continuing to curb some military expenditures.[28]

No doubt accentuated by ongoing economic problems, 'popular' Sufi discourse continued to attract the attention of urban artisnal and merchant elements whose livelihoods were the most directly disrupted thereby. Even while addressing these economic issues, in true Safavid fashion, the centre also continued to pursue a two-track, balanced response to this ongoing spiritual discord, which attempted to identify itself with both sides to, and thus transcend, the discourse.

On one hand, now in his twenties, Abbas II espoused a more public interest in Sufism, openly associating with a number of prominent figures clearly linked to such 'popular' discourse.[29]

At the same time, the shah also invited to court several key clerics associated with higher, philosophical inquiry but of proven loyalty to the centre in a clear effort to reconstitute Abbas I's court-clergy alliance and encourage these clerics, as had his great-grandfather, to promulgate orthodox discourse in Persian, and thereby still the polity's troubled spiritual waters. These clerics, as those at Abbas I's court, also supported an expanded role for the senior clergy during the absence of the Imam. Their number included Taqi Majlisi – himself earlier attacked for associating with popular religious discourse and veneration for Abu Muslim – and Mulla Sadra's own son-in-law, Fayz Kashani, who had declined a similar invitation from Safi during the years immediately following his accession. Abbas II asked the latter to lead the city's Friday prayer services, clearly hoping that Fayz, whose hostility to 'popular' Sufism was a matter of record, might exert a moderating, if not controlling, influence over Isfahan's various vociferous groups.[30] By his own admission, however, Fayz' efforts only exacerbated the city's spiritual tensions,[31] and soon thereafter he resigned the post. As after the death of Ali Karaki in the previous century, Friday prayer may have also been discontinued.[32]

In 1661, as spiritual strife persisted in the capital, if not also throughout the realm,[33] Muhammad Bek, who had also succeeded in alienating a number of key officials and the shah himself, was dismissed. The sayyid and *sadr* Muhammad Mahdi – son of Habiballah Karaki and the daughter of Lutfallah Maysi, and descendant of Ali Karaki – was appointed *vizier*, retaining the post until 1669, several years into the reign of Abbas II's successor Sulayman.[34] With minor personnel changes at the centre during Muhammad Bek's vizierate, the overall multi-constitutional dynamic at the centre remained intact[35] over the remainder of Abbas II's reign.[36]

The new *vizier* continued to try to check the export of specie and encourage trade via the overland route to the Levant.[37] From the 1660s on, however, a series of domestic crises compounded the effects of the ongoing specie drain. These included, for example, widespread drought in 1663 in Iranian Azerbaijan, as well as, from 1665 – the first year of the two-year Second Anglo-Dutch War – a series of bankruptcies among local merchants, likely compounded by the specie outflow.[38]

Karaki, whose father Habiballah's hostility to Sufism was well known, abandoned the policy of his predecessors to attempt to identify the court simultaneously with the realm's opposing spiritual discourses. Indeed, no doubt encouraged both by Muhammad Bek's dismissal and Muhammad Mahdi's appointment, the anti-Sufi tirade only continued apace, suggesting the continued strength of 'popular' spiritual doctrines and practices over this period as well, especially in the context of the domestic crises noted above. Muhammad Tahir continued his critiques of Sufi-style practices and philosophical inquiry.[39] Shaykh Ali Amili, a descendant of Zayn al-Din Amili killed by the Ottomans in 1559, and, like Tahir, a recent arrival from the Iraqi shrine cities, maintained a vociferous anti-Sufi polemic as well, focusing on singing in particular in 1662–3. The next year Shaykh Ali denounced the former *vizier*, sayyid and relative of the shah, Khalifa Sultan, dead some ten years, for criticisms he had levelled against Shaykh Ali's ancestor.[40] Such criticisms amounted to an implicit attack on Khalifa Sultan's relative the shah himself. The public fate suffered by those who explicitly and openly attacked Abbas II[41] certainly warned such clerics of the dangers inherent in overstepping their mark. The court did not, for example, move against Tahir, who was especially careful to make clear his overall allegiance to Safavid project and moderate his polemic, or Shaykh Ali.[42] But the widespread appeal of the anti-Sufi polemic in this period was such that Fayz, for example, continued to distance himself from 'popular' Sufism, even as he condemned overzealous attacks on truly ascetic individuals.[43]

The economics of legitimacy

The 1639 Zuhab peace treaty, formally reopening overland trade, coupled with the 1657 Ottoman-Safavid trade agreement, brought long-term peace to Iran's Western borders. The resulting 'peace dividend' permitted both officials and private individuals to accumulate considerable wealth[44] and to spend considerable sums on both public and private projects of benefit to the realm's spiritual infrastructure on a scale more familiar from earlier in the century. The extent of such undertakings both suggests the limited nature of the realm's economic crises over the period and points to efforts to project the identification of the centre and its allies with, and establish a monopoly over, what constituted orthodox doctrine and practice in the face of the ongoing spiritual disorder among the lower orders of the time.

The shah and members of the royal family were associated with a number of activities in promotion of the faith. Safi was buried in Qum, site of the shrine of Fatima (d. 816), the sister of the eighth Imam, and Abbas II himself ordered repairs to the shrines in Ardabil, Qum and Mashhad, and to the Friday mosques in Kashan, Qazvin, Qum and Isfahan.[45] Dilaram Khanum, the mother of Safi and Abbas II's grandmother, built two schools, in 1645–6 and 1647–8. Maryam Bekum, Safi's daughter, built a school and a mosque.[46] Kashan's Vizier Mosque, which dates to this period, may have been built by Safi's grandmother.[47]

In the immediate aftermath of Zuhab the *vizier* Saru Taqi had commenced a number of religious building projects in the last years of Safi's reign; some of these were only completed after Abbas II's accession.[48] Between 1656 and 1663 the Tajik Hakim Daud, Abbas II's physician, erected a large mosque which retained the standard four *ayvan* plan and a two-storey arcade. However, it also featured a simpler structural pattern and brick and tile surface, which marked an interesting variation on the style which had predominated under Abbas I.[49] Other court officials made similar contributions to the capital's spiritual landscape.[50]

Private individuals, some with familiar names, also made notable contributions to the city's spiritual infrastructure,[51] thereby endorsing the legitimacy of Safavid association with, and monopoly over, the faith and proclaiming their association therewith.

If his *vizier* Muhammad Mahdi was not himself keen on 'popular' discourse, Abbas II, as earlier shahs, continued the centre's sponsorship of the annual Muharram rituals and permitted the public fractional fighting between the Haydari and Nimatis throughout the realm's cities which reached its height at Ashura. Indeed, Abbas encouraged Shi'i festivals and celebrations of all sorts, many involving illuminations of bridges or portions of the city, and many of which he himself actively stage managed. Such activities, also encouraged outside the capital, enhanced the spiritual legitimacy among the populace both of the court as their sponsor and of those clerics who took leading roles in their organisation.[52] These clerics, in the midst of the spiritual strife and economic crises described above, could not have misunderstood the practical benefits of association with such court-sponsored activities.

Officials and private individuals also actively participated in the development of the realm's economic/commercial infrastructure in the aftermath of Zuhab, and enjoyed the benefits therefrom. Abbas II built two new sarais in this period, both just North of the imperial palace; from one, which housed Ottoman merchants, the shah himself is said to have received an annual rent of 135 *tumans*.[53] His grandmother Dilaram Khanum, whose two schools have been mentioned above, also built two sarais in the city. The first housed merchants from Qum, Kashan, Natanz, and specialised in dried fruit and carpets. The second, with some 490 rooms over two stories, housed rich Indian merchants from Bandar Abbas – Sunni, Shi'i and Hindu – who sold, among other things, turbans threaded with gold and silver. These sarais appear part of Abbas II's effort to make his own mark on the city by developing a new *maydan* just northwest of that established by his great-grandfather and by embellishing and expanding the imperial bazaar linking Abbas I's *maydan* and the older, traditional Maydan-i Harun-i Vilayat.[54]

Saru Taqi too built sarais during his tenure as *vizier* and dedicated the revenues therefrom to the mosque he built.[55] Ali Quli Khan, the governor of Tabriz, also built a sarai in the capital in this period, near the bazaar of the Multani gold-lace-makers; this sarai and the bazaar were reserved for Hindu merchants, including money-changers, bankers and cloth merchants.[56]

Two further bridges were constructed in this period, the Hasanabad, which could be raised and lowered and connected the Hasanabad gate with the Shiraz road, and the Rivulet Bridge which, with its seventeen arches, connected the two sections of the Saadatabad Chahar Bagh.[57]

Other infrastructural undertakings further projected the centre's authority. In this period the Ali Qapu assumed its final form, with the forebuilding and the great hall being commenced in 1643, just years after Zuhab, during the vizierate of Saru Taqi, and completed, under the *vizier*'s supervision, soon afterward.[58] In 1643–4, at the shah's order, Saru Taqi completed a hall facing the *maydan*. The audience hall of Chihil Sutun in the imperial palace was completed in 1647, during the vizierate of Khalifa Sultan.[59] Too, in a virtual repudiation of the violence at the centre which marked the early years of Safi's reign, Abbas II ordered a mausoleum built for the three sons of Isa Khan Safavi killed in 1632, all of whom, as children of a daughter of Abbas I, were princes and his own relatives.[60] In 1659–60, during Muhammad Bek's vizierate, the shah also established one of the city's great gardens, Chahar Bagh-i Saadatabad, laid out on both sides of the Zayanda Rud West of the Hasanabad bridge built some ten years before. The great amirs built their own gardens on all sides of this great high-walled structure outside of which were located baths, a mosque and shops.[61]

Others followed suit. After 'giving' his first mansion, built in the Hasanabad quarter, to Safi, Saru Taqi built another in the Abbasabad quarter. Ali Quli Khan, the governor of Tabriz who also built a sarai in the city, had a household of some 1,500 cavalry, 300 eunuchs and other officials and workshops for jewellers, tailors, saddlers and sword-makers.[62] The magistrate of Isfahan built a mansion next to that of Saru Taqi in Abbasabad as did Najaf Quli Bek who, in 1664, was sent by Abbas on mission to India. Maryam Bekum, Safi's daughter, had a mansion near the Hasanabad gate. Mirza Razi, a grandson of Abbas I who, though clumsily blinded by a eunuch, was nevertheless skilled in algebra and astronomy, built a grand mansion South of the Hasanabad quarter.[63] Indeed, such quarters as the Abbasabad section and the Khaju suburb underwent substantial development during Abbas II's reign. The latter housed a number of the mansions named above and others as well.[64]

Despite the hardships endured by the Armenian community as a whole, like other elites its wealthier elements, especially those involved in the long-distance trade, retained sufficient wherewithal to embellish the area to which the community was moved between 1655 and 1659.[65] In 1655, nearly twenty years after Zuhab, work commenced on the famous All Saviour's Cathedral, often known in the Persian sources as the Vank Cathedral. The Cathedral was completed in 1664, three years after Muhammad Bek's dismissal and in the midst of Muhammad Mahdi Karaki's vizierate. In fact, between 1658 and 1666 six new Armenian churches were built, making a total of twenty-four in the area. Wealthy Armenians also built a number of grand mansions along the river.[66] Indeed, its scapegoating aside, the court generally continued attentive to the community, allowing Armenians to manage their own affairs and responding to Armenian complaints of pressure from Catholic missionaries.[67]

'The Persian interlude'

Developments in other realms of the cultural expression also attest to the widespread accumulation of wealth in the century's middle years and the continued widespread interest in, and the vitality of, Persian as the realm's dominant cultural discourse.

Court-sponsorship of things Persian continued apace over the period. The career of Muin Musavvir, a student of Riza Abbasi, spanned the period 1635 to 1697. His contributions to some five *Shahnama*s, other manuscript and single-page illustrations consistently feature his distinctive style – his round-faced figures, for example, being slimmer than others of the period – itself rooted in that of his master.

Non-court demand for such output was also strong in this period but exhibited an interest in the more traditional. The artists of the day continued able to accommodate themselves to all tastes. One Afzal al-Husayni produced both a popular style of figure illustration and was working on a *Shahnama* between 1642 and 1651. Muhammad Qasim, Malik Husayn Isfahani and others completed a number of miniatures for a 1648 *Shahnama*, now at Windsor. Malik Husayn's son, Muhammad Ali, however, produced pictures of young men seated with bottles of wine and fruit, of the popular single-page type in the style of Riza Abbasi. Muhammad Yusuf produced illustrations both for that same *Shahnama* and portraits of young dandies.[68]

Artists' receptivity to the non-Iranian highlights the contemporary eclecticism. The works of Bahram Sufrakish, two dated to 1640–1, two years before Abbas II ascended the throne, depict Indian figures and utilise distinctly European styles, particularly in their landscape backgrounds. The flower paintings produced by his contemporary Shafi Abbasi, present at the courts of both Safi and Abbas II, exhibit European, Persian and apparently Mughal influences. Indian figures and settings also figured in the works of Shaykh Abbasi, who may have been a student of Bahram and whose earliest work dates to 1647.[69] The post-Qandahar wall paintings of Chihil Sutun, some completed by Shaykh Abbasi and some depicting standing figures and seated groups in European costumes, display a similar coexistence of styles.[70]

From late in Abbas I's reign in particular ceramics production was, as already noted, infected with a similar dynamism. A new taste for inscriptions or ornamental bands scratched through a black background, seen in works from Kirman, revived a technique of late fifteenth century Northwestern Iran. A water pipe dated to 1658–9 displays vegetation similar to that in the paintings of Riza Abbasi and Afzal al-Husayni while the arabesque medallions on another are familiar from contemporary manuscript illumination. Too, under the influence of Chinese imports, domestic ceramic wares incorporated blue and white Chinese themes and Chinese-style landscapes with arabesque medallions, a style which had not marked ceramic production prior to the turn of the century which had featured more distinctly 'Persian', especially animal and floral, motifs. The use of additional colours also dates to this period. These styles and the Kirmani ware continued popular into the century's later decades, suggesting their status as import substitutes. Production of such items, like that for single-page illustrations noted above, reflects healthy domestic, non-elite demand. Indeed, the indigenous demand for single-page illustrations made itself felt in contemporary ceramics production as single-figures appeared on small dishes, bottles and multi-neck vases produced in this period.[71]

The Kirmani ceramics were, in fact, of sufficient quality to attract the attention of Dutch and English traders based in Bandar Abbas seeking alternatives to Chinese porcelain when, following the Ming dynasty's collapse in 1643–5, porcelain exports were curtailed until *c.* 1683.[72]

Kirman also continued as a centre of carpet production in this period. Some carpets utilised the vase-carpet technique and, like the Kirmani ceramics, were produced for both the court and non-court Iranian market as well as further afield, particularly India.[73] Isfahan and Kashan also continued as centres for the production of Polonaise carpets in silk with gold and silver brocade. Persian silk-weaving featured familiar, and traditional, scenes of wine-drinking as well as flowers. That the figures in the former are attired in clothes similar to those in the figures in the paintings of both Afzal al-Husayni and Muhammad Yusuf suggests continued interaction between the two crafts; the silk or cotton painted trousers worn by women in the former's illustrations seem typical of contemporary higher fashion. Similarly, the brocaded silk on metal ground at Imam Ali's shrine in Najaf, produced after 1642, is reminiscent of the silver door facing the Ardabil shrine dated to the 1630s and 1640s.[74]

Although the literary output of the period has yet to be well studied, the mid-seventeenth century is known for the further refinement of the Indian style of poetry at the hands of such poets of the period as Saib Tabrizi (d. 1676–7).[75] Typical of the regional sweep of Persian culture, Saib, son of a Tabrizi merchant who accompanied his father to Isfahan, spent his youth in India before returning to and settling in the Safavid capital. Saib was especially well known for his panegyric poetry during the reigns of Safi, Abbas II and Sulayman.[76]

Summary and conclusion

Such challenges as the admittedly unquantifiable outflow of specie and as well as ongoing, and associated, spiritual strife, ought not to overshadow the positive features of Abbas II's twenty-four-year reign. Although four individuals held the post of *vizier* over the period, their

respective administrations exhibit notable continuity of both composition and policy. There are as many, if not more, signs of a healthy,
dynamic economy, and culture, than not.

Indeed, the centre's own self-confidence is mirrored in the period's
court chronicles. The authors of these texts continued, as Quinn noted
with regard to the chroniclers of Abbas I's reign, to commence their
narratives from early in the Safavid period itself, but left out the lengthy
political or spiritual/familial lineages from which the shahs of the previous century had derived much needed legitimacy. *Abbasnama*, the court
history of the Tajik Qazvini, begins, after a preface which is mainly
personal in nature, with Abbas II's own birth.[77] In his *Qisas al-Khaqani*
Shamlu but very quickly traces the connection between the Safavid
house and Imam Musa, the seventh Imam; similarly the main account
commenced with a very brief recounting of Safavid history from Ismail
to the end of Safi's reign.[78] Even those of Chihil Sutun's wall paintings
which were completed following the retaking of Qandahar, connected
this 'Eastern' victory of Abbas II with the 'Eastern' ventures of Ismail,
Tahmasp and Abbas I.[79]

Overall, there are many grounds on which to suggest that, in marked
contradiction to Chardin's famous, and oft-quoted, declaration, at Abbas
II's death in 1666 the realm was at least as prosperous as, and as stable,
and its prospects as bright as they were in 1629, at the death of his
great-grandfather, if not more so.

7

Meeting the Challenges
Shah Sulayman (1666/68–1694)

The smoothest accession to date

In the later hours of the morning in which Abbas II died of an unspecified illness, the *yuzbashi* Sulaman Aqa called together the 'amirs and notables' of the inner circle then travelling with the shah. With the doors closed he informed them both of Abbas II's death and of the necessity of choosing the new shah before they left the building.[1] The two most direct and available candidates for succession were Abbas II's two sons, the nearly twenty-year-old Safi Mirza and the seven-year-old Hamza. Some argued for the younger son but the *vizier* – a sayyid and descendant of Ali Karaki – argued for the older. Safi was selected and his accession took place in November of 1666.

Two very bad harvests, a violent earthquake in Shirvan and Cossack raids in the Caspian area, however, all suggested that the ceremony had been performed at an inauspicious time.

A second accession ceremony was therefore held in March 1668 in the capital itself: Sabzavari, Isfahan's *Shaykh al-Islam*, officiated at the ceremony at the Chihil Sutun palace. This was attended by 'all the amirs and notables and learned men and *ulama* (religious scholars)', all of whom stood when Sabzavari gave the *khutba*, in Arabic and Persian. Sabzavari thereupon went to the *minbar* of the Royal Mosque where he delivered the *khutba* for the people of the city. Although the crowd grumbled at being called together when, in the *khutba*, Sabzavari substituted the name of the new shah for that of the old, they understood there was a new ruler; indeed, the second accession also saw the shah take a new name, as Safi II became Sulayman.[2]

The transition between Abbas II and Sulayman was the smoothest in Safavid history to date. Indeed, that he, like his father the son of a Circassian woman, was put forth and accepted, without challenge, by the centre's key constituencies – Qizilbash, Tajik and *ghulam* – demonstrates the extent to which these different elements could work with each other to insure the future of the broader Safavid project.[3]

The realm's borders also remained peaceful. Despite entreaties from anti-Ottoman interests in Mesopotamia, Basra and several European powers, and even with the Ottomans occupied in Europe and their stunning defeat at Vienna in 1683, the centre made no move to break the 1639 Zuhab treaty. Indeed, with merchants continuing to pass unchallenged between the two realms, the treaty was observed 'scrupulously' until the 1720s, and certainly contributed to a diminished sense of military urgency throughout the period.[4]

Further contributing to a sense of security, the minor incursions on the Eastern front over the period mainly originated from tribes not strictly under the influence of the Uzbek court, with which the Safavids otherwise enjoyed reasonably good relations in this period. Although the Cossack raids did considerable damage to silk-producing regions and an Iranian force sent against them was defeated, the Cossacks in turn were defeated by the Russians. When Turkman elements moved toward Astarabad they were defeated by Iranian troops in 1676–7.[5]

Socio-economic crises and responses

What crises afflicted the polity during Sulayman's reign were mainly domestic and, as earlier, of natural, socio-economic and spiritual origin.

Natural disasters in fact afflicted the realm during most of Sulayman's reign. In Isfahan the effects of the poor harvests of 1666 and 1667 were accentuated by the royal party's return to the city before measures for its provisioning could be fully organised, and prices in the city rose sharply. There was another poor harvest in 1669 and plague. The 1670s witnessed drought, harsh winters, locust swarms, famine and earthquakes. In 1678–9 some 70,000 were said to have perished from famine in Isfahan alone and officials were stoned by angry crowds. In 1681 Armenia and Azerbaijan were struck by famine. Plague broke out in Gilan in 1684–5, spread to Ardabil, where some 80,000 were said to have died, and thence to Hamadan. In 1686–7 plague struck Azerbaijan, Mazandaran, Astarabad and Isfahan itself. In 1689 plague was said to have killed thousands in Shiraz, and struck areas from Baku to Basra, Mosul and Baghdad. The early 1690s saw plague strike the North and West, especially Baku and Tiflis, Basra, and Baghdad where 1,000 per day were dying in 1691. Southeast Iran was also struck, and, two years after Sulayman's death, in 1696, Fars was hit by drought and famine.[6]

In 1667–7, in response to the initial crisis, the shah himself moved to control price inflation in the capital. Two years later, in 1669, the year after the second coronation, Muhammad Karaki, *vizier* since 1661, was replaced by Shaykh Ali Khan of the Zangana Kurds; the latter, although in fact Sunnis, had a long record of service to the Safavid project which Shaykh Ali had himself also continued.[7] Having, as Muhammad Bek before him, moved many family members and other Kurdish elements into key positions of authority,[8] Shaykh Ali embarked on a series of measures designed to cut costs and raise revenues. Quickly realising the impossibility of completely curtailing the outflow of specie, in 1670, the year after his appointment, he instituted a 5% tax on silver sent from Isfahan to the Gulf and thence to India. He also attempted to extend control over the sugar, used at court and by the common people.[9] The *vizier* also imposed a tax on the capital's Armenian churches and, in the 1670s especially, continuing earlier scapegoating policies, renewed efforts to convert Armenians.[10]

Although, coincident with an especially harsh winter and resulting high prices and food shortages in 1672, Sulayman briefly dismissed Shaykh Ali[11] he was reappointed some fourteen months later, in the midst of rumours of a possible war with the Ottomans. Resuming his efforts to enhance the realm's revenues, the *vizier* moved to curb military expenditures and sent tax-collectors to the provinces demanding taxes and imposed fines where these were in arrears. With customs revenues having been higher under Abbas II, in 1674 the shah instituted the farming out of the collection of customs duties which led to a measurable decline in fraud. He also reaffirmed the policy of taxing Armenian churches and, in 1683, ordered a census of Kirman's Zoroastrians to reassess their poll tax liability.[12]

As to foreign trade Shaykh Ali attempted to reform the administrative arrangements for the supply of Caspian silk to Isfahan and to require contractually that the Dutch buy whatever amount of silk actually arrived therefrom in the capital. The *vizier* rejected Dutch negotiating strategies and, following the Dutch seizure of Qishm in 1684 as part of an effort to get out of treaty obligations, a Dutch team arriving in Isfahan to negotiate a new treaty was refused a royal audience until the island was evacuated. The new treaty was favourable to the VOC, but contained provisions for submission to Iran of detailed lists of VOC imports and exports.[13] As the bulk of Iranian silk continued to move through Ottoman territory to Europe, not via the Gulf or Russia, and as India remained Iran's main trading partner,[14] the court overall evinced increasingly less interest in meeting Dutch demands.

Although some of Shaykh Ali's measures were apparently successful,[15] ultimately the natural disasters, regional and such world-wide economic developments which affected trade over the period were out of Iran's control.[16] In addition, Iranian efforts to control the export of specie continued to be widely circumvented by the English and the Dutch companies – in the midst of yet a third war from 1672 to 1674 – which moved specie out either to Basra or via the Gulf. The court responded with continued devaluations of coinage but the 5% bullion tax, likely unworkable anyway in view of the foreign evasion, appears to have lapsed.[17] Other internal measures, especially those which threatened to disrupt domestic political arrangements, were abandoned.[18]

At Shaykh Ali's death in 1689, five years before that of Sulayman, his post remained vacant for nearly two years before Muhammad Tahir, Tajik Qazvini notable and author of *Abbasnama*, was appointed *vizier*.[19]

The new *vizier* continued to try to stem the loss of specie, seizing Armenian exports on Dutch ships and devaluing the realm's coinage. As for the Persian Gulf silk trade, continuing Dutch anger with the court suggests ongoing efforts by the centre to maximise Iran's own revenue position; in any case VOC silk purchases over these later years appear to have been minimal.[20]

Spiritual challenges and complex responses: Baqir Majlisi and Safavid Shi'ism

By this period, at least, Abbas I's new *maydan* had become a centre for wealthier merchants and tradesmen and the court's own social, economic and political activities[21] while, from at least mid-century, the 'dirtier' or messy crafts and trades were generally located in and around the older Harun-i Vilayat square and the old Congregational Mosque.[22] While for the former business was apparently booming,[23] the general deterioration and run-down appearance of the latter noted by Chardin[24] signalled a downturn in the old *maydan*'s fortunes which certainly dated from Abbas I's establishment of his new *maydan* to the southeast and the later establishment, by court and private figures, of sarais, bazaars, schools, mosques and private dwellings in and around this new centre, elsewhere in the city and in the suburbs as well.[25] The natural and economic calamities of the second Safavid century, Sulayman's reign in particular, seem to have accentuated this decline: in 1704, ten years after Sulayman's passing, the Dutch painter de Bruyn spoke of the old *maydan* as being used mainly as stables, with only the poorer guilds still carrying on any business there.[26]

The old *maydan* was also therefore a major focal point of such venues of 'popular' entertainment as the coffee-house, open from dawn until late into the evenings, where people met to drink coffee or different sorts of cordials, smoke tobacco and opium, listen to recitations of poetry and stories and, relatively freely, discuss the affairs of the day. The area was also where the 'popular' classes traditionally celebrated the main religious festivals.[27] Given the connection between the polity's urban commercial and artisnal/craft classes and darvish-oriented, that is 'popular', forms of Sufi inquiry and practice, from earlier in the century at least,[28] the old *maydan* and especially its coffee-houses were certainly venues for the telling of tales from the *Shahnama*, the Abu Muslim traditions and other messianic stories together with various practices associated with 'popular' Sufism. The latter's ongoing appeal is suggested by the continued anti-Sufi polemic during Sulayman's reign and points to these elements' continued search for spiritual meaning outside 'orthodox' parameters, a search only heightened by the natural and socio-economic adversities described above.[29]

The centre's response to this ongoing spiritual unrest was to resume the multi-level, balancing approach of Khalifa Sultan and his successor

Muhammad Bek in which the latter's successor Karaki had been less interested. Although the centre's own preferences in the argument were clear, that policy continued to aim to identify it with both/all sides to, and thus transcend, the dispute.

The prominent role played by which Muhammed Baqir Sabzavari in Sulayman's accession signalled an effort by the centre to identify with, if not outright favour the side of, the philosophically minded clerical elite, as it had during the reigns of Abbas I and Abbas II. Indeed, the court also honoured the philosophically oriented Husayn Khvansari (d. 1687–8) – a student of Mir Damad, Taqi Majlisi, and Sabzavari, whose daughter he married, and who had taught at the Maysi school – and Sulayman entrusted him with some court assignments. At Khvansari's death, the shah erected a mausoleum for him. Khvansari's son by Sabzavari's daughter, Aqa Jamal (d. 1710), also a student of Taqi Majlisi,[30] and other prominent practitioners of philosophical inquiry. Many of these were themselves students of the philosophically minded clerical associates of earlier courts, and were also active during Sulayman's reign.[31] Debates on issues of law and philosophy among and between these scholars were vigorous over the period.[32] Some of these discussions even addressed the permissibility of practices at court.[33]

Sabzavari, as his associate Fayz Kashani before him, in fact himself attempted to steer a middle course on the question of Sufi discourse. In *c.* 1676, for example, Sabzavari penned an essay on singing in which, on one hand he asserted the authority of the senior clerics trained in the rationalist religious sciences during the occultation, including himself and, on the other, charted a position which fell just short of the complete condemnation of singing offered by pseudo-Ardabili, Muhammad Tahir, Mir Lawhi and Shaykh 'Ali Amili.[34] Other court associates also took up the debate.[35]

Shaykh Ali Khan's twenty-year vizierate also witnessed special attentiveness to various Hijazi sayyids who visited the capital[36] and to the polity's own Tajik sayyids.[37] The centre also took pains to stress its identification with the faith: a miniature showing Ismail proclaiming Twelver Shi'ism as the realm's established faith is associated with a history of Ismail I dated to the late 1670s, whose author greatly embellished this event.[38]

The anti-Sufi discourse continued apace, however. Muhammad Tahir continued his own tirades against philosophical inquiry, although he was careful, as he had been under Abbas II, to demonstrate his loyalty to the larger Safavid project by dedicating various essays to the shah himself.[39] Mir Lawhi continued his polemics[40] and, undaunted by Sabzavari's court connections, Shaykh Ali Amili, in an essay composed in 1676–7, three years before Sabzavari's death in 1679, attacked Sabzavari's essay on singing.[41] At least one of the several attacks on Sabzavari's pro-court position on Friday prayer originated among opponents of singing and Sufism[42] and represented at least an indirect attack on the revival of the court-clerical alliance which had marked the reigns of Abbas I and Abbas II.

The appointment of Taqi Majlisi's son Muhammad Baqir (d. 1698–9[43]) as Isfahan's *Shaykh al-Islam* in 1687,[44] eight years after Sabzavari's death and during Shaykh Ali Khan's vizierate, indicates the centre's continued preference for an approach to this continued spiritual strife which attempted to identify the court with, and thus transcend and maintain its authority in the face of, such arguments.

The Majlisi family, Lebanese in origin, was by this time well established on the capital's clerical scene,[45] and Taqi Majlisi's nine daughters, at least one of whom was herself a prominent legal scholar, contracted marriages with Iranian clerics, including sayyids, who were, or subsequently became, well-established scholars in their own right, as did their children.[46]

Baqir Majlisi himself was himself both personally aware of and connected to the period's opposing currents of thought. On one hand, he had studied with such key figures on the capital's spiritual scene as Fayz Kashani, a key target of opponents of Sufism and philosophy, and Khalil Qazvini, whose philosophical, if not 'popular' Sufi, tendencies were well known, and both of whom had accepted commissions from Abbas II at the same time as his own father.[47] Via these and his father's own teachers and associates, Baqir Majlisi was in fact linked to all the major scholars associated with the court–clerical alliance which had underpinned the reigns of Abbas I and Abbas II and such scholars of Sulayman's reign as Sabzavari and Husayn Khvansari. Majlisi had also continued the legacy of the scholars of both the first and second court–clerical alliance, including his father, as a promulgator in Persian of the faith's key doctrines and practices.[48] Too, well prior to his appointment, his loyalty to the Safavid project, like that of his father and his father's associates, was well established.[49] Indeed, as a sign of the court's favour he had received financial assistance from the court for the project of *hadith* compilation which eventually resulted in *Bihar al-Anwar*, parts of which he dedicated to Shah Sulayman.[50]

On the other hand, before his own father's death Majlisi had also studied with Shaykh Ali Amili and Muhammad Tahir, both fierce opponents of popular Sufism and, certainly in the latter's case, philosophical inquiry generally. Majlisi also studied with Hurr-i Amili, whose own anti-Sufism was well known, and was himself on record with some, albeit perfunctory, reservations about 'popular' religious doctrines and practices.[51]

With such connections Majlisi was better positioned than his father, Fayz or Sabzavari to strike a middle ground between the contemporary spiritual extremes. This he did by grounding his discourse firmly in the revelation of the Imams themselves. Thus *Bihar*,[52] drawing on his earlier 'primers', focused squarely on the Imams as the ultimate sources of knowledge on all matters of doctrine and practice.[53] As such Majlisi challenged contemporary polemics focusing on alternative messianic personages, reinforced the position of senior clerics, including himself, as delegated by the Imam to interpret issues of jurisprudential and theological import and to undertake such matters of daily practical import to the community as the conduct of Friday prayer and the collection and distribution of religious taxes, during the occultation[54] and firmly linked these clerics to, and thereby legitimised, the broader Safavid project.[55] Indeed, even Majlisi's exposition of issues in medical theory and practice in *Bihar* also bespoke both an effort to reconcile potentially conflicting elements of the Galenic, 'rationalist', medical tradition with the understanding of illness and wellness on offer in the Imams' *hadith*s and, thereby, attests to the continued popularity of each.[56]

Simultaneous with this focus on the Imams, however, Sulayman's court continued, and expanded on, its role as chief promoter of all manner of 'popular' religious practices. The court's involvement in Muharram ceremonies insured that these, especially, were festivals of 'public entertainment' rather than purely 'devotional' in nature. Elaborate ceremonies were also mounted in the provincial capitals. Yazid was ritually cursed and burned, and the Ottomans were also cursed. Lavish banquets were also organised for such events as Ghadir Qumm – marking the Prophet's designation of Ali as his successor.[57] The shah himself also embellished several of the capital's *imamzada*s and other 'popular' religious sites.[58] Additionally, suggesting continued attention to the shah's status as head of the Safavid Sufi order, such court chronicles as *Nasab Nama-yi Safaviyya*, completed in 1679 by a descendant of Safi al-Din's own spiritual guide (*murshid*) Shaykh Zahid of Gilan, accorded special attention to the Sufi origins of the Safavid project.[59]

The court's continued 'redirection' of 'popular' dissatisfaction with existing socio-economic and political circumstances to the most visible of the realm's religious and ethnic minorities, as during the earlier *vizier*ships of both Khalifa Sultan and Muhammad Bek, may be counted as part of this struggle for the hearts and minds of the 'popular' classes. Thus, following his appointment as the capital's *Shaykh al-Islam* and still during the vizierate of Shaykh Ali Khan, whose anti-Armenian measures have been noted, Majlisi, otherwise tolerant of Christians and Jews – as 'People of the Book' – ordered the destruction of the idols of Isfahan's Indian community. The latter's presence as financiers and merchants in the city had, in fact, only been growing concomitant with, if they were not the direct cause of, the realm's economic problems, and widespread popular resentment with the Indians in this period was noted by contemporary resident foreigners.[60]

At the same time as the centre was moving to associate itself publicly both with philosophical, Sufi discourse and with 'popular' practices the court also moved to associate itself openly with well-known opponents of both Sufi doctrine and practice and of philosophical inquiry. Muhammad Tahir who, no doubt mindful of the fate of Mulla Qasim, had continued to moderate the tone of his criticisms – he also reportedly visited Fayz in Kashan where the latter had removed himself after resigning his Isfahan post. Muhammad Tahir was appointed Qum's Shaykh al-Islam in this period. Hurr-i Amili, like Shaykh Ali, an Arab outsider who came to Iran late in life, was appointed Shaykh al-Islam in Mashhad. Like both Shaykh Ali and Muhammad Tahir, with whom he studied, Shaykh Hurr was well-known opponent of Sufi doctrines and practices and, just as Muhammad Tahir had moderated his own rhetoric, he had also studied with Husayn Khvansari, a philosophically minded associate of the court and, like Muhammad Tahir, supported the performance of Friday prayer during the occultation, the pro-court position.[61]

In the context of these policies, together with the physical separation of Muhammad Tahir and Shaykh Hurr from the capital and the subsequent deaths of both, as well the deaths of Mir Lawhi and Shaykh Ali,[62] in the years following Majlisi's appointment as *Shaykh al-Islam* the vociferousness of the polemics against 'popular' Sufi tendencies and philosophical inquiry began to abate to the extent that its nature and scope as an ongoing discourse independent of these scholars is harder to trace.[63] Moreover, to the extent that the realm's alternative spiritual, and especially messianic, polemics had, if only implicitly, questioned the legitimacy of the Safavid shahs, foreign travellers' consistent reports of Sulayman's popularity among the people[64] also point to the success of the centre's spiritual balancing policies.

The discourse of architecture and art

All of the centre's various constituencies, 'old' and new, continued their involvement in both spiritual and secular 'cultural' undertakings, attesting to their successful integration into the larger project whose spiritual discourse was officially Shi'i and whose cultural discourse was Persian.

As earlier, the centre led the way. Like Safi before him, Abbas II was buried in Qum, site of the shrine of Fatima. From 1677 to 1680, Sulayman ordered repairs to a number of extant buildings in Mashhad, including the shrine of Imam Riza, damaged during an earlier earthquake, and several schools.[65] Sulayman's Circassian mother and daughter endowed property to the Shi'i shrines in Iraq, under formal Ottoman control since 1639, as did other female courtiers. Abbas II's mother built a mosque and a nearby school in the capital's Abbasabad suburb. In 1679–80 the *vizier* Shaykh Ali Khan, who in 1678 had built a sarai Northwest of the city, built a mosque in the city's Khaju quarter. The *vizier* also built a school in Hamadan to which he dedicated as *vaqf* the revenues of various villages, sarais, and shops.[66] Another court official erected a marble *mihrab* in a mosque in Isfahan's Imamzada Ismail in 1688,[67] and the same year the daughter of the court physician Nizam al-Din Muhammad erected the famous Ilchi Mosque. The governor of Fars made endowments in Shiraz.[68] *Ghulams*[69] and wealthy non-court figures, including women,[70] also built schools and made endowments in the period.

Other, apparently more minor figures were also active in their contribution to the realm's religious infrastructure in this period. In 1677–8 one Hajji Mirza Muhammad donated the revenues of three shops to the repair of a public water foundation adjacent to the Abdallah Shushtari School, attesting to a confluence of interests between merchants and clerics. In 1688–9 one Muhammad Qasim, apparently a darvish of some sort, built a mosque and an alleyway to connect the Hakim Mosque and the Imperial Bazaar.[71] Other contributors are difficult to identify.[72] Such undertakings represented pledges of loyalty to the project but also attested to both the prominence of non-court elements on the local scene and to the limited impact of the above-mentioned financial/economic crises on the polity.

Projecting political authority, the 'secular' buildings erected in this period included the capital's spectacular Hasht Bihisht (Eight Paradises) palace, built between 1666 and 1669 in the Northeastern end of the Chahar Bagh. As many other Safavid structures, this palace exhibited aspects of both the new and the familiar: Canby notes that the structure's 'elevation and divisions of spaces' attest to 'the continuing originality of Safavid architects' while its irregular, octagonal plan recalled a late fifteenth-century *khanga* (Sufi lodge) found elsewhere in the city, and a pavilion built by Tahmasp in Qazvin. The palace's vaulted small rooms were decorated in a style which recalled the Ali Qapu's hunting scenes. The roof, with its huge vault pierced at its apex by a high drum with an inner dome, had its Timurid predecessors. Indeed, the 'Eight Paradises' design – eight rooms with a central hall, the latter representing the sun and the former the eight paradises of the Islamic tradition – was reminiscent of structures in Aqquyunlu Tabriz. The colour scheme of bright yellow glaze combined with bright apple green, turquoise and cobalt blue of the stone paste tile was popular in the 1660s and is found also in those parts of the Shah Mosque which Sulayman refurbished as well as the city's Armenian Church of the Holy Mother of God. The spandrels featuring flowers and insects recall those in drawings found in the albums of Shafi Abbasi and are rendered in the style of Riza Abbasi's student Muin Musavvir.[73]

In *c.* 1690, toward the end of Sulayman's nearly thirty-year reign, the Talar-i Ashraf was built to the Southwest of the Ali Qapu and became the site of extravagant receptions.[74] Sulayman also undertook substantial additions to the Abbasabad Chahar Bagh.[75]

A number of court figures built especially lavish mansions in the capital over this period. Hajji Hedayat, an *amir* who kept order during Isfahan's great famine of 1669, built such a mansion in a small suburb on a branch of the Zayanada Rud; this area, by Chardin's time, contained some 150 houses and four bazaars. The *sadr*, who had married a sister of Abbas II, built a mansion as well.[76]

Despite the vicissitudes visited upon the Armenians as one of the most prominent of the capital's minority groups, the community, and especially its merchants, continued to enjoy a singular position at court and in the realm's commercial life, no doubt owing to their continued dominance of the overland route to the Levant ports, the realm's most important trade outlet to the West, over this period.[77] The community accumulated sufficient wherewithal to continue to build and to embellish churches over this period, including the All Saviour's Cathedral, completed during the reign of Sulayman's predecessor.[78]

Sulayman's court was also noted for its patronage of major painters. The latter's output exhibited an ability to move between traditional Persian and European themes and styles of expression and, moreover, to mix the two. European influences are visible in the works of Shafi Abbasi, Ali Quli Jabbadar, whose career continued until 1716, and Muhammad Zaman, in court employ from at least 1674–5. A *Shahnama* copied between 1663 and 1669 and illustrated between 1693 and 1698 contains both traditional and European-style paintings. The illustrations which embellished histories of the dynasty, including several versions of the *Alam Ara-yi Shah Ismail* completed in this period, featured both traditional and 'European' styles.[79] The same artists were sufficiently skilled also to satisfy the varied tastes of the non-court market[80] and, as their predecessors, to work in such other media as lacquer penboxes, mirror covers and caskets.[81]

The fine carpets produced over this period reveal a similar ability to greet the foreign. Carpets continued to be exported to Europe still utilising the Polonaise style, the latter visible in a 1671 carpet produced for Abbas II's tomb in Qum. Indeed, the carpets, cotton covers and clothes, including fur-lined coats, robes and waistcoats, visible in paintings completed in the 1660s and 1670s, show a taste for Indian cloths, including cotton, silks and jewels both at court and outside court circles, as well as fine glassware imported from Venice. The latter was popular both at and outside the court.[82]

The continuing strength of non-court demand over the period, despite the economic crises noted above, is further attested by the continued production of blue and white ware by Kirmani and Mashhadi potters, with styles of pottery decoration continuing to exhibit interaction with other media, including illuminated manuscripts, carpets and bookbindings.[83] The domestic market also supported the production of lustreware, based in Kashan or Isfahan, which incorporated distinctly novel shapes – such as 'tulip vases' – and designs. These items utilised a technique of manufacture featuring the application of a coppery lustre over cobalt blue, yellow, turquoise or transparent glaze, with decoration of landscape, with or without animals, suggesting demand for such items among those aware of, but unable to afford, the gold and silver vessels produced for the court and other elites.[84]

The 'Persian interlude' also continued over Sulayman's reign: Iranian ceramics remained in great demand abroad, even after China resumed porcelain exports *c.* 1683. Indeed, Iranian potters' development of the colour *grisaille* (grey) and their dynamic use of patterns in this period reflect continued attention to, and the ability to satisfy, the export market.[85] Local metalworkers also worked from Mughal and Deccan products to develop new items to satisfy domestic demand.[86]

Summary and conclusion

The dearth of contemporary Persian-language sources on the reign of Sulayman[87] has encouraged reliance, often uncritical, on the Western sources. These uniformly depict Sulayman as a pawn in the hands of the haram, as cruel, fond of women and alcohol, indifferent to political and administrative matters, and portray his twenty-eight years of rule as a period in which corruption and bribery were 'rife' and flourished alongside pomp and ceremony.[88]

In fact, however, the realm itself experienced its smoothest transition between rulers to date and, in the face of a series of natural, socio-economic and concomitant spiritual challenges, the centre and its associated elements mounted a credible, and varied, series of responses. Throughout the period the realm's different key constituencies displayed only continued and, indeed, expanded ability to interact with each other in the interests of the larger project. Such interaction and loyalty was certainly further encouraged by the prosperity experienced by a number of sectors of Safavid society – more than court and non-court elites alone – due, at least in part, to the 'long peace' of the latter half of the seventeenth century. Indeed, Chardin waxed eloquent in his physical description of Isfahan and its suburbs in this period, noting its thousands of palaces, forty-eight 'colleges', 162 mosques, 1,800 'spacious caravansarais', and 'really fine bazaars', and drew comparisons between the Iranian capital's population and that of London.[89]

8

Denouement or Defeat
The Reign of Shah Sultan Husayn
(1694–1722)

The institutionalisation of transition

Shah Sulayman died in his bed from illness, at the age of forty-seven, having reigned a few years short of three decades. Less than two weeks later, in August 1694, with Sulayman's body on the way to the shrine of Fatima in Qum for burial – where both Safi and Abbas II were also interred – the eldest of Sulayman's seven sons, twenty-six-year old Sultan Husayn acceded to the throne with the help of his aunt Maryam Bekum, herself the wife of the *sadr*, and other court attendants. Pomp marked the coronation: drums and trumpets sounded and lions and elephants paraded in Abbas I's illuminated square, and robes of honour were bestowed on various notables.[1]

The smoothness of Sultan Husayn's accession, like that of his father, underlines the degree to which, between and among each other, the realm's various key constituencies were still co-operating more than competing.

At the same time, the external challenges which had, for example, followed the deaths of Ismail and Tahmasp were also not an issue at this point. As at Sulayman's accession and during his reign, notwithstanding the 1697–1701 occupation of Basra by pro-Persian forces, Ottoman-Persian relations remained peaceful. Safavid-Mughal relations over Shah Sultan Husayn's reign were also for the most part peaceful and the Afghan risings and subsequent movements, *c.* 1709, owed nothing to Indian encouragement. To the North, although Peter the Great railed against the treatment of Russian merchants, a Russian naval squadron threatened Baku in 1700 and the Russians may have encouraged the revolt of a local commander in Shirvan in early 1709, there were no formal hostilities between Russia and Iran over this period. Indeed a formal treaty with Russia concluded in 1717, five years before the Afghan capture of Isfahan, rectified some of these perceived injustices.[2]

Elsewhere a series of Baluchi incursions into Kirman and Yazd beginning *c*. 1698–9 were turned back by Georgian levies which also re-pelled a Baluchi attack on Qandahar in 1704. A rising in Kurdistan during the midst of the Baluchi raids into Kirman and Yazd was also put down.[3]

In fact, at the outset of Sultan Husayn's reign the realm comprised roughly the same territory as that at the death of Abbas I, minus Baghdad and its environs and some Eastern areas lost during Safi's reign.

The balancing of interests: Safavid pluralist discourse continued

The several administrative manuals composed in this period, two written after the 1722 Afghan seizure of Isfahan to be sure, suggest the presence of a relatively developed, formally structured administrative bureaucracy at the central and provincial levels.[4]

Nevertheless, throughout Sultan Husayn's reign, and despite the various challenges facing the centre, the centre apparatus itself continued to reflect the same multi-constitutional (Turk, Tajik, *ghulam*) bases, and the informality, familiar from earlier in the century. Thus, of the period's five *vizier*s, the Tajik sayyid Mirza Muhammad Tahir, appointed *vizier* in 1694, served until 1699. He was succeeded by a Shamlu who served until 1707, followed by Shah Quli Khan Zangana (d. 1715), son of the former *vizier* and Sunni Kurd Shaykh Ali Khan. He was followed by Fath Ali Khan, the former's son-in-law, who served to 1720, and then a Bekdilu Shamlu until the fall of Isfahan. The many *sipahsalar*s of the period were drawn from tribal groups, mainly the Shamlu, and the *ghulam*. The *qurchibashi*s remained tribal in origin, mainly Shamlu and the Zangana Kurds. The *qullaraqasi*s were both tribal and Georgian *ghulam*, after the Sunni Fath Ali Khan. The several *sadr*s continued to be Tajik sayyids, and one, the grandson of the former *vizier* Khalifa Sultan and husband of Safi's daughter Maryam Bekum, served for twenty-six years.[5] The centre's other high offices were peopled by tribal elements[6] even as other key posts were occupied by Tajiks, including many sayyids.[7]

The provincial bureaucracy for the most part continued to mirror the central during this period, being dominated by members of prominent local Tajik, and often sayyid, families[8] even as the governorships were occupied by a variety of individuals, including tribal figures.[9] The frequency with which the Shamlu appear at both this and the centre suggests their continued pre-eminence among the Qizilbash, first apparent during the reign of Abbas I.

The provinces were formally obliged to send cash and goods to the centre, maintain locally based troops and acknowledge various centrally appointed officials such as a *vizier*, and local fief-holders may have held a post at, or were appointed by, the centre.[10] Nevertheless, local officials continued to exercise considerable autonomy of the centre, even frequently exercising control over key local posts.[11] Too, revenues from *khassa* lands were usually directed toward meeting local expenses, though financial assistance from the centre could be forthcoming.[12]

The period's various military expeditions continued to comprise the mixture of tribal and non-tribal elements familiar from earlier in the century.[13] The Safavid force sent against Afghan forces at Gulnabad in March 1722, for example, included Arab cavalry, Georgians, *qullar* elements, and tribal cavalry, and was commanded by the Shamlu *vizier*, the Georgian *qullaraqasi*, the local rulers of Arabistan and Luristan and a chief of the Qizilbash Kuhgilu.[14]

The court's policies toward non-Muslim Iranians continued as nuanced as before. As earlier in the century, so this period also witnessed sporadic campaigns for the conversion of Armenians and Zoroastrians, thus focusing blame for economic and other ills on these and other minorities whose involvement in the specie export, for example, was well known.[15]

Nevertheless, the rich Armenian merchants who continued to dominate the realm's overland trade, especially the silk trade, also continued to enjoy the centre's backing in foreign trade negotiations, the indigenous Armenian Church consistently enjoyed the court's support against Catholic missionary efforts – though this angered the Pope and the French – and the community was permitted to manage its own affairs.[16] Moreover, some of the harsher measures, additional taxes and humiliations visited on the Armenian population more generally, which caused some to leave the city and the realm, were subsequently withdrawn[17] and Sultan Husayn, as his predecessor, is known to have visited All Saviour's.[18] The various improvements made to the community's churches over the period suggest the continuing good health of the community's position, as well as its wealth.[19]

Foreign and domestic challenges and responses

The challenges which presented themselves during Sultan Husayn's reign were familiar.

Specie outflow remained a matter of concern, as attested by the centre's continued efforts to check its export, ranging from outright bans – in 1699 and 1713 – to the imposition of duties on its export.[20] The companies' continued flouting of such measures was rooted in the profits to be made in the export of specie which greatly outweighed those from trade in such other items as silk. Indeed, with world market conditions continuing to determine demand for Iranian silk, at Sultan Husayn's accession the VOC had purchased no silk at all since 1691. Between 1697 and 1710, despite a new treaty in 1702, the VOC bought silk only in 1703 and 1704, and bought only small amounts in 1711 and 1713. Although the amount purchased in 1714 was markedly higher, this was the final year in which the VOC purchased Iranian silk. In fact, as Iran's best silk was being delivered to private concerns, especially for shipment West via the Levant, a trade still controlled by the Armenian long-distance merchants, there was little silk of adequate quality for the companies anyway. The centre's relative lack of interest in dealing with the companies therefore continued, the more so given their complicity in the specie outflow; usually only lower-ranking officials attended any trade negotiations with, for example, the Dutch.[21]

Certainly aggravated by the specie outflow, widespread famine was said to have caused riots in Isfahan during the shah's year-and-a-half sojourn outside the capital to visit the shrine and tombs of Safavid rulers in Qum and a subsequent lengthy stay in Mashhad, beginning in August of 1706, some twelve years after his accession.[22] During this same period, perhaps taking advantage of such adversities, Lazgi tribes raided Georgia from the North and, in 1709, a local commander in Shirvan rose against the centre. Foreign sources refer to agitation in Kurdistan, Luristan and Mashhad and, *c.* 1713, Baluchi raids into Kirman, Uzbek moves toward Mashhad and Mughal and Afghan movements around Qandahar.[23]

The centre responded quickly to all these challenges. Sultan Husayn himself dispatched readily available Georgian forces which speedily crushed the unrest in Isfahan, and all was quiet when the royal party returned to the capital the following year.[24] Also, however, the court replaced a number of officials at the central and provincial levels, ordered Isfahan's clerics to undertake a variety of special measures to address the root causes of the riots and itself redirected income from its rented properties for the same purpose.[25] A 1704 Qandahar rising by the Ghalzai Afghans was put down but the rebellion's leader, Mir Uvais, was pardoned. In 1709, however, Mir Uvais rose again and defeated a mixed Persian-Georgian force sent from Isfahan allied with local Abdali Afghans. Although a further punitive expedition against him fizzled out, as Mir Uvais thereafter caused no further trouble he was left alone and died in Qandahar in 1715.[26]

In 1715 wheat prices in Isfahan hit new highs and caused further unrest.[27] The following year pestilence broke out in the silk-producing areas along the Caspian, a rising by Gilani peasants against local author-ities curtailed the availability of silk from the region and food riots were reported in Tabriz and Isfahan. In 1718 the pestilence spread further. Concomitantly, Uzbeks, Arabs and Baluchis launched various incursions and Tartar elements invaded Khurasan.[28]

Once again the centre did not fail to respond. In the context of the 1715 food crisis, in Isfahan the capital's *darugha* was fired. In 1715, at the death of the Sunni Kurdish *vizier*, Shah Quli Khan Zangana, his son-in-law Fath Ali Khan Daghistani, previously the *qullaraqasi*[29] was appointed *vizier* and immediately undertook a series of measures to raise revenue.[30] These included additional levies on merchants and renewed efforts to force non-Muslim subjects, including the Banyan traders and at least one prominent, previously exempted, Armenian family, to pay the *jizya* tax.[31] With some success, the centre also strove valiantly to make headway on both specie export and the silk trade.[32] At the same time, however, Iranian silk continued to move West via the overland route at a price which still produced a better return to such private merchants as the Julfans than the Gulf route. With the centre consequently still relatively uninterested in the Gulf silk trade, VOC representatives were, as before, consistently and conspicuously slighted during many of the period's trade negotiations.[33]

Maintaining the spiritual balance

The most vociferous opponents of philosophical inquiry and Sufi doctrine and practice were gone from the scene by the time of Sultan Husayn's accession. Nevertheless, low-level sniping by like-minded figures continued,[34] as did criticisms of those Twelver scholars, dead and living, who advocated an expanded authority for senior clerics as arbiters of issues of doctrine and practice during the Imam's occultation, and those of the living who enjoyed close ties to the court.[35] The socio-economic problems discussed above can only have encouraged the ongoing recourse to Sufi inquiry to which this sniping attests.

Coupled with the above responses to the economic problems, the centre also strove to maintain its spiritual authority by continuing to balance its identification with the various opposing parties to the realm's spiritual discourse and thus maintain its image as transcending particularist polemics.

On one hand, the centre further expanded its public association with the faith, and especially its more orthodox interpretations. For a start, Sulayman's body was sent to Qum for burial. Then, with prompting from Baqir Majlisi, the capital's *Shaykh al-Islam*, who was accorded a prominent role in both the ceremonies marking Sulayman's burial and Sultan Husayn's accession – including delivering the *khutba* in Sultan Husayn's name – the new shah issued a *firman* banning wine, ordering the destruction of all wine in the royal wine cellars and forbidding other excessive practices and displays.[36] Although this *firman* soon went the way of its many predecessors, attesting to the limits of both the clerical and court power in the face of human shortcomings, Sultan Husayn's reign apparently witnessed noticeably fewer public, and certainly fewer official, displays of such excess.[37]

Maryam Bek, Safi's daughter and Sultan's Husayn's aunt and the wife of the *sadr*, is identified with a mosque and school dating to 1703, to whose endowment she added continuously until 1718. In a bow to the opponents of philosophy the endowment deed for the school forbad the teaching of several works of Ibn Sina.[38]

In 1704–5, six years after Majlisi's death and ten years after his own accession, the shah commenced the building of the Chahar Bagh school, bazaar and a three-storey sarai complex, located along the Eastern side of the Chahar Bagh south of the Hasht Bihisht Palace. The entire complex, this period's most spectacular project, was paid for, in the tradition of Timurid, Turkish and Safavid female patronage, by the shah's mother. The school's dome was modelled on that of the Royal Mosque of Abbas

I and, if the quality of the tile-work did not equal that of earlier projects, it nevertheless incorporated some unusual building features which recalled and, in some ways, actually surpassed various individual structures dating to the reign of Abbas I, arguably including the Royal Mosque itself.[39]

Attesting to the larger historical context of the undertaking, the original *vaqf* deed was dated to 1706 and the school was officially inaugurated in 1710–11, respectively simultaneous with and in the aftermath of the 1706 disorders in the capital, the Uzbek attacks of the same year, and the large number of personnel changes at the central and provincial levels. The school's opening ceremony was attended by key officials and members of the polity's chief domestic constituencies, from court eunuchs to Tajik sayyids to Twelver clerics. Each thereby, in the midst of the above-mentioned challenges, reaffirmed its loyalty to the shah, to the larger Safavid project of which he was head and, and, especially as well, that project's distinctive association with Twelver Shi'ism.[40]

Further acknowledging the influence of the 'orthodox lobby', the study of philosophy was banned at the school in favour of concentration on *hadith, fiqh* and Qur'an commentary (*tafsir*).[41] Indeed, the 1706 *vaqf* document named the school's first chief teacher as Sayyid Muhammad Baqir Khatunabadi (d. 1715). Sayyid Muhammad was descended from a family said to have come to Iran from Madina in the 1470s. Both Sayyid Muhammad and his father *Sayyid Ismail* (d. 1703–4) were close associates of the court during Sultan Husayn's reign. At Sayyid Ismail's death both his son and their relative Muhammad Salih, a son-in-law of Baqir Majlisi, were given robes of honour by the shah. Baqir Khatunabadi, who had been named *Shaykh al-Islam* of Isfahan in 1703, frequently attended the shah, accompanied the royal party on its sojourn to Mashhad in 1706–7, and was gifted with 100 *tumans* by Sultan Husayn in 1707.[42] In 1712 Baqir Khatunabadi was made the realm's first *mullabashi*, chief cleric, and accorded complete authority over all the realm's religious affairs, a scope of authority equivalent to that accorded Ali Karaki during Tahmasp's reign.[43]

The Chahar Bagh complex was completed *c.* 1714, when a door costing some 800 *tumans* and containing great quantity of silver was added to the structure, but the court continued to add *vaqf*s until at least 1716. There were also endowments to cover expenses relating to the school and such non-school expenses as stipends for the faithful in Najaf, for several to perform the *hajj*, for expenses associated with Muharram ceremonies and for the maintenance of both male and female sayyids. In keeping with the centre's attention to the public welfare, excess revenues were directed to the city's hospices.[44]

The court also continued attentive to the religious infrastructure outside the capital, in both Qazvin and the shrine cities, for example.[45] In 1712 a daughter of Shah Sulayman was married to the superintendent of Imam Riza's Mashhad shrine, further cementing links between the Safavid house and key Tajik Twelver sayyids.[46]

The contributions to Isfahan's religious landscape by others at the centre also advanced the centre's identification with the faith. A sister of Sultan Husayn built a two-storey school, to the Northwest of Abbas I's *maydan* in the bazaar, and a bathhouse; revenues from the latter were dedicated to the school's upkeep.[47] The link between a number of prominent clerical associates of the court – including Baqir Khatunabadi, *Shaykh al-Islam* and the realm's first *mullabashi*, and Muhammad Husayn Tabrizi, the last *mullabashi* – with a school built *c.* 1695 by the black eunuch Aqa Kamal, denotes an active working relationship between these two key constituencies in this period, one familiar and the other a 'new' element. Indeed the presence of Aqa Kamal, who in 1695–6 became, in effect, the finance minister and is also associated with the Chahar Bagh school project, along with the above-mentioned administrative manuals produced in this period, further attests to the relative bureaucratisation of the Safavid project.[48] The large number of prominent officials, including eunuchs, who performed the *hajj* in this period also demonstrates the concern of the Safavid elite across constituencies with their spiritual credentials.[49]

Other elites and non-elites – including doctors,[50] merchants[51], and small craftsmen[52] – made similar contributions, such affirmations of their loyalty to the faith attesting to their commitment to the centre and the project itself. A variety of other *vaqf* endowments, apparently private, anonymous or otherwise unidentifiable, for the religious infrastructure are also dated to this period.[53] In fact, the great expansion of *vaqf* endowments over this period itself attests also to an effort by court and private donors alike to enhance the health of the polity's cultural, economic and social life,[54] all the more important in such troubled times.

It is noticeable also that the titles accorded Sultan Husayn in the period's building inscriptions, in projects undertaken both by court-based and non-court sponsors, gave special prominence to the 'grander' claims. Thus, for example, Sultan Husayn is variously referred to as the 'shadow of Allah (*zill Allah*)' and as 'the just sultan . . . the spreader of the precepts of Islam (*al-sultan al-adil . . . nashir ahkam al-Islam*)'.[55] He is also described as the 'shadow of Allah' in a court chronicle completed by a Tajik sayyid for the shah in 1703–4, suggesting continuing support of this constituency for the Safavid project. This text in particular seems to have revived the tradition of the universal history which distinguished such chronicles as *Habib al-Siyar* of Ismail's reign and *Lubb al-Tavarikh* and *Nusakh-i Jahan Ara* of Tahmasp's. These had sought to link the Safavid shahs directly both to earlier kings and to the Imams and thereby further enhance their legitimacy and authority but were superseded by dynastic histories during the reign of Abbas I.[56]

If all these undertakings projected the centre's identification with the anti-philosophical dimensions of the faith, simultaneous efforts were made to identify with the Hellenic legacy, philosophical inquiry and Sufi activity, none of which can be said to have been dead over the period. In his massive *hadith* compilation *Bihar al-Anwar* Baqir Majlisi, the capital's *Shaykh al-Islam* who had officiated at Sultan Husayn's accession and won a ban on wine from the shah, attempted to reconcile elements of Greek medical discourse with the statements of the Imams on medicine and health. Shaykh Muhammad Jafar, who briefly held the post at Majlisi's death, was interested in philosophical and *irfani* inquiry as was Jamal Khvansari (d. 1710), son of Husayn, who penned a number of essays to the shah[57] and accompanied Sultan Husayn and Baqir Khatunabadi, the future rector of the Chahar Bagh school – whose founding documents proscribed the teaching of philosophy – on the shah's journey to Mashhad in 1706–7. Indeed Jamal's father Husayn Khvansari, also a proponent of philosophical inquiry, had been a student of both Baqir Khatunabadi and his father Sayyid Ismail at the Lutfallah Maysi school, and Sayyid Ismail. Sultan Husayn spent long hours in conversation with the latter, who had been interested in both philosophy and theology, having studied with Rajab Ali Tabrizi, himself a student of Mir Findiriski.[58]

The contemporary critiques of Sufism and philosophy/*irfan* only further attest to the continued presence of both in this period and confirm suggestions of an increasingly active distinction between the two by this period.[59] Indeed, although the inscriptions of such schools as that of the Potters, built in 1693–4 near the Harun-i Vilayat square, whose *vaqf* document mentioned Baqir Majlisi, and the above-mentioned endowments of merchants and craftsmen, proclaimed loyalty to the Safavid project, the buildings were clearly directed to 'popular' elements seeking spiritual explanations for the crises, natural and otherwise, afflicting the realm and the city.

The court itself was continually, and visibly, mindful of this latter constituency. Sultan Husayn continued the centre's patronage of the capital's 'popular' religious edifices.[60] The same Ismail Khatunabadi who, with his son Muhammad Baqir, were such close associates of Sultan Husayn's court – the latter being the first rector of the Chahar Bagh school where teaching in *hadith*, *fiqh* and *tafsir* were the rule – further embellished the tomb of Baba Rukn al-Din, dating from the Abbas I period. This was a popular gathering place during festivals, and the location of Mir Findiriski's tomb and Sayyid Ismail's own final resting place.[61] A *yuzbashi* funded work on Isfahan's Imamzada Ismail, to which the shah himself had ordered repairs.[62]

Contemporary sources attest to the shah's careful attention to certain distinctively Sufi practices historically associated with the Safavid order and to Tajik acceptance of the Safavid-Sufi connection.[63] Contemporary travellers' accounts further attest to the sponsorship, both by the court and realm's economic elite, of other 'popular' rituals distinctive to the faith.[64] These and the shah's above-mentioned dedication of *vaqf* to sponsor Muharram ceremonies, as during earlier reigns, bespeak the centre's efforts to influence, via sponsorship, the style and substance of spiritual discourse of such key distinctive ceremonies.

The development of the city's non-religious landscape further advanced the authority and legitimacy of the shah and the larger Safavid project.

The best-known of the court's achievements in this regard was the Farahabad Chahar Bagh, dated to *c.* 1711, when the shah is said to have travelled to the area outside Isfahan's city centre and ordered the *yuzbashi*, Ibrahim Aqa, involved also in repairs to the Imamzada Ismail, to construct a new garden and commanded others build houses nearby. Just as the Chahar Bagh complex outshone Abbas I's Shah Mosque, this new garden complex, certainly took its name from, and dwarfed, Abbas I's Caspian garden palace of the same name.[65] By this time Sultan Husayn also had already carried out repairs to the Chihil Sutun complex and redesigned and redecorated a garden complex associated with his father Sulayman's Hasht Bihisht.[66] Other members of the family followed suit: the school and mosque built by Maryam Bek *c.* 1703–4 were associated with a mansion she built herself, located outside the walled city, near the Hasanabad gate.

Merchants emulated the centre: the chief merchant, on whom see below, had a large mansion in the Abbasabad suburb of the city.[67]

An economic snapshot: a plethora of taxes

The centre's devotion of financial resources to such projects, especially in the aftermath of the 1706 disturbances, is universally lamented in the secondary sources as evidence of the shah's indifference both to the events of the day and to his own duties, and responsibilities, as ruler.[68]

Detailed data on the centre's budget, let alone the polity's overall income and expenses, balance of payments or even specie outflow is lacking, to be sure.[69] However, the combined notes of such travellers to and residents in Iran as Olearius, du Mans, de Thévenot, Chardin, Kaempfer and Sanson, and other sources, suggest that by this time the centre had recourse to a myriad of measures with which to tap the chief sources of the realm's wealth – agriculture, artisnal/craft production and short and longer-distance trade/commerce.[70]

In rural areas, where the bulk of the population still resided, taxes – in cash and kind – were levied on animals, pastures, gardens, orchards and trees, houses, wells and mills. There were also additional levies or services required when the centre mounted a military campaign. Corvee labour could also be requisitioned from peasants on crown and private land. By this period the centre was also promoting sharecropping agreements and maintaining and regulating the irrigation system, all to boost further production on crown and non-crown land.

In the steadily growing cities[71] craft/artisnal and commercial life func-
tioned on both a private, independent basis, but also as sponsored by the
court. The latter itself maintained some thirty-two workshops of artisans
and craftsmen, each headed by a chief (*bashi*) who also administered the
corresponding guild in the town.[72] There were nearly thirty other non- or
semi-skilled 'professions' – from camel-drivers to grave-diggers – whose
trades, considered 'dirty [and] immoral', were not organised profession-
ally. Wrestlers, jugglers, beggars, acrobats and puppet-show operators
were supervised directly by a central official, while coffee-houses and
brothels, as well as dancers and singers, gambling house operators,
pigeon-trainers and keepers of cannabis and wine shops were supervised
as a group by another department. Blood-letters and circumcisers were
supervised by the shah's personal barber.[73]

Iranian merchants were organised into groups based on their common
line of business, religion, place of origin and nationality; the chief merchant (*malik al-tujjar*) was appointed by the shah from one of their
number.[74] As with the centre's involvement with rural irrigation, on the
urban scene the centre's building of bazaars both promoted economic
activity and allowed the centre to oversee the affairs of these professions.

All of these elements were liable for a host of direct taxes in cash and
in kind as well as the corvee, organised by their guild chief or merchant
leaders.[75] The centre also used the guilds to influence, if not control, the
quality and flow of goods, their prices and weights and measurements
and to force sales of its own goods at artificially low or high prices.[76]
Through guild leaders the centre also acquired its own finished products.
There was a personal head tax and a house tax. Religious minorities paid
the *jizya*, the non-Muslim head tax.[77]

In lieu of regular cash salaries,[78] local and central government officials
were often given assignments on sources of revenue – land, customs
duties, etc. – a system in place since early in Islamic history.[79] These
officials also charged fees for their services.[80]

All ranks of officials also gave an annual 'gift', in cash or kind, to their
superiors and similar 'gifts' on such special occasions as Nawruz, the
Persian New Year. Holders of the above-mentioned assignments on revenue, and even small landowners, were expected to make extra gifts.
Tribal elements might include in their gifts cash and/or military forces for
use by the centre. Foreign companies were also expected to provide gifts,
pay fees and render services to local and central officials. The latter
included provision of ships for transport of the court's goods. Indeed the
royal workshop system produced luxury items both for the court itself
and for export to Europe and India; all profits accrued therefrom passed
directly to the court. The court also received one-fifth of all booty taken
in war and the shah was heir to the estates of those who died without
heirs or who went bankrupt.[81]

Taken together, such a variety of means to extract wealth both minimised the centre's need to raise and have on hand, let alone spend,

substantial amounts of cash to finance day-to-day central or local administrative 'running' costs let alone any of the great architectural projects of
the day. Indeed, the Farahabad project in particular made extensive use
of corvee labour.[82] Such a system also allowed the centre to spread the
costs of such undertakings among a variety of sources, depending on the
strength or weakness of one or the other sector.

Perhaps more importantly, such projects – undertaken on such scale
as to equal if not outshine those of Abbas I – complemented both the
variety, already detailed, of short-and longer-term 'practical', i.e. economic and political, responses of centre to the misfortunes of the time
and the centre's already-discussed enhancement of the realm's spiritual
legitimacy and secular/political infrastructure.

Taken together, all these undertakings bespeak simultaneous efforts to
project both power and legitimacy, all the more important following the
disturbances which had rocked the capital in 1706 and 1715, not to
mention the other largely internal economic and political challenges to
both the realm's stability and his authority in 1706. In this instance
Sultan Husayn's efforts recalled the extent of similar, and ultimately
successful, projects undertaken during Abbas I's reign which illustrated
the centre's perception of the challenges it faced in that period. The
secular and non-secular projects undertaken by both non-court elites
and non-elites over the period, in turn, projected their reciprocal loyalty,
as individuals and representatives of larger constituencies, to both the
person of the shah and, hence, to the larger project itself.

Creativity and consumption

Indeed the strength of activity, and creativity, on other 'cultural' fronts
does not suggest a system under fundamental social or economic challenge but rather the continued strength of elite and non-elite purchasing
power and, therefore, the limited impact of the various economic crises
discussed above. Nor is there any suggestion of the sudden appearance
of, let alone any innate, hostility to things foreign, let alone Christian
and/or Western.

Court-sponsored painting, for example, flourished over the period,
both addressing and incorporating the European, as it had during
the reign of Sultan Husayn's predecessors, and evolving new styles.
Indeed, although Muhammad Zaman died *c.* 1700, the work of his son
Muhammad Ali displayed advances on his father's work and his debt to
European styles; his figures, for example, are more 'delicately modelled',
'not puffy-eyed and ponderous like those of his father', and his painting
of Sultan Husayn reflects a different use of lighting.[83]

Styles and techniques continued to cross media boundaries. By the
mid-1690s the above and other artists are associated with a new style
of pen box,[84] the lush floral motifs evident in early eighteenth-century
border-illuminated manuscripts feature also in the 1714 silver door of

the Chahar Bagh school[85] and a ewer of the period is decorated with panels of tulips of the type found in album covers. Lustreware was clearly influenced by metalworking patterns and these, in turn, by manuscript illumination and bordering.[86]

Evidence from court paintings also attests to the continued production both of such luxury items as textiles and objects made of precious metals, such as dagger sheaths and jewelled hilts, for the socio-economic elite.[87]

The continued presence of lustreware, enamel work and steel objects points to both the continued strength of purchasing power of both court and non-elite elements, the realm's continued productive capacity and, in particular, producers' awareness of, and ability to adapt to, changing domestic and foreign tastes.[88]

Denouement or defeat?

Sultan Husayn is uniformly disparaged in the European and secondary sources and blamed for the fall of the capital and, by extension, the dynasty itself to the Afghans in 1722, albeit three decades after he assumed his throne.[89]

At the outset of his reign, however, there was little hint that he might be the 'last' ruler of the longest-ruling dynasty in Iran's Islamic history. Even given the diversity of actions taken by the centre in response to the challenges discussed above, there was no evidence of continuous, widespread and profound discontent among the populace generally or, more importantly, the realm's key politico-military and socio-economic constituencies sufficient to present a serious challenge to the broad configuration of interests behind the ruling house, let alone the latter's legitimacy in particular.

As for foreign threats, there was little hint of any renewed threats from the realm's traditional enemies, the Ottomans or the Uzbeks. Indeed, the Safavid military, comprising some centre-based elements with the bulk of the troops dispersed throughout the provinces, was best suited to respond to just such large-scale ground expeditions as had been launched by these enemies in the early seventeenth and sixteenth centuries, their well-heralded approach having always allowed adequate time for the assembly of a sufficiently credible Safavid force to, eventually, repel the invaders. Following the initial Safavid offensive strategy which carved out the Safavid realm this essentially defensive military strategy, together with fortuitous turns of events among the Safavids' opponents and such peace treaties as that of Amasya, in 1555, and, especially, Zuhab in 1639, had secured the realm against its traditional external enemies for more than two hundred years. As for minor incidents of unrest and incursions in border areas, in the early, and even later, years of Sultan Husayn's reign, the deployment of local forces had usually proved sufficient.[90]

In 1717, in the aftermath of food riots in Tabriz and Isfahan and with treaties with Russia and the VOC secured, in Qandahar Mir Uvais' son Mahmud murdered and seized power from Mir Uvais' successor and brother. The centre, occupied with a Kurdish rising in Hamadan and the seizure of Persian islands in the Gulf by Omani Arabs, opted for the short-term measure of recognising Mahmud as the local potentate. When Mahmud sacked Kirman in November of 1719,[91] as the Omani threat fizzled out, the centre turned its attention East. Despite the fall of the *vizier* Fath Ali Khan in December 1720,[92] an expeditionary force was raised and, at its approach, the Afghans – as had the Uzbeks so often in the past – withdrew. The relief force, under Qajar leadership, was thereupon directed against the rather too-independent ruler of Sistan.

Following the Sistanis' defeat of this force, in the late summer of 1721, Lazgi tribesmen seized the capital of Shirvan and, in October, Mahmud reappeared at Kirman. Stiff local resistance caused Mahmud to withdraw toward Yazd. Driven off by the Yazdis as well, in March 1722 Mahmud reached Gulnabad, less than 18 miles to the East of Isfahan. There the Shamlu commander's apparent failure to capitalise on the initial successes of his much larger force allowed Mahmud to exploit a narrow opening and Safavid forces, snatching defeat from the jaws of victory, fled to Isfahan. Three days later, the Afghan, realising the extent of his victory, commenced his siege of the city.[93]

The shah's continued presence in the capital throughout the subsequent half-year siege served as a rallying point for tribal and non-tribal military forces based near to and far from the capital. These forces responded to the centre's messages for assistance and penetrated the Afghan lines to enter the city.[94] The population of Isfahan, including those who, spurred on by stories of the brutality of advancing Afghan forces, had retreated to the city from outlying areas, showed no signs of defecting but rather protested vigorously the court's failure to counter the Afghan threat.[95]

Nevertheless, the siege could not be broken and six months later, in October, with the English East India Company reporting that all hopes of its being raised had faded, Mahmud received Sultan Husayn at the latter's own Farahabad palace where the shah named the Afghan leader as his successor. This ceremony was thereafter repeated at the royal palace in the city centre, with the shah being brought from prison to reprise his earlier performance.[96]

Epilogue
Poetry and Politics –
The Multiplicity of Safavid Discourse

In his perceptive analysis of the panegyrics of the great Safavid poet Saib Tabrizi, Jafariyan notes Saib's poetry described the shahs of his day as leaders of the Safavid Sufi order, as promoters and propagators of Twelver Shi'ism, as Alid sayyids, as defenders of Iran from its Uzbek and Ottoman enemies, as the Shadow(s) of Allah on earth, as defenders of the *shaf* (the law) and as providers of *'adl* (justice) and security.[1] References to the ruler as Shadow of Allah on earth were not unique in pre-Safavid Iranian history. Too, many other rulers were portrayed as defenders of the law and as providers of justice and security. However, these references together with Saib's additional references to the shahs' roles as Sufi leaders, promoters of the faith, sayyids and defenders of the realm against these particular enemies, highlight features unique to the centre's public discourse during the Safavid period and point up its distinctly multi-faceted, inclusive nature and broad appeal.

Efforts to project such a broad appeal were in evidence from early on. Ismail's own poetry spoke simultaneously to aspects of Sufi and Shi'i, Tajik Persian, and even Christian, discourse widely extant on the urban and rural scenes in the late fifteenth and early sixteenth centuries. Indeed, Ismail portrayed himself, and was portrayed, simultaneously as the servant and embodiment of each of these traditions, mediator between and, therefore, transcendent ruler over them all. Appeals to, and thus recognition of, any one element did not therefore entail the exclusion of any of the others, and hence facilitated the transfer of the allegiances of Turk and Tajik affiliates of the region's earlier tribal polities to the Safavid project. Moreover, for more than a quarter-century of his leadership of the order and the polity itself, after the 1501 capture of Tabriz, Ismail's 'words' were matched by practical actions. Marriages, appointments, grants of land and/or recognition of existing local rulers' autonomy so successfully aligned Turk and Tajik to each other and to the ruling house that the resulting, broadly based polity was sufficiently strong to survive domestic and foreign challenges, especially given the fortuitous Ottoman turn to the Southwest after Chaldiran.

So dependent on a single personality was the Safavid project to this point, however, that the hierarchical configuration of Turk and Tajik interests arranged around Ismail at the polity's centre could only have fractured with his death. During the half-century reign of Ismail's son Tahmasp, therefore, the polity experienced, first, a decade or more of civil disorder and consequent foreign invasion. There followed, however, the rise of a reconstituted, and familiar, Turk-Tajik alliance, hierarchically organised, together with a reconstituted, and similarly familiar, broad and inclusive discourse and actions/policies which centred on the person and presence of the new shah as spokesman, mediator and transcendent ruler in whom both Turk and Tajik could see their discourses mirrored, their interests expressed and thus legitimised. As with Ismail's death, however, so the death of his son Tahmasp, in 1576, voided these arrangements.

The subsequent fourteen years of civil war which threw up, and marked the reigns of, his sons Ismail II and Khudabanda, brothers by a single Mawsillu woman, revealed the extent to which interests in and loyalty to the broader project had, in less than a century, broken down particularist interests. Turk, Tajik and now also more recently arrived Northerners struggled both between and against but also, and more importantly, alongside and with each other for mastery of the political centre. Indeed, that Ismail II's Sunni flirtation, intended to reach out to still-strong Sunni sympathies among Tajiks and placate the Ottomans and thus solidify his own personal position, received such short shrift from the military-political centre, reveals the depth of commitment of the polity's key constituencies to Twelver Shi'ism as the realm's established faith. This commitment persisted despite the fact that few were conversant with more than its very basic doctrines and practices, as other forms of spiritual expression contined to remain popular at the elite and non-elite levels – as one aspect of the broader Safavid project's hitherto overall successful discourse.

The scale of the internal and external military-political and domestic spiritual challenges which faced Khudabanda's son Abbas at his 1587 accession called forth perhaps the most wide-ranging and transformative responses of the period. On one hand, although long-standing Qizilbash tribal elements retained their military, and thus, political predominance throughout, non-Qizilbash tribal and newly arrived *ghulam* constituencies were now accorded greater, and in some cases formal, status and positions in the realm's military-political and administrative spheres. The newly expanded centre oversaw both a series of successful domestic and foreign military undertakings and a similarly large-scale programme of secular and non-secular building projects which reinforced the transcendent political and spiritual authority of the shah, and thus the larger Safavid project itself, in the face of considerable challenges to both.

The enlarged centre also embarked on an effort to connect with elements outside the region. The latter included Armenian and Western political, commercial-economic and religious constituencies, Arab clerics and even Chinese potters.

As manifested in particular by their acceptance of political and administrative appointments, or the funding of religious and cultural undertakings, indigenous elites and non-elites in particular declared their loyalty to the shah, and thereby each other's traditions and discourse and, thus, the broader, inclusive, fundamentally multi-constitutional nature of the project itself. The military-political stability and economic growth and the new foundations laid for the faith itself by additions in material infrastructure and personnel which marked the later years of Abbas' reign generated a new self-confidence at the centre. This was reflected in the diminishing preoccupation of the period's court chronicles with the distant, pre-Safavid past in favour of grounding the roots, and legitimacy, of the polity in the very distinctly, and distinctive, more-recent Safavid past.

The success with which the newer elements were incorporated into, and came to identify with, the broader project without displacing those already in place is most clearly manifest in the increasing smoothness which marked subsequent transitions between rulers and the degree of continuity in the domestic and foreign policies which were pursued and spirituo-culture discourse which was projected by subsequent, different configurations of Turk, Tajik and *ghulam* at the centre. Indeed, the balanced allocation of key posts at the centre among these three constituencies was the chief common and continuous feature of Safavid politics for the duration, even if the personalities themselves changed, or were changed. This process was certainly facilitated by the growing wealth accruing to the realm over the century, especially in the aftermath of the 1639 Zuhab treaty, which both elites and non-elites clearly enjoyed.

These later years were hardly trouble-free, to be sure. In addition to the clashes at the centre during the reigns of Abbas I's first two successors there were certainly bursts of officially sanctioned religious and/or ethnic intolerance, especially against Armenians, Jews and Banyans. These latter outbursts – during the vizierates of Khalifa Sultan, Muhammad Bek and Shaykh Ali Khan especially – were almost always associated with larger economic crises either alone, or in combination with other, 'natural', disasters, however, and these minority elements served as scapegoats to deflect 'popular' attention from the centre's own inability, despite its best efforts, to resolve problems whose causes, in fact, were essentially outside its influence but whose impact on 'popular' elements was especially telling.

But, during Sultan Husayn's reign in particular – as witnessed by the riots in Isfahan during the second decade of his reign, the torching of Baqir Khatunabadi's house in the third or, during the Afghan siege of Isfahan, the riots over the court's inability to defend the city – not all of the people were fooled all of the time. Too, some senior clerics objected to this official intolerance: aside from his actions against Indian idols abetted, if not initiated, by the same Shaykh Ali Khan vizierate, even Baqir Majlisi was certainly more tolerant of Christians and Jews than is usually assumed. In fact, moreover, the Safavid centre generally sided with indigenous, especially elite, Armenian interests against those of foreign Christians. And, if these Armenians, owing to the crucial role of some, at least, in long-distance trade, had been forcibly brought to Isfahan, ongoing Armenian church-building and embellishment attests that they enjoyed, and were officially encouraged in their, freedom of worship. Even Christian *ghulam* were permitted to continue their own distinct rites and practices just as in the first Safavid century nominal Shi'ites had been permitted to give expression to Sunni historical interpretations of Islamic history. As for the Indians, though their rising numbers in the later seventeenth century attracted attention and, in the midst of economic crises, animosity, in the same time frame various court and non-court elites, including eunuchs and clerics, entrusted their funds to Isfahan's Indian merchants. On balance, the Safavid record on minorities certainly stands in favourable contrast to that of contemporary Europe.[2]

Over the period there were also both episodic and ongoing spiritual challenges to Safavid spirituo-religious legitimacy. Early in the period the messianism of these movements mainly attracted tribal elements, especially when the deaths of Ismail and Tahmasp removed the key figures around whom the elites and levies of the polity's different tribes had become organised. Over the sixteenth century and during the second Safavid century especially, commensurate with urban expansion, political disarray at the centre and socio-economic and natural crises, such messianic discourse attracted the support of some tribal but also, and increasingly, elements of the expanding urban population. In Isfahan the worse affected of the latter were those located around the city's traditional centre, the Harun-i Vilayat square. Least able to weather the combination of external economic and internal 'natural' misfortunes over the seventeenth century, they sought meaning and solace in messianic 'Sufi' discourse and practice. The growing popularity of such movements in turn provoked middle- and lower-ranking clerics who turned also on court-based clerics whose philosophical interests and personal associations appeared to encourage such unorthodox discourse, but whose associated theological and jurisprudential writings both legitimated both their own affiliation with the established political institution and the exclusivity of their leadership position within the community during the Imam's absence. The resulting domestic spiritual disorder, which grew coincident with the polity's economic problems, was of increasing concern to the centre.

Overtly alternate messianic discourse was anathema, and over the period those tribal or urban elements which went so far as to question the legitimate rule of their *pir*/the shah paid the ultimate price. However, over the seventeenth century in particular, except for brief moments the centre, adhering to its traditional tendency to strive to transcend particularist polemics, attempted to forge and maintain links with all parties to those ongoing, opposing spiritual polemics which fell short of such overt challenges to the larger project rather than moving brutally to crush such movements.

On one hand, court-associated clerics were sent to preach in Isfahan's mosques, many strategically located in the precincts of the bazaar itself. Senior clerical associates of the court provided a growing body of Persian-language resources on the basics of Twelver doctrine and practice for use in such campaigns. Some also undertook regular preaching. Others turned to scholarship in the religious sciences both to advance the cause of the Safavid project itself in the face of such discord but also to enhance both their own authority in the community during the Imam's absence and the legitimacy of their involvement with the political establishment. All of these clerics were well-known for their interests in philosophical inquiry, if not also 'high' Sufism.

Simultaneously, however, by means of appointments to various political and religious posts the centre both undertook to associate itself with some of the more vocal critics of 'popular' Sufi-style and philosophical discourse and to sponsor, and thereby identify with, 'popular' religious and spiritual discourse, structures, events and practices – even during Saru Taqi's vizierate though not during that of Muhammad Mahdi Karaki – and thereby to offer 'official' alternatives to contemporary messianic polemics.

Taken together these efforts, aided by the timely passings of key opponents of Sufi and philosophical doctrine and practice and the centre's ongoing 'material discourse' in support of its authority, the 'policy of transcendence' succeeded in lowering the volume of the realm's competing polemics by the end of Sulayman's reign while maintaining the legitimacy of the latter's authority; hence, the policy was continued, with similar success, during the reign of Sultan Husayn.

Much attention has been paid to the centre's 'foreign' trade relations and, especially, movements of silk and specie, this especially in the light of the recent, and much-needed, mining of the records of the Gulf-based foreign trading companies. To be sure, efforts over the second Safavid century in particular bespeak the centre's continued concern with maximising silk exports and checking the export of specie. Too, this material suggests that of far greater importance to the realm's well-being over the period was the continued vitality of both the overland trade routes, from the Eastern Mediterranean through Iran to India, and domestic economic activity – agriculture, especially, and domestic production and trade. Also clear is the initial apparently compatible politico-economic expectations, and needs, of the court and the foreign trading companies which then increasingly diverged as the centre realised that company representatives, beholden both to tiers of 'higher-ups' abroad and to the exigencies of the world market, could not set their own political and economic/commercial agendas and policies, or even purchases, let alone act as spokesmen for their home governments' policies in the region. Attempts by Abbas to construct an anti-Ottoman alliance with the European powers, as similar efforts both by Ismail and the Safavids' Aqquyunlu forebearers, therefore came to nought. Hence, if the Safavid centre appeared to foreign observers to grow a tad inward-looking in the latter part of the century, particularly after the 1639 Zuhab treaty with the Ottomans, this is understandable given the centre's growing understanding that the domestic and the regional mattered, and would continue to matter, more.[3] Compared to dealing with company representatives, usually impotent and often petulant, peace on the Western marches was attainable, if at a price, and promised, and produced, better and broader political and economic returns.

Any such inward focus did not obtain in all spheres of life. Safavid artists and artisans were consistently well attuned to growing demand from and changes in the increasingly sophisticated domestic and external markets, and proved interested in and capable of incorporating 'the foreign' over the period. Overseas and domestic markets remained interested in their output, and, that the latter included elite and non-elite points to the economic benefits enjoyed by a number of sectors of Safavid society in the aftermath of Zuhab.

If, despite its many and varied efforts, the centre was unable to control specie outflow it was hardly oblivious to the domestic damage wrought by changes in Iran's place in the period's world trade patterns, especially as these were exacerbated by similarly uncontrollable natural calamities. During the reign of Sultan Husayn, for example, the centre's response was as nuanced and complex as that adopted in response to the domestic spiritual discord. Aside from the scapegoating of indigenous minorities, a policy not unknown in the West in our own age, the centre was alert to the interests and demands of key merchant/commercial and producing elements, sacking incompetent officials, pursuing tax measures and undertaking, and encouraging others to undertake, appropriate social welfare activities and seeking to spread the financial burdens thereof widely and broadly. Paralleling, and presupposing, these 'practical' measures, concomittant centre-sponsored secular and non-secular building projects further advanced the centre's claims to continued political and spiritual authority and legitimacy.

Even if it was, or tried to be, more than the sum total of its component elements, the centre emerges not as the sole actor on the military-political, socio-economic, or the 'cultural' and spiritual spheres but rather, and perhaps merely, the largest and most important one. Comprised of multiple constituencies itself, the centre set the tone in different spheres of the realm's activities, articulating a discourse intended to transcend those of its, and other, individual constituents. Short of such direct, overt challenges to the authority of the shah as the projected apex of this transcendent discourse, or key, individual components thereof, the centre generally tolerated different discourses and expressions and limited its intervention in affairs outside the capital. To be sure, changing tastes and preferences at the centre might mean that patronage of some activities was limited or curtailed. In such cases, however, provincial elites and the realm's non-elites often replaced the court elites as patrons thereof.

As large as the centre and its associated bureaucracy became over the project's second century, however, Safavid Iran can hardly be equated with a modern nation-state. Such a term connotes a highly centralised adminstrative apparatus with a monopoly on military and, in its totalitarian versions, political power and formal lines of administrative practice and procedure, as well as fixed, internationally agreed upon borders, a single language, and a generally homogeneous population.[4]

Instead of 'state', therefore, such terms as 'project', 'polity' and 'realm' appear herein. The first in particular has been intended to suggest disparate groups engaging in a broader, common activity but whose interests and agendas are potentially, if not inherently, in conflict. Consequently also, the term 'shah', with its absolutist connotations, has been used sparingly. At all times the Safavid project was, and was 'run' by, a composite of precisely such disparate groups. Indeed, over the period the number of both the realm's constituencies and those constituencies which enjoyed a 'place at the table' of the project's centre only grew. In the early sixteenth century the project was dominated by the military-political power of the Turk and the administrative expertise and broader cultural discourse of the Tajik united in loyalty under, by and to, the heterodox spiritual and Persian cultural discourse with which Ismail I projected his own identification. By contrast, at his peaceful accession in the last years of the seventeenth century Sultan Husayn and the larger project of which he was now acknowledged as head commanded the recognition, if not always the continuous affection, of an array of foreign commercial, political and religious interests as well as indigenous Muslim, Christian and foreign artisnal and commercial and religious classes, and more importantly, enjoyed the allegiance of Turk and non-Turk tribal, Tajik, and *ghulam* military, political and administrative and other court elements. The fortunes of all of these had benefited from long-term internal and external peace and stability and concomitant economic growth delivered by the Safavid project. Great clerical families – Karaki and Majlisi – administrative families – Jabiri, Khuzani and Kujuji – and sayyid families – Marashi, Shahristani – owed the origins or enhancement of their fortunes to their participation in the Safavid project, as did families of historians, medical practitioners, astrologers and artists.

Binding all these together was Twelver Shi'i spiritual and Persian cultural discourse – the former itself, subject as it was to its own internal tensions, sufficiently complex to lie much less heavily on the populace than later Persian and most Western secondary sources would have it. At the apex of this diverse, multi-constitutional, multi-discourse project stood the ruling shah himself, less an absolute, or absolutist, ruler than the mediating embodiment of the discourse of, and therefore the transcendent figure over, the realm's increasingly larger number of components. The narrow, particularist interests of the latter had been steadily overcome over the period: where disorder had followed the deaths of Ismail I and Tahmasp, concomitant with the broadening of the number of its component constituencies, increasing institutionalisation and economic growth noted above, the smooth successions of Sulayman and Sultan Husayn show that the Safavid project itself had succeeded in becoming bigger than any one of its rulers and associated key political personalities.

Saib's panegyrics thus accurately reflected the complex, multi-constitutional nature of the broader Safavid project as it had evolved to this point, broad enough so that each of the realm's individual constituent elements, rural and urban, elite and non-elite, Muslim and non-Muslim, indigenous or foreign, perceived itself to have a vested interest in the present, and future, thereof.

Aftermath

Small wonder, then, that for most the capture of Isfahan and Sultan Husayn and even the crowning of Mahmud the Afghan did not herald the project's end. Sultan Husayn's third son, the young Tahmasp (1704–32), appointed crown prince by the shah during the siege, broke out of the city and fled to the former capital of Qazvin. There, in November, after Isfahan's fall, and supported by Bakhtiyari elements and troops based in various provincial cities, Azerbaijan, Georgia and Luristan, as well as Shahsevan and Qajar elements, he proclaimed himself Tahmasp II.[5] Although he fled Qazvin at the approach of an Afghan force and the city was occupied, the Qazvinis themselves rose up against the Afghans who thereupon withdrew to Isfahan. There Mahmud, fearing a uprising, ordered the murder of Sultan Husayn's key supporters and officials and later also a number of other princes, including the former shah's sons and brothers. A number of villages near Isfahan continued to hold out against the Afghans, however, as did, for some nine months, the city of Shiraz.

Another refugee from Isfahan, Mirza Ahmad, a descendant of Sulayman's daughter by the Marashi sayyid administrator of the Mashhad shrine, fled to Kirman and Fars with an army which at one point is said to have numbered some 6,000. Pursued by Tahmasp's and Afghan forces, he made his way to Bandar Abbas but was eventually captured by the Afghans and executed in 1728. Several figures rose claiming to be Tahmasp's younger brother, Ismail. One of these, based in Lahijan, is said to have raised an army of 12,000, including some Qizilbash elements who defected from the Ottomans. Another pretender appeared among the Bakhtiyari and attempted to establish a base at Shushtar, a key base of the Safavids' sixteen-century rivals the Mushasha.[6]

Even as the Afghans were struggling against such continued resistance, the Ottomans, in co-ordination with the Russians, sent forces through Georgia toward Kirmanshah and Hamadan – ostensibly on the side of Tahmasp II. Local communities were as opposed to the Ottomans as to the Afghans and, although the Ottomans finally took Tabriz in 1725, they faced fierce local resistance both there and at Irivan, which they finally seized in 1724. Tahmasp II, still locked in struggle with the Afghans, tried in vain to save Hamadan, itself defended by a nephew of Sultan Husayn. With Hamadan's conquest in 1724, the Ottomans were, finally, masters of Western Iran, including the long-coveted silk-producing regions. An Ottoman-Russian treaty concluded the same year divided Western Iran and limited the movements therein of Tahmasp II, who had defeated an Afghan force near Qum. Throughout the occupation local tribal elements, including Bakhtiyari, Lur and local Arab elements kept up their resistance to the Ottomans, as did both Tahmasp II and the Afghans.[7]

In 1726 Mahmud was assassinated, victim of internal Afghan intrigues, and was succeeded by his cousin Ashraf. Faced with the Ottoman threat, Ashraf turned to the Safavid legacy to rally the opposition, ingratiating himself with Sultan Husayn and accepting service from some Safavid commanders against Ottoman forces. The Ottomans, attempting to trade on the same legacy, proclaimed their intention to restore Sultan Husayn to power, at which Ashraf sanctioned the shah's murder.[8] Although Ashraf subsequently defeated an Ottoman force near Hamadan later in 1726, the continued tenuousness of the Afghan position in the country and, especially, the continuing threat posed by Tahmasp II forced Ashraf to cede most of Western Iran to the Ottomans. In 1729, following the 1726 capture of Mashhad and in the context of the 1729 occupation of Herat and Qandahar by Tahmasp II's forces led by his new *vakil* Nadir Quli Bek Afshar, the future Nadir Shah, Ashraf agreed a treaty with the Russians which allowed Russian traders to reside in Iran.[9] The Afghans retreated toward Isfahan where Ashraf, unsure of the population's loyalty, ordered the execution of many prominent figures and even maltreated the representatives of the foreign trading companies. In the ensuing Afghan-Safavid confrontation at Isfahan, the former were decisively defeated and, in November 1729, but seven years after its capture, the forces of Sultan Husayn Safavi's son Tahmasp II, led by Nadir Afshar, entered Isfahan. Ashraf's forces were defeated again near Shiraz, and melted away, some travelling East and others moving toward the Gulf. Ashraf himself apparently perished near Qandahar. Tahmasp subsequently moved against Ottoman forces in Azerbaijan and laid siege to Irivan. He withdrew from the latter to seek the enemy in Iraq where he was defeated. The Ottomans, yet again not following up on their success, opted for a treaty in which, concluded in its final version by Nadir in 1733 after he had deposed Tahmasp, recognised the border as specified by the terms of the Zuhab treaty nearly a century before. A treaty concluded with Peter the Great the year before, ten years after Isfahan's fall, had returned to Iran all territories the Russians had seized in the intervening years.[10]

The retaking of Isfahan fulfilled popular expectations and hopes. Indeed, by all indications, especially as attested by the extent of urban and tribal resistance, the populace at large was genuinely convinced, or at least hoped, that the Afghan 'interlude' would, in fact, amount to no more than that. Even the Dutch continued to accept the validity of treaties reached with the Safavids.[11] In fact, three years later, in 1732, when the Afshar Nadir deposed Tahmasp, he did so in favour of the latter's infant son who, as Abbas III, 'ruled' for some four years. Nadir further aligned himself with the Safavid name by contracting marriages for himself and his son into the Safavid house, in the manner of the many earlier marriages between prominent Qizilbash tribal elements and members of the Safavid house. Thus, in the aftermath of Nadir's 1736 own ascent to the throne as Nadir Shah, his 1738–9 retaking of Qandahar and his subsequent, spectacular invasion of Mughal India and the 1740 execution of both Tahmasp and Abbas III, Nadir and his family were well affiliated to the house, both by marriage and by membership of one of the original Qizilbash tribes, and could project themselves, at least, as well within the Safavid tradition, if not as heirs.[12] If Nadir disestablished Shi'ism, recalling the similar, if similarly unfruitful, effort of Ismail II in the context of a need to broaden his domestic support, at the same time Nadir was careful to devote considerable attention to, and designate as his new capital Mashhad, home of the shrine of the eighth Shi'i Imam, to whose chief officials, given their own intermarriage with the Safavid house, he was related.[13] That in 1747 Nadir was assassinated, an experience enjoyed by English and French kings but no sitting Safavid shah, by fellow Afshar and rebel Qajar elements, suggests his marked failure to project the combined aura of legitimacy, authority and transcendence with the same degree of success as more than two centuries of Safavid shahs.

Indeed, throughout the period from Nadir's claiming of the throne, his 1743–6 wars with the Ottomans and his assassination – after but eleven years as shah – there continued to be no shortage of Safavid pretenders. The number thereof attests to the continued appeal of the Safavid project in the region and discontent with some of Nadir's policies, especially around Ardabil, in Daghistan/Shirvan region and in Tabriz, let alone rejection of his legitimacy.[14]

Following Nadir's murder, even as Iran experienced political fragmentation, the Safavid name retained its prestige: Ali Mardan of the Bakhtiyari tribe established a measure of authority in Central Iran in the name of Ismail III (d. 1773), another grandson of Sultan Husayn. The Zand leader Karim Khan (d. 1779) captured this Ismail, styled himself the latter's *vakil*, as Nadir had been to Tahmasp II and, in 1765, established himself in Shiraz. Only when, soon thereafter, Karim Khan changed his official title to that '*vakil* of the people' and rejected attempts to be declared shah, may overt lip-service to the idea of Safavid dynasty be understood to have ended.[15] Within but a few decades, however, the Qajars, another of the original Qizilbash tribes, commenced their rise to power.

That chroniclers throughout the years immediately following 1722 and even into the Qajar period continued to refer to the Safavid period and, unsurprisingly, disparaged the reigns of the last several shahs only further attests to the continued power of the Safavid project, if increasingly as an historical ideal whose legacy could be contested and claimed as subsequent rulers strove to bolster their own positions.

That legacy was contestable precisely because the Safavid project was more than just a political undertaking, encompassing achievements in all the realms of human endeavour. To be sure, the impact of that legacy on later times is still not well understood. Eighteenth-century Iran, even on on its terms, remains poorly studied.[16] Floor has discussed some aspects of the Safavid economic legacy. The Safavid artistic and architectural legacy has yet to be addressed specifically in any great detail, but Canby, for example, citing oil painting on canvas, lacquer ware, glass, European styles of painting, and carpet production, has noted that Iranian art of the eighteenth and nineteenth centuries 'developed on the foundations that were laid in the Safavid period'. Although her study ends at 1738 Crowe has noted that Iranian potters, for example, remained aware of the Qing ceramic legacy, even as the latter came under Japanese influence.[17]

By contrast, the legacy of Safavid-period developments in religion has been better studied. As the first period since the disappearance of the Imam in which Twelver Shi'ism was not merely tolerated but given safe haven, the Safavid emerges as a key period in the faith's history. These two centuries witnessed the development of an elaborate infrastructure of schools, mosques and shrines – in Isfahan, Mashhad and Qum, where the last four Safavid shahs were buried, for example – which allowed the country to develop as a major centre of Twelver scholarship alternative to, albeit not eclipsing, the centres of scholarship, and population, located outwith Safavid domains. As a result, where the few major Twelver clerics of the sixteenth century were still resident outside Iran the much larger number of the faith's chief figures of the seventeenth century were based in Iran, either by birth or immigration. The realm's consequent vibrant, dynamic spiritual life gave birth to a reinvigorated Usuli dynamic and Akhbari rejoinder. New life was given also to philosophical/metaphysical discourse and an opposition thereto also emerged. Subsequent polemics and developments in Usuli doctrine and practice, which culminated in the doctrine of 'the deputyship of the legist (*vilayat-i faqih*)' have attracted growing interest[18]. By contrast, the study of post-Safavid Iran-based philosophical/metaphysical discourse is relatively much less advanced.[19]

This is to address developments in but a few of post-Safavid Iran's realms of human activity which, as with the Safavid story itself, being led by both the textual and even most 'non-textual' sources, is overwhelmingly slanted toward the urban. Developments outside the major centres of population and particularly among the majority, non-literate population await further study and, in particular, detailed consideration of a broader range of such non-textual sources as are mentioned in the Introduction which may well correct much of our current understanding.

In considering precisely such different realms of human activity, however, it is worth remembering that the pre-modern period, whatever the geography, was not, perhaps by definition, afflicted by the 'division of knowledge' as we are. The latter encourages consideration of events and trends separately to each other rather than against the background, and as aspects, of a larger whole, in the manner in which, in reality, they unfolded.

Taking such broader parameters into account, the Safavids inherited from previous establishments the political control of a region long accustomed, from pre-Islamic times, to a diversity of both composition and discourse. Indeed, the present volume commenced with references to the longevity and diversity of the Achaemenian empire. The formal concept of *Iranzamin* or *Iranshahr*, dates at least from the Sassanians (*c.* 221–651), who created a polity as large in area and size, and as diverse, as that of the Achaemenians.[20] The term, insofar as it can be defined by an outsider, reflects an effort to assert the reality of the distinctly Iranian, or Persian, experience without regard to such transient political realities as individual rulers and dynasties, changing borders and boundaries. The term 'Persianate' used by Marshall Hodgson (d. 1968)[21] perhaps captures something of the meaning of *Iranzamin* in English, although the term refers to the period after the Islamic conquest of the mid-seventh century and much of Iran's pre-Islamic heritage remained influential throughout the region for centuries thereafter.[22]

The Safavid polity was never as large physically as those of the Achaemenians or Sassanians. Nor do Safavid historians seem to have taken special inspiration from these pre-Islamic polities. Nevertheless, the longevity of the Safavid project may be most usefully explained in terms of the success with which Safavid society, as these earlier undertakings, expanded to recognise, include and transcend the diverse elements and discourses extant in the region at the time. If this tendency is not distinctly Persian, it is nonetheless familiar over the history of many of the peoples who have dwelt in and around that plateau which extends from the Mesopotamian lowlands to the Oxus river and South to the Persian Gulf and Indian Ocean.

Appendix I
Key Dates

1334	death of Shaykh Safi al-Din, 'founder' of the Safavid order
1456–9	marriage of sister of Uzun Hasan Aqquyunlu to Junayd Safavi
1460	death in battle of Junayd, succession of his son Haydar as head of the Safavid Sufi order
1467	death of Jahan Shah Qaraquyunlu
1471–2	marriage of daughter of Uzun Hasan to Haydar Safavi
1473	Ottomans defeat Aqquyunlu at Bashkent
1478	death of Uzun Hasan Aqquyunlu
1487	birth of Ismail, third son of Haydar Safavi
1488	death in battle of Haydar, succession of Ismail as head of Safavid Sufi order
1501	**Ismail captures Tabriz**
1508	fall of Baghdad to Safavid forces
1510–11	fall of Khurasan to Safavid forces
1512	Uzbeks defeat Safavids in Khurasan; loss and recapture of Herat; rising of Ismail's half-brother in Tabriz
1514	Ottomans defeat Safavids at Chaldiran; loss and recapture of Tabriz
1515	Portuguese consolidate control over Hormuz island in Persian Gulf
1517	Ottomans enter Cairo
1524	**death of Ismail; accession of Tahmasp** onset of first civil war Uzbeks commence series of five incursions into Khurasan, lasting to 1540
1532	first of series of Ottoman invasions, lasting until 1555
1533	Tahmasp's *firman* naming Ali Karaki deputy of the Imam
1533–4	Tahmasp's first repentance (*tawba*)
1534	death of Ali Karaki Ottomans take Arab Iraq, including Baghdad, Najaf and Karbala

1536	revolt of Alqas, half-brother of Tahmasp; end of first civil war
1555	Amasya treaty with Ottomans cedes Arab Iraq to Ottomans
1555–6	Tahmasp's second repentance
1556	arrest of future Ismail II
c. 1556	completion of Chihil Sutun palace in Qazvin
1557	execution of Shaykh Zayn al-Din Amili by the Ottomans
1561–2	Tahmasp returns the rebel Bayazid to the Ottomans
1563–4	following a dream in which he sees the Imam, Tahmasp issues *firman* banning *tamgha* and other practices
1567	Tahmasp sends *Shahnama* to Ottoman Sultan Selim II
1574	Nuqtavi risings at illness of Tahmasp
1576	**death of Tahmasp** onset of second civil war **accession of Ismail II**
1577–8	**death of Ismail II; accession of Muhammad Khudabanda**
1578–90	Ottoman incursions into Safavid territory
1579	murder of Khudabanda's wife Khayr al-Nisa Marashi, mother of Abbas I
1585	fall of Tabriz to the Ottomans
1587	**accession of Abbas I**
1590	peace treaty signed with Ottomans Abbas' moves against risings of his two brothers in Isfahan and the defeat of Yaqub Khan Dhul-Qadr mark end of second civil war Isfahan designated capital (?)
1592	rising of Nuqtavi Darvish Khusraw in Qazvin
1594	Mughals take Qandahar
1595	death of Muhammad Khudabanda
1596–7	purging of Takkalu
1598–9	Eastern Khurasan (including Mashhad and Herat) retaken from Uzbeks
1599	work on Abdallah Shushtari school commences
1602	work on Lutfallah Maysi Mosque commences
1602–3	Azerbaijan (including Tabriz) retaken from Ottomans work begins on Naqsh-i Jahan maydan in Isfahan
1604–5	Armenians forcibly deported from Julfa to Isfahan
1606–7	further Armenian deportations to Isfahan
1607–8	Shirvan retaken from Ottomans
1611	work on Royal Mosque commences
1613	Armenian Church of Mary built in Isfahan
1620–1	death of Shaykh Bahai
1622	Qandahar retaken from Mughals
1623–4	Kurdistan, Eastern Iraq (including Baghdad and Shi'i shrine cities) retaken from Ottomans

1624	Khalifa Sultan, son-in-law of Abbas, appointed *vizier*
1627–8	Bethlehem Armenian Church built in Isfahan
1629	**death of Abbas I; accession of his grandson as Safi**
	rising of Gharib Shah in Gilan
1630	Ottomans occupy Hamadan
1631	rising of Darvish Riza in Qazvin
	death of Mir Damad
1632	fall of Khalifa Sultan alliance at court
1633–4	two decades of anti-Abu Muslim essay-writing commences
1634	Saru Taqi becomes *vizier*
	more than twenty Armenian churches now active in Isfahan
1635	Ottomans plunder Tabriz; Safavids sue for peace
	death of Riza Abbasi
1637	Olearius arrives in Iran
1638	Ottomans capture Baghdad and Shiʿi shrine cities
	Qandahar lost to the Mughals
1639	treaty of Zuhab signed with Ottomans
	rising of reincarnated Darvish Riza
	Safi visits Qazvin
1640	death of Mulla Sadra
1641	last year of EIC purchase of Iranian silk
1642	**death of Shah Safi; accession of his son as Abbas II**
c. 1643	VOC begins export of Iranian specie to India
1643	work commences on Ali Qapu
1643–5	China curtails exports of porcelain
1645	Dutch bombard Gombroon and occupy Qishm
	Saru Taqi killed
	Khalifa Sultan reappointed *vizier*
	new *vizier* launches campaign against minorities and immorality and devalues currency
1647	completion of audience hall of Isfahan's Chihil Sutun
1648	further currency devaluation
1649	Safavids retake Qandahar from Mughals
1650	death of Isfahan's *Shaykh al-Islam* Alinaqi Kamrai
	Muhammad Baqir Sabzavari appointed capital's *Shaykh al-Islam*
1651–2	Hasanabad/Khvaja bridge in Isfahan built
1653	death of the *sadr* Habiballah Karaki
	his son Mirza Muhammad Karaki appointed *sadr*
1654	Abbas II invites Fayz Kashani to lead Isfahan's Friday prayers
	Abbas II commissions work from Taqi Majlisi
1654–5	severe winter; death of Khalifa Sultan
	Armenian *ghulam* Muhammad Bek appointed *vizier*
	Georgian official in Isfahan dismissed from post

1655	work commences on All Saviour's Cathedral in Isfahan
1657	further Ottoman-Safavid trade agreement reached
	Muhammad Bek launches anti-minority campaign
	and forbids export of specie, which bans lasts until 1661
	Qajar official dismissed from post
1657–8	Rivulet bridge completed in Isfahan
1658	VOC exports record amount of Iranian specie
	between 1658 and 1666 six new Armenian churches built in Isfahan
1659	death of Taqi Majlisi
1659–60	Chahar Bagh-i Saʿadatabad laid out in Isfahan
1661	dismissal of Muhammad Bek, the *vizier*
	appointment of Mirza Muhammad Karaki, the *sadr*, as *vizier*
1663	widespread drought in Azerbaijan
1665–6	series of local bankruptcies
1666	**death of Abbas II and first accession ceremony of Safi II**
	Chardin arrives in Iran
	poor harvest
	work on Hasht Bihisht palace commenced
1667	poor harvest
1668	**second accession ceremony of Safi II as Sulayman**
1669	poor harvest; plague; famine in Isfahan
	Muhammad Karaki, the *vizier*, replaced by the Kurd Ali Khan Zangana
	new *vizier* adopts anti-Armenian measures
1670	tax on exported silver imposed
1672	harsh winter, inflation and food shortages
	vizier briefly dismissed from post
1674	tax farming of customs duties
1678–9	famine in Isfahan as result of decade of drought, harsh winters, locusts
1679	death of Baqir Sabzavari, Isfahan's *Shaykh al-Islam*
1680	death of Fayz Kashani
1681	famine in Armenia and Azerbaijan
c. 1683	China resumes export of porcelain
1684	Dutch seize Qishm
1684–5	plague in Gilan spreads to Ardabil and Hamadan
1687	Baqir Majlisi appointed Isfahan's *Shaykh al-Islam*
	death of Muhammad Tahir, opponent of Sufism
1689	death of the *vizier* Ali Khan
1689–91	plague in Shiraz, Eastern Iraq
c. 1690	Talar-i Ashraf built in Isfahan
1691	Muhammad Tahir Qazvini appointed *vizier*
	death of Shaykh Ali Amili
1693	death of Shaykh Hurr-i Amili

1694	**death of Sulayman; accession of Sultan Husayn**
	firman issued banning wine
	Carmelites expelled from Isfahan
1696	Fars struck by drought and famine
1697	Carmelites allowed to return to Isfahan
1699	death of Muhammad Baqir Majlisi
	Shamlu appointed *vizier*
	specie exports banned
1703	Baqir Khatunabadi named Isfahan's *Shaykh al-Islam*
1704–5	commencement of work on Chahar Bagh complex
1706	Sultan Husayn embarks on visit to Qum and Mashhad
	food riots in Isfahan
1707	the Sunni Kurd Shah Quli Khan Zangana (d. 1715), son of
	the former *vizier* Shaykh Ali Khan, appointed *vizier*
1709	second rising of Mir Uvais
1710–11	inauguration of Chahar Bagh school
c. 1711	Farahabad Chahar Bagh built outside Isfahan
1712	*firman* issued forbidding Catholic missionary efforts among
	Armenians
	Baqir Khatunabadi named first *mullabashi*
1713	specie exports banned
1714	last VOC purchase of Iranian silk
1715	rises in wheat prices cause unrest in Isfahan
1716	pestilence in Gilan, food riots in Tabriz and Isfahan
	certain harsh measures against Armenians withdrawn
	Isfahan's *darugha* replaced
	death of *vizier* the Kurd Shah Quli Khan Zangana,
	appointment of Fath Ali Khan Daghistani
1717	Russo-Iranian treaty
	Mir Uvais' son Mahmud seizes power in Qandahar
1719	Mahmud sacks Kirman
1720	fall of the *vizier* Fath Ali Khan
1722	March – battle of Gulnabad
	fall of Isfahan
	November – Tahmasp II proclaimed in Qazvin
1724	Russians seize Hamadan
1725	Ottomans seize Tabriz
1726	Mahmud the Afghan assassinated; succeeded by Ashraf,
	defeats Ottoman force near Hamadan
	Ashraf executes Sultan Husayn
	Tahmasp II takes Mashhad
1728	Mirza Ahmad Marashi captured and killed by
	Afghans
1729	Tahmasp II takes Herat and Qandahar from Afghans
	November – Tahmasp II enters Isfahan
	Russo-Iranian treaty

1732	Nadir deposes Tahmasp II in favour of the infant Abbas III
	Russo-Iranian treaty returns to Iran all territories seized since 1722
1733	Iranian-Ottoman treaty
1736	Nadir Afshar becomes Nadir Shah
1738–9	Nadir retakes Qandahar, invades India
1740	Nadir executes Tahmasp II and Abbas III
1747	Nadir assassinated
1750	Sulayman II proclaimed in Khurasan

Appendix II
Key chronicles and travellers

Below is a list of the key chronicles and travellers mentioned in the text, together with their dates of composition, however approximate, and the standard published versions thereof, if available. Further references to these sources may be found via the index. On the chronicles, see also Quinn, *Historical*, 13–29, 145–8. For other contemporary and, especially, earlier primary sources, see also Woods, *The Aqquyunlu*, 215–35. For an introduction to some of period's foreign travellers, see Stevens, 'European Visitors', and Lockhart, 'European Contacts'. Matthee's bibliography of primary sources (*The Politics*, 254–61) contains a listing of Persian and European-language source materials. For a more extensive listing of Persian sources, including local histories, etc., see Savaqib's bibliography, cited in the Introduction, above, n8.

Pre-1501 sources

1479–80
Treatise of the Hanafi cleric Ahmad Pakaraji. See 2002 paper of A. Morton (in the bibliography).

Fazlallah Khunji Isfahani (d. 1521), *Tarikh-i Alam Ara-yi Amini*, covers up to 1491. This was published by V. Minorsky as *Persia in AD 1478–1490, An Abridged Edition of Fazlallah b. Ruzbihan Khunji's Tarikh-i Alam Ara-yi Amini* (London, 1957) and by Woods as Khunji-Isfahani, Fazlallah b. Ruzbihan, *Tarikh-i Alam-Ara-yi Amini*, with the abridged English translation by Vladimir Minorsky, edited, revised and augmented by J. Woods (London, 1992).

1497–1508
Sanudo, Venetian traveller.

Reign of Ismail I (1501–1524)

1508

Edition of *Safvat al-Safa*, originally completed in 1358 by Tavakkul b. Ismail b. Hajji Ardabili, known as Ibn Bazzaz. This is a history of the Safavid house but the 1508 copy portrayed the family as descended from Imam Ali. Tahmasp commissioned a further edition in 1533 (see Quinn, *Historical*, 13–14). See also reference to the 1542 manuscript below, as noticed by Togan. The work, edited by G. R. Tabatabai, was published in Ardabil in 1373/1994. It has appeared in German, edited and translated by H. Zirke (Berlin, 1987). A lithographed edition by A. Tabrizi was published in Bombay in 1329/1911.

Ismail Safavi, *divan* of poetry. Excerpts have been published in English by V. Minorsky, and see also Thackston (both in the bibliography). For editions, see also Tourkhan Gandjei, *Il Canzoniere di Sah Ismail Hata'i* (Naples, 1959), and Ibrahim Aslanoghlu, *Sah Ismail Hatayi (Divan, Dehname, Nasihatname ve Anadolu Hatayileri)* (Istanbul, 1992).

Reign of Tahmasp (1524–1576)

Tarikh-i Habib al-Siyar, completed in 1524, by Ghiyas al-Din Khvan-damir (d. 1535–7). The standard edition is that edited by J. Humai, in 4 vols, 3rd ed. ([Tehran], 1362), and earlier editions, including 1333/1954. See also W. Thackston's translation (Cambridge, MA, 1994). The author's grandfather was himself a historian and his son Amir Mahmud composed a 1550 'sequel' to the *Habib*, on which see below.

1539–42

Membré, the Venetian envoy. See A. Morton's translation of his travelogue cited above under Membré.

1542

Yahya b. Abd al-Latif Husayni Qazvini, *Lubb al-Tavarikh*. The standard edition is that edited by J. Tehrani [Tehran], 1314/1937. An edition edited by A. Navai was published in 1985. There is also a lithographed edition published in [Tehran] in 1363.

1542

Mir Abul-Fath's revision to *Safvat al-Safa*.

1550

Amir Mahmud, son of the above Khvandamir, completed a continuation of his father's work. This has been published as *Iran dar Ruzegar-i Shah Ismail va Shah Tahmasp*, Gh. R. Tabatabai, ed. (Tehran, 1370/1991). A less reliable edition is *Tarikh-i Shah Ismail va Shah Tahmasp (Zayl-i Tarikh-i Habib al-siyar)*, M. A. Jarrahi, ed. (Tehran, 1991).

1552
Qadi Ahmad b. Muhammad Ghaffari Qazvini, *Nigaristan*. This has been published as *Tarikh-i Nigaristan*, A. M. Mudarris Gilani, ed. (Tehran, 1340/1961, 1404). See also reference to his 1563–4 *Nusakh-i Jahan-Ara* below.

1563–4
Ahmad b. Muhammad Ghaffari Qazvini, *Nusakh-i Jahan-Ara*. This has been edited by H. Naraqi and published as *Tarikh-i Jahan-ara* (Tehran, 1342/1963).

1564–5
Khurshah b. Qubad Husayni was the Indian envoy to Tahmasp's court between 1545–7 and remained there until 1564. He completed his account thereof in Calcutta. The British Museum MS Add 153 copy was completed in 1564–5 (Jamali, xxvi). The work was published as *Tarikh-i Ilchi-yi Nizam Shah*, M. R. Nasiri and K Haneda, eds (Tehran, 2000).

1570
Abdi Bek Shirazi, *Takmilat al-Akhbar*. The published text is cited.

Tahmasp Safavi, *Tadhkira-yi Shah Tahmasp*. This has been edited and published by A. Safari, ed., 2nd ed. (Tehran, 1363). See also P. Horn, ed., 'Tazkirah-i Shah Tahmasp', *ZDMG* 44 (1890), 563–649; 45 (1891), 245–91.

The Second Civil War (1576–1587)

1576–7
Budaq Qazvini, *Javahir al-Akhbar*. The published text is cited.

1577
Hasan Rumlu, *Ahsan al-Tavarikh*, 1577. This has been translated as *A Chronicle of the Early Safawis, being the Ahsan al-Tavarikh of Hasan-i Rumlu*, C. N. Seddon, transl. (Baroda, 1934), though without 'the poetry, Quranic quotations, and exaggerated descriptive passages (v)'. The standard Persian edition is that edited by A. Navai and published in Tehran in 1349/1970 but Seddon also edited a Persian edition which appeared with the English translation.

after 1584
Qadi Nurallah Shushtari, *Majalis al-Muminin* 2 vols (Tehran, 1354).

1586
G. B. Vechietti, Italian traveller. His 'A Report on the Conditions of Persia in the year 1586' (in Italian), was published by H. F. Brown in *English Historical Review* (1892), 314–21.

1590–1
Qadi Ahmad Qummi, *Khulasat al-Tavarikh*. The standard edition is that edited by I. Ishraqi, 2 vols (Tehran, 1359–1363/1984). It has been translated into German and edited by H. Müller as *Die Chronik Hulasat altawarih des Qazi Ahmad Qumi* (Wiesbaden, 1964) and by E. Glassen as *Die frühen Safawiden nach Qazi Ahmad Qumi* (Freiburg, 1970). See also his *Calligraphers* cited below.

Reign of Abbas I (1587–1629)

1596
Sharaf Khan Bidlisi, *Sharafnama*, 2 vols (Cairo, nd).

1598
Mahmud b. Hedayatallah Afushta Natanzi, *Nuqavat al-Asar*. This has been published by I. Ishraqi, and is cited.

c. 1606
Qadi Ahmad Qummi, *Gulistan-i Hunar*. This has been translated and published as *Calligraphers and Painters, A Treatise by Qazi Ahmad, son of Mir Munshi (c.* AH *1015/*AD *1606)*, V. Minorsky, ed. and transl. (Washington DC, 1959). A Persian edition, edited by A. S. Khvansari, appeared [in Tehran] nd.

1611–12
Jalal al-Din Munajjim Yazdi, *Tarikh-i Abbasi*. The author was the court astrologer. This has been published and is cited.

1616–29
Iskandar Bek Munshi completed volume one of his *Alam Ara-yi Abbasi* in 1616 and the final volume in 1629. This has been edited and translated by R. Savory as *History of Shah 'Abbas the Great*, 2 vols (Boulder, Co, 1978). Vol. 2 has a short index but a longer, more extensive English-language index, compiled by R. Bernhard, appeared as vol. 3 of the work in New York, 1986. The standard Persian edition is that edited by I. Afshar, 2 vols, (Tehran, 1350/1971) but has no index. The Bernhard index (343–55) includes a comparative table for Afshar's Persian edition. A new, less reliable, three-volume Persian edition, edited by M. I. Rizvani, was published in Tehran in 1377/1998–9. Munshi's additions to his chronicle, until his death in 1633, have been published as part of *Zayl-i Tarikh-i Alam Ara-yi Abbasi*, on which see below ad 1633.

1617–21
Pietro della Valle. See *Delle conditioni di Abbas Ré di Persia* (Venice, 1628; Tehran, 1976); *I viaggi di Pietro Della Valle: lettere dalla Persia*, a

cura di F. Gaeta e L. Lockhart (Rome, 1972); *Viaggi di Pietro della Valle, il pellegrino*, 2 vols (Venice, 1681; Brighton, 1843).

1624–5
The Russian traveller Kotov was in Isfahan. His account was edited and translated by Kemp, in his *Russian Travellers*, cited in the bibliography.

1625–26
Mirza Hasan Junabadi, *Rawzat al-Safaviyya*. This has been edited by G. R. Tabatabai Majd and published in Tehran, 1378/1999.

Reign of Safi (1629–1642)

1633
Iskandar Beg Munshi's addition to his earlier chronicle ends with his death. This material, together with material from *Khuld-i Barin* on Safi, was edited by S. Khvansari and published as *Zayl-i Tarikh-i Alam Ara-yi Abbasi* (Tehran, 1317/1938). See n1 of Chapter 5.

1635–9
Fazli Isfahani Khuzani, *Afzal al-Tavarikh*, a three-volume history of the Safavids to the death of Abbas I. The text was begun in 1616–17, and the second volume of which was being revised in India in 1639 and the third in 1635. The work has not been published but Melville, Morton and Abrahams are collaborating on further work with the text, and Melville is directing production of a CD version of the text. See the articles on the text by Melville and the Edinburgh thesis of Abrahams.

1637
Adam Olearius. The standard edition is *Vermehrte newe Beschreibung der Muscowtischen und Persichen Reyse sodurch gelgenheit einer holsteinischen Gesandschaft an den Russichen Zaar und König in Persien geschehen* (Schleswid, 1656; fasc. reprint, Tübingen, 1971).

Reign of Abbas II (1642–1666)

1641–2
Muhammad Masum Isfahani, *Khulasat al-Siyar*. This has been published in Tehran in 1368/1989, and is cited. The texts covers the period 1627 to 1641–2.

1660
Raphael du Mans, superior of Capuchin mission in Isfahan, lived in Iran between 1664 and 1696. See his *Estat de la Perse en 1660*, Ch. Scheffer, ed. (Paris, 1890).

Reign of Sulayman (1666–1694)

1664
Jean de Thévenot. See his *Relation d'un Voyage fait au Levant 2, Suite du Voyage de Levant* (Paris, 1674).

1664–74
Valiquli b. Daud Shamlu, historian and poet, composed *Qisas al-Khaqani* and died after 1674. This has been published in 2 vols and is cited.

1666
Muhammad Tahir Qazvini, *Abbasnama*. The text covers the years 1642 to 1666. It has been published and is cited. Muhammad Tahir's brother composed *Khuld-i Barin*.

1666–7, 1669, 1672–7.
Jean Chardin. The standard edition of his account is *Voyages du chevalier Chardin, en Perse, et autres lieux de l'Orient* L. Langlès, ed., 10 vols and map (Paris, 1810–11). See also Ferrier's abridgement, cited above.

Contemporary to Chardin
John Ogilby. See his *Asia, The First Part: An Accurate Description of the Empire of the Great Mughal* (London, 1673).

1667
Muhammad Yusuf Valih Qazvini, *Khuld-i Barin*. That part of this lengthy chronicle covering the reign of Ismail to the end of the second civil war, was edited by M. H. Muhaddath and published in Tehran in 1372. The sections which cover the reigns of Safi and Abbas II have been edited by M. R. Nasiri and published as *Iran dar Zaman-i Shah Safi va Shah Abbas-i Duvvum (1038–1071)*, a single volume, in Tehran in 1380/2001; the latter was not available to the present author at the time of writing. M. H. Muhaddath edited and published in a single volume the sections on the Timurids and Turkish dynasties (Tehran, 1379/2000). The author was the brother of Mirza Muhammad Tahir, the author of *Abbasnama*.

1668
Jean-Baptiste Tavernier, who, between 1632 and 1668 made some six trips in Iran. See his multi-volume *Les Six Voyages de J. B. Tavernier . . . en Turquie, en Perse et aux Indes* which has been published in Paris in 1676, 1679, 1682; 3 parts, Utrecht, 1712; Le Haye, 1718, among others.

1673/4–1679
Muhammad Tahir Nasrabadi, *Tazkira-yi Nasrabadi*. The standard edition is cited.

1674
The Venetian traveller Bembo. His account has yet to be published. A. Welch is preparing an English translation. See his 'Safavi Iran', cited.

1675–6
Anonymous, *Alam ara-yi Safavi*. This work, edited by Y. A. Shukri, was published in Tehran in 1350/1971. See the entry below on *Alam ara-yi Shah Ismail*.

After 1675–6
Anonymous, *Alam ara-yi Shah Tahmasp*. This has been edited by I. Afshar and published in Tehran in 1370/1991.

1677–8
John A Fryer. See his *A New Account of East India and Persia, being 9 Years Travels, 1672–1681*, (London, 1698; 3 vols, W. Crooke, ed. London, 1909–15; New Delhi, 1992).

1678
S. Nimatallah Jazairi, *al-Anvar al-Numaniyya*. This is cited in the bibliography.

1679
Shaykh Husayn b. Abdal Zahidi, *Nasab Nama-yi Safaviyya*, or *Silsilat al-Nasab-i Safaviyya*. This was edited by Kazimzadah and published in Berlin in 1342/1924.

1680s
Anonymous, *Alam ara-yi Shah Ismail*. This work, edited by A. M. Sahib, was published in Tehran in 1349/1970. McChesney ('Alam Ara-yi Shah Ismail', *EIr*, 1 (1985), 796) suggests this is the same as the also anonymously authored *Alam ara-yi Safavi*. See, however, Quinn, *Historical*, 145; Wood, 'The Tarikh-i Jahanara', 91. Shukri, edited of *Safavi*, argues for differences between the two texts.

1680s
Ross Anonymous. See Morton's 'The Date and Attribution'. The author was one Bijan. This has been published as *Jahangusha-yi Khaqan: Tarikh-i Shah Ismail*, A. D. Muztarr, ed. (Islamabad, 1984).

1683–4
E. Kaempfer, a German doctor who lived in Isfahan and was in the service of the VOC until 1688. See his *Am Hofe des persischen Grosskönigs: 1684–1685*, published in Leipzig in 1940; Tübingen, W. Hinz, ed., in 1977 and 1984. See the paper by Brakensiek cited in the bibliography.

1683–91
Nicolas Sanson. See *Voyage ou relation de l'état présent du Royaume de Perse* (Paris, 1695).

1686
Sayyid Abd al-Husayn Husayni Khatunabadi, *Vaqai al-Sinin val-Avvam* (Tehran, nd), 508–9. The author died in 1693. Not a court chronicle per se, this Persian language text records events after 1686 as added by the author's descendants.

Reign of Sultan Husayn (1694–1722)

1692–1700
Muhammad Nasiri, *Dastur-i Shahryaran*. This has been published, as noted in the bibliography of primary-language sources. The last date cited herein is 1700.

1703–4
Sayyid Hasan Astarabadi, *Tarikh-i Sultani*, (I. Ishraqi, ed., 2nd ed., Tehran, 1366).

1704
Cornelius de Bruyn (various spellings). See *Reizen over Moskovie, door Persie en Indie* (Amsterdam, 1711, 1714). English translations from the French original were published in London in 1737 and 1759. The French version – *Voyages de Corneille Le Brun par la Moscovie, en Perse, et aux Indes Orientales* – was published in Amsterdam in 1718 and – as *Voyage au Levant* – in Paris in 1725.

After 1712
Mirza Rafia Ansari, *Dastur al-Muluk*. There is little known of the author, except that he was likely of the capital's well-known Jabari family which had served the court from Ismail's reign. The last date cited in the text is 1712. This has been published by Danishpazhuh, as noted in the bibliography. C. Marcinkowski has recently completed a translation of Ansari's text, as *Mirza Rafia's Dastur al-Muluk. A Manual of Later Safavid Administration. English Translation, Comments on the Offices and Services, and Facsimile of the Unique Persian Manuscript* (Kuala Lumpur, 2002). I. Afshar is scheduled to produce a new version of this text based on the recent discovery of the remainder of the manuscript of which Marcinkowski has indicated he will produce a new translation.

1717
John Bell. See *Travels from St. Petersburg to Various Parts of Asia* (2 vols, Glasgow, 1763; 1 vol., Edinburgh, 1805).

Post-1722 sources

Judasz Tadeusz Krusinski (d. 1756), the Polish procurator of the Jesuits, in Isfahan from 1704. Close to the Afghan court after capture of Isfahan, he left the capital for Europe in 1725. There are a number of French editions and English translations of his account. Matthee (258) cites *The History of the Revolutions of Persia*, 2 vols (London, 1728), but see also Lockhart, *The Fall*, 516–25, who notes the alterations of du Cerceau, whose translation *The History of the Late Revolutions of Persia* has also been repeatedly published from Paris, 1728 to New York, 1973.

Mirza Ali Naqi Nasiri, *Alqab va Mavajib-i Dawrah-i Salatin-i Safaviyya*, Y. Rahimlu, ed., Mashhad, 1372. This was completed during the reign of Tahmasp II (d. 1732), the son of Shah Sultan Husayn, who proclaimed himself shah in Qazvin following the 1722 fall of Isfahan.

M. S. Tehrani (Varid), *Mirat-i Varidat*, M. Sefatgol, ed. (Tehran, 1383/ 2004). The author was born in 1676 in India, and there had strong Sufi, especially Chishti, connections. He was alive at least as late as 1705, and the text includes references from as early as 1688 to Nadir Shah's 1738–9 invasion of India. The work addresses the rise of the Safavids and, especially, their fall, including the fall of Isfahan, Tahmasp II, and Nadir Shah. It is epecially interesting for its apparently first-hand information on Khurasan and Sistan in this period, and the capture of Mashhad by Malik Mahmud Sistani.

Qutb al-Din Nayrizi, *Fasl al-Khittab*, written after 1722. Portions appear in Jafariyan, ed., *Ilal*, 259f, and idem, *Safaviyya dar Arsa-yi Din*, 3: 1355–81. The author, a Dhahabi shaykh, died in 1759.

Mukafatnama written by an anonymous former court official between two and four years after Isfahan's fall, and published by R. Jafariyan, in his *Ilal*, 63–169; idem, ed., *Safaviyya dar Arsa-yi Din*, 3: 1191–297.

Tadhkira al-Muluk, an administrative manual written sometime after the 1725 assassination of Isfahan's conqueror Shah Mahmud, for Shah Mahmud's nephew and successor Ashraf (1725–9); Lockhart (*The Fall*, 513–14) dates it to 1726. This has been published as Minorsky, V., ed. and transl., *Tadhkirat al-Muluk, A Manual of Safavid Administration, (c. 1137/1725)*, London, 1943.

Qutb al-Din Nayrizi, *Tibb al-Mamalik*, written after 1729 and published in R. Jafariyan, ed., *Ilal*, 215–35; idem, ed., *Safaviyya dar Arsa-yi Din*, 3: 1324–37.

Shaykh Ali Hazin, *The Life of Sheikh Mohammed Ali Hazin*, F. C. Belfour, transl. (London, 1830). The author was born in 1692, left Iran for India in 1734, completed his memoirs and died there in 1742 and 1779 respectively. The Persian text, entitled *Tazkirah-i Hazin*, was published in Isfahan in 1334/1955. Belfour's edition of the Persian was published in London in 1831.

Muhammad Muhsin, *Zubdat al-Tavarikh*, I. Afshar ed. (Tehran, 1375). The author was an official at Nadir Shah's court, and wrote this account at Nadir's command for the latter's eldest son in 1741–2.

Mirza Muhammad Mahdi Kawkabi Astarabadi, *Tarikh-i Nadiri*, composed *c.* eleven years after Nadir Shah's 1747 assassination. This text was published in Iran in 1282/1865 and 1293/1867. A French translation, *Histoire de Nader Chah*, undertaken by W. Jones (d. 1794) at the order of the king of Denmark, was published in London in 1770. *Tarikh-i Jahangusha-yi Nadiri*, reproducing a 1757 illuminated manuscript by the same author, with an introduction by Abd al-Ali Adib Burumand, was published in Tehran in 1991/2.

Mirza Muhammad Marashi, *Majma al-Tavarikh*, A. Iqbal, ed. (Tehran, 1362). The author was a descendant of Shah Sulayman. The chronicle covers the period 1708–9 to 1792–3.

Abul-Qasim Qazvini, *Favaid al-Safaviyya*, M. Mir Ahmadi, ed. (Tehran, 1990). The account was completed in India *c.* 1796.

Muhammad Hashim Asaf, *Rustam al-Tavarikh*. The author completed the text in 1831. An edition done by M. Mushiri has been published at least three times in Tehran (1348/1969, 1352, 2538).

Muhammad Tanukabuni (d. 1884–5), *Qisas al-Ulama* (Tehran, nd), a Persian-language clerical biography.

M. A. A. Pashazada, (d. 1310/1892), *Inqilab-i Islam bayn al-Khavass val-Avvam*, R. Jafariyan, ed. Qum, 1379.

Notes

Preface and Acknowledgements

1 L. Lockhart, *The Fall of the Safavi Dynasty and the Afghan Occupation of Persia* (Cambridge, 1958), 32–33, 70, 71n1, 72–3, the latter citing Browne, *A Literary History of Persia*, 4 (Cambridge, 1924, 1953), 120.

2 Newman, *The Formative Period of Period of Shi'i Law: Hadith as Discourse Between Qum and Baghdad* (Richmond, Surrey, 2000).

Introduction

1 Lockhart, *The Fall*, 16; R. Savory, *Iran Under the Safavids* (Cambridge, 1980) 103, 226; R. Stevens, 'European Visitors to the Safavid Court', *Iranian Studies*, 7(3–4) (1974), 441.

2 A collection of Savory's articles on early Safavid political history appeared as *Studies on the History of Safawid Iran* (London, 1987).

3 Volume 6 of *The Cambridge History of Iran*, 'The Timurid and Safavid Periods', P. Jackson and L. Lockhart, eds, appeared from Cambridge University Press in 1986, but the bulk of the volume's article had been written in the previous decade. Earlier, papers from a colloquium on Isfahan, the Safavid capital from the early seventeenth century, held at the Fogg Museum of Art, Harvard University, were published in 1974 as a special issue of the Society for Iranian Studies' journal *Iranian Studies* (*IS*).

4 This account draws on Browne, esp. 103f, 118–20, 372–3, 403–4, 406–10, 426f; *Tadhkirat al-Muluk, A Manual of Safavid Administration, (c. 1137/ 1725)*, V. Minorsky, ed. and transl. (London, 1943), esp. 13–14, 16–19, 23–6, 30f, 41; Lockhart, esp. 16–18, 21–34, 70–9; Savory, *Iran Under*, 76–103, esp. 93–95, 216–20, 226–54, esp. 226–8, 233–4, 238–41. See also Savory, 'The Safavid Administrative System' in Peter Jackson, et al., eds, *The Cambridge History of Iran*, 6: 351–72, and his more recent 'Safawids: Dynastic, political and military history', *EI²*, 8: 765–71. Savory's analyses parallel those of Minorsky (23–4), and both, in turn, presupposed the work of Browne (4: 84–120, esp. 116f); indeed, in *The Fall* Lockhart (esp. 16f) paid special tribute to Browne and Minorsky. See also M. Dickson's review of *The Fall* in *Journal of the American Oriental Society*, 82(4) (1962), 503–17.

5 The 1988 papers were published as *Études Safavides, sous la direction de Jean*

Calmard, (Paris-Teheran, 1993). The 1993 papers appeared as *Safavid Persia, The History and Politics of an Islamic Society*, C. Melville, ed. (London, 1996). In 1998 some forty specialists in this period based in Russia and Asia, continental Europe, the UK, the US and Iran attended the Third International Round Table in Edinburgh. Abstracts of the latter papers may be viewed at: http://www.arts.ed.ac.uk/eisawi/events/RoundTable.html, and a selection thereof has been published as *Society and Culture in the Early Modern Middle East: Studies on Iran in the Safavid Period*, A. J. Newman, ed. (Leiden, 2003).

6 Papers presented that year at the British Museum by some twenty-four scholars from Iran, Russia, Europe and the US have been published as *Safavid Art and Architecture*, Sheila R. Canby, ed. (London, 2002). *Safavid Iran and Her Neighbours*, M. Mazzaoui, ed. (Salt Lake City, 2003) stems from a gathering of some fourteen, mainly US-based, scholars in the same year.

7 The Iran Heritage Foundation, the University of Manchester's Centre for Historical Research on the Middle East and the Centre for Near and Middle Eastern Studies at the University of London organised 'Iran and the World in the Safavid Age' in London in September 2002. Bert Fragner convened the Fourth International Round Table in Bamberg, in July 2003. In November 2003, the Armenian Educational Foundation, the Armenian Society of Los Angeles and the G. E. von Grunebaum Center for Near Eastern Studies (University of California, Los Angeles) sponsored 'New Julfa: The Fourth Centennial, 1604/5–2004'. The Fifth International Round Table is set to meet in Italy.

8 See their works as referenced herein. See also M. Mir Ahmadi, *Din va Madhhab dar Asr-i Safavi* (Tehran, 1984) and idem, ed., Abul Hasan Qazvini, *Favaid al-Safaviyya* (Tehran, 1990). See also the work of M. K. Yusuf Jamali and N. Ahmadi cited below. Special mention should be made of the special issues of *Kitab-i Mah, Tarikh va Jugrafiyya* devoted to the Safavid period, the most recent being 68–69 (1382/2003), edited by M. Sefatgol. Note should also be made of M. Parsadust's recent *Shah Ismail-i Avval* (Tehran, 1375), *Shah Tahmasp-i Avval* (Tehran, 1377) and *Shah Ismail-i Duvvum va Shah Muhammad* (Tehran, 1381). In his *Tarikhnigari-i Asr-i Safavi va shinakht-i manabi va maakhiz* (Shiraz, 2001), J. Savaqib offers an extensive listing of sources on the period in many languages.

9 References in both Browne (4: 46n2) and Lockhart (e.g. 26n1, 28n2) to the 1815 *History of Persia* of Sir John Malcolm (d. 1833) suggest aspects of this framework were on offer in the previous century. On disagreement as to the nature and meaning of *khassa* and *mamalik* lands in the seventeenth-century European sources, let alone the Persian sources, see n14 of Chapter 2.

10 Such sources include *The Life of Sheikh Mohammed Ali Hazin*, F. C. Belfour, transl. (London, 1830), whose author was born in 1692, left Iran for India in 1734, and completed his memoirs and died there in 1742 and 1779 respectively; *Zubdat al-Tavarikh*, I. Afshar, ed. (Tehran, 1375), written in 1741–2 by Muhammad Muhsin, an official at Nadir Shah's court, at Nadir's command for his eldest son, and several years after which Nadir Shah engineered his own designation as monarch; *Majma al-Tavarikh*, A. Iqbal, ed. (Tehran, 1362) written by Mirza Muhammad Khalil Marashi, a descendant of Shah Sulayman, which covers the period 1708–9 to 1792–3; *Favaid al-Safaviyya*, M. Mir Ahmadi, ed. (Tehran, 1990), by Abul Hasan Qazvini, completed in India *c.* 1796; *Rustam al-Tavarikh* by Muhammad Hashim Asaf, completed in 1831, and published at least three times (Tehran, 1348, 1352, 2538); and the Persian-language clerical biography *Qisas al-Ulama* (Tehran, nd) of Muhammad

Tanukabuni (d. 1884–5). On *Rustam al-Tavarikh* as 'not a reliable historical account', see B. Hoffmann, 'A Nineteenth Century Glimpse of Safavid Persia', paper presented at the *Fourth International Round Table on Safavid Studies*, Bamberg, July 2003.

The *Mukafatnama*, written in jail by a former court official between two and four years after Isfahan's fall while members of the Safavid family were being executed around him, and recently published by R. Jafariyan, and post-1722 works by the Sufi shaykh Qutb al-Din Nayrizi (d. 1759), also contain reflections on reasons for the realm's collapse. Less negative, pre-1722 accounts, if historically problematic for different reasons, are only infrequently consulted by Western scholars. See the reference to Abu Talib Mir Findiriski in n37 of Chapter 8.

11 See S. Quinn, *Historical Writing during the Reign of Shah Abbas* (Salt Lake City, 2000), an exemplary study of the political-religious 'agendas' of various sixteenth- and early seventeenth-century court chroniclers, and her other works listed herein.

12 In the seventeenth century such foreign residents include, particularly, for example, the Frenchman Jean Chardin, who was in Iran in 1666–7, 1669 and between 1672 and 1677 and whose *Voyages en Perse* features prominently in Western accounts of the period. I. McCabe, P. Loloi and J. Ghazvinian have begun to explore the varied agendas of such foreign residents as Chardin and Père Judasz Tadeusz Krusinski (d. 1756), the procurator of the Jesuits in Isfahan. McCabe, for example, has suggested that Chardin's writings reveal more about the religio-political climate of contemporary France than Safavid Iran, and that his critique of the Safavid court was a less-than-veiled attack by Chardin, a Huguenot and, as such, an arch opponent of the established Catholic Church in France, on French absolutism. See J. Ghazvinian, 'British Travellers to Iran, 1580–1645'; P. Loloi, 'The Image of the Safavids in English and French Literature of the Sixteenth to Eighteenth Century'; I. McCabe, 'Beyond the Lettres Persanes: Safavid Iran in the Political Discourse of the French Enlightenment', all presented at *Iran and the World in the Safavid Age*, London, September 2002. See also n44 of Chapter 5. On Chardin's 'greedy and imperious' character, according to a Venetian contemporary, see A. Welch, 'Safavi Iran Seen Through Venetian Eyes', in Newman, ed., *Society and Culture*, 105. On Krusinski, see also n26 in Chapter 8, below, and on E. Kaempfer, a German doctor who lived in Isfahan in 1683–4, see n70 of the same chapter. A list of these foreign accounts appears in Appendix II. On the dates of Chardin's sojourn in Iran, see J. Emerson, 'Chardin', *Encyclopaedia Iranica (EIr)* 5(4): 369–70. Comments by all foreigners in Iran over this period on the affairs of the court and the haram merit special care, as neither was routinely accessible by the public, let alone Westerners. For conflicting accounts of 1690s' events based on French-Dutch enmity, see Matthee, 'Negotiating Across Cultures: The Dutch Van Leene Mission to the Iranian Court of Shah Sulayman (1689–1692)', *Eurasian Studies* 3(1) (2004), 50f, 56n62 and esp. 61–2. The same article addresses conflicting European and Iranian expectations and perceptions more generally.

13 The early work of Wallerstein (b. 1930) dealt especially with African politics. 'World system theory', an outgrow of 'dependency theory' as initially enunciated by Andre Gunder Frank (b. 1929), underlay the work of Samir Amin (b. 1931) on 'unequal development', the 1976 establishment of the Braudel Center at SUNY, Binghamton, the founding of the Center's journal *Review* and, for Ottoman studies especially, such works as Wallerstein, et al., 'The Incorporation

of the Ottoman Empire into the World Economy' in H. Islamoglu-Inan ed., *The Ottoman Empire and the World Economy* (Cambridge, 1987), 88–100.

In the Safavid case in particular, concern with foreign trade has come to over-shadow domestic economic activity although the latter, W. Floor has argued, was far more important to the Safavid economy. Similarly, although the rural pro-portion of the population far outnumbered the urban, which stood at between 10 and 15% of the total of *c.* nine million, the available primary sources are overwhelmingly skewed toward life among the latter. See Floor, 'Commerce, vi. From the Safavid Through the Qajar Period', *EIr*, 6: 69; idem, *The Economy of Safavid Persia* (Wiesbaden, 2000), 2–5 and 301, where he suggests that 'agri-culture, and its ancillary activities, was the most important sector of the econ-omy in Safavid Persia employing about 80% of the population.' See also nn70, 71 of Chapter 8.

14 On 'Ottoman decline' theory, see H. Inalcik and D. Quataert, eds, *An Economic and Social History of the Ottoman Empire, 1300–1914*, 2 vols (Cambridge, 1994), especially S. Faroqhi's 'Crisis and Change 1590–1699' (411–636) on the stereotypical view that the Ottoman empire reached its peak during the reign of Sulayman 'the Magnificent' (*reg.* 1520–66). See also, more recently, H. Lowry, *The Nature of the Early Ottoman State* (Albany, 2003). Thanks to S. Blake and G. Garthwaite for directing my attention to these sources.

15 See, for example, W. L. Cleaveland, *A History of the Modern Middle East* (Boulder/Oxford, 1994), 52–6; B. Lewis, *The Middle East, 2000 Years of History from the Rise of Christianity to the Present Day* (London, 1995), 117–19.

16 Contemporary with the Safavids only the Ottomans and Romanovs and, in China, both the Ming and its successor the Qinj, and, in Japan, the Tokugawa shogunate, endured longer.

17 This notion of constituency builds on G. R. Garthwaite, 'An Outsider's View of Safavid History: Shah Ismail Reconsidered', paper delivered at the Third International Round Table on Safavid Persia, Edinburgh, August 1998. Thanks to the author for making available a copy of his paper and for providing refer-ences to Pamela Crossley's discussion of 'simultaneous rulership' on which he himself drew. See Crossley, 'The Rulerships of China', *The American Historical Review*, 97 (December 1992), 1468–83; idem, *A Translucent Mirror, History and Identity in Qinj Imperial Ideology* (Berkeley and London, 1999), esp. 9–29. Our discussion above of simultaneous, universal rulership in Iran under the Achaemenians draws on Garthwaite's *The Persians* (Malden and Oxford, 2005). On Zoroastrianism, see ibid., 93f.

18 The Ilkhanid Sultan Uljaitu (d. 1316) was a Buddhist, became a Sunni Hanafi, a Shafii, and then, supposedly upset with intra-Sunni disputations, a Twelver Shi'ite; he is said to have reconverted to Sunnism before his death. See M. Mazzaoui, *The Origins of the Safawids, Shi'ism, Sufism, and the Ghulat* (Wiesbaden, 1972), 38, 40. Gawhar Shad, the wife of Timur's son Shah Rukh (d. 1446), built a mosque next to the shrine of the eighth Shi'i Imam, Ali Riza (d. 818), in Mashhad. See also J. Calmard, 'Le Chiisme Imamite sous Les Ilkhans', in D. Aigle, ed., *L'Iran Face à La Domination Mongole* (Tehran, 1997), 261–92. See also G. Lane, *Early Mongol Rule in Thirteenth-Century Iran: A Persian Renaissance* (London, 2003). Members of Iran's native Christian com-munity, the Nestorians, were sent as ambassadors to Europe by the Ilkhans and intermarried with the ruling family. See Garthwaite, *The Persians*, 104, 142, 146. See also 'Christianity', *EIr*, 5: 523f.

19 J. Woods, *The Aqquyunlu: Clan, Confederation, Empire*, rev. ed. (Salt Lake City, 1999), 82–3, 89, 102–3, 105–9, 259n77, n78, n79. See also L. Hunarfar, *Ganjinah-i Asar-i Tarikhi -i Isfahan* (Isfahan, 1344), 95; A. Godard, 'Isfahan' in *Athar-i Iran, Annales du Service Archeologique de l'Iran* (Paris, 1937), 26. On Jahan Shah, who had also claimed divine approbation for his rule and also displayed a healthy interest in Shi'ism, see V. Minorsky, 'Jihan Shah Qaraquyunlu and his Poetry', *Bulletin of the School of Oriental and African Studies (BSOAS)* 16(2), (1954) 271–97, esp. 281; a descendant of Jahan Shah founded the Shi'i Qutbshah dynasty in India in 1481. See also F. Sümer, 'Kara-koyunlu', *EI²*, 4: 584–8, esp. 588; J. Calmard, 'Les rituels shiites et le pouvoir. L'imposition du shiisme safavide: eulogies et malédictions canoniques', in Calmard, ed., *Études Safavides.*, 113. Although Timur also had claimed divine approval for his rule and his discourse evoked associations which attested to the importance of his Turco-Mongol constituency, he and his immediate successors were known for their patronage of Shi'i shrines. On Timur's projection of the legitimacy of his rule across different particularist discourses, and the consequent notion of 'simultaneous rulership', see Garthwaite, 'An Outsider's View'; Woods, 'Timur's Genealogy' in M. Mazzaoui and V. Moreen, eds, *Intellectual Studies on Islam, Essays Written in Honor of Martin B. Dickson* (Salt Lake City, 1990), 85–125; H. R. Roemer, 'The Successors of Timur', in Peter Jackson, et al., eds, 6: 142; R. Pinder-Wilson, 'Timurid Architecture', in Peter Jackson, et al., eds, 6: 745–6.

For an introduction to Twelver Shi'ism, see M. Momen, *An Introduction to Shii Islam* (New Haven and London, 1985). On 'the just sultan' and 'the just Imam' as references to the hidden twelfth Imam, see our 'The Myth of the Clerical Migration to Safawid Iran: Arab Shi'ite Opposition to Ali al-Karaki and Safawid Shi'ism', *Die Welt des Islams*, 33 (1993), 71n13; n4 of the following chapter. On Davani, see n56 of the following chapter.

20 The names, dates and geographical boundaries with which these messianic movements came to be identified – the Babai-Biktashis in Anatolia; the Hurufis, influential from Khurasan to Anatolia and Syria; Shaykh Badr al-Din in Western Anatolia; *Ahl al-Haqq* in Kurdistan; the Nurbakhshi in Southwestern Iran and the Mushasha in Southern Iraq – were often bestowed by both later adherents, and later scholars, and suggest a greater clarity of doctrine and practice, let alone sharp distinctions between them in both, than probably obtained at the time. On these orders see I. P. Petrushevsky, *Islam in Iran*, H. Evans transl., (London, 1985), 260–4, 291–300; B. S. Amoretti, 'Religion in the Timurid and Safavid Periods', in Peter Jackson, et al., eds, *The Cambridge History of Iran*, 6: 610–29; J. Baldick, *Mystical Islam* (London, 1989), 71–7, 94, 96, 100–4, 111; Woods, 3f. Useful contributions on individual movements include J. Birge, *The Bektashi Order of Dervishes* (London, 1937), 32f; H. Norris, 'The Hurufi Legacy of Fadlullah of Astarabad', in L. Lewisohn, ed., *The Legacy of Medieval Persian Sufism* (London, 1992), 87–97; S. Bashir, 'Enshrining Divinity: The Death and Memoralisation of Fazlallah Astarabadi in Hurufi Thought', *The Muslim World* 90 (Fall, 2000), 289–308; idem, 'The Imam's Return: Messianic Leadership in Late Medieval Shi'ism', in L. Walbridge, ed., *The Most Learned of the Shi'a* (New York, 2001), 21–33; T. Graham, 'Shah Ni'matullah Wali, Founder of the Ni'matullahi Sufi Order', in Lewisohn, ed., *The Legacy*, 173–90; B. G. Martin, 'A Short History of the Khalwati Order of Dervishes', in N. Keddie, ed., *Scholars, Saints, and Sufis* (Berkeley and London, 1978), 275–305; H. Algar, 'Naqshbandis and Safavids: A Contribution to the Religious History of Iran and

Her Neighbors', in M. Mazzaoui, ed., *Safavid Iran and Her Neighbors* (Salt Lake City, 2003), 7f. On the geographical distribution of these movements, see also Woods, 3. On these and other movements' various millenarian risings throughout the region, see also Adel Allouche, *The Origins and Development of the Ottoman–Safavid conflict (906–962/1500–1555)* (Berlin, 1983), 39–41.

21 Woods, 108–9.

22 Woods, 9, 83–4, 107, 150, 211; Allouche, 48f; G. Sarwar, *History of Shah Ismail* (Aligarh, 1939), 24f, 30f, 94–5. See also V. Minorsky [C. E. Bosworth], 'Uzun Hasan', *EI²*, 10: 963–7, esp. 967; idem, *Tadhkirat*, 190. A daughter of Junayd married a tribal notable of Ardabil. See M. Szuppe, 'La participation des Femmes de la Famille Royale à l'Exercice du Pouvoir en Iran Safavide au XVIe Siècle (première partie)', *Studia Iranica*, 23(2) (1994), 235.

23 Sarwar (17–43, esp. 33–9) offers an account of the events of this period based on the often-indiscriminate use of Safavid sources composed over the sixteenth and seventeenth centuries. Allouche's (39–64) account is somewhat more careful. See also Woods, 280n41 and 281n44 on the date of Ismail's entrance into Tabriz. For later reports that Ismail ordered his followers to eat the body of the defeated Uzbek chief Shaybani Khan, see n89 of Chapter 2.

On Tabriz as an important trade entrepot even before the rise of the Safavids, see n75 of Chapter 4.

1 Laying the Foundations: Ismail I (1488–1524)

1 Fazlallah Khunji Isfahani (d. 1521), the ferociously anti-Safavid and anti-Shi'i Sunni historian to Uzun Hasan's son Yaqub (d. 1490), wrote that the order's members praised Junayd as 'the Living One, there is no God but he' and that followers from Anatolia and elsewhere viewed Junayd's successor Haydar as Allah and neglected such daily religious duties as prayer. See Khunji's *Persia in AD 1478–1490, An Abridged Edition of Fadlallah b. Ruzbihan Khunji's Tarikh-i Alam Ara-yi Amini* (London, 1957), V. Minorsky, ed., 4, 61–80, 1f. J. Woods has produced a new edition of the text (London, 1992), which includes Minorsky's original abridged translation and additional notes. On Khunji, see also A. Jacobs, 'Sunni and Shi'i Perceptions, Boundaries and Affiliations in Late Timurid and Early Safawid Persia: an Examination of Historical and Quasi-Historical Narratives', unpublished PhD dissertation, School of Oriental and African Studies, University of London, 1999, 81–103. On a similarly anti-Safavid Arabic-language treatise composed in 1479–80 by a contemporary Hanafi cleric and the latter's role in expelling Junayd from Syria, see A. Morton's 'Maulana Ahmad Pakaraji and the Origins of Anti-Safavid Polemic', paper presented at *Iran and the World in the Safavid Age*, University of London, September 2002.

2 Minorsky, 'The Poetry of Shah Ismail I', *Bulletin of the School of Oriental and African Studies (BSOAS)*, 10 (1942), 1006a–1053a, esp. 1042a, 1043a, 1044a, 1047a, 1048a. See also G. Garthwaite, 'An Outsiders View', citing Minorsky (1047a); W. Thackston, 'The *Diwan* of Khata'i: Pictures for the Poetry of Shah Ismail', *Asian Art*, I(4) (Fall 1988), 37–63. Thanks to G. Garthwaite for directing me to the latter source. See also J. Calmard, 'Popular Literature Under the Safavids', in Newman, ed. *Society and Culture*, 317–18; A. Karamustafa, 'Esma'il I. His Poetry', *EIr*, 8. On the *taj* being adopted under Haydar, as noted by Khunji, see *Persia in AD 1478–1490*, Minorsky, ed., 73; Woods, ed. 260,

265, 282. There is no reference to such headgear in an earlier history of Diyar Bakr completed for Uzun Hasan between 1469 and 1478; see H. R. Roemer, 'The Safavid Period', in Peter Jackson, et al., eds, 6: 207; Woods, *The Aqquyunlu*, 219–20. On representations of the *taj* as early as 1503, see B. Schmitz, 'On a Special Hat Introduced during the Reign of Shah Abbas the Great', *IRAN*, 22 (1984), 103–12. My thanks to G. Garthwaite for directing me to this source.

For editions of Ismail's *divan*, see T. Gandjei, *Il Canzoniere di Sah Ismail Hata'i* (Naples, 1959), and I. Islanoghlu, *Sah Ismail Hatayi (Divan, Dehname, Nasihatname ve Anadolu Hatayileri)* (Istanbul, 1992).

Yazid (d. 683) was the Umayyad caliph during whose rule the third Shi'i imam, Husayn, grandson of the Prophet, was killed at Karbala in 680, on the tenth day, Ashura, of the Muslim month of Muharram. Khidr was the companion of Moses (Qur'an, 18: 62–83) whom the Shi'a identify as the Hidden Imam.

3 Other than references to the *taj*, Khunji's history contains no evidence of Safavid identification with any distinctively, let alone exclusively, Twelver discourse to 1490. Indeed, had this been otherwise, Khunji – an avowed opponent of Shi'ism – would certainly have referred to them as such; instead he repeatedly refers to Haydar's followers as 'Sufis'. See also nn5, 62 below. Hasan Rumlu's 1577 account (*Ahsan al-Tavarikh*, Tehran, 1357, 86), that at Ismail's profession of faith in Tabriz no book of Twelver doctrine or practice was immediately available, if not absolutely accurate, certainly reflects the leadership's unfamiliarity with the details of the faith. In a further indication of poor Safavid familiarity with key texts of the faith to this time, *Qavaid al-Islam*, attributed to Hasan b. Yusuf, Allama Hilli (d. 1325), eventually located according to Rumlu, is not a title listed as a work of Hilli. Mazzaoui (*The Origins*, 80, 6, 28n2) suggested this work was Allama's *Qavaid al-Ahkam*. For a translation of Rumlu's chronicle, see n10 below.

4 See the Arabic preface to a *firman* inscribed in Isfahan's Congregational Mosque in 1505, four years after Tabriz' capture, wherein, although no specifically Shi'i claims were made, nor was there allusion to descent from the Imams, Ismail was described as 'the successor of the age (*khalifat al-zaman*) the spreader of justice and beneficence, the just Imam (*al-imam al-adil*)'. See Hunarfar, 86–8. A coin minted in Kashan in 1506 referred to him as 'the just sultan'; see H. L. Rabino, 'Coins of the Shahs of Persia', *Numismatic Chronicle*, IVth series, 1908, 357–73, ad 368; idem, *Coins, Medals and Seals of the Shahs of Iran, 1500–1941* (Dallas, TX, 1973), 26–9; S. Schuster-Walser, *Das Safawidische Persien im Spiegel Europäischer Reiseberichte, 1502–1722* (Hamburg, 1970), 45. S. Canby (*The Golden Age of Persian Art, 1501–1722*, London, 1999, 28) cites a similar inscription on a crimson velvet belt dated to 1507–8. See also the reference to *al-sultan al-adil* in a copy of *Jamal va Jalal* dated to Tabriz *c.* 1504 in n31 below. The Twelver Shi'i scholar Muhammad b. al-Hasan al-Tusi (d. 1067) had referred to the absent, or Hidden, Imam variously as 'Sultan of the Time (*sultan al-waqt*)' and 'Lord of the Age (*sahib al-zaman*)'. See our 'The Myth', nn13, 65.

5 Although in his *divan* (Minorsky, 1043a), Ismail had claimed to be a Husaynid, such claims were absent in the 1505 firman cited above. Indeed not all of the coins minted in the period even contained avowedly Shi'i formulas, let alone the Imams' names. See Rabino, 1973, 26–8. See also n3 and Allouche, 34–5, 76–7; Sarwar, 17; J. Aubin, '*Études Safavides. I. Shah Ismail and les Notables de l'Iraq Persan*', *JEHSO*, 2 (1959), 43f. A 1508 manuscript copy of the Safavid family history *Safvat al-Safa*, originally completed in 1358, portrayed the family as

descended from Imam Ali. Working independently, the Iranian historian A. Kasravi (d. 1946) and Z. V. Togan (d. 1970) concluded the Safavids were Kurdish in origin. See Togan, 'Sur L'Origine des Safavides', *Melanges Louis Massignon* 3 (Damas, 1957), 345–57. Allouche (157–66) reviews the literature on the Safavids' origins and cites Ottoman sources dating such claims to the time of Junayd, Ismail's grandfather. Quinn (*Historical*, 83f) notes the importance of genealogy within the broader Turco-Mongol tradition of historical writing. See also Mazzaoui, 47n3; Quinn, *Historical*, 13–14.

6 For the Biktashis Abu Muslim was the link between the Prophet, Ali and the later Imams. Qizilbash elements apparently venerated that order's eponymous founder Hajji Biktash who, like Ismail himself, had a Christian mother. See Birge, 33–69; K. Babayan, 'The Waning of the Qizilbash: The Spiritual and the Temporal in Seventeenth Century Iran', unpublished PhD dissertation, Princeton University, June 1993, 200–11, 219 citing, especially, I. Melikoff, *Abu Muslim: Le 'Porte-Hache' de Khorassan Dans la Tradition Epique Turco-Iranienne* (Paris, 1962); idem, 'The Safavid Synthesis: From Qizilbash Islam to Imamite Shi'ism', *IS*, 27(1–4) (1994), 143–7; idem, 'Sufis, Dervishes and Mullas: the Controversy over the Spiritual and Temporal Dominion in Seventeenth-century Iran', in C. Melville, ed., *Safavid Persia*, 124–5; Calmard, 'Popular Literature', 318–22, 327, 333.

7 On the distinct appeal to Tajik Persians in Ismail's poetry, see also K. Babayan, *Mystics, Monarchs, and Messiahs: Cultural Landscapes of Early Modern Iran* (Cambridge, MA, 2002), xxviii–xxxi. On the appeal to Christians, L. Ridgeon notes that by the time of Jalal al-Din Rumi (d. 1273) Jesus had become 'interiorised . . . to the extent that he became an ideal symbol of spiritual resurrection'. Ridgeon also discusses the religious pluralism of such earlier prominent mystical figures in the region as Rumi, Suhravardi (d. 1191) and Aziz Nasafi (d. 1300), in his *Crescents on the Cross* (Oxford, 1999), 32f.

8 A modern-day Iranian commentator has suggested Ismail's claims to being the Imam or the Prophet were allegorical, even if his followers may have understood otherwise (R. Jafariyan, *Safaviyya, Az Zuhur ta Zaval*, Tehran, 1378, 65–7). See also Allouche, 155. The Venetian chronicler Sanudo, reporting on the period from 1497 to 1508, noted that Ismail himself said he was descended from the Prophet and 'that he is God'. Garthwaite, author of the above quote, suggests that the exact 'interpretation is left to the "reader" [of Ismail's poetry]', with 'the text' encouraging and allowing for variant readings. See Garthwaite, ibid., especially his citation of Crossley's 'The Rulerships', wherein Crossley argues that such simultaneous rulership, as a phenomenon of the early modern era, can be observed in Louis XIV's France, Peter the Great's Russia, the Qing's China and among the Ottomans. See also Woods, 'Timur's Genealogy'. On Ismail's discourse, see also Browne, 4: 61; Minorsky, *Tadhkirat*, 13; Allouche, 79–80, 155, 148n2; B. S. Amoretti, 'Religion in the Timurid and Safavid Periods', in Peter Jackson, et al., eds, *The Cambridge History of Iran*, 6: 638n1, 640n1; Savory, 'The Principal Offices of the Safavid State During the Reign of Ismail I (907–30/ 1501–24)', BSOAS 23(1) (1960), 91; J. Aubin, 'L'Avènement des Safavides Reconsidéré (*Études Safavides*. III)', *Moyen Orient et Ocean Indien* 5 (1988), 129; Woods, *The Aqquyunlu*, 217.

9 Woods (199) offers a map of Turkish and Kurdish tribes in the region *c.* 1400–50. Use of this particular dialect set Ismail's poetry apart from the Persian dialect which his ancestor Safi al-Din had utilised in his poetry and, in

Ismail's own time, the Turkish and Persian poetry of the Herat-based Timurid ruler Sultan Husayn Bayqara and the Persian poetry composed by contemporary Ottoman rulers. See also n.34 below and the sources in n2.

10 After its conquest in 1508, Khan Muhammad Ustajlu, whose brother had already married a sister of Ismail, was designated governor of Diyar Bakr. At his death, that brother succeeded him as governor and tribal khan. Another Ustajlu was governor of newly captured Tabriz. See Hasan Rumlu, *A Chronicle of the Early Safawis, being the Ahsan al-Tawarikh of Hasan-i Rumlu*, C. N. Seddon, transl. (Baroda, 1934), 41; Sarwar, 53; M. Haneda, *Le Chah et les Qizilbash, Le Systeme militaire safavide* (Berlin, 1987), 86–7; K.-M. Röhrborn, *Provinzen und Zentralgewalt Persiens im 16. und 17. Jahrhundert* (Berlin, 1966), transl by K. Djahandari as *Nizam-i Iyalat dar Dawrah-yi Safaviyya* (Tehran, 1978), 43; Szuppe, 'La participation', 1994, 215–16, 215n19, 220n42, 221, 224; Woods, 197.

As for the Shamlu, before Tabriz Ismail's father Haydar had married the daughter of Abdi Bek Shamlu. Abdi Bek married another sister of Ismail and their two sons from this marriage were later governors of Herat and Khurasan. One son, Durmish Khan, in 1503 became the first Safavid governor of Isfahan, fought at Chaldiran in 1514, suppressed a revolt by the governor of Rasht in 1518, was appointed guardian to Ismail's third son, Sam Mirza (b. 1517), and was sent to Khurasan as its governor where he died in 1525–6. His brother Husayn succeeded him both as governor of Khurasan and Sam Mirza's guardian – a post of great standing – and his daughter married Sam Mirza. Another Shamlu was made governor of Herat in 1513–14. See Szuppe, 224, 220–1, where she notes that Durmish Khan's descendants remained governors of Herat, itself a key provincial posting as it was the traditional capital of Khurasan and usually the seat of the crown prince, into the next century. See also Sarwar, 46; Haneda, 86–90; Röhrborn, 146. See also Szuppe, 'The "Jewels of Wonder": Learned Ladies and Princess Politicians in the Provinces of Early Safavid Iran', in G. Hambly, ed., *Women in the Medieval Islamic World, Power, Patronage and Piety* (London, 1998), 325–47; idem, 'Status, Knowledge and Politics: Women in Sixteenth-Century Safavid Iran', in G. Nashat and L. Beck, eds, *Women in Iran from the Rise of Islam to 1800* (Urbana and Chicago, 2003), 141–69.

11 The former Diyar Bakr Mawsillu chief was made the shah's sealkeeper, and two others served as governor of Baghdad and guardian to Tahmasp. See Sarwar, 52–3, 70; Szuppe, ibid., 234; M. Dickson, 'Shah Tahmasb and the Uzbeks (The Duel for Khurasan with Ubayd Khan: 930–946/1524–1540)', unpublished PhD dissertation, Princeton University, 1958, 120; Woods, 191–3.

12 Haneda, 93, unsourced; Szuppe, 215–16, 220–1, 224; Woods, 195–6.

13 A Dhul-Qadr was made governor of Fars at its conquest in 1503, and the tribe 'retained' it until 1594–5. The Afshar, having participated in the conquest of Qandahar, received and held Kirman province for some generations. At Baghdad's 1508 conquest a Talish was made governor of the city and later of all of Arab Iraq; another member of this tribe was governor of Astarabad/Gurgan. See Rumlu, 47; Haneda, 75–6, 93; Szuppe, 215–16, 220–1, 224; Sarwar, 46–7, 50, 68–71; Röhrborn, 46–7; Aubin, 'Revolution Chiite et Conservatisme, Les soufis de Lahejan, 1500–1514' (*Études Safavides. II.*)', *Moyen Orient et Océan Indien*, I (1984), 5, 22; Woods, 198, 183. On the Dhul-Qadr, see P. Oberling, 'Dhul -Qadr', *EIr*, 7.

14 The seven 'Sufis' whom later chroniclers identified as companions of Ismail

included leading Shamlu, Qaramanlu, Talish and Dhul-Qadr figures. See, for example, Haneda, 72f, citing Khuzani's *Afzal al-Tavarikh*, completed in the late 1630s; Aubin, 'Les soufis', 3n12, citing *Alam Ara-yi Shah Ismail*, dated to after 1675–6; Sarwar (33) and Allouche (61) citing *Ross Anonymous*, the British Library manuscript dated by Morton to the 1680s, from which the dustjacket of the present volume is taken.

By contrast, Ghiyas al-Din Khvandamir's 1524 account (*Tarikh-i Habib al-Siyar*, J. Humai, ed. ([Tehran], 1362), 4: 448–9) mentions only two by name. His son Amir Mahmud, in his 1550 *Tarikh-i Shah Ismail va Shah Tahmasp*, M. A. Jarrahi, ed. (Tehran, 1991, 43–4), neither notes nor numbers Ismail's companions, nor does Abdi Bek Shirazi in his 1570 *Takmilat al-Akhbar*, A. Navai, ed. (Tehran, 1369, 36). See also Rumlu's 1577 *Ahsan* (12) and Iskandar Bek Munshi, *History of Shah 'Abbas the Great*, R. M. Savory, transl. (Boulder, CO, 1978), 1: 42, the first volume of which was completed in 1616. Budaq Qazvini's 1576 *Javahir al-Akhbar*, M. Bahramnizhad, ed. (Tehran, 1378), 112, mentions, but does not name, seventeen individuals as having accompanied Ismail. In his 1590 *Khulasat al-Tavarikh* [E. Eshraqi, ed. Tehran, 1359], 1: 47–9], Qummi speaks of the 'Sufis of Lahijan' but neither names or numbers them. In his 1703–4 *Tarikh-i Sultani* (E. Eshraqi, ed., 2nd ed., Tehran, 1366, 33) Sayyid Hasan Astarabadi gives seven, but does not name them. M. Szuppe (*Entre Timourides, Uzbeks et Safavides* (Paris, 1992), 57–8, 58n211, 13) has noted the unreliability of the Jarrahi edition above. A better edition is published as *Iran dar Ruzagar-i Shah Ismail va Shah Tahmasp*, Gh. R. Tabatabai, ed. (Tehran, 1370/1991).

On Khuzani, see also A. Morton, 'The Early Years of Shah Ismail in the *Afzal al-tavarikh* and Elsewhere', in Melville, *Safavid Persia*, 27–51, esp. 32f; S. Abrahams, 'A Historiographical Study and Annotated Translation of Volume 2 of the *Afzal al-Tavarikh* by Fazli Khuzani al-Isfahani', unpublished PhD dissertation, University of Edinburgh, 1999; C. Melville, 'A Lost Source for the Reign of Shah Abbas: the *Afzal al-tawarikh* of Fazli Khuzani Isfahani', *IS*, 31/ii (1998), 263–5; idem, 'New Light on the Reign of Shah Abbas: Volume III of the *Afzal al-Tavarikh*', in Newman, ed. *Society and Culture*, 63–96; Sarwar, 6; M. Haneda, 'La Famille Khuzani Isfahani (15e–17e siècles)', *SIr*, 18 (1989), 77–92; n29 below. On *Ross*, see A. Morton, 'The Date and Attribution of the *Ross Anonymous*. Notes on a Persian History of Shah Ismail I', in C. Melville, ed., *Pembroke Papers I* (Cambridge, 1990), esp. 187–8, 201; Quinn, *Historical*, 146. The work has been published as *Jahangusha-i Khaqan: Tarikh-i Shah Ismail*, A. D. Muztarr, ed. (Islamabad, 1984). On this work see also E. Sims, 'A Dispersed Late-Safavid Copy of the *Tarikh-i Jahangusha-yi Khaqan Sahibqiran*' in S. Canby, ed., *Safavid Art and Architecture* (London, 2002), 54–7. On *Alam Ara-yi Shah Ismail*, see R. McChesney, 'Alam Ara-ye Shah Ismail', *EIr*, 1:796–7, wherein McChesney urges that the work be treated with caution, and suggests it is the same as the also anonymously authored *Alam Ara-yi Safavi* which, edited by Y. A. Shukri, was published in Tehran, 1350/1971. See, however, Quinn, *Historical*, 145. Shukri, editor of *Safavi*, argues for differences between the two. The former has been published as *Alam ara-yi Shah Ismail*, A. M. Sahib, ed. (Tehran, 1349/1970). In his 'A Note on Iskander Bek's Chronology', *Journal of Near Eastern Studies*, 39(1) (1980), 53–63, McChesney also notes the need for caution with Munshi's dates. On Budaq Qazvini, see n20 of chapter 3.

15 See references to the Afshar, Dhul-Qadr, Mawsillu, Qajar, Qaramanlu, Rumlu,

Shamlu, Talish, Takkalu and Ustajlu in, especially, Haneda, *Le Chah*, 30–47, citing Khuzani and *Ross*. On these battles compare, for example, Sarwar (37–8, 62, 67, 78–9) with Rumlu (18–20, 28–9, 52–4, 69–70). See also Allouche, 61.

16 Woods, 183f. On the Takkalu, whose name suggests Takka in Southern Anatolia, see R. Savory, 'Takkalu', *EI²*, 10: 136–7. Khunji's account (59), in addition to mentioning tribal amirs and followers from Rum, Talish and 'Siyah-kuh', also mentioned the Shamlu, a term suggesting Syrian connections. The Talish are spoken of by Khunji (71) as 'clad in blue' which, as Minorsky notes (Khunji, 71n5), suggests peasant origins. Ottoman sources confirm Haydar's appeal in Rum (Allouche, 54–5). See also Woods' map (199) of tribal elements between 1400 and 1450.
     Here we do not propose to investigate the notion of 'tribe', let alone 'Turk'. On both, however, Woods' discussion (10–23) in particular repays attention.

17 Röhrborn, 112–29; W. Floor, *Safavid Government Institutions* (Costa Mesa, 2001), 85f. On the Mushasha, see also Sarwar, 55–6, Rumlu, 47, Roemer, 6: 216–17, 245, and our discussion below. On Luristan, see also M. K. Jamali, *The Life and Personality of Shah Ismail I (907–930/1489–1524)* (Isfahan, 1998), 198–9.

18 On other family members and associates who served Ismail and Tahmasp, see Savory, 'Offices . . . Ismail, 102; Aubin, 'Shah Ismail', 60–3; Roemer, 6: 213; Floor, *Safavid Government*, 35.

19 Another, a judge in Rayy, was on close personal terms with Ismail. Aubin, ibid., 47f, 64–5; Savory, ibid., 98; Floor, ibid. See also Woods, ibid., index s.v.

20 Aubin, ibid., 76–7; Floor, 'The Secular Judicial System in Safavid Persian', *SIr*, 29(1) (2000), 48; Munshi, 1: 256. An ancestor of the Isfahani family of Khvaja Afzal al-Din Muhammad Turk was made judge in the city and supervisor of the city's Congregational Mosque under Ismail; a descendant was a court poet known not to have been complimentary to Abbas II's *vizier* Saru Taqi. See Hunarfar, 48. On the Khaki Shirazi family whose members had also served the Aqquyunlu, see Aubin, ibid., 77. The continuity between the policies of the Turkish dynasties and Ismail's reign in such administrative matters as tax policy, as noted by W. Floor (A *Fiscal History of Iran in the Safavid and Qajar Periods, 1500–1925*, New York, 1998, 149–50, 216–17), was likely the result of such administrative continuities.

21 It is mainly later sources which report the harshness of the new faith's imposition throughout the realm. In his 1577 chronicle Rumlu reported (26) that at the capture of Tabriz seven decades before Ismail commanded the prayer sermon (*khutba*) be read in the name of the twelve Imams and that the first three caliphs 'be cursed in the bazaars, on pain of death to him who refused'. See also the 1564–5 *Tarikh-i Ilchi-yi Nizamshah*, authored by an Indian emissary to Tahmasp's court who arrived in Iran only in 1545 and stayed until 1564 (Jamali, xxv–xxvi), Junabadi's 1625–6 *Rawzat al-Safaviyya*, and Pashazada's mid-nineteenth century *Inqilab-i Islam*, as discussed by Jamali (299–302). The latter, whose author died in 1892, has been published by R. Jafariyan as *Inqilab-i Islam bayn al-Khavass val-Avvam* (Qum, 1379). The Indian source has been published as Khurshah b. Qubad Husayni, *Tarikh-i Ilchi-i Nizam Shah*, M. R. Nasiri and K. Haneda, eds (Tehran, 2000). *Ilchi* and *Ross* each cite 30,000 as the number of Sunnis killed at Firuzkuh, a ten-day long battle in 1504 against a local ruler (Sarwar, 47), where the more contemporary Khvandamir (4: 476), gives no

figure and the 1542 *Lubb al-Tavarikh*, whose author was actually present, (Quinn, 16) cites 1,000; Rumlu (33) has no figure. See also Jamali, 200 and, on Firuzkuh, n89 of the following chapter. Compare also later sources on the severity of forced conversion of Heratis to Shi'ism following its capture in 1510 (Jamali, 309–11 citing the later *Alam Ara-yi Shah Ismail*, contemporary with *Ross*) with Khvandamir (4: 514–15). M. Szuppe, *Entre Timourides, Entre Timourides, Uzbeks et Safavides. Questions d'Historie politique et sociale de Hérat dans la première moitié du XVIe siècle* (Paris, 1992), 128, noting but nominal persecution of Herat's Sunnis, suggests that gaining a share in Sunni property may have encouraged denunciations.

In her 'The *Tabarraiyan* and the Early Safawids', *IS*, 37/i (2004), 47–71, esp. 56–60, Stanfield-Johnson analyses the ritual cursing as addressed in eight of the period's chronicles, and notes that the later the chronicle the more elaborate the description of Ismail's measures to institute the practice. Unsurprisingly, the account of the practice in Tahmasp's reign by the Sunni Mirza Makhdum Sharifi (on whom see Chapter 3 below) is especially hostile. See ibid., 60–5.

Later sources also charge that Ismail ordered the desecration of the tombs of the poet Jami (d. 1492) and Fakhr al-Din Razi (d. 1208–9) in Herat (Jamali, 305–6, citing *Bustan al-Siyaha* of Zayn al-Abidin Shirvani (d. 1837–8). Jami's apparent hostility to Shi'ism (Algar, 'Naqshbandis', 24–5, 28–31; n21 of the previous chapter), albeit promulgated whilst based at the Sunni Timurid court, did not inhibit Ismail from association with Jami's nephew Hatifi (d. 1520–1), on which see below. See also n33 that Herat's artists remained in the city after its capture by the Safavids. *Ross* (Jamali, 173) also refers to Ismail's massacre of thousands of Sunnis at the capture of Tabas in 1504. Rumlu refers (36) to this as retribution for Chagatai attacks, not as an anti-Sunni action per se and Munshi (1: 49) raises an eyebrow to Rumlu's figure of 7,000 killed; Khvandamir (4: 480) had cited 3,000 or 4,000. During the capture of Baghdad in 1508 the tomb of the famous Sunni jurist Abu Hanifa (d. 767) was also apparently damaged. See our 'The Myth', n33. See also R. J. Abisaab, *Converting Persia, Religion and Power in the Safavid Empire* (London, 2004), 16.

By contrast, the relative ease of conversions to the new faith is suggested by the account of Nurallah Shushtari (d. 1610–11), composed in India after 1584, that at the Safavid capture of Kashan in 1503 the Shi'i cleric accompanying Ismail, Ali Karaki, on whom see below, endorsed the rulings of a local Sunni judge (*qadi*) and allowed the latter to keep his post after he cursed the three caliphs. See Nurallah Shushtari, *Majalis al-Muminin* (Tehran, 1354), 2: 233–4.

22 Aubin, ibid., 55–7; Munshi, 1: 239, 244. On Abd al-Vahhab, a Naqshbandi who, it appears, kept his Sufi tendencies secret, see also Algar, 'Naqshbandis', 9–13. On another such Sunni Naqshbandi who returned to Tabriz after its conquest, see Algar, 13–14.

23 Newman, 'The Myth', n44.

24 H. Mudarrissi Tabatabai, *Bargi az Tarikh-i Qazvin* (Qum, 1361), 22–3, 55, 59–60. Another sayyid who served both Sultan Husayn Bayqara and the Safavids was Ghiyas al-Din Khvandamir (d. 1535–7), author of *Habib al-Siyar*. Khvandamir's grandfather, Mir Khvand, also had served Sultan Husayn, as had Sultan Ibrahim Amini, author of *Futuhat-i Shahi*, a work completed in 1531 but commissioned by Ismail. On Khvandamir and Amini and their overt acceptance of Safavid legitimacy, see the following chapter ad n25.

25 As many key contemporary sources contain little or no such detailed information,

Savory, Haneda, Floor and others identify the period's office holders by recourse
to a number of, occasionally much later, sources.

26 Savory, 'Offices . . . Ismail, 100; Floor, *Safavid Government*, 17–21.
27 Savory, ibid., 101; Minorsky, *Tadhkirat*, 32, 116–17, 126, 188; Sarwar, 80;
    Floor, *Safavid Government*, 137–40; Haneda, *Le Chah*, 74–5, 144–5, 178–9.
28 Newman, 'The Myth', n25; Savory, ibid., 103. Aubin, ibid., 69: J. Calmard, et
    al., 'Sadr', *EI²*, 8: 748–51; Floor, 'The *sadr* or head of the Safavid religious
    administration, judiciary and endowments and other members of the religious
    institution', *Zeitschrift der deutschen morgenländischen Gesellschaft* (*ZDMG*)
    150 (2000), 461–500, esp. 478; Floor, 'Judicial', 19, 21f. Another *sadr*, Sayyid
    Sharif al-Din Ali, was a descendant of the well-known Sunni theologian Sharif
    Jurjani (d. 1413) who had served Timur.
        The Tajiks did not always get along with each other. See, for example,
    accounts of the feuds between the *vakil* Najm-i Thani, on whom see the follow-
    ing note, and Sayyid Sharif al-Din and his intended replacement Astarabadi, and
    the post-Chaldiran feud between the 'civil' *vakil* – on which post see below – Mir
    Shah Husayn Isfahani and the *sadr* Astarabadi in the sources cited herein, espe-
    cially Savory, and our discussion of the Uzbek campaign in Khurasan, below. On
    the office of *mustawfi al-mamalik*, see Floor, *Safavid Government*, 35, 42, and
    the following note.
29 Najm al-Din was replaced in 1509 by the Isfahani notable Yar Ahmad Khuzani,
    mustawfi al-mamalik from *c.* 1501. The latter had received land grants from
    Ismail in the Isfahan area in 1503, confirming his family's prominence therein.
    Indeed, the presence of the Khuzani family in Isfahan can be dated to the 1440s.
    Given the title Najm-i Thani (*The Second Star*) Khuzani commanded Safavid
    forces at their 1512 defeat by the Uzbeks, in which battle he was killed. The Yazdi
    notable and *sadr* Sayyid Abd al-Baqi, on whom see further below, was thereupon
    appointed *vakil* but was killed at Chaldiran. At Amir Yar's appointment, his
    brother was appointed Isfahan's *darugha* (Prefect of Police). Haneda, 'La Famille
    Khuzani', 78, 80, 82. As noted above, a descendant authored *Afzal al-Tavarikh*
    in the next century (Haneda, 83–4). Jamali (220) cites the much later Ottoman
    chronicle *Inqilab-i Islam* stating that Amir Yar married a daughter of Ismail. See
    also Savory, 'Offices . . . Ismail', 94–6; Floor, *Safavid Government*, 12, 42. On
    the post of *darugha*, see also M. Keyvani, *Artisans and Guild Life in the later
    Safavid Period* (Berlin, 1992), 70–1; Floor, *Safavid Government*, 115–22.
30 Canby, 16.
31 A copy of Muhammad Asafi's *Jamal va Jalal* was executed in Herat in 1502–3
    but, brought to Tabriz *c.* 1504, underwent very Tabrizi embellishments and the
    addition of the *taj*. The miniature entitled 'Jalal before the Turquoise Dome'
    features a doorway bearing the inscription *al-sultan al-adil* (the just ruler).
    Canby, ibid., 16–17, 29–31, 34–5; B. Brend, '*Jamal va Jalal*: a Link Between
    Epochs', in S. Canby ed., *Safavid Art and Architecture* (London, 2002), 32–6.
    See also B. Gray, 'The Arts in the Safavid Period', in Peter Jackson, ed., 6: 880;
    J. Bloom, 'Epic Images Revisited: An Ilkhanid Legacy in Early Safavid Painting',
    in Newman, ed., *Society and Culture*, 237–48; A. Welch, 'Art in Iran ix. Safavid
    to Qajar', *EIr*, 2: 622.
32 A 1514 copy of the *Gulistan* of the Iranian poet Sadi (d. 1292) featured elements
    traditional to fifteenth-century Shirazi paintings. Canby, 35. On the involvement
    of the Kazeruni mystical order in the production of such manuscripts in Shiraz,
    see n45.

33 Canby, 36, 39, citing, on metalworking, A. Melikian-Chirvani, *Islamic Metalwork from the Iranian World: 8–18th centuries* (London, 1982), 260, 279–80, 283–5. Most of Herat's artists who remained in the city after its fall to the Uzbeks in 1507 and its 1510 capture by the Safavids were forcibly removed from the city by the Uzbeks at their retaking of the city in 1528. See the sources cited in n21; E. Bahari, *Bihzad, Master of Persian Painting* (London, 1996), esp. 179–88; idem, 'The Sixteenth Century School of Bukhara Painting and the Arts of the Book', in Newman, ed., *Society and Culture*, 251–64.

34 E. Yarshater, 'Persian Poetry in the Timurid and Safavid Periods,' in Peter Jackson, ed., 6: 978; H. R. Roemer, 'The Türkman Dynasties', in Peter Jackson, ed., 6: 165; Z. Safa, 'Persian Literature in the Safavid Period', in Peter Jackson, ed., 6: 957. Ismail's ancestor Safi al-Din had composed his poetry in Persian. See Minorsky, *Tadhkirat*, 189n4. Minorsky ('Jihan Shah', esp. 282–3) notes Jahan Shah's Turkish poems were written to Persian metre. Yarshater (6: 967f), discusses the basic forms of poetry in this period – the *masnavi* (couplet) form, used for narrative, mystical and ethical works; the *qasida*, a monorhyme usually between twenty-five and seventy lines, but occasionally longer, used mainly for panegyrics; and the *ghazal*, used for lyric poetry – and the rise in the fifteenth century of the 'Indian style'. The latter sought to establish new links between previously unrelated notions and 'orchestrate' associated meanings between words, ideas and images; in essence, focusing on uncommon relationships such that the more subtle is the more ingenious.

35 Hatifi did begin, but never completed, such a poem. See Canby, 33; Z. Safa, 'Persian Literature in the Timurid and Türkman Periods', in Peter Jackson, ed., 6: 920; Yarshater, 6: 957f; J. T. P. de Bruijn, 'Safawids.III. Literature', *EI²*, 8: 774–7, esp. 775. On Hatifi, see also n58 of the following chapter. On Jami see also ad n19 of the previous chapter.

 Jami inducted into the order Husayn b. Ali Vaiz-i Kashifi (d. 1504–5), author of the famous Alid martyrological work *Rawzat al-Shuhada*, completed in 1502–3, and also a recipient of the favour of Sultan Husayn and Mir Ali Shir. The recent special edition of *IS*, 36(4) (December, 2003), M. E. Subtelny, ed., examines Kashifi and his legacy. See also Babayan, *Mystics*, 165f; n126 of Chapter 4.

36 These included: Fighani Shirazi (d. 1519), Shihab al-Din Bayani (d. 1525), Ahli Shirazi (d. 1535–6), and Fuzuli Baghdadi (d. 1562–3). See De Bruijn, ibid.; Jamali, 122f; Yarshater, 6: 979–81. To be sure, not all of these poets' compositions earned the approbation of the shah or others at the centre. See, for example, Jamali, 146–7. For a more recent discussion of Persian poetry in this period, centring on Fighani, see P. Losensky, *Welcoming Fighani, Imitation and Poetic Individuality in the Safavid-Mughal Ghazal* (Costa Mesa, 1998).

37 Pinder-Wilson, 6: 745, 728f.

38 The same year inscriptions in the name of the twelve Imams were, however, added to Isfahan's main Congregational Mosque, which dates to the Saljuk period and to which Ismail's grandfather Uzun Hasan had made additions. Hunarfar, 90–1.

39 Canby notes that the Saljuk style of the brickwork decoration, the Kufic script and the arabesque all evoke early Islamic heritage as the thin glazed strips in the facade evoke Timurid Khurasan and as the motif of the glazed insets against plain brick suggest Jahan Shah's Blue Mosque, built in Tabriz in 1465 for his daughter. The arabesque itself appears on later metalwork of this period as well.

A small school attached to the complex was built at the same time. Canby, 26–8; R. Hillenbrand, 'Safavid Architecture', in Jackson, ed., 6: 761–4, citing Hunarfar, 368, 360–9; Godard, 63–9; S. Blake, *Half the World: The Social Architecture of Safavid Isfahan, 1590–1722* (Costa Mesa, CA, 1999) 104, 169–70. For Ismail's presence in Isfahan, see Sarwar's index, s.v. On the pre-Safavid history of 'Chinese' clouds in Iranian art see Y. Kadoi, 'Aspects of Iranian Art under the Mongols: Chinoiserie Reappraised', unpublished PhD dissertation, University of Edinburgh, 2005, especially Chapter 1.

40 Ismail visited Ardabil on several occasions, notably in the spring of 1500, on his way from Lahijan to Irzinjan. In *c.* 1509–10 Ismail ordered the remains of his father Haydar reburied at the shrine. See C. Melville, 'Shah Abbas and the Pilgrimage to Mashhad' in Melville, ed., *Safavid Persia*, 221n12; Sarwar, 34, 94, 57; Canby, 12–13. See also C. E. Bosworth, 'Ardabil', *EIr*, 2: 357–60, esp. 359–60. In his own lifetime Ismail also laid plans for his own tomb at Ardabil so close to that of his ancestor Safi al-Din as to suggest that the resulting small size thereof was less an issue than its proximity to the order's eponymous founder. See R. Hillenbrand, 'The Tomb of Shah Isma'il I, at Ardabil', in S. Canby, ed., *Safavid Art and Architecture* (London, 2002), 3–8. For others of Ismail's contributions to the shrine, see also K. Rizvi, 'The Imperial Setting: Shah Abbas at the Safavid Shrine of Shaykh Safi at Ardabil', in Canby, 9–10.

41 Coins with distinctly Twelver inscriptions were minted in 1508 by the Mushasha governor of Shushtar. These murders provoked anti-Safavid outbursts among Mushasha adherents in Basra and al-Ahsa. See J. H. Shubbar, *Tarikh al-Mushashaiyin wa Tarajim Alaihim* (Najaf, 1385/1965), 216–17, 85–7.

42 Petrushevsky, 324; Calmard, 'Popular Literature', 336–7.

43 F. Daftary, 'Ismaili-Sufi Relations in early Post-Alamut and Safavid Persia', in L. Lewisohn, and D. Morgan, eds, *Late Classical Persianate Sufism (1501–1750), The Safavid and Mughal Period* (Oxford, 1999), 275–89, esp. 287, citing, however, Qummi's 1590 *Khulasat al-Tavarikh*, on which see Chapter 4 below.

44 Babayan, 'The Waning', 202–3; idem, 'Sufis, Dervishes and Mullas', 124.

45 Arjomand, *The Shadow*, 115, citing Khvandamir, 4: 611–12; Shushtari, 2: 149, 152–3, 521; Munshi, 1: 145. On Abd al-Baqi, see also P. Soucek, 'Abd al-Baqi Yazdi', *EIr*, 1: 105–6. In this period the continued involvement of the Shiraz-based Kazeruni mystical order in the production of traditional illustrated manuscripts including, for example, a *Khamsa*, perhaps accounts for the order's continued existence. See F. Cagman and Z. Tanindi, 'Manuscript Production at the Kazeruni Orders in Safavid Shiraz', in S. Canby, ed., *Safavid Art and Architecture* (London, 2002), 43–8. See also n32. Cf. Algar ('Naqshbandis', 26) that the order was wiped out after Ismail conquered Fars in 1503.

46 The Talish chief eventually received a pardon and a robe of honour, another Shamlu was appointed Herat's new governor and a Mawsillu was made governor of Qayin and given the title 'Sultan'. See Savory, 'Offices . . . Ismail', 96, citing Sharaf Khan Bidlisi, *Sharafnama*, (Cairo, nd) 2: 130f, a source completed in 1596, and the later *Ross*; Sarwar, 66–71. Cf. the shorter version of the story in Khvandamir (4: 527); Aubin, 'Les soufis', 22. On Bidlisi, see Woods, 228.

47 The Ustajlu commander later became governor of Tabriz. See Sarwar, 71; Allouche, 105–6, 106n9; Jamali, 233–5, citing Rumlu (66), the later *Alam Ara-yi Shah Ismail* and *Ross*. Khvandamir's 1524 account carries no report on this rising but see such later sources as Rumlu (66) and Qummi (*Khulasat*, 1: 128).

48 Allouche, 120–1.

49 Browne, 4: 57; Sarwar, 50–1, 65–6, 73, 78–82; Allouche, 86–7, 91, 94–6, 111–12, 114–20, 170–3; Jean-Louis Bacqué-Grammont, '*Études Turco-Safavides*, I. Notes sur le Blocus du Commerce Iranien par Selîm Ier', *Turcica*, 6 (1975), 74–5. On Ottoman-Safavid relations generally, see idem, *Les Ottomans, les Safavides, et leurs Voisins* (Istanbul, 1987); Haneda, 41–6. Ismail's loss of his Tabriz-based metalworkers ended the city's role as a key metalworking and weapons-making centre. See J. Allan, 'Safavid Loss, Ottoman Gain – Metalworking Across the Two Empires', paper presented at *Iran and the World in the Safavid Age*, University of London, September, 2002; J. Allan and B. Gilmour, *Persian Steel, The Tanavoli Collection* (Oxford, 2000), 23, 142.

50 Rumlu, 71, 74; Sarwar, 86.

51 In 1519, Ismail also lent assistance to the Jalali rebellion in Anatolia. Sarwar, 86, 88–92, Allouche, 122, 128–32; Bacqué-Grammont, *Les Ottomans*, 272–5; Floor, *Safavid Government*, 11, 178–9. On military 'reforms' undertaken after Chaldiran, see Floor, ibid., 11; R. Matthee, 'Unwalled Cities and Restless Nomads: Firearms and Artillery in Safavid Iran', in Melville, ed., *Safavid Persia*, 391.

52 Rumlu, 84–7, 255; Sarwar, 86, 89, 91–3.

53 His alliance-buildng efforts came to nought, however. Indeed, in 1522, two years after the Spaniard Magellan circumnavigated the globe, a new treaty between the Portuguese and the ruler of Hormuz further tightened the former's grip on the island. The Portuguese were also approached with a request to use their ports based in India to evade the Ottoman trade blockade of the overland trade from Iran and transport silk to the West. The Portuguese did, indeed, seize the Bahrayn islands from local Arab chiefs as specified in the 1515 treaty but, instead of turning these over to Iran, retained them for some eighty years. In 1543, the Portuguese also seized Hormuz' customs revenues and the island became a staging post for shipment of Caspian silk to Portuguese trading stations in India. On other, failed, Safavid efforts to win European assistance against the Ottomans, see Savory, 'Ismail I', *EI²*, 4: 186–7; L. Lockhart, 'European Contacts with Persia, 1350–1736', in Peter Jackson, ed., 6: 380f, 410–11; R. Ferrier, 'Trade from the Mid-14th Century to the End of the Safavid Period', in Peter Jackson, ed., 6: 420–6. See also Allouche, 122; Floor, *The Economy*, 210–13; R. Matthee, *The Politics of Trade in Safavid Iran, Silk for Silver 1600–1730* (Cambridge, 1999), 20, 27–8. On contacts between Ismail and Russia, see Matthee, 'Anti-Ottoman Concerns and Caucasian Interests: Diplomatic Relations Between Iran and Russia, 1587–1639', in M. Mazzaoui, ed., *Safavid Iran and Her Neighbors* (Salt Lake City, 2003), 105, 107.

54 Floor, *Safavid Government*, 12, 20–1, 140; Haneda, 179–80. Muhammad Bek's brother, the governor of Tabriz, had crushed the earlier rising of Ismail's half-brother.

55 Tabrizi was murdered by Rumlu elements at Ismail's death. See Khvandamir, 4: 598; Rumlu, 88–9, 90–1; Sarwar, 93–4, 104; Savory, 'Offices . . . Ismail', 93–9, 102; Aubin, 'Shah Ismail', 60–5; Floor, *Safavid Government*, 6–13, 20, 35; idem, 'The *sadr*', 478. On Qadi Jahan, see also Munshi, 1: 237.

56 Sayyid Jamal al-Din Astarabadi, appointed to the post after Chaldiran, had studied with the same Davani who both praised Uzun Hasan and his son Yaqub, the latter well known for his anti-Safavid, anti-Shi'i tendencies, and had rejected Ismail's claims to be the 'Imam of the Age'. Davani's rather perfunctory *Nur al-Hidaya* is often cited as evidence of his 'conversion' to Shi'ism. See our 'Jalal

al-Din Davani', *EIr*, 7: 132–3, and nn21, 28. Sayyid Ghiyas al-Din Mansur Dashtaki, *sadr* toward the end of Ismail's reign, who had dedicated an early essay to the Ottoman Sultan Bayazid II (reg. 1481–1512), was also at best only nominally Shiʻi. See our 'Ghiyas-al-Din Dashtaki', *EIr*, 7: 100–2; Savory, 'Offices . . . Ismail', 103. Aubin, 69. See also Floor, 'sadr', 478; Newman, 'The Myth', n25, n72. A member of Isfahan's Shahristani family of sayyids was *mustawfi al-mamalik* from 1514 to 1523. Floor, *Safavid Government*, 42; Munshi, 1: 257.

57 Rumlu, 82; Sarwar, 91; Szuppe, 217–18, 229. On Ismail's five daughters, see Szuppe, 216, 231; idem, 'La participation des Femmes de la Famille Royale è l'Exercice du Pouvoir en Iran Safavide au XVIe Siècle (seconde partie)', *Studia Iranica* 24(1) (1995), 106; Sarwar, 94. Jamali (257) lists six daughters, but notes some sources give fifteen.

58 Sarwar, 91, 25, 94; Szuppe, 1994, 229–30; Jamali, 278–9. The Shirvanshah were certainly not Shiʻites at this time. See Röhrborn, 143. Cf. Woods (16) that intermarriage between Aqquyunlu Turkish tribal elements and native Iranians was rare.

59 In *c.* 1518 a foreign merchant reported that 'the Sophy is loved and reverenced by his people as a god and especially by his soldiers, many of whom enter into battle without armour expecting their master Ismail to watch over them in the fight'. Minorsky, *Tadhkirat*, 13. Compare Allouche, 156, and Savory, 'Ismail', 91.

60 Shaykh Muhammad Al-Hasan al-Yasin, *Tarikh al-Mashhad al-Kazimi* (Baghdad, 1387/1967), 71. A coin minted in Mashhad in 1518 referred to Ismail as 'the just sultan'. On the latter term see n4 and n31 above.

61 Hillenbrand, 6: 764–5; Hunarfar, 369–79; Godard, 69–72. See also Pinder-Wilson, 6: 756f; Blake, 104, 153.

62 Szuppe, 1994, 250–1; 1995, 71. Although Khunji's earlier history of the Aqquyunlu is notably devoid of references to Safavid identification with Shiʻism (n2 above), in a work completed in 1514 Khunji clearly associates the Safavids with the faith (Jacobs, 96f).

On Qum as a Shiʻi centre from early in Islamic history, see our *The Formative*, 32f.

63 These included *Imamzada*s in Tehran in September 1514, the month after Chaldiran, and in 1519 in Amul. Work was done in 1518 in Qum, where Ismail frequently wintered, and in 1520 in Damavand's Congregational Mosque. These, and scattered carvings and tombstones, the latter including one at Natanz in 1515, also delineated territorial claims, as did Ismail's *firman*s. See those added in 1512 in Isfahan's Congregational Mosque, in mosques in Kashan in 1516 and in Simnan in 1519. See Hillenbrand, 6: 767–8; H. Naraqi, *Asar-i Tarikhi-yi Shahristanha-yi Kashan va Natanz* (Tehran, 1348/1969), 399. On the *imamzada*, the tomb of a member of the family of the one of the Imams, and listings thereof, see H. Algar, et al., 'Emamzadeh', *EIr*, 8.

64 Canby, 31, 34; Rumlu, 87; B. Gray, 'The Arts in the Safavid Period', in Jackson, ed., 6: 880f. Canby (29–35) notes the freedom of stylistic expression artists of the period enjoyed throughout the region. On Bihzad, see also Behari, 'The Sixteenth Century School'; idem, *Bihzad*. Bihzad's death date is variously given as 1514 and 1535, with the latter date favoured. See also Welch, 'Art', 622.

65 R. Hillenbrand, 'The Iconography of the *Shah-nama-yi Shahi*', in C. Melville, ed., *Safavid Persia*, 53–78, esp. 59, 60. On this *Shahnama* see also M. B. Dickson and S. C. Welch, *The Houghton Shahnameh* (Cambridge, MA and London,

1981); S. C. Welch, *A King's Book of Kings, The Shah-nameh of Shah Tahmasp* (New York and London, 1972). See also Gray, 'The Arts in the Safavid Period', 6: 880f.

66 R. Jafariyan discusses pre-Safavid Iranian Shi'ism in his 'The Immigrant Manuscripts: A Study of the Migration of Shi'i Works From Arab Regions to Iran in the Early Safavid Era', in Newman, ed., *Society and Culture*, 351–69. The following discussion derives from our 'The Myth', which questioned the long-accepted notion that large numbers of Arab Twelver scholars flocked to Iran following the Safavids' establishment of Twelver Shi'ism as the realm's official faith.

67 When the Safavids captured Baghdad in 1508, Karaki and the local Twelver leader Sayyid Kamuna, both of whom had been jailed by the local governor, were released and joined the shah. The latter was killed at Chaldiran. Karaki was with Ismail at the 1510–11 capture of Herat. See Rumlu, 46–7; Sarwar, 54–5, 79, 81; W. Madelung, 'al-Karaki', *EI²*, 4: 610.

    The equation of the *naib* of the Hidden Imam with a senior cleric empowered to undertake certain specific duties of absent Imam had been available for some centuries, although Karaki was the first Twelver cleric to articulate the concept of *niyaba amma* (general deputyship) by which those prerogatives generally could be exercised by such clerics in the former's absence. See N. Calder, '*Zakat* in Imami Shi'i Jurisprudence, from the Tenth to the Sixteenth Century, AD', *BSOAS*, 44(3) (1981), 468–80; idem, '*Khums* in Imami Shi'i Jurisprudence, from the Tenth to the Sixteenth Century, AD', *BSOAS*, 45(1) (1982), 39–47.

68 Newman, 'The Myth', 108n90. Karaki's most vociferous opponent in this period, Sulayman Qatifi (d. after 1539), rebuked Karaki in person in Mashhad *c.* 1510 for associating with, and accepting gifts from, the court. However, Qatifi completed his well-known essay on the subject only after Chaldiran, in 1518, at the urging of fellow clerical critics based outside Safavid territory to whom Chaldiran certainly gave more confidence to voice criticisms more openly. In that essay Qatifi also challenged the rulings of those clerics who argued the deputy might also collect and distribute believers' alms on behalf of the Imam. The public cursing of the Sunni caliphs, endorsed by Karaki both in 1503 in Kashan, as noted above, and in a 1511 essay dedicated to Ismail, also angered Twelvers in the Hijaz who were, they complained to Iranian coreligionists, 'chastised for this cursing and reviling'. On Karaki as the only known Lebanese migrant to Safavid Iran during Ismail's reign, see also D. Stewart, 'Notes on the Migration of Amili Scholars to Safavid Iran', *Journal of Near Eastern Studies*, 55(2) (1996), 85, 87–9.

69 Woods, 169, citing Aubin, 'La Politique Religieuse des Safavides', in *Le Shi'isme Imamite*, T. Fahd, ed. (Paris, 1970), 235–44.

70 Given the notion of stages in the attainment of human perfection – down to the inclusion of such 'falls' as those experienced by such earlier personages as Adam – evident in the discourse of such earlier Sufi figures of the region as Aziz Nasafi – and the notions of spiritual resurrection on offer in the religious discourse of the time (Ridgeon, 71), Chaldiran may have been viewed as a, perhaps necessary, step on the path of a longer, but ultimately successful, journey.

2 Reconfiguration and Consolidation: The Reign of Tahmasp (1524–1576)

1 On Tahmasp's date of birth as 1513 or 1514, see Browne, 4: 84; Sarwar, 70, citing Khvandamir; Savory, 'The Principal Offices of the Safavid State During the Reign of Tahmasp I (930–984/1524–1576)', *BSOAS*, 24, part 1 (1961), 65; idem, 'Safavids', *EI²*, 8: 768; Roemer, 6: 233; Allouche, 133n114; Szuppe, 1994, 234; Rumlu, 91. Ismail had either four (Szuppe, 1995, 106; Sarwar, 94) or six (Jamali, 239f) sons.

2 Illustrating the extent of intra-Qizilbash strife, in 1528–9 the Mawsillu governor of Baghdad was killed by his nephew who ordered the *khutba* read in the name of the Ottoman Sultan Sulayman. When the latter was killed by his own brothers the rebellion fizzled out. See Allouche, 137, citing later sources. Tahmasp's mother was a Mawsillu.

3 Many secondary sources miss the Ustajlu co-regency, but see C. J. Beeson, 'The Origins of Conflict in the Safawi Religious Institution', unpublished PhD thesis, Princeton University, 1982, 35. Beeson was a student of Dickson. On the Ustajlu see also n12.

4 Dickson, 295, 342–3. Savory ('Offices . . . Tahmasp'), 65; idem, 'Safavids', *EI²*, 8: 768), Allouche (134) and Roemer (6: 233) all suggest the civil war lasted ten years. Dickson (265–95) and Beeson (ibid.) suggest twelve, to include Sam Mirza's return to court and the execution of his Shamlu supporters. Compare Savory, 'The Safavid Administrative System', 6: 361–2; Szuppe, 1995, 106. Dickson's account of the civil war, although drawing on sources composed over the entire Safavid period, is the most exhaustive. Dickson (199–201) disputes Tahmasp's self-portrayal in his memoirs as in complete control of these events. See also Floor, *Safavid Government*, 12, 21.

5 Munshi, 1: 251–2; Aubin, 'Shah Ismail', 65, 47f; Abrahams, 'A Historiographical Study', Chapter 1; Savory, 73f; Dickson, 200; Haneda, 'La Famille', 84. On Nur Kamal and his family, see also Munshi, 1: 252; Szuppe, 1995, 67; Jafariyan (*Safaviyya*, 74) notes that Qadi Jahan's son was *vakil* for a short time. Floor, *Safavid Government*, 12, 35–6.

6 Safavid forces mounted counter-attacks coincident both with turning points in the period's intra-Qizilbash struggles and Ottoman movements in the West. See Dickson, 212f.

7 On Tahmasp's 1561–2 return to the Ottomans of Sulayman's son Bayazid who fled to Iran after his 1559 revolt against his father, see Allouche, 145; Roemer, 6: 244.

8 Allouche, 143–4; Roemer, 6: 243–4.

9 On the various dates proposed for the move to Qazvin, see Eshraqi, 'Le *Dar al-Saltana* Qazvin, deuxième capital des Safavides' in Melville, ed., *Safavid Persia*, 105; Röhrborn, 8; Savory, *Iran Under*, 63; M. Membré, *Mission to the Lord Sophy of Persia (1539–1542)*, translated with Introduction and Notes by A. H. Morton (London, 1993), xxiv; Roemer, 6: 243; M. Mazzaoui, 'From Tabriz to Qazvin to Isfahan: Three Phases of Safavid History', *ZDMG*, Supp. III, 1. XIX. *Deutscher Orientalistentag*, Wiesbaden, 1977, 514–22, esp. 517–19; Floor, *The Safavid Economy*, 197. Jacobs (167n18) discusses all the proposed dates. Qazvin appears to have been the capital by 1559, when the Ottoman prince Bayazid arrived in Safavid territory (Rumlu, 179).

10 Later sources' descriptions of the Safavid forces which repulsed Uzbek and Ottoman attacks during the civil war have been used to chart the changing

struggle for predominance at the political centre. See, for example, Haneda, *Le Chah*, 104f, citing Rumlu and Khuzani on Safavid forces during the third Uzbek invasion (1529–31). Dickson (102–3n1) carefully notes the 'frequently contradictory' nature of his – mainly non-contemporary – sources.

11 Contemporary office-holders themselves are, in fact, often identified in the (later) sources as the civil war's main protagonists. Thus, for example, with the ascendancy of the Shamlu-Ustajlu coalition, *c.* 1531, Husayn Khan Shamlu (d. 1534–5) was *vakil* and *amir al-umara* jointly with Abdallah Khan Ustajlu; both were Tahmasp's nephews. In 1531–2 Husayn Khan Shamlu married a sister of Qara Khan Ustajlu, Abdallah Khan's father, who had married a sister of Ismail. Abdallah Khan, later *amir al-umara* and minister of justice (*divanbeki*), was governor of Shirvan from 1549 until 1566 or 1567, the year of his death. See Szuppe, 1994, 221–2, 224, 238; Floor, *Safavid Government*, 12. The post of *amir al-umara* disappears from 1534 to 1567–8, when it is occupied, unsurprisingly, by an Ustajlu, the governor of Azerbaijan. The post of *vakil* followed the same pattern. The office of *qurchibashi* was held by Takkalu, one of whom was killed by a fellow Takkalu in 1529 and the second in the 1531 Takkalu massacre. The Shamlu held the post during the Shamlu-Ustajlu period, but thereafter the Afshar held the post until *c.* 1584. See Savory, 77–9; Floor, *Safavid Government*, 12, 21. On the *qurchibashi*, see Savory, 'Offices . . . Tahmasp', 79; Savory, 'The Safavid', 361–2; Floor, *Safavid Government*, 140–1; and, especially, Haneda, 144–53, 171–80, 105–10, where he also discusses the relative influence of the *qurchi*s in this period. On the suggestion that Tahmasp himself 'appointed' or 'conferred' such posts on specific individuals (e.g. Savory, 'Offices . . . Tahmasp', 78), see Dickson, 199–201, and Savory, who notes that the amirs appointed Husayn Khan as *amir al-umara* and only later informed Tahmasp. See also n4.

12 Röhrborn, 28; Haneda, 120; Szuppe, 1994, 236n112. On Tahmasp's nine, or twelve, sons see Rumlu, 209; Munshi, 1: 206–18; Szuppe, 1995, 107. Savory ('Tahmasp', *EI²*, 10: 110) says Tahmasp had thirteen sons. Haneda (127–9) also calls attention to Ustajlu dominance and their influence over Tahmasp from the outset. Changes in the tribal hierarchy under Abbas I best explain why Munshi (1: 222), writing in 1616, hailed the Shamlu as 'the greatest of all Qizilbash tribes'. See also Rumlu, 195, 197; n20 of Chapter 4.

13 In 1576 the Shamlu were governors of Mashhad and Hamadan; the Mawsillu held Tun and Tabas; the Rumlu held the posts of *amir al-umara* of Shirvan and the administrative head of the Safavid Sufi order (*khalifa al-khulafa*); the Dhul-Qadr, seal-keeper, and the governorships of Astarabad and Shiraz. The Afshar held the post of *qurchibashi* and were governors in Kirman and Sava and their traditional fief of Kuh Giluya; they were also guardians to two sons of Tahmasp by concubines; Qajars held the posts of *divanbeki* and governor of Damghan and Bistam. The Takkalu, although some were related to Tahmasp and one was guardian to Tahmasp's son Muhammad Khudabanda in Herat, apparently held two minor holdings in Gilan and one in Khurasan, suggesting some, at least, continued to be distrusted. See Haneda, 117f, citing Munshi's listing of the realm's amirs at Tahmasp's death (1: 222f), and Minorsky, *Tadhkirat*, 14–8. A Mawsillu and three Afshars were guardians of several Safavid princesses. Szuppe, 1994, 242–3; 1995, 107. On Abbas and his brothers, see Munshi, 1: 208f, and on the sons of Tahmasp's full-brother Bahram, see Munshi, 1: 219–21; W. Floor, 'The *Khalifeh al-Kholafa* of the Safavid Sufi Order', *ZDMG* 153(1) (2003), 55.

On concubines and 'slavery', see the excellent introduction in Babaie, et. al., *Slaves of the Shah*, 1f.

14 In this period little of the realm's land was under the direct administration of the court/family itself; such land was called *khassa*, or sometimes *khalisa*, land. During Tahmasp's reign these lands included Tabriz, the former capital, Qazvin, the new capital, Isfahan and Simnan. Kashan was *khassa* from the middle of Tahmasp's reign until his death in 1576, briefly again in 1579 and from 1585 to the death of Hamza Mirza. Yazd was *khassa* from the middle of Tahmasp's reign until 1586. Röhrborn (169–71) notes much disagreement about the nature and meaning of *khassa* and *mamalik* lands in the seventeenth-century European sources, let alone the Persian sources and (195–9) that before Abbas I the difference was not that distinctive or important. Cf. Floor, *Safavid Government*, 80–1, 85–90; idem, *A Fiscal*, 107f. Chardin (cited by Minorsky, *Tadhkirat*, 26) famously said that Shah Safi (reg. 1629–42) first introduced the *khassa* system. Röhrborn (169–71) is especially critical of foreign residents' discussions of the categories of land and notes that no Persian sources define these categories of land in the manner on offer in the foreign sources.

15 In theory, these lands would have had a separate administrative system at the centre, but information on such structures in this period is scanty and contradictory. Röhrborn, 177, 183f. On provincial autonomy, see Röhrborn, 40, 69, 81, 92, 103–4, 108–9, 111. The centre did attempt to influence the appointment of local officials where maladminstration was an issue. See, for example, Röhrborn, 147, citing Munshi, 1: 147–50, 161. Röhrborn (152f) notes that the centre's power to hire and fire the local *vizier* in Khurasan, a key province as seat of the crown prince, was exceptional. See also n41. Floor, *Safavid Government*, 80–123.

16 Szuppe, 1994, 234, 236–7, 238n115, 240.

17 Szuppe, 1994, 218–19, 236n112, 223–4, 236–7, 239, 242–3; idem, 1995, 110, 113, and further below. Compare Savory, 'Tahmasp', *EI²*, 10: 110; Munshi, 1: 218–19. Both princes became major land-owners in Sistan and Qandahar. According to a later source, Ibrahim was later appointed *vakil c.* 1570–1; see Haneda, 140–1. Cf. Floor, *Safavid Government*, 12.

18 Tahmasp's sons, brothers and cousins held the governorships of Shirvan, Qarabagh, Ardabil, Hamadan, Kashan, Fars – where the Dhul-Qadr were the guardians – Qandahar, Sistan, Qain, Mashhad, Sabzavar, Astarabad, Mazandaran and Lahijan, though with guardians nearly always drawn from the leading tribes. See Röhrborn, 59f; 62–8. See also Haneda, 111n20; Savory, 'Ismail II', *EI²*, 4: 188. On Ibrahim, born in 1543–4 and sent East in 1556–7, the year after his marriage to his uncle Tahmasp's daughter Gawhar Sultan, daughter of a concubine, see Qadi Ahmad Qummi's *Gulistan-i Hunar*, published as *Calligraphers and Painters, A Treatise by Qadi Ahmad, son of Mir Munshi (c. AH 1015/AD 1606)*, V. Minorsky, ed. and transl., (Washington, DC, 1959), 3–4; Munshi, 1: 219–20; Szuppe, 1995, 113.

19 Masum Bek was named *divanbeki* and then *vakil c.* 1550–1, and led expeditions in 1551–2 against the Ottomans at Irzirum and 1563–4 in Mazandaran. On the Takkalu rising, those Takkalu who remained loyal and the Takkalu lands Masum Bek received thereafter, see Rumlu, 184–5; Szuppe, 'Kinship Ties Between the Safavids and the Qizilbash Amirs in the Late-Sixteenth Century: a Case Study of the Political Career of Members of the Sharaf al-Din Ogli Tekelu

Family', in Melville, ed., *Safavid Persia*, 83–6, 84n23; Szuppe, 1994, 237. See also Szuppe, *Entre Timourides*, 109f.

20 Munshi, 1: 213–14.

21 In *c.* 1530, during the Takkalu period, Tahmasp's brother Bahram was appointed governor of Herat, with a Takkalu guardian and Tajik *vizier*; a prominent Herati Tajik was Bahram's guardian (Dickson, 188–9). After the 1533 retaking of Herat, during the Shamlu-Ustajlu period, the Shamlu governor thereof appointed Ruhallah Khuzani Isfahani *vizier* for Mashhad and the affairs of the shrine; the latter's grandson authored *Afzal al-Tavarikh*. Other Khuzanis included the *vizier* of Azerbaijan and governor of Shirvan and Shakki and Gharjistan, and another who served an Ustajlu governor. See Röhrborn, 158–9; Qummi's 1590 *Khulasat*, 1: 94; Haneda, 'La Famille Khuzani', 84–6, 88. On the Savji and Kujuji family, see Aubin, 'Shah Ismail', 63–4; Munshi, 1: 253. On Qummi, see n23 below; Quinn, *Historical*, 19.

22 Munshi, 1: 229–30; 233–4, 237–9, 240–1, 244; Qummi, *Khulasat* 2: 1002; Röhrborn, 189; Aubin, 56, 57nn1, 63, 79–80. All the chief accountants of this period, the overseers of the royal workshops, secretaries and others in the royal retinue as well as the physicians of the day were Tajiks. Many were sayyids. Munshi, 1: 254–9, 261–6; Aubin, 'Shah Ismail, 57n1, 78. In *c.* 1573 a member of Isfahan's Shahristani sayyid family was *mustawfi al-mamalik*, as a predecessor had served Ismail after Chaldiran. See Floor, *Safavid Government*, 42.

23 Röhrborn, 160. The family of Ahmad Qummi, a Husayni sayyid and author of *Khulasat al-Tavarikh*, had long served the Safavids. His father, known as Mir Munshi (d. 1582), had studied with Mansur Dashtaki (d. 1541), Tahmasp's nominally Shi'i Tajik sayyid *sadr* who had opposed Ali Karaki. Mir Munshi served three years on the staff of Nur Kamal Isfahani and then, for some eleven years, he served the *vakil* Qadi Jahan Qazvini and then held various provincial posts. He eventually became *vizier* in Mashhad under Ibrahim, son of Tahmasp's brother Bahram. See Qummi's *Calligraphers*, 1–10, 76–9.

24 Röhrborn, 151f, 156, 160, 163, 167–8; Jafariyan, *Safaviyya*, 74.

25 Khvandamir embellished accounts of the dreams of Shaykh Safi al-Din so that these foretold Ismail's rule and the adoption of the distinctive Safavid *taj*. That he completed the chronicle in India, having fled repeated Uzbek attacks after Ismail's death, suggests Khvandamir even endorsed such discourse when outside Safavid territory. See Quinn, *Historical*, 15–16, 63f, 72–3, 78–9; idem, 'The Historiography of Safavid Prefaces', in Melville, ed., *Safavid Persia*, 1–25, esp. 4; Jacobs, 104–65. In *c.* 1474 Khvandamir's grandfather, Sayyid Muhammad, known as Mir Khvand (d. 1498), commenced for Sultan Husayn Bayqara's *vizier* Mir Ali Shir what would become *Rawzat al-Safa fi sirat al-anbiya* which reflects some Shi'i sympathies. Jacobs, 12–49; Quinn, *Historical*, 14; Babayan, *Mystics*, 298–9.

Like Mir Khvand, Sultan Ibrahim Amini had also served Sultan Husayn. *c.* 1519–20, he accepted a commission from Ismail to undertake what he finally delivered to Tahmasp in 1531 as *Futuhat-i Shahi*, a world history whose second section covered the birth and reign of Ismail to 1513, the year before Chaldiran. Amini's interpretations of Shaykh Safi's dreams endowed Ismail with both spiritual and political legitimacy. See Quinn, *Historical*, 15, 70–1. See also ibid., 80, 84, 90, 151–2.

26 Amir Mahmud included a detailed accounting of Ismail's ancestors, portraying the early Safavid shaykhs as devout Twelver Shi'ites and the house itself as

descended from Imam Musa, though in a manner which paid homage to certain pre-Islamic notions of Persian kingship. He also equated the reign of Ismail with the caliphate itself, reflecting the competing claims to Muslim legitimacy extant in the region as a whole, the Ottomans under Sulayman especially. See Quinn, 17, 65, 73–4, 79. Babayan (*Mystics*, 301) notes that Amir Mahmud also referred to Ismail as *sahib qiran* (master of an auspicious conjunction), a title which emphasised that military successes were the result of divine favour and which was also given Ismail by Tahmasp's brother, and Amir Mahmud's contemporary, Sam Mirza (d. 1567).

27 Jacobs, 166–81, Quinn, 16–17, 84. Although Qazvini was denounced as a leader of the city's Sunnis in 1552, died in jail several years later and his sons fled to India, such denunciations and such treatment were unusual. See also n93 below. On Qazvin's Sunnis, see also n35 of the following chapter. See also R. McChesney, 'The Central Asian Hajj-Pilgrimmage in the Time of the Early Modern Empires', in M. Mazzaoui, ed., *Safavid Iran and Her Neighbors* (Salt Lake City, 2003), 129–56, esp. 133, discounting Ottomanists' suggestions that the rise of the Savafids per se accounts for Sunni Central Asian pilgrims' difficulties in performing the *hajj* in this period in particular, and over the Safavid period more generally. On calligraphy albums assembled for Bahram, see n74 below.

28 Togan, 355.

29 Jacobs, 182–99, esp. 186; Quinn, 17, 86–7; Babayan, *Mystics*, 302–3. *Nigaristan* has appeared as *Tarikh-i Nigaristan*, A. M. Mudarris Gilani, ed. (Tehran, 1340/ 1961, 1404). *Nusakh-i Jahan-Ara* has been published as *Tarikh-i Jahan-ara*, H. Narqi, ed. (Tehran, 1342/1963).

30 Blake, 153; Hunarfar, 380, 384–5. For similar inscriptions dating to 1548 and 1554 in other mosques, see Hunarfar, 386–8.

31 An effort to appoint a governor in Mazandaran succeeded only temporarily, but Tahmasp did secure payment of regular tribute from Gilan. Roemer, 6: 245; Röhrborn, 112f, 142; Minorsky, *Tadhkirat*, 170.

32 Rumlu, 270n2; Roemer, 6: 245; Savory, *Iran Under*, 64.

33 Georgia had been an area of interest for the Ottomans, the earlier Turkish dynasties, and the early Safavids, as the province of mainly Christian rulers whose palaces and churches held great riches. As in the past both booty and Georgian, Circassian and Armenian prisoners were brought back. Some of the latter converted and received military training, but the military and political importance of these elements, called *ghulam*, over Tahmasp's reign was, by all accounts, relatively insignificant, especially vis-à-vis Qizilbash levies whose numbers are estimated as *c.* 100,000. See Röhrborn, 71–6; Cf. Savory, *Iran Under*, 65–6; Savory, 'Tahmasp', *EI*², 10: 109; Roemer, 6: 246–7. Members of more prominent families in the region in fact chose to enter into *ghulam* service. See H. Maeda, 'On the Ethno-Social Backgrounds of the Four *Gholam* Families from Georgia in Safavid Iran', *SIr*, 32(2) (2003), 243–78, and our discussion of the *ghulam* during Abbas I's reign in Chapter 4 below.

34 Tiflis retained autonomy until *c.* 1569 and Kurdistan until Abbas I's reign. The Lurs, perhaps in return for autonomy under Ismail, fought with Tahmasp against the Uzbeks; even under the Ottomans they retained some freedom of action. Some Kurds and Lurs had Shiʿi connections. Röhrborn, 112–18, 120–3, 143.

35 Intermarriages between Turk and Tajik were unusual during the Qaraquyunlu and the Aqquyunlu periods. Woods, 16.

36 On the children of Ismail by the Mawsillu Tajlu Khanum, including Tahmasp,

see Szuppe, 1994, 234; idem, 1995, 107. On Tahmasp's eight daughters, see Munshi, 1: 218f; Szuppe, 1994, 216, 231, 239–40. Savory ('Tahmasp', *EI²*, 10: 110) notes Tahmasp had thirteen daughters. Szuppe (1995, 111–18) lists the marriages of members of the Safavid house in the seventeenth century. See also idem, 1994, 236n113. Khan Ahmad would be defeated in battle in 1592 by Tahmasp's grandson Abbas I but his daughter by that marriage, Yakhan Bekum (b. *c.* 1586–7), would marry Abbas. On Amira Dabbaj, see also below ad n51.

37 A sister of Tahmasp who married Abdallah Khan Ustajlu (d. 1566–7), himself a grandson of Shaykh Haydar, had previously been married to the Shirvanshah Sultan Khalil who had also married a daughter of Ismail. Their grandson, Salman Khan, was governor of Qazvin, and married back into the family in the 1580s. See Szuppe, 1994, 216, 221–2, 223–4, 229–31, 238–9; idem, 1995, 90f, 110, 114, 118; Savory, 'Offices . . . Tahmasp', 78; Munshi, 2: 1063. On the Marashi family, see Calmard, 'Marashis', *EI²*, 6: 510–18. On Abdallah Khan see also n11 above.

38 Membré, the Venetian envoy in Iran between 1539 and 1542, notes that local sayyids and Qadi Jahan Qazvini wore the *taj*. See Membré, xiv, xvii, xx, 41; Morton, 'The *Chub-i Tariq* and Qizilbash Ritual in Safavid Persia', in Calmard, ed., *Études Safavides.*, 241n57.

39 Babayan, 'The Waning', 139, 203–6, idem, 'Sufis, Dervishes', 124–5; idem, 'The Safavid Synthesis', 143–7; idem, *Mystics*, 145f. On heterodox beliefs among some Takkalu which may have encouraged these traditions, see below ad n91.

40 On the first repentance, see Rumlu, 113; Röhrborn, 105; Bidlisi, 2: 160; Qummi, *Khulasat*, 1: 224–6; Dickson, 277–8, citing Tahmasp's own memoirs, *Tadhkira-yi Shah Tahmasp*, A. Safari, ed., 2nd ed. (Tehran, 1363), 30, which do not mention the specific prohibitions but record a dream in which Tahmasp received commands on certain matters. For a text of this *firman* inscribed in a Kashan mosque in 1534, see A. Navai, ed., *Shah Tahmasp Safavi, Majmua-i Isnad ba Mukatibat-i Tarikhi . . .* (Tehran, 1368), 513–14. See also Matthee, 'Prostitutes, Courtesans, and Dancing Girls: Women Entertainers in Safavid Iran', in R. Matthee and B. Baron, eds, *Iran and Beyond, Essays in Middle Eastern History in Honor of Nikki R. Keddie* (Costa Mesa, 2000), 145; Keyvani, 129, 133n30; Naraqi, 203f, esp. 211–13, 216–18; Membré, xvi. On the second repentance see Jacobs, 167, 167n18; Qummi, *Khulasat*, 1: 386; Bidlisi, 2: 184; Rumlu, 173; Röhrborn, 105–6, 118. See also n63. Thanks to Dr Sefatgol and Dr Floor for their assistance in checking these dates. For similar *firman*s in 1571 and 1573 in Kashan's 'Imadi mosque, see Naraqi, 214–15, 219–20; A. Kalantar Zarrabi (Suhayl Kashani), *Tarikh-i Kashan*, I. Afshar, ed. (Tehran, 2536), 531–2.

41 Röhrborn, 104, 154–5, Rumlu, 173; Qummi, *Khulasat*, 1: 392, 438, 2: 974, 987; Bidlisi, 2: 183. An Isfahani sayyid had been appointed administrator (*mutavalli*) of the shrine and Mashhad's *Shaykh al-Islam* in 1554 was recalled to court. Röhrburn therefore suggests that provincial governors were charged with the enforcement of religious edicts and that Ibrahim was therefore being charged to act where the Qizilbash governor and these other officials had failed. See also Rumlu, 192; Röhrborn, 106. In 1569–70 another local governor was admonished about corruption and sinful behaviour. See Röhrborn, 106, and Rumlu, 192. The latter cites Tahmasp the same year as dismissing local authorities in Jirun who were 'doing much evil'. Röhrborn also refers (107) to an undated *firman* of Tahmasp appointing the *mutavalli* at the Ardabil shrine and acknowledging irreligious behaviour on the part of the public at large.

42 On the dream, *firman*s and their dates, see Qummi, *Khulasat*, 1: 449–50; Bidlisi, 2: 198. Tahmasp's memoirs (30) link the earlier repentance with a dream. See also Fragner, 6: 545. Floor (*The Economy*, 45) notes that Tahmasp's successors restored the *tamgha*. See also Floor, *A Fiscal*, 149–50, 163, 174, 217f; Woods, 13, 144–5. Thanks to W. Floor for his help in tracking down relevant references. This was about the same time as the position of *sadr* was split, on which see Floor, *A Fiscal*, 89. Babayan (*Mystics*, 309f) also discusses Tahmasp's dreams.

43 In his 1667 *Khuld-i Barin* (M. H. Muhaddath, ed., Tehran, 1372, 280, 482–3), Muhammad Yusuf Valih Isfahani cites Tahmasp as having banned parties at court but may have been conflating this incident with Tahmasp's comment on panegyric poetry, discussed below. See also nn71, 72. See also our discussion of the publishing history of this text in the appendix.

44 Qummi, *Calligraphers*, 163–4; n43 above. See also our discussion below.

45 Secondary sources suggest Tahmasp moderated or suppressed veneration of himself as divine; later copies of Tahmasp's *divan* omitting earlier references proclamation of himself as *mahdi* and similar claims of his predecessors. See, for example, Arjomand, *The Shadow*, 110n9, citing Aubin, 'La Politique', 239, itself unsourced, and later sources. See also Babayan, *Mystics*, 91–2, 100, 297, 312 and 343n60. Indeed, some *firman*s of the period lack the titles for Tahmasp which had been ascribed to Ismail. See Hunarfar, 150–5 and a similar *firman* of 1525 in Tabriz in Naraqi, 216–18. The 1533–4 *firman* cited below also lacked such titles.

46 Hunarfar, 91–4. Cf. Canby, 46; Hillenbrand, 'Safavid Architecture', 6: 770; Blake, 150.

47 For a 1548 coin minted in Yazd, see Rabino, 'Coins of the Shahs of Persia', 370. For an undated coin minted in Qazvin referring to Tahmasp as 'the just sultan', see Rabino, ibid., 369. See also idem, *Coins, Medals and Seals*, 29–30, noting the distinct Shi'i message of the coins, bearing the names of the Imams. On contemporary poetry equating Tahmasp and the Imam, see n70.

48 A. K. S. Lambton, *State and Government in Medieval Islam; An Introduction to the Study of Islamic Political Theory; the Jurists* (London, 1981), 266; Arjomand, *The Shadow*, 179.

49 Canby, 47–9; Hillenbrand, 6: 771. The well-known 'Ardabil carpets' derive their name among Western scholars for likely having been commissioned for the new building. See S. Blair, 'The Ardabil Carpets in Context', in Newman, ed., *Society and Culture*.

50 See further our discussion below, ad n91.

51 This woman, on whom see n54, had been offered to the grandson of the founder of the Nurbakhshi order. She financed a mosque in Taft, in Yazd province, next to a well-known Nimatallahi centre, further underlining the alliance between the court and the order, if not also the dependency of the latter on the former. See Szuppe, 1994, 226, 231, 238, 251; idem, 1995, 117. On Amira Dabbaj, see above ad n36.

52 The son of this union was Mir Ghiyas al-Din Muhammad (d.1589–90). Known as Mir Miran-i Yazdi, he built palaces and sarais in Yazd. His own son married the daughter produced by the union of Ismail II with the daughter born from the union of Tahmasp's sister with Nur al-Din Baqi Yazdi. As brother-in-law Nur al-Din Yazdi mediated between Tahmasp and his brother Alqas during the latter's revolt. Szuppe, 1994, 226, 225; Woods, 16; Graham, 192; Arjomand, *The Shadow*, 116. See also Aubin, 'Shah Ismail', 39–40, 59; Rumlu, 36; Munshi, 1: 123–4.

53 Ghaffari's 1563–4 *Nusakh* and Abdi Bek Shirazi's 1570 *Takmilat al-Akhbar*, on which see n70, play down Abd al-Baqi's Sufi connections, focusing only on his political career. See Quinn, 'Rewriting Nimatallahi History in Safavid Chronicles', in L. Lewisohn and D. Morgan, eds *Late Classical Persianate Sufism*, 201–22, esp. 208–10, where she notes that in his earlier chronicle Khvandamir had specifically discussed the order when recounting Abd al-Baqi's appointment as Ismail's *sadr* and then *vakil*. Graham (192) notes that the famous Nimatallahi poet Vahshi Bafqi (*c.* 1532–83) even composed several poems in honour of Tahmasp. On a Naqshbandi scholar of the time, see Algar, 'Naqshbandis', 16. See also Arjomand, *The Shadow*, 112–13; Babayan, *Mystics*, 114n91.

54 The sister subsequently married into the Nimatallahi order. Munshi, 1: 232. See also Szuppe, 1994, 228; Arjomand, *The Shadow*, 115; Graham, 191.

55 Röhrborn, 144; Szuppe, 1995, 112.

56 Daftary, 'Ismaili-Sufi Relations', 275–89, esp. 287. Cf. Arjomand, *The Shadow*, 113–14.

57 Arjomand, 76–7; Shubbar, 85–7; Röhrborn, 118–20, noting Ahvaz' independence later in the century; Roemer, 6: 216–17. In 1565–6 Tahmasp also suppressed a messianic tribal rising. See Arjomand, 110n10, citing Qummi, *Khulasat*, 1: 455.

58 See M. Bernardini, 'Hatifi's *Timurnamah* and Qasimi's *Shahnamah-yi Ismail*: Considerations for a Double Critical Edition', in Newman, ed., *Society and Culture*, 3–18; B. Wood, 'Shah Ismail and the *Shahnama*', paper presented at the Second Edinburgh *Shahnama* Conference, Edinburgh, March 2003. See also idem, 'The *Shahnamah-yi Ismail*: Art and Cultural Memory in Sixteenth-Century Iran', unpublished PhD dissertation, Harvard University, 2002. On Hatifi see also Abdallah Hatifi, *I Sette scenari*, M. Bernardini, ed. (Napoli, 1995).

The father of Muhammad Mumin, supervisor of Tahmasp's library and the renowned calligrapher who tutored Tahmasp's son Sam Mirza in this art, had also served Sultan Husayn. See D. J. Roxburgh, 'Bahram Mirza and His Collections', in S. Canby, ed., *Safavid Art and Architecture* (London, 2002), 39.

59 Hillenbrand, in Melville, ed., *Safavid Persia*, 69.

60 The illustration 'The Court of Gayumars' occupied Sultan Muhammad for some three years. Canby, 50–1, fig. 33, citing S. C. Welch, *Wonders of the Age* (Cambridge, MA, 1979), 25, 50; Peter Jackson, ed., 6: plate 37 (between pages 808 and 809). See also Welch, 'Art', 623.

61 Hillenbrand, 54–6. This project occupied only a handful of artists whose illustrations are, therefore, more stylistically uniform and far fewer in number than the *Shahnama*. Gray, 6: 885; Canby, 52–4; Welch, 'Art', 623.

62 Canby, 78, citing Munshi. On the dating of Qazvin as the capital, see n9.

63 Canby, 78, 96; Qummi, *Calligraphers*, 142–4, 182–3; Gray, 6: 893. *Chihil Sutun* post-dates Tahmasp's 1533–4 *firman* and his second *tawba* of 1555–6. On Muzaffar Ali, see n72. The walls of a palace completed in Nain *c.* 1565–75, whose owner remains unknown, feature similar scenes and poetry; indeed, six of the eight subjects on these walls feature in Qazvin's *Chihil Sutun*. Their form and content recall Ilkhanid motifs. Gray, 6: 892–4; Canby, 69. On Muzaffar Ali, see also Qummi, *Calligraphers*, 186, 191. On the palace, see also W. Kleiss, 'Chehel Sotun, Qazvin', *EIr*, 6: 116–17.

64 Canby, 72, 74, 76; Gray, 6: 889f. On Ibrahim's artists, see Qummi, *Calligraphers*,

78, 141–4; Gray, 6: 890. See also M. Shreve Simpson, *Sultan Ibrahim Mirza's 'Haft Awrang': A Princely Manuscript from Sixteenth-Century Iran* (New Haven, 1997); Welch, 'Art', 623–4.

65 Canby, 76, noting the distinctive Khurasani styles of manuscript illustration.

66 A *Khamsa* completed in Shiraz in 1548 exhibits the continuing tendency to follow a mainly Timurid style of illustration; after 1560 styles become more complex. See Qummi, *Calligraphers*, 28–9, 30–1, 67, 75, 188, 192–3, 32–4, 183–4, 80, 147, 165, 186, 190; L. Marlow, 'The Peck Shahnameh: Manuscript Production in Late Sixteenth-Century Shiraz', in Mazzaoui and Moreen, eds, 230.

67 Canby, 77 and figs 62, 63. On carpet weaving in Kashan over the period, see also Naraqi, 369–75. On similar patterns in contemporary metalwork, see Canby, 77–8, citing Melikian-Chirvani, *Islamic metalwork*, 263. Qummi's *Calligraphers* attests to the numerous skills of Safavid artisans: calligraphers worked in ceramics, were painters and actively co-operated with builders. See, for example, 24, 60–2, 124–5, 147–8.

A *simurgh* in Persian legend is a gigantic, winged monster in the shape of a bird with the head of a dog and the claws of a lion. By some accounts the creature is immortal and has a nest in the Tree of Knowledge.

68 Canby, 60; Gray, 6: 885–6.

69 Canby, 56–8. See also Canby, 51f; Hillenbrand, 54; Gray, 6: 883.

70 Abdi Bek, an employee of the shah's chancellery who eulogised Tahmasp's *Chihil Sutun* palace at Qazvin and dedicated his chronicle *Takmilat al-Akhbar* to a daughter of Tahmasp, also authored poetry which equated the shah with the Hidden Imam himself. See R. Jafariyan, *Safaviyya dar Arsa-yi Din, Farhang, va Siyasat* (Qum, 1379/2000), 1: 493–503, esp. 496; Szuppe, 1994, 244; Quinn, *Historical*, 18.

71 See Safa, 6: 954; Munshi, 1: 274–5; Qummi, *Calligraphers*, 135; n76 below. Later scholars (e.g. Safa, 6: 955) claim Tahmasp's censure of Muhtasham caused a widespread exodus of Persian poets abroad. In fact, among skilled artisans and scholars travel within the larger realm of 'Persianate culture', particularly Mughal India where Persian was the language of the court, was quite common. See Yarshater, 6: 980; de Bruijn, 774–7, esp. 775. S. Dale, in his 'A Safavid Poet in the Heart of Darkness: The Indian Poems of Ashraf Mazandarani', *IS*, 36(2) (2003), esp. 199–200, dismisses 'Shi'i religious intolerance' in favour of the relative wealth and corresponding 'scale of patronage' as a reason for poets' migration to India (a version of this article is available in Mazzaoui, ed., *Safavid Iran*, 63–80). For other artisans who migrated across 'borders' of their own volition in the later years of Tahmasp's reign, see Qummi, *Calligraphers*, 165–6, 79–80, 81–2, 89, 102–3, 124, 126–31, 138–41, 168, 185, 190. See also Haneda, 'Emigration of Iranian Elites to India During the 16th–18th Centuries', in *L'Héritage Timouride. Iran-Asie Centrale-Inde XVe–XVIIIe siècles*, M. Szuppe, ed. (Tashkent/Aix-en-Provence, 1997), 135. Calmard ('Shi'i Rituals and Power II. The Consolidation of Safavid Shi'ism: Folklore and Popular Religion', in Melville, ed., *Safavid Persia*, 167) notes that Muhtasham in fact remained in Safavid territory and continued to produce important non-religious poetry, including a clever chronogram on the accession of Ismail II. See also Calmard, 'Popular Literature', 329–30; A. Ahmad, 'Safawid Poets and India', *Iran* 14 (1976), 117–32. On Muhtasham's tomb in Kashan, see Naraqi, 191–3. On poets still at court later in Tahmasp's reign, see Qummi, *Calligraphers*, 94–5, 150–1, 154. On Iranian merchants travelling to India, see n10 of Chapter 4.

72 Qummi, *Calligraphers*, 93. See Membré (32, 45) that the Shah's *tawba c.*
    1533–4 did not end revelry. See also Canby, 54–5, (citing Qummi, ibid., 186),
    51–2, 55, 76, pl. 63; Peter Jackson, ed., 6, plate 67 (between pages 872 and 873).
    In *c.* 1573, in Qazvin, Muzaffar Ali and two other younger artists, Zayn al-
    Abidin and Sadiqi Bek Afshar, contributed to an illustrated manuscript of the
    Garshaspnama, a story centring on a ruler in the *Shahnama*; the figures in the
    illustrations recall the long-necked youths found in Qazvin-style portraits of
    the previous decade. See Canby, 83–4; Gray, 6: 891–2. On Muzzafar Ali, who
    taught the painter Siyavush, and his service to the court after Tahmasp's sup-
    posed disenchantment with the arts, see Canby, 51–5; Qummi, *Calligraphers*,
    186, 191. The artist Shaykh Muhammad left Tahmasp's court to serve the
    latter's nephew Ibrahim in Herat. See Canby, 72, 74, 76, 85, 88, 105–7.
73 The court at Yazd supported Vahshi Bafqi who wrote *qasida*s in praise of
    Tahmasp. Shiraz and Kashan also supported literary circles. See the sources cited
    in the preceding notes.
74 She died at Tabriz, owning lands in Shirvan, Tabriz, Qazvin, Rayy, Isfahan. See
    Szuppe, 1994, 234, 238, 243, 244, 245, 247–9, 251; Mudarrissi, *Bargi*, 25;
    Qummi, *Calligraphers*, 146–7. On her political activities, see Rumlu, 139;
    Szuppe, 1995, 67, 76–7.
    Calligraphy albums compiled for Mahin Banu and Tahmasp's brother Bahram
    by the same Dust Muhammad reflected an attempt to project a bridge of continu-
    ity between practitioners of the art from the late seventh century to the late
    1530s. See Gray, 6: 886; D. J. Roxburgh, 'Bahram Mirza', 37–42. On Dust
    Muhammad, see also Gray, 6: 886; Hillenbrand, 'The Iconography', 71n3.
75 Szuppe, 1994, 240, 244.
76 Szuppe, 1994, 241, 244, 248–9, 250. She amassed a great fortune, had her own
    court and was the recipient of Abdi Bek's *Takmilat al-Akhbar*. Muhtasham's
    qasida to her generated her father's disparaging comment about panegyric
    poetry, cited above.
77 Qummi, *Calligraphers*, 93–4, 97–8, 133, 186, 190–1; Gray, 6: 891–2, 897;
    Szuppe, 1994, 237–8; Munshi, 1: 34, 323, 339, 384, 421. The manuscript illus-
    trator Sadiqi Bek was an Afshar. Muhammad Khan Takkalu (d. 1556–7), the
    guardian of Muhammad Khudabanda whose sister-in-law was Tahmasp's Maw-
    sillu wife Sultanum Bekum, Khudabanda's mother, sponsored the painting of the
    inside of the shrine of the Imam Riza in Mashhad by a Herati painter. See
    Szuppe, 1994, 237; Haneda, 111; Qummi, *Calligraphers*, 187.
78 Dickson, 127n1, 178, 147, 261, 277–8. Tahmasp would be buried in Mashhad.
    See also Qummi, *Calligraphers*, 162; Rumlu, 207.
79 Mudarrissi, 21–2, 121f, 130–4. Although distinctly Shi'i in tone, the fullest
    account of Tahmasp's correspondence with the Uzbek Ubayd Khan, dated to
    c. 1530, is found only in the later *Afzal al-Tavarikh*, authored by a Khuzani, and
    hence, as with many such later accounts of earlier events, is to be treated with
    some care. See Dickson, 180–7, esp., 180n1, and 191–3.
80 Calmard, 'Shii Rituals and Power, II', 142–3; Membré, 43, AD 1540; 25–6.
    Although the woman is not identified, it is known that Tahmasp's full sister
    Mahin Banu never married. See above n74.
81 Mudarrissi, 22, 60f, 148f. Canby (154) notes that in 1540–1 Tahmasp presented
    to the Mashhad shrine a set of gold plaques whose design recalled a 1524 set of
    ivory cartouches of ivory produced for Ismail's cenotaph at Ardabil.
82 Hillenbrand, 'Safavid Architecture', 6: 770.

83 Hillenbrand, in Melville, 69–70, 77n75 where the illustration is dated to the mid-1530s, as the Shamlu-Ustajlu regency was giving way to that of the Ustajlu.

84 An illustration from a contemporary copy of Nizami's *Khusraw and Shirin* also features a banner on which is written 'All victory is with God' and a standard with the words 'Allah, Muhammad, Ali'. See U. al-Khamis, 'Khusraw Parviz as Champion of Shi'ism? a Closer Look at an Early Safavid Miniature Painting in the Royal Museum of Edinburgh', in B. O'Kane, ed., *The Iconography of Islamic Art, Studies in Honour of Robert Hillenbrand* (Edinburgh, 2005), 202.

85 Mir Ala al-Mulk (d. 1582), onetime military chaplain to the shah and *sadr* of Gilan after its conquest, was also buried there. Mudarrissi, 21–2, 23–5, 28, 42, 64–70, 121f, 147–50; Munshi, 1: 234.

86 N74 above; Rumlu, 184.

87 Blake, 153; Hunarfar, 369–78. The date of Minshar's arrival in Safavid Iran is not known, nor is his last place of residence. He is, however, known to have been in India for some years. See our 'The Myth', n94. See also n95 and n23 of the following chapter.

88 Blake, 170; Hunarfar, 362.

89 See our 'The Myth', 95f.

Reports of cannibalism during Ismail's reign which began to circulate in this period cannot have encouraged orthodox Twelver clerics. These reports are contained in the 1564–5 *Tarikh-i Ilchi-yi Nizamshah*, on which see n21 of the previous chapter, and were repeated in such later sources as Mirza Hasan Junabadi's 1625–6 *Rawzat al-Safaviyya* (Tehran, 1378/1999, 724). See S. Bashir, 'Sacred Power and Human Embodiment in Fifteenth Century Iranian Religion', paper delivered at the Fourth International Round Table on Safavid Studies, Bamberg, July 2003. Jamali (211–14) cites Junabadi's graphic account (241) of Ismail's command, a century earlier, to his followers to eat the body of Shaybani Khan Uzbek following the Safavids' 1510 defeat of the Uzbeks. By contrast, in his 1577 account Rumlu (54–5) mentions no such incident nor does Munshi, writing in 1616 (1: 62–3). See also Sarwar, 62–3, citing the later *Ross*. See also N. Falsafi, *Zindigani-yi Shah Abbas-i Avval*, 2: 125–7, citing Junabadi who opened the above account (241) by stating 'it is related that', in fact suggesting this was a story he had heard.

Later sources state that after the 1503 battle of Firuzkuh (n21 of the previous chapter) Safavid soldiers ate the flesh of a local commander but only after 'solemn and sworn oaths' guaranteeing the safety of Safavid soldiers had been broken. See, for example, Qummi, *Khulasat*, 83; Munshi, 47–8; Falsafi, 2: 125–6n2, citing Junabadi (177–9). In his earlier chronicle Khvandamir (4: 476–8), however, mentions no such incident. See also Szuppe, 1995, 83n129, citing *Ilchi*, Amir Khvand's 1550 *Tarikh-i Shah Ismail va Shah Tahmasp* and Munshi. Thanks to Dr K. Babayan for directing me to Falsafi.

Standards carried into battle during Tahmasp's reign seem to have featured only the very basic Shi'i declaration 'Ali is the *vali* of Allah; there is no god but Allah'. Allan, *Persian Steel*, 258, citing Munshi, 114; Membré, 1994, 24. See, however, Allan, ibid., 267f, on some standards with more explicitly Shi'i slogans which may date to this period.

90 Not coincidentally, the prayer usually included an invocation of the ruler's name, thus legitimising his rule. On the Ottomans' use of Friday prayer as such, see Allouche, 137.

91 Tahmasp banned recitation of these stories and ordered that storytellers who

refused were to have their tongues cut out. See Babayan, 'Sufis', in Melville, ed., 124–5; idem, 'The Safavid Synthesis', 143–7; Calmard 'Popular Literature', in Newman, ed., *Society and Culture*, 318–21. On Takkalu beliefs, see Calmard, ibid., 336–7.

92 The *firman* is translated by Arjomand in his 'Two Decrees of Shah Tahmasp Concerning Statecraft and the Authority of Shaykh Ali al-Karaki', in Arjomand, ed., *Authority and Political Culture in Shi'ism* (Albany, 1988), 252–6. Cf. Babayan, *Mystics*, 306–7. See also the discussion of Karaki's formulation of the 'general deputyship' ad n67 in the previous chapter.

93 See our 'The Myth', 100–4. Although later Shi'i sources ('The Myth', n80) suggest Karaki expelled all Sunni clerics from the realm, in fact many prominent Sunnis remained, including Mirza Jan Shirazi (d. 1586), another student of Davani. See Munshi, 1: 246; n37 of the following chapter. On the continued presence of less prominent Sunnis in the capital Qazvin, for example, see n35 of the following chapter.

94 See our 'The Myth', ibid. On Ottoman anti-Safavid-propaganda *c.* 1540, see Jafariyan, *Safaviyya dar Arsa-yi Din*, 1: 87f. In his 'Husayn b. Abd al-Samad al-Amili's Treatise for Sultan Suleiman and the Shi'i Shafii Legal Tradition', *Islamic Law and Society*, 4(2) (1997), 156–99, esp. 167–8, D. Stewart suggests Shaykh Husayn and Zayn al-Din's recourse to dissimulation of their faith (*taqiyya*), to pass as Sunni jurists, secured them Ottoman employment. See also Stewart's excellent 'The Genesis of the Akhbari Revival,' in M. Mazzaoui, ed., *Safavid Iran and Her Neighbors* (Salt Lake City, 2003), 182f, especially his reference to Zayn al-Din's criticisms of Iranian scholars' neglect of legal studies (186).

Shaykh Hasan Karaki (d. 1530), whom Stewart ('Notes on the Migration', 88–9) suggested did not visit Iran, is reported as having done so by Qummi in his *Khulasat* (1: 75, 2: 931–2) a reference not, however, cited in 'The Myth', 92n59.

95 Zayn al-Din's young son was not removed to Iran: he and an associate later studied in the shrine cities with Abdallah Yazdi (d. 1573) and Ahmad Ardabili (d. 1585); Yazdi left Iran between 1553 and 1558. See also Newman, 'Towards a Reconsideration of the Isfahan School of Philosophy: Shaykh Bahai and the Role of the Safavid Ulama', *SIr*, 15(2) (1986), 176n35; R. Jafariyan, 'Munasibat-i Isfahan va Hijaz dar Dawrah-yi Safavi', paper delivered at the conference Isfahan and the Safavids, Isfahan, February, 2002, 13–14. On these and Hijazi Twelvers who avoided Safavid entanglements in this period, see our 'The Myth', 104–8. Soon after his arrival in Iran Shaykh Husayn contracted a marriage alliance with his fellow Arab Ali Minshar on whom see also n87 and n23 of the following chapter. Shaykh Husayn's son Shaykh Bahai (d. 1620–1), Minshar's son-in-law, also reported his father as having interpreted a *hadith* as referring to the appearance of Ismail I (Qummi, *Khulasat* 1: 75). On scholarly criticisms of Zayn al-Din and Ali Karaki, – the former as having adopted Sunni juristic methodologies – see nn137, 138 of Chapter 4.

96 Shaykh Husayn, having pleaded for another post, was later appointed *Shaykh al-Islam* of Mashhad and then, *c.* 1567, of Herat where he served some nine years. He performed the pilgrimage but chose not to return to Iran and died in Bahrayn in 1576. See D. Stewart, 'The First *Shaykh al-Islam* of the Safavid Capital Qazvin', *Journal of the American Oriental Society*, 116(3) (1996), 387–405; Newman, 'Towards', 169–72; Munshi, 1: 233. Stewart (394) quotes a later poem written by Shaykh Husayn to his son Shaykh Bahai, who would have been about thirteen when his father brought him to Iran and who was not

permitted to accompany his father on the *hajj*, in which Shaykh Husayn appears to have regretted his Safavid associations. On Ali Karaki's son, see Stewart, 395, citing Munshi, 1: 244–5. Sayyid Husayn's Lebanese father, who died in 1530, never emigrated to Safavid territory (Newman, 'The Myth', 91–4). On Shaykh Husayn's supposed Akhbari tendencies, see Stewart, 'The Genesis', 186–8. On the Karaki family see also Jafariyan, 'Nufuz-i Davistsalih-yi Khandan-i Muhaqqiq-i Karaki dar Dawlat-i Safaviyya', paper presented at the Fourth International Round Table on Safavid Persia, Bamberg, July 2003, 17f. On Friday prayer, see further our 'Fayz al-Kashani and the Rejection of the Clergy/State Alliance: Friday Prayer as Politics in the Safavid Period', in L. Walbridge, ed., *The Most Learned of the Shi'a*, (New York, 2001), 34–52, esp. 34; Stewart, 398; Arjomand, 'Two Decrees', 253; n90.

 97   Dickson, 247, citing Qummi's 1590 *Khulasat* and Junabadi's 1625–6 *Rawzat al-Safaviyya*.
 98   Budaq Qazvini, 231; A. Soudavar, 'The Early Safavids and Their Cultural Interactions with Surrounding States' in N. Keddie and R. Matthee, eds, *Iran and the Surrounding World* (Seattle and London, 2002), 103–5.
 99   Rumlu, 176–7, 182, 184, 186–92, 195, 197–8; Keyvani, 154–5. Savory, 'Ismail II', *EI²*, 4: 188; Munshi (1: 125) implies Tahmasp's fear that his son might move against him.
100   On Bashkent, see especially Woods, 87–9.

3 The Second Civil War: Ismail II (1576–1577) and Khudabanda (1578–1587)

 1   Szuppe, 1994, 230; 1995, 107–8.
 2   Haydar's guardian was his relative Masum Bek Safavi, whose son took his place at Masum Bek's death.
 3   Haneda, 131, 134. See also Szuppe, 'Kinship Ties', 82–3; idem, 1994, 234, 238; 1995, 107. The account herein is drawn from such contemporary sources as Rumlu (202f, 292–3) and Qummi (*Khulasat*, 1: 609f, 2: 626–7). See also Haneda, 128, citing W. Hinz, 'Schah Esmail II. Ein Beitrag zur Geschichte der Safaviden', *Mitteilungen des Seminars für orientalische Sprachen* 26 (1933), 19–100, esp. 46–7; Szuppe, 1995, 77f; Savory, *Iran Under*, 69; Roemer, 6: 250–1.
 4   Munshi, 1: 217.
 5   Munshi, 1: 315f, 323, 327–8. Among the Takkalu, Musayyib Khan, related both to the Safavid house by blood – his mother was Ismail II's aunt – and to the Mawsillu by marriage, was promoted to khan, affianced to a daughter of Tahmasp, designated ruler of the tribe and given lands around Rayy. Other Takkalu amirs held lands in nearby Hamadan, and the Turkman, related to the Takkalu, held land in Kashan and Qum. See Szuppe, 'Kinship Ties', 86f; idem, 1994, 237–8; n 10. See also Munshi, 1: 34, 323, 339, 384, 421. Compare Bidlisi, 2: 222.
 6   Rumlu, 204–9. Qummi, *Khulasat*, 1: 603, 607, 609, 2: 615–33. See also Szuppe, 'Kinship Ties', 82–3; Qummi, *Calligraphers*, 10–11. Szuppe (1995, 82–3) notes that in the Turco-Mongolian system any male family member might claim succession. The murder of potential pretenders and their allies was a 'new' feature of the period; indeed, Tahmasp had not ordered the murder of his half-brother Alqas. The Ottomans also followed a policy of 'political'

murder. See Munshi, 2: 1288; Mazzaoui, 'The Religious Policy of Safavid Shah Ismail II', in Mazzaoui and Moreen, eds, 54–5; Roemer, 6: 251. In her 'Mirza Makhdum Sharifi: A 16th Century Sunni *sadr* at the Safavid Court' (unpublished Ph D thesis, New York University, 1993), 105–7, R. Stanfield suggests that Ismail II's actions bespeak awareness of threats to his precarious hold on the leadership posed by family members, his own experience of having been arrested by his father and the earlier revolts of the Alqas and Sam Mirza. Rumlu (204–5) notes Ismail was even suspicious of those who freed him from prison.

7   Rumlu, 210–11, 295; Szuppe, 1995, 83–4, 84n137; Qummi, *Calligraphers*, 10–11. Rumlu (211) notes Ismail took opium to relieve recurrent colic. See also Munshi, 1: 336–41; Roemer, 6: 252–3; Savory, *Iran Under*, 69–70.

8   Rumlu, 212–13; Qummi, *Khulasat*, 2: 656–69; Munshi, 327–9; Szuppe, 1994, ibid.; Bidlisi, 2: 223–4; Roemer, 6: 253–5.

9   Szuppe, 1995, 68–9. Other Shirazi allies of the Shamlu were among the key Tajik administrators of Khudabanda's reign (ibid., 68–70). Khudabanda's first wife was the granddaughter of Qadi Jahan Qazvini and a Gilani notable. See Szuppe, 1994, 230; idem, 1995, 108.

10   Khayr al-Nisa also had removed Kashan province from Turkman tribal control and had executed a family rival who had been given protection from the Ustajlu commander sent to quell his rebellion. Qummi, *Khulasat*, 2: 658, 662, 693–7; Qummi, *Calligraphers*, 95n294; Szuppe, 1995, 84–100. Röhrborn (199) suggests that Khayr al-Nisa also tried to seize other provinces for the centre. On the careful role of Musayyib Khan Takkalu in these events, see Szuppe ('Kinship Ties', 89–90). Szuppe notes (1995, 97n208) the Ustajlu complainants included a relative of Tahmasp.

11   Bidlisi, 2: 228–9, 245–6; Savory, *Iran Under*, 73–5; Roemer, 6: 259–61; Röhrborn, 200–1.

12   Szuppe, 1995, 108. Qummi, *Khulasat* (2: 848–63) and Bidlisi (2: 248–9) give October 1587; compare Savory, 75; Roemer, 6: 261; McChesney, 'A Note', 63. Some accounts suggest Khudabanda remained in Qazvin for a time and was then blinded, with his other sons, Abbas' younger brothers, Abu Talib and Tahmasp, and died nine years later in the city. On a marriage alliance between Murshid Quli Khan and the Turkman, see further below ad n47.

13   Bidlisi, 2: 223f; Roemer, 6: 257–8, 266; Savory, 71–5; n11.

14   Floor, *Safavid Government*, 12, 14–15.

15   Floor, ibid., 141. The post of sealkeeper was held mainly by the Dhul-Qadr into the late 1630s. See Floor, ibid., 70–2 and our discussion on Pari Khan's uncle Shamkhal Sultan below.

The *qurchis*, not independent of direct Qizilbash control, were also not a major military force. Over Tahmasp's reign the total number of Qizilbash troops numbered between 85,000 and 100,000. Since large numbers of these troops were stationed in the provinces and mustering them took time, a smaller force, *c*. 60,000, might appear. This force might in practice also include Kurdish, Georgian and other non-Qizilbash tribal elements whose leaders owed allegiance to the centre. By comparison, at Tahmasp's death in 1576 Munshi (1: 228) numbered 'the *qurchis* of the royal bodyguard' at *c*. 4,500; other sources cite 3,000. In this period Safavid princes also had their own *qurchis* whose commanders, like the centre's *qurchibashi*, were all Qizilbash amirs. See Minorsky, *Tadhkirat*, 15, 32; Röhrborn, 70–7; Haneda, 105–10, 144–53, 171f, esp. 176n57; Floor, ibid., 133–7.

16 Under Ismail II, Ali Quli Khan Shamlu (d. 1588–9), the grandson of Durmish Khan Shamlu, who had married a daughter of Haydar (Szuppe, 1994, 224), and himself was married to Abbas' aunt Zaynab Bekum (Szuppe, 1995, 118; Munshi, 1: 316), was sent to Herat as both governor and Abbas' guardian with an order from Ismail II and Khayr al-Nisa to murder his charge; this was voided by their deaths. Ali Quli Khan was also married to another tribal daughter (Szuppe, 1994, 239), and both of his sons married into the Safavid household (Szuppe, 1994, 224). Bidlisi (2: 228–9) mentions an Ustajlu governor of Khvaf, a Qajar governor of Mashhad and a Rumlu governor of Nishapur. That Rumlu, who completed his universal history *Ahsan al-Tavarikh* just after the accession of Muhammad Khudabanda in 1577, referred so highly to Ismail I, Tahmasp and Khudabanda suggests continued tribal support for the house. See Quinn, *Historical*, 18.

   During Khudabanda's reign Safavid Iraq was divided among tribal amirs. The governor of Kashan was a Turkman (Röhrborn, 40, 43) and Ardabil and its dependencies and Hamadan were held by Ustajlu chiefs (Qummi, *Khulasat*, 2: 851f). The Shamlu and Ustajlu held key areas in Khurasan in this period as well. The Dhul-Qadr held the governorship of Qum and Kashan as well as Shiraz (Qummi, *Khulasat*, ibid.). Khuy was held by a Mawsillu and Shirvan by a Rumlu (Rumlu, 213; Bidlisi, 2: 225–6). In 1579–80, the Afshar governor of Qarabagh and the Mawsillu governor of Tabriz beat back the Ottoman challenge (Bidlisi, ibid.). Provincial officials might reside outside their assigned provinces (Röhrborn, 44).

17 Aubin, 'Shah Ismail', 76–7; Savory, *Iran Under*, 70–2, 74, 76; Munshi, 1: 256–7, 417–20; Roemer, 6: 254f; Floor, *Safavid Government*, 37. See also Szuppe, 1995, 84–5, 88–9, 95, 100; S. Gholsorkhi, 'Pari Khan Khanum: A Masterful Safavid Princess', *IS*, 28(3–4) (1995), 143–56; K. Babayan, 'The "Aqaid al-Nisa": A Glimpse at Safavid Women in Local Isfahani Culture', in G. Hambly, ed., *Women in the Medieval Islamic World, Power, Patronage and Piety* (London, 1998), 353f; Bidlisi, 2: 223–4; Floor, 'Judicial', 48. Jabiri was succeeded by another Tajik. See Floor, 37; Munshi, 1: 259.

18 Shah Inayatallah Isfahani, member of a prominent Isfahani family of sayyids and *naqib*s who had held the post of military chaplain under Tahmasp, was *sadr al-ikhassa* under Ismail II. He was dismissed under Khudabanda but was allowed to return to Isfahan. See Aubin, 'Shah Ismail', 79–80; Munshi, 1: 237–8; Floor, 'sadr', 480.

19 Floor, *Safavid Government*, 36, 42; Qummi, *Calligraphers*, 99; Munshi, 1: 254–6; Savory, 'Offices … Tahmasp', 76; Röhrborn, 156–7; Haneda, 'La Famille Khuzani', 86. The son of the Tajik sayyid *Shaykh al-Islam* in Shiraz under Tahmasp came to court during Khudabanda's reign, was made military chaplain and enjoyed the shah's special favour. See Munshi, 1: 237.

20 Qummi, *Calligraphers*, 97, 97n304; Munshi, 2: 1319; Floor, *Safavid Government*, 37. Another family member was *vizier* of the Takkalu sealkeeper and later became *vizier* of Khurasan (Aubin, 63). A Husayni sayyid relative of the Abd al-Vahhabi sayyids was inspector general (*muhtasib al-mamalik*), a post with roots in early Islamic history, under Tahmasp and into the early years of Abbas I's reign (Munshi, 1: 239; Aubin, 56; Keyvani, 68–70). A relative was mayor (*kalantar*) of Tabriz during Khudabanda's reign under a Mawsillu governor (Munshi, 1: 239–40). For other Tajik officials who kept their posts over this period, see also Munshi, 1: 246, 257; Qummi, *Calligraphers*, 99. On physicians,

poets, calligraphers, see Munshi, 1: 263–5, 266f. On the *kalantar*, see Keyvani, 65–6; Floor, 'Judicial', 45–9.

   Budaq Munshi Qazvini, in his universal history to the year 1576, *Javahir al-Akhbar*, having traced Tahmasp's line back to Imam Musa (102–3), then dedicated its conclusion to Ismail II (238), perhaps to secure an appointment under the new ruler. See also Nizhad's preface (17, 27, 30) and the text itself (58). The published text commences with a history of the Qaraquyunlu. Qazvini's grandfather had served the Aqquyunlu and he himself served in minor official posts during Tahmasp's reign.

21 The Husayni sayyid Mirza Ibrahim Hamadani, for example, was a *qadi* in Hamadan during Tahmasp's last years, through the civil war and into Abbas I's reign. See Munshi, 1: 261, 1: 239, 1: 240–1.

22 Mudarrissi, *Bargi*, 151–2.

23 Munshi, 1: 233, 234–5; Newman, 'Mir Damad', *EIr*, 6: 623–6. As noted above, Shaykh Husayn Amili had been dismissed as Qazvin's *Shaykh al-Islam* in favour of Sayyid Husayn Karaki. Stewart suggests that after the 1576 death of Ali Minshar, Isfahan's *Shaykh al-Islam* and Shaykh Husayn's son-in-law, Shaykh Husayn's son Baha al-Din, known as Shaykh Bahai, succeeded Minshar. See his 'The Lost Biography of Baha al-Din al-Amili and the Historiography of Safavid Shah Ismail II's Reign', *IS*, 31(2) (1998), 187–8. See also Munshi (1: 234–6, 247). In 1577 Bahai declared his loyalty to Khudabanda by dedicating to him an essay on weights and measures, a standard work. See Aqa Buzurg Muhammad Muhsin Tehrani, *al-Dharia ila Tasanif al-Shi'a* (Tehran and Najaf, 1353–98), 23: 321. On Minshar, see also n87 of Chapter 2.

24 Several of Tahmasp's daughters had married Georgians and Circassians. See also n33 of the previous chapter; Szuppe, 1995, 84–9; Floor, *Safavid Government*, 72.

25 The fortunes of these elements fluctuated with those of their patrons: Shamkhal Sultan fell as his niece Pari Khan was challenged. At Hamza's murder Farhad Bek was imprisoned and his palace was plundered by Khudabanda's Afshar troops. After Abbas I was enthroned Farhad Bek became agent of Murshid Quli Khan Ustajlu, Abbas' prime supporter. At the latter's murder in 1588 Farhad Bek was again jailed, lost all his goods, was poisoned and died; his mansion was remade into a palace. See Munshi, 1: 493–5, 594–6; Qummi, *Khulasat*, 2: 852–3, 855–7, 873, 895; Blake, 86–8, citing, esp., Mahmud b. Hedayatallah Afushta Natanzi, *Nuqavat al-Asar*, E. Eshraqi, ed., 2nd ed. (Tehran, 1373), 233–42. The latter was completed in 1598. See Quinn, *Historical*, 20; R. McChesney, 'Four Sources on Shah Abbas's Building of Isfahan', *Muqarnas 5* (1988), 105.

26 Szuppe, 1994, 224, 225–6, 233; 1995, 77f, 108, 111–13, 115–16; Haneda, 78n124.

27 Szuppe, 1994, 225, 239; 1995, 114–15, 117; Munshi, 1: 232. Khalilallah's father, Mir Miran (d. 1589–90), maintained ties to some rebel Afshar elements supportive of Hamza when Abbas I's star was in the ascendancy. Though he himself paid for this error in judgement, as so often in Safavid history the centre's anger with the father did not visit itself on his sons: Khalilallah himself held a post in Yazd and a son married two of Tahmasp's daughters. Szuppe, 1994, 225–8, 237; 1995, 114, 117; Munshi, 1: 232. On a later Yazdi-Afshar marriage alliance, see Chapter 4 ad n30.

28 The family had given refuge to the young Ismail when he was fleeing from the Aqquyunlu. Maryam's daughter would marry her cousin Abbas I – both were

grandchildren of Tahmasp. See Szuppe, 1995, 229, 229n86, 231, 239; 1995, 114. The marriage with Khan Ahmad Khan may have followed the short-lived effort to appoint a governor in the area. See Roemer, 6: 245. See also Röhrborn, 163, on a 1567–8 *firman* attaching Gilan to Khurasan.

29 Szuppe, 1994, 219; 239–40.

30 Szuppe, 1994, 218, 222, 236n112, 240.

31 Szuppe, 1994, 219, 223–4, 237, 239; 1995, 116. On Tahmasp's daughters, see also Szuppe, 1994, 239; 1995, 110; Szuppe, 'Kinship Ties', 86. Compare Savory, 'Tahmasp', *EI²*, 10: 110; Munshi, 2: 1244.

32 Szuppe, 1994, 232; 1995, 115.

33 In their 1577 and 1590 chronicles respectively, Rumlu and Qummi consistently refer to the Hidden Imam's deputy solely with reference to the latter's leading the Friday prayer in place of the Imam, in which prayer the ruler's name would have been mentioned, and his position thus legitimised by, the Hidden Imam's representative. Absent are references to any other of the deputy's jurisprudential and practical duties and responsibilities, the latter including, for example, the collection and distribution of believers' alms and tithes. See n90 of the previous chapter; nn67, 68 of Chapter 1; Newman, 'The Myth', n55.

34 At his recovery Tahmasp treated both sons with leniency. See Qummi, *Calligraphers*, 164. The Nuqtavi rising was put down by the local Mawsillu governor. After the Andijan rising the Nizari Ismailis adopted a form of dissimulation (*taqiyya*) which allowed them to pose as Twelver Shi'a for the remainder of the Safavid period; the imam of this period married a Safavid princess. In 1627 Abbas I exempted the Andijan Shi'a from certain taxes. Amoretti, 6: 644–6; Arjomand, *The Shadow*, 198–9; Daftary, 'Ismaili-Sufi Relations', 287–8; A. Amanat, 'The Nuqtavi Movement of Mahmud Pisikhani and his Persian Cycle of Mystical-materialism', in F. Daftary, ed., *Medieval Ismaili History and Thought* (Cambridge, 1996), 290. See also Eshraqi, ' "*Noqtaviyya*" à l'époque Safavides' in Newman, ed., *Society and Culture*, 341–9; Melville, 'New Light', 83–4, on the order's suppression according to Khuzani's *Afzal al-Tavarikh*.

35 Johnson, in her 'Sunni Survival in Safavid Iran: Anti-Sunni Activities during the Reign of Tahmasp I', *IS*, 27(1–4) (1994), esp. 127–33, notes that in his later years Tahmasp pursued a stricter anti-Sunni policy in the capital of Qazvin, including, for example, a differential taxation policy for Qazvin's Sunni and Shi'i population. She also notes that those who could afford bribes could escape harassment. See also Stanfield, 74–85. Kashan is also known to have been a Sunni centre. See also R. A. Jurdi, 'Migration and Social Change: The Ulama of Ottoman Jabal Amil in Safavid Iran, 1501–1736' (unpublished PhD dissertation, Yale University, 1998), 146–7, 156, 158; Jafariyan, *Safaviyya dar Arsa-yi Din*, 1: 81. On the Naqashbandis' continuing influence in Qazvin in this period, see Algar, 'Naqshbandis', 21–3, 27.

36 Munshi, 1: 237, 2: 703, 703n9; Stanfield, 32f, 91–4. See also S. Gholsorkhi, 'Ismail II and Mirza Makhdum Sharifi: An Interlude in Safavid History', *IJMES* 26 (1994), 477–88; Jurdi, 144f; Aubin, 'Shah Ismail', 80; Jafariyan, *Safaviyya dar Arsa-yi Din*, 1: 74–80, 452–64; Floor '*sadr*', 480; n18 above.

37 Ismail II was said to have consorted with Sunni darvishes and, following his accession, to have objected to the ritual Shi'i cursing of the first three caliphs and the Prophet's wife Aisha, to have ordered poetry praising the Imams erased from the capital's mosques, to have ordered protection for Mirza Makhdum when he delivered a sermon, to have punished any who cursed the caliphs, to have shown

favour to such other Iranian Sunni scholars as Mirza Jan Shirazi, to have reclaimed land grants given to prominent sayyids and Shiʻi clerics and to have urged these to turn to the Sunni Shafii school. See Gholsorkhi, ibid.; Aubin, 'Shah Ismail', 79–80, 69–70; Qummi, *Khulasat*, 1: 607; Munshi, 1: 213–18, 237; 319–23; Szuppe, 1995, 108; Mazzaoui, 'The Religious Policy', 49–56, esp. 53, citing Rumlu; Stanfield, esp. 95f; Stanfield-Johnson, 65–67. On Mirza Jan, a well-known Sunni teacher in Shiraz during Tahmasp's reign who came to court during Ismail II's reign but fled to India at the latter's death, see nn39, 40; n93 of the previous chapter; Munshi, 1: 246.

When Sayyid Husayn Karaki opposed changing the Shiʻi inscriptions on the realm's coins the shah is said to have plotted the death of both Sayyid Husayn and Ali Karaki's son. See D. Stewart, 'The Lost Biography', esp. 180–3, 196–203. The latter work addresses Hinz, 'Schah Esmaʻil II', long the standard work on Ismail II, and other primary-language sources on Ismail's II anti-Shiʻi activities. See also Gholsorkhi, 'Ismail II', 480–5, esp. 482; Jurdi, 'Migration and Social Change', 144–58; Stanfield, esp. 98–9; Munshi, 1: 214. Floor (*The Economy*, 78) notes that coins minted under Ismail II did not feature the formal Shiʻi profession of faith (*shahada*) but attested simply to the sufficiency of 'Ali and his family' and that at Ismail's death, the Shiʻi *shahada* was reinstated. Cf. Munshi, 1: 324. For a cleric who fled to India as a result of Ismail's pro-Sunni policy, see Munshi, 1: 234.

38 Stanfield (103–4) cites Bidlisi (2: 222) that Ismail wanted to reconcile Sunnis and Shiʻis to each other. See also ibid, 105. On the treaty, see Roemer, 6: 252.

39 Munshi names some Mawsillu-Turkman and Takkalu amirs as concerned with Ismail's Sunni sympathies; based on their subsequent support for Ismail II as he moved against Mirza Makhdum and for Khudabanda's succession, Ustajlu, Shamlu, Dhul-Qadr and Afshar elements may have expressed similar concerns. See, especially, Munshi, 1: 317–30, esp. 320–3. See also Gholsorkhi, 480, 483–4; Stanfield, 116; Stewart, 200; Qummi, *Khulasat*, 2: 648–9; Mazzaoui, ibid., 54. Ibrahim b. Malik, whose father had served Ibrahim b. Bahram in Mashhad and returned to Qazvin at Tahmasp's request to embellish the palaces there, fled Iran at this point as well (Qummi, *Calligraphers*, 145) as did Mirza Jan Shirazi, on whom see n37. On Musayyib Khan Takkalu's role, see Szuppe, 'Kinship Ties', 88–9. Stanfield (119–38) analyses Mirza Makhdum's theological and jurisprudential arguments with key Shiʻi doctrines.

40 Ahmad Ardabili, who had himself studied under Mirza Jan Shirazi, remained in the Ottoman-controlled shrine cities throughout the civil war, as did his two prominent students Shaykh Zayn al-Din's own son Hasan (d. 1602–3) and his relative and associate Sayyid Muhammad Amili (d. 1600). Both later abandoned a pilgrimage to Mashhad for fear Abbas I would press them into government service. Ardabili also challenged Karaki's writings on accepting remuneration from the court but his departure from Iran likely stemmed from his rejection of certain Sufi beliefs in the potential for unification with the divine and the manifestation of the divine in the human belief which Ismail I especially had encouraged. See J. Cooper, 'Some Observations on the Religious Intellectual Milieu of Safawid Persia', in F. Daftary ed., *Intellectual Traditions in Islam* (London, 2000), 149; J. Cooper, ed. and transl., 'The Muqaddas al-Ardabili on *taqlid*', in Arjomand, ed., *Authority and Political Culture*, 263–6. On Hijaz- and Gulf-based scholars' continued rejection of Safavid entanglements in this period, see our 'The Myth', esp. 104–8; R. Jafariyan, 'Munasibat', 13–14. See also n95 of

Chapter 2. On the tolerance of the Ottomans to Shi'i clerics, see M. Salati, 'Toleration, Persecution and Local Realities: Observations on the Shi'ism in the Holy Places and the Bilad al-Sham (16th–17th centuries)', *Convegno sul Tema La Shi''a Nell'Impero Ottomano* (Roma, 1993) 121–48.

41 One of these movements proposed an attack on Ottoman territory. See R. Savory, 'A Curious Episode of Safavid History', in C. E. Bosworth, ed., *Iran and Islam* (Edinburgh, 1971), 461–73, citing Munshi, 1: 401f. Qizilbash tribes active in crushing these risings included elements of the Afshar, Dhul-Qadr and Takkalu.

42 Hillenbrand, 'Safavid Architecture', 6: 773–4. See Hunarfar, 164–5, 389–91. See also Hunarfar, 134–5, for a distinctly Twelver Shi'i style inscription in Isfahan's Congregational Mosque dating to 1584. See also Blake, 150.

43 Tahmasp's body was interred there before being moved to Mashhad. Some of the princes killed at Ismail II's accession were also buried in Qazvin. Ismail II's body remained in the Qazvin shrine until 1587 when Abbas I removed it to the shrine of Imam Riza himself in Mashhad. Khayr al-Nisa was also buried in Qazvin, until Abbas moved her also to Mashhad. The wife of Salman Khan Ustajlu, a daughter of Tahmasp, was buried in the Qazvin shrine at her death in 1583. At his death Khudabanda's Inju *sadr* was also buried in the Qazvin shrine. See Mudarrissi, *Bargi*, 25–8.

44 On these artists, see Qummi, *Calligraphers*, 191, 187, 191, 7, 188, 138–40. Canby, 80f, esp. 83–5. On Shaykh Muhammad, see Canby, 72, 74, 76, 85, 88, 105–7, and our discussion in the previous chapter. Soudavar (105, citing Budaq Qazvini), notes that Ismail II sent some fifty illustrated manuscripts to the Ottoman Murad III who launched the series of incursions into Iran noted above, probably, as with his Sunni 'flirtation', to forestall such incursions. See also Welch, 'Art', 624. On Ismail II's *Shahnama*, see B. Robinson, 'Ismail II's Copy of the *Shahnama*', *Iran*, 14 (1976), 1–8, esp. 1 and 6–7, where Robinson lists the painters who contributed to the project.

45 Gray, 6: 891–2; Canby, *The Golden*, 89; 87; idem, *The Rebellious Reformer. The Drawings and Paintings of Riza-yi Abbasi of Isfahan* (London, 1996), 23.

46 Canby, *The Golden*, 88–90; Gray, 6: 896.

47 Szuppe, 1995, 113; Canby, *The Golden*, 87–8; Haneda, 121; Qummi, *Khulasat*, 2: 1024. Ibrahim's wife, Gawhar Sultan Khanum, Ismail II's own half-sister, destroyed much of her husband's library to deny it to her half-brother. See Qummi, *Calligraphers*, 184.

48 Canby, *The Golden*, 88–90. Evolution in carpet design is discernible over the latter half of the century. In Herati carpets the appearance of Chinese scroll clouds and large palmettes echoes similar ornaments on ceramics in the last decades of the century. These suggest continued interaction between carpet design and ceramics, bookbinding and manuscript illustration. See Canby, *The Golden*, 90–1.

49 From 1576 to 1580 Qummi was *vizier* to the chief financial administrator. He was *vizier* to a Takkalu *amir* when, in 1581, Khudabanda appointed him administrator of *vaqf*. Qummi, *Calligraphers*, 12, 15; Haneda, 123–4. He completed his *Calligraphers c.* 1596–7.

50 Savory, *Iran Under*, 67–8.

4 Monumental Challenges and Monumental Responses: The Reign of Abbas I (1587–1629)

1 Abbas' Ustajlu patron Murshid Quli Khan was soon designated the sixteen-year-old shah's *vakil*. The Ustajlu chief – whose own Tajik *vizier* was designated Abbas' *vizier* – was allotted the province of Isfahan, which had been the personal holding of Tahmasp and then of his grandsons Hamza and Abu Talib. The Ustajlu were also entrusted with guarding Khudabanda and his son, Abbas' full brother, Abu Talib. See the sources in the following notes.

2 Munshi, 2: 557; 548–9; Szuppe, 1995, 113–14; Floor, *Safavid Government*, 13, 37.

3 Munshi (2: 559–60) suggests that many Shamlu and Shi'a were killed when Herat fell. The Uzbeks approached Mashhad, where Murshid Quli Khan's brother was governor, but withdrew, as they often had during Tahmasp's reign, at the rumoured approach of a Safavid army.

4 Khudabanda died in 1595. Among the Tajik allies of Murshid Quli Khan killed was Abu Talib's Tajik *vizier* Mirza Muhammad Kirmani, of the Tabrizi Kujuji sayyids, who was Abbas' first *vizier*. Munshi, 2: 551–60, 577–81, 612, 1319; Qummi, *Khulasat*, 2: 669.

5 Those who challenged Abbas included the governor of Shiraz, Yaqub Khan Dhul-Qadr, in alliance with Takkalu, Turkman, Shamlu, and Afshar amirs. Even the governor of Isfahan, Yuli Bek, the *ghulam* of Hamza who had replaced Farhad Bek, associated himself with the claims of Abbas' two brothers. In *c.* 1593–14 Rustam Mirza (d. after 1616–17), a great-grandson of Ismail I via the latter's son Bahram, organised a revolt in Sistan. Deserted by his Qizilbash supporters, Rustam fled to India where Akbar (reg. 1556–1605) encouraged his anti-Abbas activities. Munshi, 2: 585, 591, 595–604, 612, 659–60, 692, 1177; Natanzi, 374–5; Szuppe, 1995, 108.

6 On the role of the son of the *sadr*, Mir Miran, of the Nimatallahi sayyid family which had provided administrators since Ismail I's reign, see Munshi, 2: 551–5, 599–601. See also n120.

7 These were accused of collaboration with the Ottomans during the occupation of Tabriz. See Savory, 'A Curious Episode', 469; idem, 'The Office of *Khalifat al-Khulafa* under the Safavids', *Journal of the American Oriental Society*, 85 (1965), 497–502, esp. 501. See also Floor, 'Khalifeh', 70; n122.

8 N34 of the previous chapter.

9 Eshraqi, 347–8; Babayan, 'The Waning', 46–64, noting (citing Munshi 2: 648) the influence of astrology in these events; idem, *Mystics*, 3–6, 90–3, 103f. See also Munshi, 2: 646–50; Natanzi, 514–28. Both Munshi (2: 647) and Natanzi (515) attest to Darvish Khusraw's widespread popularity.

10 Munshi, 2: 649–50. Babayan ('The Waning', 62) notes apparent Shamlu involvement. See Amanat, 'The Nuqtavi Movement', 281–97, esp. 290f; Arjomand, *The Shadow*, 198–9, 74; Babayan, ibid., 175f. On the later account of Fazli Isfahani, who commenced his three-volume history of the Safavids in 1616–17, see Melville, 'New Light', 83–4; Abrahams, 'A Historiographical Study', 103f. A. Dadvar (*Iranians in Mughal Politics and Society, 1606–1658* (New Delhi, 2000, 217) mentions several Nuqtavi poets who fled to India during this period although elsewhere (203f, 211f) he suggests economic reasons for their flight. Indeed, of those artisans and craftsmen whose reasons for travel to India are known in this period most left for economic reasons (293–8). For a further

example thereof, see also E. Lambourn's 'Of Jewels and Horses: the Career and Patronage of an Iranian Merchant under Shah Jahan', *IS*, 36(2) (2003), esp. 221. In his 'Emigration of Iranian Elites to India During the 16th–18th Centuries' (in *L'Héritage Timouride. Iran-Asie Centrale-Inde XVe-XVIIIe siècles*, M. Szuppe, ed. (Tashkent/Aix-en-Provence, 1997), esp. 131f, 135f, Haneda notes the high percentage of Iranians among the Mughal elite, adding that such immigration was not limited to a specific period in Safavid history and noting that many went to India of their own free will and kept contact with their homeland. See also n128 below and n49 of chapter six.

The details of contemporary Nuqtavi discourse provided by such hostile sources as Munshi and Natanzi ought to be judged with some care. See, for example, Babayan, *Mystics*, 19–20, 47–54. See also Babayan, ibid., 57f, 67f for a reconstruction of that discourse based on later and unidentified Nuqtavi sources.

11 See our 'Towards', 177–8.
12 Munshi, 2: 583–4, 587–8, 612f; Roemer, 6: 266–7. That the 1555 Amasya treaty had stipulated similar restrictions suggests the reappearance of this practice, perhaps following 'the Sunni interlude' discussed in the previous chapter.
13 Munshi, 2: 602f, 609f; Quinn, 'The Historiography', 14.
14 Munshi, 2: 597. Röhrborn (48–9) dated their creation as a corps under Abbas to 1587 or 1590, but such elements had formed a small force under Tahmasp. See Floor, *Safavid Government*, 166f; n15 of Chapter; 3; n33 of Chapter 2; n33 below.
15 Pietro Della Valle, the Italian patrician who spent four years in Iran from 1617, even meeting Abbas I, numbered the *ghulam*s at 30,000, of whom half were soldiers. See Floor, *Safavid Government*, 170; Röhrborn, 77. Chardin, however, albeit later, estimated that 1,000 *ghulam*s served the shah and 3,000 eunuchs resided at the court. See Babaie, et al., *Slaves of the Shah*, 15. On Chardin's reliability, see n44 of Chapter 5 below, and n14 of our Introduction. The post of *qullaraqasi*, head of the *ghulam*s, held for some years by the Armenian *ghulam* Allahvirdi Khan himself, receives decidedly little attention by Munshi; it is not listed as one of the realm's key posts (2: 1317f) and is mentioned only occasionally in the text of his chronicle itself (e.g. 597). The other *qullaraqasi*s of the period included the first, a Dhul-Qadr chief, who held the post for a year and, after Allahvirdi Khan, another Armenian convert Qarachaqay Khan (d. *c.* 1624–5). Cf. Floor, *Safavid Government*, 172, 21. A Georgian Armenian *ghulam* was *sipahsalar* for a decade, though a Shamlu succeeded him at his death. Munshi, 2: 1260, 1120; Floor, ibid., 21. On Della Valle, see J. Gurney, 'Pietro Della Valle: the Limits of Perception, *BSOAS*, 49(1) (1986), 103–16; idem, 'Della Valle, Pietro', *EIr*, 7. See also n24.
16 Farhad Khan was especially prominent in the wars against the Uzbeks. On the decidedly mixed composition of Safavid forces – including elements of the Ustajlu, Bayat and Dhul-Qadr, Rumlu, Shamlu, Afshar, Qajar, *qurchi*s and *ghulam*s and even 'Isfahani' musketeers – and their commanders sent against the Uzbeks and revolts in Gilan, see Munshi, 2: 635–7, 689, 668, 674, 624, 633, 621, 711–12, 717–23, 748–64. On Farhad Khan, see Munshi, 2: 617–30, 638, 760–3. The Qaramanlu had figured in both the Qaraquyunlu and Aqquyunlu confederations (Woods, *The Aqquyunlu*, 195–6). On the Ustajlu commander of the 1603 expedition against the Ottomans, see below and n28.
17 Allahvirdi Khan featured prominently in later Ottoman campaigns. On the

1603, 1615 and other Ottoman campaigns, the different contingents which made up the respective Safavid forces on each occasion, and their commanders, see Munshi, 2: 825f, 839f, 851–2, 1103f, 1119f. On Allahvirdi Khan himself, see ibid., 2: 578, 690, 719, 1083–4. On a campaign led jointly by Farhad Khan and Allahvirdi Khan, see ibid., 2: 748–64. The 1602–3 campaign to take Bukhara was jointly commanded by a *ghulam* and a Shamlu, but both Allahvirdi Khan and Ganj Ali Khan, along with Ustajlu and Qajar forces, also participated. See ibid., 2: 810–22. McChesney's careful 'A Note' (53–63) argues for revisiting all of Munshi's dates. On Allahvirdi Khan, see also Maeda, 'On the Ethno-Social Backgrounds of the Four *Gholam* Families', 262f.

Among other Armenians who, having converted, became prominent figures at the centre was Yusuf Khan, governor of Shiraz who, in conjunction with tribal amirs, commanded troops in a 1616–17 counterattack against the Georgians. See Munshi, 2: 1260, 1113f. Qarachaqay Khan, the Armenian *ghulam* from Georgia, led a mixed force against the Ottomans in 1616, and was governor of Mashhad 'and most of Khurasan' at the time of his death in 1624–5; his son Manuchir was appointed governor of Mashhad at his father's death and was counted by Munshi as one of the realm's twenty-one *ghulam* amirs, on whom see below. See Munshi, 1: 184; 2: 1120, 1260, 1316. On Ganj Ali Khan, see Munshi, 2: 1261–2.

18 Later campaigns clearly reflect this tribal predominance. See, for example, details on the 1617–18 campaign against the Ottoman Khalil Pasha's move East in Munshi, 2: 1160f. The 1622–3 retaking of Baghdad involved a similarly complex force; Baghdad's new governor was a Georgian *ghulam* who was also the governor of Hamadan, but the new governor of Mosul was of the Imanlu subclan of the Afshar. See Munshi, 2: 1215f, 1229f.

19 A number of Takkalu were, as noted by Munshi (2: 707), purged *c.* 1596–7; see also Munshi, 2: 1137f; Szuppe, 'Kinship Ties', 93–5. The Dhul-Qadr were disciplined by Abbas as were the Bayat and Mokri (Munshi, 2: 631, 1018). On the heterodoxy of Takkalu religious beliefs and practices dating to the previous century, see ad n91 of Chapter 2, citing Calmard, 'Popular Literature', 337. See also Szuppe, ibid., 94.

20 Minorsky, *Tadhkirat*, 16–18, citing Munshi, 2: 1309–23. Both the order of prominence in which Munshi lists these key tribes and their names – Shamlu, Ustajlu, Dhul-Qadr, Qajar, Afshar, and Turkman, followed by such others as the Rumlu, Bayat and Talish – are roughly familiar from the previous century. Missing are the Takkalu, on whom see the previous note. The post of *vakil* was empty after Murshid Quli Khan Ustajlu's death. See Floor, *Safavid Government*, 13. Isa Khan, son of Masum Bek Safavi, was *qurchibashi* from 1612 to 1631, where an Afshar and a Qajar held the post earlier in Abbas reign. Floor, ibid., 142.

By 1629 the Shamlu, whom Munshi describes as 'the chief of the Qizilbash tribes', held seven of the seventy-three Qizilbash *amir*-ships, nearly 10%. The Dhul-Qadr held six while the Ustajlu and the Afshar each held three (2: 1309f), suggesting a diminution of Ustajlu pre-eminence over Abbas' reign. Not surprisingly, therefore, when discussing tribal positions at Tahmasp's death in 1576, Munshi also hailed Shamlu pre-eminence at Tahmasp's death (1: 222) though the Ustajlu in fact were dominant at the time (n12 of Chapter 2). See also n24 below. Based on a nineteenth-century Persian source, N. Kondo discusses the Afshar in the Urmiyya in his 'Qizilbash Afterwards: The Afshars in Urmiya from the Seventeenth to the Nineteenth Century', *IS*, 32(4) (1999), 537–56.

21 Munshi, 2: 1309f. See also Minorsky, ibid., 16–17. On the designation and incorporation of the 'Shaykhavand' as such a tribe, see below ad n27. The Taji-buyuk tribe, on whom see ad n94 below, would also appear to have been incoporated into the Qizilbash in this time period.

22 Munshi (2: 1316) listed fourteen *ghulam* amirs but noted that some twenty-one had, in fact, become amirs during Abbas' reign. Cf. Minorsky (ibid., 17–18, 17n7), who used the lower figure. Thus, of the total of ninety-four amirs in Munshi's list, twenty-one or 22% were *ghulam*s and seventy-three, or 78%, were drawn from the now-expanded Qizilbash confederation; Minorsky gives 20% and 83% respectively. The ranking of *khan* was also bestowed on non-Qizilbash officials (Röhrburn, 40), clearly, like the granting of the *taj* (n.38 of Chapter 2) and the granting of *amir*-ships, attesting to efforts to incorporate 'new' elements into the larger project.

23 Röhrborn (50f) notes that Fars was the first to have such a governor, in 1595–6; Astarabad had a *ghulam* governor in 1604–5. In 1592–3 a *ghulam* was governor of Qazvin (Munshi, 2: 622), perhaps suggesting the latter was no longer the capital city. See also n92.

24 The Shamlu, related to the house by marriage, and Dhul-Qadr each held seven such key administrative posts at Abbas' death (Minorsky, ibid., 18), further hinting at the rising influence of the Shamlu over Abbas' reign (see n20). When the Georgian *sipahsalar*, who held the post for some ten years, died in 1626, a Shamlu succeeded him (Floor, *Safavid Government*, 20–1). In the provinces Röhrborn shows (51–7) that Herat was held by the Shamlu almost continuously throughout Abbas' reign; Farhad Khan Qaramanlu held it for a time, but between Shamlu governors. Azerbaijan, another key front-line province, was held in turn by the Shamlu, Qaramanlu and Turkman. Hamadan, which could be a front-line province, was held by the Shamlu, Ustajlu and Bayat; the latter also held Nishapur *c.* 1624–5. A Shamlu centurion was sent to India as ambassador and another was governor of Rayy *c.* 1604. Mashhad, when not in Uzbek hands, was held by the Ustajlu and the Qajar. Astarabad was held by the Afshar and Turkman, Farhad Khan Qaramanlu and a Qajar before it was given to *ghulam*s *c.* 1603–4. The Afshar held Kirman, then the Ustajlu, then the Turkman. Ustajlu and Qajar chiefs held the governorships of Marv, Herat, Kirman, Hamadan (Haneda, 201) as well as Astarabad. The Shamlu also held such key central posts as the position of chief officer (*ishikaqasibashi*) of the haram *c.* 1617. See Munshi, 2: 753, 773, 866, 768, 795, 114, 1315f; Haneda, 201. Röhrborn, 51–8; Melville, 'Shah Abbas and the Pilgrimage to Mashhad', 214.

   The Qajar and Qaramanlu held Fars briefly, but for the most part it was held by the Dhul-Qadr from 1586 until the *ghulam* Allahvirdi Khan was given it in 1594–5. Although at his death in 1613 Allahvirdi's son Imam Quli Khan became its governor, Dhul-Qadr tribal levies continued to furnish the bulk of the province's military forces. See also Savory, *Iran Under*, 81–2. Although Haneda (204f) suggests that at the provincial level tribal elements became mixed with the *ghulam* and lost their distinct tribal identity, such that the *qurchi*s represented the only true, pure tribal element, Munshi, for example, identifies Safavid military forces as members of a named tribe, as do contemporary European sources. See also Haneda, 208. Röhrborn (75) dismisses Chardin's figures on the numbers of *qurchi*s in the reign of Abbas I (Minorsky, ibid., 32).

25 Munshi, 2: 1295, 598, 613, 1068–9, 1309; see also Savory, 'Offices . . . Tahmasp', 79; Floor, *Safavid Government*, 141. The Afshar had held the post over

Tahmasp's reign. A Qajar held the post from 1591 to 1612, when he was dismissed, and killed, for corruption. Isa Khan Safavi, grandson of Masum Bek (d. 1569), then held the post until Abbas' death in 1629.

26   Floor, 'Judicial', 22–3, 24. Of the two identifiable holders of the post in the period, a Shamlu, the *qurchi* Ali Quli Khan, became *divanbeki* and *ishikaqasi-bashi* during Abbas' reign and held the post for two decades. Haneda, 201–2. The Dhul-Qadr held the post of sealkeeper over the period. See Floor, *Safavid Government*, 72.

27   Munshi, 2: 1309f; Minorsky, *Tadhkirat*, 16–18. On the marriage, see Munshi, 2: 1069, 1302; Hunarfar, 594.

28   Munshi, 2: 707, 1262. On the campaign itself, see Munshi, 2: 825f.

29   Gilan, of course, presented problems for Abbas throughout his reign, especially his early years. Even after the betrothal, Khan Ahmad himself had revolted and was defeated by the Qaramanlu commander Farhad Khan in 1592, after which he fled to the Ottoman court and died there in 1597. See Munshi, 2: 621–4; Szuppe, 1995, 114, 118. Khan Ahmad, on whom see also the previous chapter ad n28, was a patron of the arts, poet and musician. See also Marlow, 240–2.

30   Szuppe, 1995, 117, 118, 114; 1994, 231, 225. The centre also continued its patronage of the Nimatallahi order. On work done in 1589–90 and 1601 to the Mahan shrine of Shah Nimatallah, see Hillenbrand, 'Safavid Architecture', 6: 792–3. See also Blair, 'The Ardabil Carpets'. Mir Miran himself sided with the Afshar against Abbas but a son who remained loyal was rewarded. See Munshi, 1: 232; 2: 606; n6. On this marriage, yet another example of such Turk-Tajik alliances in the period, see Szuppe, 1994, 228. Even the grandson of Abbas' eldest son Muhammad Baqir, the future Shah Safi, married a Circassian, Anna Khanum.

31   Munshi, 1: 257; 2: 1147, 1170, 1261, 1234–5; Floor, '*sadr*', 480–2; Babayan, personal communication; H. Mudarrissi, *Misalha-yi Sudur-i Safavi*, Qum, 1353/ 1974), 16; Floor, *Safavid Government*, 42. Thanks to K. Babayan for facilitating access to *Misalha*. On the emigration of another Shahristani to, and his career in, India, see Haneda, 'Emigration', 135–6.

32   Another of Abbas' sons-in-law was the Shahristani warden of the shrine of Imam Riza in Mashhad. On Abbas' daughters, see Hunarfar, 594. See also Babayan, 'The Waning', 79–80, 114; Munshi, 1: 236, 238; 2: 1146, 1187, 1234–5, 1261, 1302, 1320. Khalifa Sultan's grandson, *sadr* during the reign of Sultan Husayn, would marry a daughter of Safi, Maryam Bekum. See Chapter 8, below. Many thanks to K. Babayan for her help on the sayyid/*sadr* connections over this period.

33   On the political benefits in the Caucasus accruing from Abbas I's association with Allahvirdi Khan, himself from a family of Georgian landed military elites, see Maeda, 'On the Ethno-Social Backgrounds of Four *Gholam* Families', 262–6. See also ibid., 247–53, on the service to the court of the Baratashvili clan, whose lands were never formally subdued by the Safavids, and 255–7 on that of the Mirimandze clan, others of whom married into the Safavid house and whom Tahmasp had left in control of the Somkhiti region.

34   See, for example, the example of the Georgian Khusraw Mirza/Rustam Khan (d. 1658) who, though head of the *ghulam*s under Abbas' successor Safi and later *divanbeki* and *sipahsalar*, renewed churches and had a Christian marriage. See N. Gelashvili, 'Iranian Georgian Relations During the Reign of Rostam (1632–1658)', paper presented at 'Iran and the World in the Safavid Age',

London, 2002. See also H. Maeda, 'Shah's Slave or Georgian Noble? Unknown History of Georgian *ghulam*s', paper presented at the Fourth International Round Table on Safavid Studies, Bamberg, July 2003; idem, 'On the Ethno-Social Backgrounds of Four *Gholam* Families', esp. 257f. Perhaps the very nominalism of these Christians' conversion precluded such formal liaisons as marriages with Turks or Tajiks.

35 Floor, *Safavid Government*, 37, 42, 53, 56, 202; Munshi, 2: 913–17, 1034, 612–13, 915–16, 1318–21. See also A. H. Morton, 'An Introductory Note on a Safawid *Munshi*'s Manual in the Library of the School of Oriental and African Studies', *BSOAS*, 33(2) (1970), 357–8. See also Babayan, 'The Waning', 105–6, 313; Floor, ibid., 37. The Kujuji Tabrizi sayyids were also represented. After the Urdubadis the next longest-serving *vizier* was the sayyid Khalifa Sultan, son of the *sadr* and son-in-law of Abbas himself, who, like his *qurchibashi* relative Isa Khan, held the post into the reign of Abbas' successor Safi. Khalifa Sultan's predecessor as *vizier* was another relative, Salman Khan, Abbas' brother-in-law and a grandson of Tahmasp, who served from 1621 to 1624.

On Abbas' recourse to 'cabinet' consultation, see Floor, *Safavid Government*, 31, and for such meetings during the reigns of his successors, see n4 of Chapter 7.

36 Munshi, 2: 1317–8, 1261; Floor, '*sadr*' esp. 480–2. A Shirazi Inju sayyid, unrelated to the house, was *sadr* for nearly ten years. The post of *majlis nivis* was also held by Tajik sayyids in this period. Floor, *Safavid Government*, 56–7.

37 Munshi, 2: 1321–2; Floor, *Safavid Government*, 42–3. Hatim Bek Urdubadi had briefly held this post before his promotion.

38 Mudarrissi, *Bargi*, 152–4, 154–8, 158–60, 160–4, 164–9. A prominent Marashi was sent on diplomatic missions to the Ottomans and the Deccan in this period (ibid., 22–3, 60). On the *suyurghal*, see Chapter 8.

39 Blake (*Half*, 15–27, esp. 18, 20–1) argues for 1590 as the date for the designation of Isfahan as the capital over the usually cited date of 1597–8. Compare R. McChesney, 'Four Sources', 114–15, 117; Munshi, 2: 607–11, 724–5; Canby, 95, 95n5. See also C. Melville, 'New Light', 81; n72.

40 Blake, 22–3, citing Junabadi, 759. See also n131 below.

41 The Qaysariyya Gateway was begun in 1611 and, when completed in 1617–18, after victories against the Ottomans, balanced out the gateway of the Shah Mosque on the opposite side of the square finished the year before. The former, completed by the premier court painter Riza Abbasi (see n49) and others, included a now barely visible representation of the 1598 victory over the Uzbeks and a giant likeness of the archer Sagittarius, under whose zodiac sign the new square was founded in 1602. See Blake, 23–7, 107n35.

42 The same Riza Abbasi embellished the palace's inner walls with portraits and scenes of birds and animals in landscape reminiscent of book illumination and with paintings which included scenes of drinking youths. Abbas installed therein a door from Najaf. Cannon seized from the Portuguese at Hormuz in 1622 were set on either side of the gate. Blake, 62–5, 82; Hunarfar, 416–26; cf. Hillenbrand', Safavid Architecture', 6: 782–4; Canby, 96. On Chahar Bagh, see also Hunarfar, 465–7, 479–93; Hillenbrand, 6: 777; Godard, 88–94.

43 Blake, 95–7; idem, 'Contributors to the Urban Landscape: Women Builders in Safavid Isfahan and Mughal Shahjahanabad', in Hambly, ed., 410; Haneda, 'The Character of the Urbanisation of Isfahan in the Later Safavid Period', in Melville, ed., *Safavid Persia*, 369–87. On Hormuz, see also Floor's forthcoming *The Persian Gulf in the Safavid Period, A Tale of Five Port Cities*.

44 Abbas remitted Tabrizi immigrants' taxes for one year and built a market, sarai, bazaar and houses, bought from local peasant cultivators some 1,000 *jarib*s of land and provided the immigrants interest-free loans. See Blake, 185–6; Munshi, 2: 1025–34.

45 Hillenbrand (6: 789, 781–2) notes that the *maydan* itself can be seen as a huge version of such a courtyard, as found in mosques, sarais, schools and even houses. The four *ayvan*s are the four portals centred on each side of the square, two of which lead into mosques and two lead into the Ali Qapu and Qaysariyya Bazaar respectively.

46 Canby, 96, 101–2, citing, on Mazandaran and Astarabad, Munshi, 2: 1059, 1065–6. See also Naraqi, 66; Zarrabi, 471–2. Melville ('From Qars to Qandahar: The Itineraries of Shah Abbas I', in Calmard, ed., *Études Safavides.*, 213f, 222f) regards each of these sets of palaces as establishing 'new capitals' and, given Abbas' seemingly constant movement, suggests the realm had no real capital in this period. Matthee (*The Politics*, 44) notes that Abbas moved Georgian Jews to Farahabad and that Jews were involved in the silk trade; n85. See also ad n108.

47 Blake, 158; Haneda, 378; Hunarfar, 470–5. Godard, 123. Cf. Hillenbrand, 6: 796; Canby, 121.

48 Maysi (d. 1622–3), descendant of a cleric who had avoided association with the Safavids in the previous century (Newman, 'The Myth', 91–2), had been given an appointment to the Mashhad shrine by Tahmasp. Shushtari (d. 1612–13) had studied in Najaf with the émigré Ardabili. See Munshi, 1: 249, 2: 1229–30, 1069–70; n138. The city's other mosques included the 1602 Maqsud Bek Mosque, the 1605 Sufrachi Mosque, the 1610 Jarchi Mosque, the 1624 Bagh-i Khaji and the 1625 Aqa Nur Mosques, on which see further below.

49 Blake, 140, 147–50; Munshi, 1: 249, 2: 1229–30; Hunarfar, 401–5; Blake, 140, 147–50; Canby, 98–9; Hillenbrand, 6: 784–6. On Maysi, see also below.
   The calligrapher Ali Riza Abbasi, responsible for a number of architectural inscriptions, is not to be confused with the painter Aqa Riza, later known as Riza Abbasi. See Babaie, et al., *Slaves of the Shah*, 116–17; n41.

50 The 1614 *vaqf* document, organised by the shah and Muhibb Ali Bek, a Shamlu and *ghulam* head of the royal household and the imperial treasury, lists thirty-seven students residing in the mosque, their stipends, twenty-three mosque officials and more than fifty servants. See Blake, 144–7; R. McChesney, '*Waqf* and Public Policy: The *Waqf*s of Shah Abbas, 1011–1023/1602–1614', *Asian and African Studies*, 15 (1981), 178–81; Canby, 97. Blake notes that the Mosque's cash expenses exceeded cash income, but that the mosque's income in-kind exceeded that received in cash. On Muhibb Ali Bek, see also Munshi, 2: 1169–71.
   Nearby also a pre-Safavid school was refurbished in this period and over the century, owing to its proximity to the nearby Lutfallah Maysi Mosque, gradually became known as the Lutfallah Maysi School. Blake, 158; Hunarfar, 657n1; M. Tabrizi, *Faraid al-Favaid dar Ahval-i Madaris va Masajid*, R. Jafariyan ed. (Tehran, 1994), 297, 297n1. Tabrizi was a student of Baqir Majlisi, Jamal Khvansari and Muhammad Salih Khatunabadi, on whom see below. I am indebted to R. Jafariyan for directing me to this source and to Dr M. Sefatgol for facilitating access to it. Maysi himself alludes to the school as having been built for him in his 'Risala-yi Itikafiyya', A. A. al-Rizvanshahri, ed., *Miras-i Islami*, R. Jafariyan, ed., 1 (Qum, 1373), 313–37. See also Abisaab, *Converting Persia*, 81–5.

51 Hillenbrand, 6: 786–9; Blake, 143–4. According to Chardin (Blake, 143) the mosque contained a Qur'an said to have been copied by the eighth Imam, Ali Riza, and the bloodstained robe of the third Imam, Husayn, martyred at Karbala, which was believed to have magical powers. The Western school also contained a sun-dial of Shaykh Bahai, the son of Shaykh Husayn Amili, on whom see further below.

52 Hunarfar, 427–65, esp. 402, 429, 430–3; McChesney, 'Waqf', 178–81. See also Babayan, *Mystics*, 234–5, citing N. Khoury, 'Ideologies and Inscriptions : The Epigraphy of Masjid-i Shah and the Ahmediye in the Context of Ottoman-Safavid Relations', forthcoming in *Muqarnas*.

53 Munshi, 2: 955; Melville, 'Shah Abbas and the Pilgrimage', esp. 193, 196; McChesney, 'Waqf', 169–70, 181–2; Hillenbrand, 6: 789, 790–1.

54 Mudarrissi, *Barqi*, 28; Munshi, 2: 702f.

55 Mudarrissi, *Barqi*, 29; 83, 86.

56 Naraqi, 233–4, 385–6, 395. Hunarfar, 876. Repairs on the Natanz Congregational Mosque date to this period. On Abbas' Kashan tomb, see below.

57 Blake, 119; Melville, 216; Jafariyan, 'Munasibat', 16–17 (citing the text of the *vaqf* from Vali Quli Shamlu, *Qisas al-Khaqani*, H. S. Nasiri, ed., Tehran, 1371/ 1992, 1: 186f), 19. On the latter source, see Chapter 6 below. See also McChesney, 'Waqf', 171. A 1608 *vaqf* dedicated items to the shrine in Najaf (McChesney, ibid., 173).

58 Munshi, 2: 1070. On an attack on the Ottomans Mir Damad composed for the shah, see Jafariyan, *Safaviyya dar Arsa-yi Din*, 1: 85–6; idem, 'Nufuz', 28.

59 See our 'Towards a Reconsideration', esp. 175f; Stewart, 'A Biographical Note on Baha al-Din al-Amili (d. 1030/1621)', *JAOS*, vol. 111(3) (1991), 563–71; idem, 'Taqiyyeh as Performance: The Travels of Baha al-Din al-Amili in the Ottoman Empire (991–93/1583–85)', *Princeton Papers*, Spring 1996, Vol. IV, 1–70; McChesney, 'Waqf', 174, 178. On reports that Bahai objected to official efforts to convert Iranian Jews, see n140.

60 Qummi, *Khulasat*, 931–2. Shaykh Husayn cited the text from Sayyid Hasan b. Jafar Karaki (d. 1531) who, in fact, had journeyed to Safavid territory but returned to, and died in, Lebanon (Newman, 'The Myth', 108n90); n68 of Chapter 1. On two prominent Arab clerics who avoided associating with Abbas, see n40 of the previous chapter.

61 The original tomb dates to 1453–4, in the reign of Jahan Shah Qaraquyunlu. See Blake, 171; Hunarfar, 341–53, esp. 346; Godard, 47–57; P. Varjavand, 'Darb-i Imam', *EIr*, 7.

62 Blake, 171; Hunarfar, 521–40.

63 By Chardin's time, Isfahanis were said greatly to have venerated the site. Many prominent figures of the later Safavid period were buried there, including Mir Findiriski (d. 1640–1), Mirza Rafi (d. 1671–2) and Sayyid Ismail Khatunabadi (d. 1704–5), on all of whom see further below. See Blake, 170–1; Hunarfar, 493–500, 543–6, 631–3; Godard, 123–9.

64 Naraqi, 150f; Zarrabi, 430f. Naraqi (155f) describes inscriptions on the tomb. See also Melville, 'Shah 'Abbas and the Pilgrimage', 217, 228n117, where Melville adds that Chardin noted that many believed Abbas was buried in Ardabil and that Olearius claimed he saw Abbas' tomb there. Cf. 'Emamzada' in *EIr*, which lists some 130 such sites throughout the country but identifies the Imam in question as Imam Musa, from whom the Safavids claimed descent.

Abbas' clear attempt to embellish further this shrine and thereby Kashan itself came to naught, as all four of his successors were buried in the shrine of Fatima in Qum. See n45 of Chapter 6.

65 *Ayd-i qurban* commemorates Abraham's sacrifice of a ram to Allah instead of his son. Travellers reported that the latter affair occasioned violent anti-Sunni demonstrations. Calmard, 'Shi'i Rituals', in Melville, ed., *Safavid Persia*, 143–54; H. Mirjafari, 'The Haydari-Nimati Conflicts in Iran', *IS*, 12(3–4) (1979), 135–62; J. Perry, 'Toward a Theory of Iranian Urban Moieties: The Haydariyyah and Nimatiyyah Revisited', *IS*, 32(1) (1999), 51–70. See also, more recently, B. Rahimi, 'The Rebound Theater State: The Politics of the Safavid Camel Sacrifice, 1598–1695 C. E.', *Iranian Studies* 37(3) (2004), 451–78; Babayan, *Mystics*, 222, citing the account of Ashura by the Russian Kotov in the capital in 1624–5. On Kotov, see n124 below.

66 On Abbas' various *vaqf* donations to the Shrine and repairs and embellishments ordered thereto, see Morton, 'The Ardabil Shrine in the Reign of Shah Tahmasp I', *Iran*, 12 (1974), 36, 54–6; ibid., 13 (1975), 40, 42, 52–3, 54–7; Hillenbrand, 6: 792; Canby, 102, citing Munshi, 1: 536; 2: 873, 900, 955, 1033, 1057; Canby, 115; McChesney, '*Waqf* and Public Policy', 170f; Blair, passim, esp. 137; M. Medley, 'Ardabil Collection of Chinese Porcelain', *EIr*, 2: 364–5; K. Rizvi, 'The Imperial Setting: Shah Abbas at the Safavid Shrine of Shaykh Safi at Ardabil', in Canby, ed., *Safavid Art and Architecture*, 9–15. On the continuing influence of the house itself in Ardabil in this period, as evidenced by the ongoing economic activities of its women, see F. Zarinebaf-Shahr, 'Economic Activities of Safavid Women in the Shrine-City of Ardabil', *IS*, 31(2) (Spring, 1998), esp. 257–9.

67 A. H. Morton, 'The *Chub-i Tariq* and Qizilbash Ritual in Safavid Persia', in Calmard, ed., 234–5. On the *tawhidkhana*, see also Minorsky, *Tadhkirat*, 55. See also Floor, 'Khalifeh', 71–3. Reports of cannibalism in the previous century (n89 of Chapter 2) circulating in this period no doubt also bolstered Abbas' Sufi credentials in the same manner as the references to the 'Sufis of Lahijan' which also began to circulate in this period (n14, Chapter 1). See also the text ad n7 and n123.

68 The 'Peck' *Shahnama*, dated to 1589–90, contains interesting visible variations to the Timurid-style of manuscript illustration generally followed in Shiraz until mid-century. See Marlow, 229–43. U. al-Khamis, in a personal communication, notes that Abbas' *Shahnama* was never completed. Perhaps the answer lies in the painters' interests, if not the necessity, in this period in producing single-page illustrations such that, as noted by Gray, 6: 898, these painters 'rivalled one another in virtuosity of penmanship and richness of design', tendencies which, as will be seen, only grew over the century. On this *Shahnama* see Canby, 105. On the non-royal market for single-page illustrations from the *Shahnama* itself, see E. Sims, 'Two 17th Century Firdausi Manuscripts: The Windsor and the Rashida *Shahnama*s', paper presented at 'Shahnama: The Visual Language of the Persian Book of Kings', Edinburgh, March 2001. On Riza's painting of Russians, see the following note. Two *Shahnama*s were, however, produced in Shiraz in 1600 and 1601. See Babaie, et al., *Slaves of the Shah*, 116, 183n24.

On Sadiqi Bek, see also A. Welch, 'Art', 621–2, 625. On a second *Shahnama* commissioned in 1614, see ibid., 625. On Riza Abbasi, in particular, see also Canby, *The Rebellious Reformer*. Munshi notes that Sadiqi Bek exhibited similar independence of convention. See Canby, 20, citing Munshi, 1: 273. See also A. Adamova, 'On the Attribution of Persian Paintings and Drawings of the Time of Shah 'Abbas I', in Hillenbrand, ed., *Persian Painting from the Mongols to the Qajars* (London, 2000), esp. 23f; Gray, 6: 699. In that both his father and his son also served the court Riza's family was similar to that of the period's multi-generational administrators, historians and clerics already discussed. The *nisba* Abbasi itself, though Riza was reluctant to use it until *c.* 1610, was likely bestowed upon him by the shah *c.* 1600. Canby, ibid., 22. See also, more generally, Canby, *The Golden Age*, 105–6; idem, *Reformer*, 23, 39f, 68; Gray, 6: 897–903. On the other artists, see also Canby, *The Golden Age*, 72, 74, 76, 83–5, 87, 88–9, 105–7; Qadi Ahmad, *Calligraphers*, 101, 191, 187, 188; Munshi, 1: 271–2; A. Welch, 'Painting and Patronage under Shah Abbas I', *Iranian Studies* 7(3–4) (1974), 458–507; Babaie, et al., *Slaves of the Shah*, 114–38.

69 See the sources in the previous note and, on the possible influence of Dutch painters from this period, see n77. Riza Abbasi also produced portraits of two Russian ambassadors to the court in the late sixteenth century. See A. Adamova, 'Persian Portraits of the Russian Ambassadors', in S. Canby, ed., *Safavid Art and Architecture* (London, 2002), 49–53; n114.

70 Blake, 119. The royal sarai itself, of two storeys, with 140 rooms, mosques and schools, housed merchants from Ardabil and Tabriz; the former sold blankets, carpets and shawls and the latter sold silk goods. Muslins from Qazvin were available along with Kirmani and Mashhadi porcelain fine enough to compete with the Chinese product. The upper rooms were occupied by goldsmiths and jewellers, and in the middle of the structure were rich Indian merchants, probably cloth dealers.

71 Hunarfar, 395–401; Blake, 107–15; Hillenbrand, 6: 779.

72 Naraqi, 310–18, 322, 414; Hunarfar, 863; Floor, *The Economy*, 32, 36–40. For an overview of Iran's sarais and Safavid sarais, see M. Y. Kiani, M-Y. and W. Kleiss, 'Caravansary', *EIr*, 4: 798–802; W. Kleiss, 'Safavid Caravanserais', in S. Canby, ed., *Safavid Art and Architecture* (London, 2002), 27–31.

73 On the Ottomans' earlier oppression of the Armenians in Julfa, the flight of richer Armenians to Iran, their welcome by Abbas and the hopes of those remaining in Julfa for rescue by Abbas, see H. Papazian, 'Armenia and Iran. vi. Armeno-Iranian Relations in the Islamic Period', *EIr*, 2: 472. On the deportations generally, see Papazian, ibid.; E. Herzig, 'The Deportation of the Armenians in 1604–05 and Europe's Myth of Shah Abbas I', in Melville, ed., *Pembroke Papers*, 59–71; I. McCabe, *The Shah's Silk for Europe's Silver* (Atlanta, 1999), 35f; V. Ghougassian, *The Emergence of the Armenian Diocese of New Julfa in the Seventeenth Century* (Atlanta, 1998), 17f; Munshi, 2: 857, 859, 933. For later deportations, see ibid., 2: 1179f. McCabe's analysis is also on offer in Babaie, et al., *Slaves of the Shah*, 49–79. Matthee (*The Politics*, 84–9) suggests Abbas must have planned the Armenian settlement in Isfahan sometime before, perhaps suggesting an earlier date for Abbas' decision to designate Isfahan as the new capital. On Iran's Nestorian Christian population, see n18 of the Introduction.

74 Ghougassian, 29; McCabe, 49–53.

75 The most important routes crossed through Eastern Anatolia, where they linked up with routes from Syria and the Upper Euphrates and Tigris' region to the South, and the Black Sea ports to the North, to converge on Tabriz before running South across the central Iranian plateau to Hormuz and thence India and China, and eastwards, South of the Alburz mountains, to Herat, Qandahar, Kabul and India or North to Bukhara, Central Asia and China. On the Levant

route, see n84 below. For an overview of Iran's trade and commercial position in the larger region, see Lockhart, 'European Contacts', 6: 373f; Ferrier, 'Trade from the Mid-14th Century to the End of the Safavid Period', 6: 410f, 420–7; Allouche, 6–29; Matthee, *The Politics*, 15–7; Allouche, 21–2; B. Fragner, 'Social and Internal Economic Affairs', in Peter Jackson, ed., 6: 524–7; Floor, *The Economy*, 197–203; Woods, 30. Given its prominent role as a key city in this trade, Tabriz, consistently described as a thriving commercial centre in the pre-Safavid period, was, unsurprisingly, the capital of Jahanshah Qaraquyunlu and of the Aqquyunlu under Uzun Hasan and the focal point of Ismail I's early efforts.

76 Matthee, *The Politics*, 23–4; Herzig, 'The Rise of the Julfa Merchants in the Late Sixteenth Century', in Melville, ed., *Safavid Persia*, 305–23.

77 The English companies included the Russia Company, chartered in the 1550s, the Spanish Company formed in 1577, the Eastland Company in 1578, formed to handle Scandinavian and Prussian trade, the Levant Company, chartered in 1592 as a fusion of the earlier Turkey and Venice companies, the former founded in 1581, and the East India Company (EIC), founded in 1600. On the EIC see also R. Mukherjee, *The Rise and Fall of the East India Company* (New York, 1974), especially 35, 61. On the Levant Company, see A. Wood, *A History of the Levant Company* (London, 1935, 1964). See also, more generally, R. Ferrier, 'Anglo-Iranian Relations, i. From the Safavids to the Zands', *EIr*, 2: 41–4; Ferrier, 'East India Company (The British)', *EIr*, 8; Ferrier, 'The Terms and Conditions under which English Trade was Transacted with Safavid Persia', *BSOAS* 49(1) (1986), 48–72; R. Davis, *The Rise of the Atlantic Economies* (Ithaca, 1973). The Russia Company, seeking to bypass the East–West trade in spices, silks and dyes dominated by the Venetians and Ottomans and a market for English cloth, first made contact with Tahmasp who, in 1566, signed a treaty guaranteeing the company the toll-free trade rights. Matthee, *The Politics*, 30–2; Lockhart, 6: 383f; Ferrier, 6: 416, 428f; n84; idem, 'The Terms', 50–3. The Dutch United East India Company (VOC) was chartered in 1602. For an overview of Iranian-Dutch relations from 1623 to 1759, see also Floor, 'Dutch-Persian Relations', *EIr*, 7. Still understudied, as Floor notes, is the influence of the many Dutch artists and artisans in Iran on commissions from the court or prominent elites.

78 Matthee, *The Politics*, 87–8, 91–2, 15; Floor, *The Economy*, 61, 77, 219.

79 In 1590, at the start of his Uzbek campaign, Abbas was said to have melted down his silver and gold plate service to raise the funds to pay the army. In 1593 Abbas initiated currency reform. See Floor, *The Economy*, 29–30, 78–80, 183, 222–3; Matthee, *The Politics*, 115; n82.

80 Abbas also sent Julfan merchants to Venice and special parcels of silk to Spain and Russia in an attempt to interest these powers in direct commercial, and political, relations.

For an overview of foreign arrivals in Iran over this period, see Lockhart, 6: 394–7; Stevens, 'European Visitors'. On dealings with Russia in this period, see Matthee, 'Anti-Ottoman', 110f. On the English especially, see Ferrier, 'Anglo-Iranian', 41f; idem, 'The Terms', 53–6. On the Carmelite missionaries, sent from Rome and allowed to settle in Isfahan in 1608, but whose efforts among Iranian Armenians were opposed by the court, see F. Richard, 'Carmelites in Persia', *EIr*, 4: 832–4. On the French Capuchin monks who first arrived in 1628 and whose charge in the region involved the conversion of Armenians and Muslims, see Richard, 'Capuchins in Persia', *EIr*, 4: 786–8. On the Portuguese

Augustinians, who had been in Iran operating from Hormuz since 1572 but who lost their position with the fall of Hormuz, see C. Alonso Vanes, 'The Hormuz Convent and the Augustinians (1572–1621)', paper presented at 'Iran and the World in the Safavid Age', University of London, September 2002. On the Jesuits, see n67 of Chapter 6.

In 1616 and 1618 Abbas also ordered Persian translations of Psalms and the Gospels. See K. J. Thomas, 'Chronology of Translations of the Bible', *EIr*, 4: 203; K. Thomas and F. Vahman, 'Persian Translations of the Bible', *EIr*, 4 (1990), 211; Richard, 'Carmelites', 832–3.

The court painter Riza Abbasi produced portraits of Russian ambassadors to the court in 1588–9 and 1594. See n69.

81 Matthee, *The Politics*, esp. 93f, 115f, 145–6; idem, 'Merchants in Safavid Iran: Participants and Perceptions', *Journal of Early Modern History*, 4(3–4) (2000), 238–9.

82 In 1623, during the Baghdad campaign, Abbas had to pay his troops in leather coins and cloth, the latter obtained by trade with the EIC. In 1626 the Dutch observed the poverty of Isfahan owing to the campaigns to recover Baghdad and Qandahar, the latter in 1624. Matthee, *The Politics*, 111, 115; Floor, *The Economy*, 29; n79. In his *The First Dutch-Iranian Commercial Conflict* (Costa Mesa, 2004), not available to the present author, Floor reviews the terms of the 1627 VOC treaty with the shah which specified Dutch imports would be paid for in Iranian silk and a 1632 agreement which, though never fulfilled, reflected increasing Iranian demands for cash payments for silk.

83 With the retaking of Tabriz, Shirvan and Irivan in 1606–8 the Safavids regained control over key silk-producing areas and transit zones. Matthee, *The Politics*, 76. On the role of the Armenians in the trade see also, idem, 'Merchants', passim, esp. 238–9, 240–2; McCabe, 87; Ghougassian, 67; Papazian, ibid. On the silk monopoly, see below.

84 The Levant trade route passed from the Eastern Mediterranean ports via Baghdad to Kirmanshah to Hamadan to Isfahan and thence either North to the Caspian or South via Shiraz to the Persian Gulf, or East to India. See Matthee, *The Politics*, xix, xxi; Herzig, 'The Volume of Iranian Raw Silk Exports in the Safavid Period', *IS*, 25(1–2) (1992), 62; Floor, *The Economy*, 200–46, esp. 216f. On the companies' consistent failure over the period to redirect the silk trade from the overland routes to the Levant to the Gulf route, see Matthee, *The Politics*, 93–4; Floor, *The Economy*, 172–5, 203f, 216f, 254–7; Floor, 'The Dutch and the Persian Silk Trade', in Melville, ed., *Safavid Persia*, esp. 325f, 349f. The Russia Company wound up business in the 1580s, and trade through Russia remained insignificant over the period. See Herzig, 'The Volume', 71; Floor, *The Economy*, 221, 232f.

85 Further families were removed from Armenia to Isfahan in 1606–7 and 1618. Blake, 188–9; Hunarfar, 505–20; Godard, 165–9; Munshi, 2: 858–61, 933; Ghougassian, 83f, 204–7, 208–10, 291–2. On the churches built during Abbas' reign, the last being the Bethlehem Church, dating to 1627–8, see also J. Carswell, *New Julfa, The Armenian Churches and Other Buildings* (Oxford, 1968), 37, 41, 43, 46, 48, 50. See also Canby, 96. On the 1604 decree, see also Matthee, *The Politics*, 84f; Floor, *A Fiscal*, 130. On Abbas' attendance at Armenian feast days, in 1619, for example, see McCabe, 89; Ghougassian, 57–8; Babaie, et al., *Slaves of the Shah*, 69, 89–90. On the Tabriz refugees, see above ad n44.

Other centre elements were involved with the Armenian venture: an Ustajlu *amir* protected the Armenians at Julfa during the Ottoman advance in 1603 (Munshi, 2: 829f; n28) and Abbas' 1614 decree mentions the involvement of the *ghulam* Muhibb Ali Bek (Hunarfar, 507), on whom see n86. Floor (*The Economy*, 57) notes also the transportation of a number of Tabriz-based Muslim merchants to Isfahan in 1607. On Jews and the silk trade, see Matthee, *The Politics*, 44; n46.

On Shaykh Bahai's rulings on interaction with Christians, see n140 below. See also nn136, 137.

86 Floor, *The Economy*, 44f; Matthee, *The Politics*, 72–4. These royal merchants included Muhibb Ali Bek, the *ghulam* head of the imperial household and the imperial treasury, from 1616 to 1623 and, from 1623 to 1632, the *ghulam* Mulayim Bek who negotiated silk trade agreements with the VOC. Floor (103–5) notes that good relations between the centre and indigenous merchant elements were all the more important as the court occasionally borrowed money from them, directly or through certain purchases. On Muhibb Ali, see Matthee, *The Politics*, 44, 84, 89, 102. See also Blake, 122–3, 142–3, 144–5, 185; Munshi, 2: 1170–1; Minorsky, *Tadhkirat*, 127–8, and below. On Mulayim Bek, see Matthee, *The Politics*, 44, 84, 109–11, 116; McCabe, 148. See also Babaie, et al., *Slaves of the Shah*, 63.

87 Matthee, *The Politics*, 67–8, 115; Floor, *The Economy*, 29–30, 79–80, 181–4, 222–3, 331; Allan, *Persian Steel*, 116f; n81. Citing Tavernier, the Antwerp merchant who made a number of trips to Iran between 1632 and 1668, Matthee has suggested the centre's encouragement of Iranian pilgrimage centres, including Mashhad, as well as Isfahan's *imamzada*s was part of a policy to discourage Iranian pilgrims from going on pilgrimage to the Iraqi shrines and/or the Hijaz and thereby limit specie outflow. See Matthee, *The Politics*, 68; idem, 'Between Venice and Surat: The Trade in Gold in Late Safavid Iran', *Modern Asian Studies* 34(1) (2000), 243. See also W. Floor and P. Clawson, 'Safavid Iran's Search for Silver and Gold', *IJMES* 32 (2000), 345–68. See n36 of Chapter 7 on other reasons for such encouragement later in the period. On coinage in this period, see Floor, *The Economy*, 65f, 75f; Matthee, 'The Safavid Mint of Huwayza: The Numismatic Evidence', in Newman, ed., *Society and Culture*, 265–91. Dadvar (329–48) discusses Iranian merchants in India over the century.

Note also Abbas' efforts to assist Central Asian Sunnis traversing Iran in their performance of the pilgrimmage *c.* 1595 and in the 1620s (McChesney, 'The Central Asian', 145, 146f).

88 Hunarfar, 444–5, 434–6. A 1627 *firman* in Isfahan's Dhul-Fiqar mosque, privately built in 1543, had reduced taxes for some of the same guilds named in the 1628 *firman*. See Hunarfar, 385–6. Keyvani (135) notes a 1629 *firman* in the Shah Mosque addressed to Isfahan's barbers as part of a more general tax reduction to various tradesmen, which Hunarfar (434–6) ascribes to Abbas' reign.

89 Naraqi, 224–5, 230–3; Zarrabi, 532–4. A *firman* of Jahanshah Qaraquyunlu was inscribed in this mosque as was Tahmasp's 1534 *firman* banning various non-Islamic practices. See ad n40 in Chapter 2; Naraqi, 203–38, esp. 211f.

90 The *firman* announcing the tax was inscribed in Yazd's Congregational Mosque (Keyvani, 159). Floor (*The Safavid Economy*, 325) estimates some 30% of the urban population was involved in textile and leather crafts.

91 See, for example, Munshi, 2: 633; 1063f, 1187; Szuppe, 1994, 238–9; Floor,

Safavid Government, 37. On Abbas' responsiveness to an earlier earthquake in Shirvan, see Munshi, 1: 928–9.

92 Gilan and Mazandaran, important silk-producing lands, became crown land in 1598 and 1599 respectively, with *ghulam*s as governors. Qum had been made *khassa* in 1597 and from 1606 Astarabad was so designated. Abbas' mother Khayr al-Nisa held Simnan, Damavand and some other areas as *khassa* in 1578–79. Röhrborn, 90–1, 173, 177–8, 181; Matthee, *The Politics*, 75; Munshi, 2: 621, 625, 633–4. The *firman* described ad n90 suggests both that locally based troops may not have been paid by the centre and that local taxes were used for local military purposes.

93 The mosque inscription described it as being built 'during the caliphate of the most just, most dignified, most courageous, greatest Sultan, King . . . of the Arabs [this at a time when Eastern Iraq and the shrine cities were still held by the Ottomans] and Persians . . . Shadow of Allah on the two Earths, *ghulam* of . . . the Prince of the Believers Ali b. Abi Talib . . . the Musavid . . . the Husaynid'. See Blake, 152; Hunarfar, 475–6. On the post itself, see Munshi, 2: 1120n7. The occupant of the post *c.* 1616–17 also had military responsibilities, and remained in office for some years. See ibid., 2: 1123, 1200, 1259–60, 1265–7, 1270.

94 Blake, 152; Hunarfar, 477–9. *Tadhkirat al-Muluk* does not list this tribe but Munshi (2: 648) describes them as having been ordered to arrest Darvish Khusraw. Malik Ali's position attests to the continued influence of tribal elements at court over this period. See also Munshi, 2: 941, 1100–1. On Malik Ali, see also nn107, 122.

95 McChesney, 'Waqf', 179. See also Babaie, et al., *Slaves of the Shah*, 90f.

96 See n61 above.

97 Blake, 168; Hunarfar, 148.

98 Hunarfar, 479; Godard, 122; Munshi, 1: 261.

99 Blake, 152; Hunarfar, 467–70; Godard, 99–101. Keyvani (143) calls Maqsud Bek a coppersmith. Cf. Munshi, 2: 1111.

100 Blake, 152; Hunarfar, 620–1. On the Buyid mosque see also Tabrizi, 341.

101 Blake, 153; Hunarfar, 501–4. Nur al-Din's brother, Aqa Mumin, built a bathhouse nearby. The 1629–30 Persian-language inscription refers to the justdeceased Abbas as 'the Husaynid' and to Safi as 'the just ruler (Padishah-i Adil)'.

102 The layout of the *maydan* where these were located resembles the Naqsh-i Jahan square in miniature. The *vaqf* document dates from 1605. The same Ali Riza Abbasi whose work appeared in Isfahan's mosques from this period contributed to the inscriptions. See Munshi, 2: 1261–2; Hillenbrand, 6: 793–5; Canby, 116–7. See also S. Babaie, 'The Mosque of Ganj Ali Khan in Kirman: *Shahsevani* Loyalty and the Index of Belonging', paper presented at the Fourth International Round Table on Safavid Studies, Bamberg, July 2003; Babaie, et al., *Slaves of the Shah*, 94–7.

103 Mudarrissi, *Bargi*, 29.

104 The traditional four *ayvan* plan is followed but absent any symmetry. The communal areas are to the East not the *qibla* side or within the entrance complex. Hillenbrand (6: 790–1, 795–6) noted that both this school and Ganj Ali Khan's Kirman complex attests that the emphasis on size, and the wealth to produce it, were not confined to Isfahan in this period. See also Blake, 88; Canby, 117; Babaie, et al., *Slaves of the Shah*, 92–4.

105 Babaie, et al., *Slaves of the Shah*, 95; Blake, 88–91. According to Chardin, the

Khan's mansion in Shiraz, the seat of his power inherited from his father, out-shone the Isfahan house.

106 Blake, 89, 91. On Rustam Khan, see n34, n108; Munshi, 2: 944. At Rustam Khan's death, his brother inherited the mansion. At the latter's death without heir the shah inherited the mansion and gave it to the *sadr*, his own relative.

107 Blake, 32–3, 95, 74; Hillenbrand, 6: 779; Hunarfar, 487–93; Canby, 100; Munshi, 2: 578; Babaie, *Slaves of the Shah*, 92–3. On the bridge's date of completion, see Melville, 'New Light', 63–9.

108 Blake, 123–4. In 1614 the sarai was dedicated to the Shah Mosque. From this same time period dates a sarai in the city in the name of Ali Quli Khan, possibly a reference to Ali Quli Khan Shamlu, Abbas' tutor who died when the Uzbeks seized Herat in 1588–9, or the brother of Rustam Khan Qaramanlu, the latter killed in battle in 1606 (Munshi, 2: 944). The latter seems probable as he is identified with a mansion in Isfahan, on which see below. See Blake, 43, 119, 89; n122.

109 Blake, 122–3.

110 Blake, 117f; Hillenbrand, *Islamic Architecture: Form, Function and Meaning* (New York, 1994), 331–76. On coffee and coffee houses, see further below.

111 Melville, 'Shah Abbas', 212–13; Matthee, *The Politics*, 67. On Zaynab Bekum, see Szuppe, 1995, 118, 113.

112 Naraqi, 310–18, 322, 414. On the *ribat*/sarai, see Kiani and Kleiss, esp. 798.

113 Ferrier, 'Women in Safavid Iran: The Evidence of European Travellers', in Hambly, ed., 401–2, citing Chardin, who described the sarai as 'one of the finest and roomiest' in the country.

114 Canby, *The Golden Age*, 106–7; Gray, 6: 896–7; Canby, *Rebellious*, 65f. See also the work of Muhammad Qasim, who produced one of the few life-time portraits of Abbas himself, as discussed in Adamova, 'Muhammad Qasim and the Isfahan School of Painting', in Newman, ed., esp. 208; n68. Shiraz was also a centre of armour production and arms feature in a drawing produced by Riza Abbasi (Allan, *Persian Steel*, 143, 155). On a family of steel-makers of this period, see J. Allan, 'Abbas, Hajji', *EIr*, 1: 76–7. On Riza's portraits of Russian ambassadors, which may have been influential in the development of his style, see n69.

115 Canby, 109, 111, 115.

116 Canby, 112–17; idem, *Reformer*, 177; Gray, 6: 911–12; Matthee, *The Politics*, 67; Welch, 'Art', 625; L. Golombek, 'Riza Abbasi's Wine Pot and Other Problems of Safavid Ceramics', in Canby, *Safavid Art and Architecture* (London, 2002), 95–100. Later in the century Chardin (Canby, *The Golden Age*, 115) named Shiraz, Mashhad, Yazd, Kirman, Zarand and Isfahan as the main centres of ceramic production. See also Floor, *The Economy*, 322–3. On water pipes and the popularity of smoking, see also Matthee, 'Tobacco in Iran', in *Smoke, A Global History of Smoking*, S. L. Gilman and Z. Xun, eds (London, 2004), 58–67.

117 Canby, 103–5. On the centres of textile production see esp. Floor, *The Economy*, 325. Inside Iran, over the late fourteenth and early fifteenth century domestic centres such as Yazd and Kashan were important centres of textile and other manufactured items, such as ceramics, whose goods were sold at home and abroad (Floor, *The Economy*, 322–4). See also D. Walker, 'Carpets. ix. Safavid Period', *EIr*, 4: 866–75, which includes pictures of Polonaise carpets. Walker notes the paucity of carpets from the sixteenth century but characterises carpet production from Abbas' reign on as increasingly commercialised.

118 Quinn, *Historical*, 19–23, 28–9, 43–5, 57–60. See also her 'The Timurid Historiographical Legacy: A Comparative Study of Persianate Historical Writing',
in Newman, ed., *Society and Culture*, 19–31; idem, 'The Dreams of Shaykh Safi
al-Din and Safavid Historical Writing', *IS*, 29(1–2) (1996), 139. On Qadi
Ahmad, see n23 of Chapter 2. Yazdi's son and grandson were also court astrologers and historians, and, as such formed the second 'multi-generational family of Safavid historians, the first being Mir Khvand, his grandson Khvandamir
and the latter's son Amir Mahmud. See Quinn, 'Rewriting Nimatallahi History', 205. Yazdi's chronicle has been published as Mulla Jalal al-Din Munajjim
Yazdi, *Tarikh-i Abbasi ya Ruznama-yi Mulla Jalal*, S. Vahid Niya, ed. (Tehran,
1366/1987). For a medical 'dynasty' whose members served the court through
the reigns of Tahmasp and Abbas I, see our 'Safavids – Religion, Philosophy
and Science', 783.
   Sadly, if understandably, Savory's translation of Munshi's chronicle does not
include the Turkish-language poetry Munshi had included therein, a further
testament to his loyalty to the dynasty and its origins and a reminder of the
potential gulf between 'ruler' and 'ruled'.

119 Quinn, *Historical*, 87–8. The interest in Timurids among Safavid historians is
paralleled by that among such painters of the period as Riza Abbasi who, from
1612 to 1620, made direct use of paintings and drawings of Bihzad. See Canby,
Rebellious, 129–30, 110. The Timurids' religious eclecticism and tolerance of
minorities, and their patronage of both Islamic and distinctly Persian cultural
projects, can only have informed the interest in, if not also reinterpretation of,
things Timurid in this period.

120 Quinn, *Historical*, 75, 80–1, 87; idem, 'Notes on Timurid Legitimacy in Three
Safavid Chronicles', *Iranian Studies* 32 (1998): 149–58; idem, 'The Dreams of
Shaykh Safi al-Din', 139–40. Quinn ('Rewriting', 209) notes that Qadi Ahmad
also did not downplay the Nimatallahi associations of Ismail's *vakil* Abd al-Baqi
Yazdi, as had later Tahmasp-period chronicles. Of course, by now the family was
well linked to the family via numerous marriages, as recounted above.

121 A copy of *Afzal*'s third, final volume had been completed some four years
earlier in India in 1635. See Melville, 'New Light', 69. The Khuzani family had
served Ismail and Tahmasp. During the second interregnum, one member of the
family supported the pro-Abbas faction in Mashhad, and his son was briefly
Abbas I's *vizier* before he fell with his ally the Ustajlu Murshid Quli Khan. Fazli
himself was *vizier* to a Qajar governor. On the family see n14 of Chapter 1;
Haneda, 'La Famille Khuzani', 83, 87, 89.

122 Morton, 'The Early Years of Shah Ismail', esp. 32f; nn66, 122.

123 Quinn, *Historical*, 100–23. See also Qummi and Munshi's accounts of Ismail's
victory at Firuzkuh, as well as mention in Junabadi's 1625–6 *Rawzat* (241) of
Ismail's order to his troops to eat the body of Shaybani Khan Uzbek, on which
see also n89 of Chapter 2. Falsafi (2: 125–6n2) cites another report of cannibalism in Qummi dating to Khudabanda's reign and also (2: 126–7) cites Junabadi
(724) and Yazdi (224, ad. 1010/1601) implicating Malik Ali Sultan in such
activities. Munshi (2: 1100–1), however, notes Malik Ali's reputation as a wit
and a jester. See also Floor, 'Khalifeh', 62–4 and Dadvar, 268, the latter citing
Falsafi. As noted above (n67) references to the 'Sufis of Lahijan' also first appear
in these chronicles; see n14 of Chapter 1, citing Qummi's *Khulasat* and Fazli's
Afzal. Such references may have offset the impact of the challenge to Abbas by
other Lahijani Sufis in 1592–3 and again *c.* 1614–16. See the text ad n7, n128.

124   Canby, *Rebellious*, 77f; text above ad n113. The Russian traveller Kotov (n65 above) describes darvishes in the capital (Allan, *Persian Steel*, 313, citing P. M. Kemp, transl. and ed., *Russian Travellers to India and Persia, 1624–1798: Kotov, Yefremov, Danibegov* (Delhi, [1959], 25).

125   Having travelled to India, where he studied Hinduism and the occult sciences, he wrote works on Yoga and Hinduism and on the vocations in society. Abbas I is famously said to have queried Mir Findiriski's frequent attendance at cock-fights. See S. H. Nasr, 'The School of Ispahan', in M. M. Sharif, ed., *A History of Muslim Philosophy* (Wiesbaden, 1966), 2: 922–6; H. Dabashi, 'Mir Damad and the Founding of the "School of Isfahan" ', in *History of Islamic Philosophy*, S. H. Nasr and H. Dabashi, eds (New York/London, 1996), 626–7; Newman, 'Mir Damad' *EIr*, 6: 623–6.

126   Babayan, 'The Waning', 253, citing Sadr al-Din Muhammad Shirazi, *Kasr Asnam al-Jahiliyyih*, M. T. Danishpazhuh, ed. (Tehran, 1340/1962), 3; Cooper, 'Some Observations', 151–2. See also Babayan, *Mystics*, 165f, 176f, 213f, on the historical links between guilds and Sufi Alid movements, focusing especially on *Futuvvatnama-yi Sultani*, the undated work of Kashifi (d. 1504–5), which has been translated by J. R. Crook as *The Royal Book of Spiritual Chivalry* (Chicago, 2000). See also n35 of Chapter 1. On this date for *Kasr*, see Muhsin al-Amin, *Ayan al-Shi'a* (Damascus, 1935-) 17: 293. On Sadra see also nn133, 136 below. Abisaab (*Converting Persia*, 82–5) notes Lutfallah Maysi's anger at the ignorance of Shi'i doctrine and practice among local craftsmen and merchants and Maysi's self-promotion of his superior Arab/clerical background. See also n131 below.

127   Babayan, 'The Waning', 195f.

128   Munshi, 2: 1096–9; Babayan, 'The Waning', 68; Savory, 'The Office of "Khalifat" ', 501; Floor, 'Khalifeh', 68. Dadvar (268) attributes the emigration of 'the Iranian sufis' to India to this 'massacre', but lists only nineteen such Sufis as having emigrated to India over the period and these for a variety of reasons (269–79). On the Lahijani Sufis, see also the text ad n7 and nn 67, 123, and n14 of Chapter 1. Another son of Abbas, Imam Quli, was blinded in 1626–7 (Munshi, 2: 1288). The Ottomans also now tended to eliminate such rivals (n6 of Chapter 3, citing Munshi, 2: 1288). Also perhaps following Ottoman policy Abbas gradually ceased sending his sons to important provincial centres (Röhrborn, 61–8).

129   Munshi, 2: 1174, 1176; Babayan, 'The Waning', 62–3. See also Fazli Khuzani's account as discussed by Abrahams, 104.
      Such accounts point to the presence of a complex view of illness and wellness extant among all segments of Safavid society. See our 'Baqir al-Majlisi and Islamicate Medicine: Safavid Medical Theory and Practice Re-examined', in Newman, ed., *Society and Culture*, 371–96.

130   Matthee, 'Coffee in Safavid Iran: Commerce and Consumption', *JESHO*, 37 (1994), esp. 24–30; A. Al-i Davud, 'Coffeehouse', *EIr*, 6(1): 1–4; Floor, *The Economy*, 140–3. On poets of this period, see also P. Losensky's forthcoming research on the poet Alinaqi Kamrai (d. 1620–2). See also A. Tamimdari, *Irfan va Adab dar Asr-i Safavi*, 2 vols (Tehran, 1372–3), a discussion of Persian poetry from this period as yet unexplored by Western-language writers.

131   Of such essays by Shaykh Bahai see, for example, I. Kanturi, *Kashf al-Hujub* (Calcutta, 1914), 5, 256, 262, 287; Tehrani, 13: 61, 3: 340, 5: 63; Khatunabadi, 500; Newman, 'Towards', 191f, on Bahai's Persian-language *Jami*

Abbasi. For such essays by Mir Damad, see Kanturi, 360, 375; Tehrani, 1: 407, 5: 156. For Majlisi, see Kanturi, 256, 265–6, 270; Tehrani, 2: 260, 6: 389, 13: 305, 15: 68, 313, 18: 369–70, 22: 258. For a Persian-language essay on the *hajj* by the *vizier* Khalifa Sultan, see Tehrani, 1: 16.

The opposition to Lutfallah Maysi, for whom Abbas built a mosque in the new *maydan*, expressed by Isfahan's craft and merchant elements (Abisaab, *Converting Persia*, 85; n126 above) suggests they, at least, objected to these evangelistic efforts, if not also to the transferral of activities from the old, traditional city centre to the new which the siting of Maysi's mosque in the new *maydan* betokened.

132 See our 'Mir Damad'; H. Dabashi, 'Mir Damad'; I. Netton, 'Suhrawardi's Heir? The Ishraqi Philosophy of Mir Damad', in Lewisohn and Morgan, eds, 225–46. Both Bahai and Mir Damad were also interested in medicine. See our 'Safavids – Religion, Philosophy and Science', 783.

133 See, most recently, S. Rizvi, 'Reconsidering the Life of Mulla Sadra Shirazi: Notes towards an Intellectual Biography', *Iran* 40 (2002), 181–201, and his forthcoming *Mulla Sadra: Philosopher of the Mystics*. See also Cooper, 'Some Observations', 150–2; idem, 'From al-Tusi to the School of Isfahan', in *History of Islamic Philosophy*, S. H. Nasr and H. Dabashi, eds (New York/London, 1996), 585–96; H. Ziai, 'Mulla Sadra: His Life and Works', in Nasr and Dabashi, eds, 635–42; S. N. Nasr, 'Mulla Sadra: His Teaching', in Nasr and Dabashi, eds, 643–62. For earlier sources on Sadra and the others mentioned herein, see our 'Safavids – Religion, Philosophy and Science', *EI²*, 8: 781–2, 787. On Sadra's arguably most famous philosophical contribution, see F. Rahman, 'al-Asfar al-Arbaa', *EIr*, 2: 744–7.

134 Newman, 'Towards', 179–85, 190–6; idem, 'The Nature of the Akhbari/Usuli Dispute in Late-Safawid Iran. Part Two: The Conflict Reassessed', *BSOAS*, 55(2) (1992), 258–9; Newman, 'Fayz', esp. 37–8, 40–1, the latter citing a 1619 discussion on the prayer by Fayz Kashani (d. 1680), a student of Bahai and Mulla Sadra, and Sadra's son-in-law.

135 Where his father's teacher Zayn al-Din had held lay believers were not in all situations obliged to the lead of senior clerics and Ahmad Ardabili argued for the obligatory nature of such a relationship (*taqlid*), both having avoided all Safavid associations during their lifetimes, Bahai was a proponent of *taqlid* in all religious matters. See our 'Usuliyya', forthcoming in *EI²*. Munshi (2: 1070) records 'violent arguments . . . on theological matters and problems of *ijtihad*' – the exercise of judicial interpretation absent sole recourse to the faith's key revealed texts – between Abdallah Shushtari and Lutfallah Maysi, both recipients of the shah's favour. See also Abisaab, *Converting Persia*, 85–6. See also nn137, 138.

136 On Bahai see our 'Towards', 185–90; Abisaab, *Converting Persia*, 87; n140 below. On Sadra's residence in Kahak, see our 'Fayz', 38. See also D. MacEoin, 'Mulla Sadra', *EI²*, 7: 547–8. From this period probably dates Sadra's *Sih Asl*, a denunciation of some clerics for seeking worldly power coupled with a condemnation of 'sincere spiritual [i.e. Sufi] practices as innovation', a tradition of balanced refutation evident also in the works of Hafiz and Rumi. See Cooper, 'Some Observations', 151.

Bahai's strict rulings on the impurity of goods made, and consumption of animals slaughtered, by 'infidels' (Abisaab, *Converting Persia*, 64–6) may have been an effort to reaffirm his credentials among his 'orthodox' critics as well as delimit the Ottomans, who permitted both, as imperfect Muslims. Indeed, Abisaab (ibid., 67) notes his other, more tolerant, rulings on relations between Muslims and Christians per se. See also n137.

137 On Majlisi, see our 'Fayz', 40–1; S. M. Mahdavi, *Zindigi-nama-yi Allama-yi Majlisi* (Tehran, 1378) 2: 351f. A 1619 ban on wine issued by the shah, although it exempted many, including non-Muslims and foreigners, may have been part of effort to cool various 'popular' passions and allay the concerns of some 'orthodox' elements. See Jafariyan, *Safaviyya dar Arsa-yi Din*, 1: 381–2.

On Astarabadi, often accounted the 'founder' of the Akhbari movement within Twelver Shi'ism, his critique and Akhbarism itself in this period see, most recently, Stewart, 'The Genesis'. See also our 'The Nature of the Akhbari/ Usuli Dispute'; n138.

138 Abdallah Shushtari and his own son Jafar disagreed on the legality of the performance of Friday prayer by the cleric as the deputy of the Hidden Imam just as Zayn al-Din and Shaykh Husayn had disagreed with Ali Karaki on the same issue. In his *Jami Abbasi*, a legal manual written in Persian, Bahai himself acknowledged the contemporary controversy over the prayer's legality. See our 'Towards', 195; idem, 'Fayz', 35–8; n130; n31 of Chapter 6. Stewart ('The Genesis', 181–2) notes additional criticisms of Shaykh Zayn al-Din by his own son and others in addition to Astarabadi.

139 Babayan, 'The Waning', 105–6, 313; Floor, *Safavid Government*, 37. See also our discussion above. Zaynal Khan Shamlu's position, as either chief officer of the Supreme Divan (*ishikaqasibashi*) or *sipahsalar*, or both during 'Abbas' last years, is unclear in the sources. See Munshi, 2: 1283; Muhammad Masum Isfahani, *Khulasat al-Siyar* (Tehran, 1368/1989), 33, 55; Babayan, 'The Waning', 109, 111; Roemer, 6: 280. On the first office, see Minorsky, *Tadhkirat*, 47. Its previous holders from at least 1591–2, had also been Shamlu (Munshi, 2: 1309, 922, 810, 614). On Isfahani's *Khulasat* see n1 of the following chapter. Babayan's charts of the members of the various 'cabinets' over the period are also available in Babaie, et al., *Slaves of the Shah*, 139f.

140 On the Jews in this period, see the references herein (nn46, 59, 85), nn26, 30 of Chapter 6, and nn56,77 of Chapter 7. Gurney (114) refers to Lar as a centre of Jewish learning in this period. See also Kemp, 21–3. Netzer, ('Conversion, iv. Of Persian Jews to Other Religions', *EIr*, 6: 235), cites efforts c. 1613 and 1620 to convert Jews, over the objections of such court clerics as Shaykh Bahai.

141 Farhad Khan Qaramanlu's execution was not only down to his failure of battle but also to suspicions over his loyalty to the shah. As was frequently the case over the period, individual disloyalty as not taken as a sign of family disloyalty, and Farhad's brother was not killed. See Munshi, 2: 755–60. Yaqub Khan Dhul-Qadr's disloyalty did not forestall the advancement of other members of the tribe, as noted above in n20. Even in 1596–7 some Takkalu elements still enjoyed the shah's favour. See Szuppe, 'Kinship Ties', 92–5.

5 Shifts at the Centre and a Peace Dividend: Shah Safi (1629–1642)

1 These included Abbas' son-in-law the Tajik sayyid Khalifa Sultan, *vizier* since 1624, and Isa Khan Safavi, another son-in-law and *qurchibashi* since 1612. Also present were Abul-Qasim Evughlu, *ishikaqasi* (defined as 'usher' by Minorsky, *Tadhkirat*, 77, 138) of the haram since 1617, and, the *ishikaqasibashi*

Zaynal Khan of the Bekdilu, apparently a Shamlu subclan. On Abul-Qasim, see Munshi, 2: 717, 947, 975, 1147; Floor, *Safavid Government*, 169. On Zaynal Khan, see Munshi, 2: 1194, 1172, 1233, 1283, 1309–10 and n138 of the previous chapter. For these events, see Muhammad Masum Isfahani, *Khulasat*, 33, 11–18, 311f.

Isfahani's chronicle covers the years 1627 to 1641–2, through the accession of Abbas II. The author, apparently related to the *vizier* of Lahijan and governor of Qarabagh, held a court position which entailed travel with Safi. This text has yet to be subjected to the sort of analysis undertaken by Quinn for the pre-Safi court chronicles. The sections of Valih Isfahani's 1667 *Khuld-i Barin* which cover the reigns of Safi and Abbas II, edited by M. R. Nasiri and published as *Iran dar Zaman-i Shah Safi va Shah Abbas-i Duvvum (1038–1071)*, a single volume, in Tehran in 1380/2001, were not available to the author at the time of writing. Munshi, author of *Tarikh-i Alam Ara-yi Abbasi*, added material to this work until his own death in 1633, several years after Safi's accession. To produce a text which covered the entirety of Safi's reign, S. Khvansari published this additional material of Munshi together with that on Safi until the latter's death in 1642 from *Khuld-i Barin* as *Zayl-i Tarikh- i Alam Ara-yi Abbasi* (Tehran, 1317/1938) which volume was also not available to the present author. Thanks to W. Floor and M. Sefatgol for their assistance with this bibliographical information.

2   Sam's father was Muhammad Baqir, murdered in 1614 after being implicated in a plot against his father. The fate of Abbas' three uterine brothers, Hamza Mirza (d. 1586), Abu Talib and Tahmasp (d. 1619–20) has been discussed. Hasan Mirza, Abbas' brother by a Gilani notable, had been killed in 1577 by Ismail II. In 1620–1 and 1626–7 Abbas blinded his own sons Muhammad Mirza and Imam Quli respectively. Another son died a natural death. See Munshi, 1: 208–13, 2: 612, 614, 692, 825, 1099, 1177, 1187, 1288, 1303; 1288n. See also Savory, *Iran Under*, 94–5; Babayan, 'The Waning', 90n207. On Khudabanda's brothers and their fates, see Munshi, 1: 213f.

3   Munshi (2: 1302–3) noted the speed of the accession process 'to preserve the stability of the realm and to guard against possible mischief, because the capital was full of [all?] sorts and conditions of men . . . if the future Shah Safi had not been at the capital when the news of the death of Shah Abbas was published, serious riots and insurrections might have resulted . . . Large numbers of troops were stationed in Isfahan, some of whom reliable and some not.'

4   Abbas I had appointed no *vakil*, the post of *qullaraqasi* was vacant at his death, and the post of *sipahsalar* was also less important than it had been. Khalifa Sultan and Isa Khan retained their posts and Zaynal Khan Shamlu was now appointed *vakil* and *sipahsalar*. Abbas' *sadr*, the Tajik sayyid Rafi al-Din Muhammad Shahristani, like the first two above a son-in-law of the shah, also remained in his post. Khusraw Mirza, the Georgian governor of Isfahan whose brother's daughter was a wife of Abbas, was appointed *qullaraqasi* and given the name Rustam Khan. Babayan, 'The Waning', 105–6, 313; Floor, *Safavid Government*, 13, 16, 18, 21, 37, 142, 172; Floor, '*sadr*', 482, 483n134. On Rustam Khan's earlier career, including his campaigns in Georgia and Baghdad, see Munshi 2: 1168, 1250, 1280; Babayan, 'The Waning', 108. See also Munshi 2: 1069, 1146–7, 1261. Thanks to K. Babayan for her assistance with the various *sadr*s.

5   Mir Damad, a descendent of Ali Karaki, read the prayer at the ceremony. Other clerics who attended included: Mirza Habiballah, son-in-law of Lutfallah Maysi and the son of Sayyid Husayn Karaki, and hence another relative of Ali Karaki,

and Hasan Ali Shushtari, the son of Abdallah, for whom Abbas had built a school. See Munshi, 2: 1300ff; Isfahani, 35–9. See also Sayyid Abd Husayn Husayni Khatunabadi, *Vaqai al-Sinin val-Avvam* (Tehran, nd), 508–9.

Khatunabadi (d. 1693) was a student of Taqi Majlisi and Muhammad Baqir Sabzavari (d. 1679). On the latter, an associate of Khalifa Sultan, see the following chapter. Not a court chronicle per se, Khatunabadi's Persian-language text records events to the year 1686, with additional entries being added by his descendants.

6 Isfahani (41–2) notes payments to various courtiers, *ghulam*s, *qurchi*s, musketeers, those in the royal workshops and other military and political officials at court and in the provinces. Imam Quli Khan, son of the of the *ghulam* Allahvirdi Khan, and governor of Fars, Lar and Bahrayn, was said to have received as a gift a sum equivalent to the total of Fars' tax burden for one year. Isfahani noted the resulting outpouring of support among the large numbers who attended the accession ceremonies at the Shah Mosque, itself completed several years thereafter. See also Matthee, *The Politics*, 119.

7 Baghdad was administered by a Georgian, appointed by Abbas in 1622–3, and later commander in all of Persian Iraq and warden of the Iraqi Shi'i shrines, and one of the *ghulam*s raised to *amir*-status. See Munshi, 2: 1223, 1226–7, 1316; Roemer, 6: 283–4.

8 Matthee, *The Politics*, 121, and our discussion below. On Qishm see also Floor's *The First Dutch-Iranian Commercial Conflict* (Costa Mesa, 2004), unavailable to the present author. Although Isfahani does not offer great detail on Safavid military forces over Safi's reign, their composition over the period appears to have been as complex as during Abbas' reign. See, for example, Isfahani, 190, 262.

9 Munshi, 1302–3; Babayan, 'The Waning', 93–6.

10 Isa Khan Safavi, three of his sons and the grandson of the son who had allowed himself to be identified with claims to the succession at Abbas' death, were all killed. The sons of all Abbas' daughters were blinded. Zubayda Bekum, Abbas I's daughter and Safi's aunt, and Isa Khan's wife who had put forth the claim of her own son and may have tried to poison Safi, seem also to have been killed. Khalifa Sultan, Abbas' Tajik *sayyid vizier* and son-in-law, was put under house arrest. His four sons were blinded, as were those of the *sadr*, another son-in-law. The sons of the guardian of the Mashhad shrine, himself yet another of Abbas' sons-in-law, were also blinded. See Isfahani, 124–5, 132; Babayan, 'The Waning', 99, 113–14. Yusuf Aqa, master of the *ghulam*s of the royal haram and supervisor of Isfahan's Armenian community, was also executed. A relative who was governor of Shirvan, and a key figure in the royal silk monopoly, also lost his post. See Matthee, *The Politics*, 120–1 and our discussion below.

11 Several months later a son of Imam Quli Khan – himself son of Allahvirdi Khan and formerly head of all the *ghulam*s – who claimed to be a son of Abbas rose in Georgia. At this Imam Quli Khan and his family all were killed. The province of Fars, which had been governed by Imam Quli Khan, was seized as crown land. See Babayan, 'The Waning', 109, 114n271, 109, 109n259; Roemer, 6: 283–5 notes a rising among the Mushasha following the murder of Imam Quli Khan in 1632. On Rustam Khan see further below. In the same time frame Mulayim Bek, the royal factor, or court merchant, responsible for silk deliveries, purportedly became involved in an embezzlement scheme such that by 1632 he lost any role in the silk trade whatsoever. Matthee, *The Politics*, 124. See also Savory, 'Cerag Khan Zahedi', *EIr*, 5: 263.

12 The Tajik Mirza Abu Talib Urdubadi, the son of Abbas' *vizier* Hatim Bek, was *vizier*; the *ghulam* Rustam Bek was *sipahsalar*, head of the musketeers, and *divanbeki*; the Georgian Khusraw Mirza, now renamed Rustam Khan, was head of the *ghulam*, but was replaced by the *ghulam* Siyavush Bek. The Evughlu apparently held the post of the *ishikaqasi* of the haram, in the form of the brother of Abul-Qasim, the post's previous holder. The new *sadr* was Habiballah Karaki, son of Sayyid Husayn Karaki who had displaced Bahai's father as Qazvin's *Shaykh al-Islam* under Tahmasp. Tajik sayyids held other key administrative posts. See Munshi, 2: 1147; Isfahani, 61, 94, 172, 247, 380; Babayan, 314, 114n268; Floor, *Safavid Government*, 20, 237, 185; idem, 'Judicial', 22. On Rustam Bek, see also Babayan, ibid., 102; Floor, 'Judicial', 22; idem, *Safavid Government*, 18, 21, 185.

13 Urdubadi was executed. Rustam Bek remained *sipahsalar* and head of the musketeers and *divanbeki*. The *ghulam* Siyavush Bek remained *qullaraqasi*, Karaki remained *sadr* and the Evughlu retained sway over the haram. A Dhul-Qadr was appointed *qurchibashi* and a Shamlu was designated *ishikaqasibashi*. See Babayan, 'The Waning', 314–15; Floor, *Safavid Government*, 142, 172; idem, 'Judicial', 22. On Saru Taqi, see Floor, 'The Rise and Fall of Mirza Taqi, The Eunuch Grand *Vizier* (1043–55/1633–45), *Makhdum al-Omara va Khadem al-Foqara*', *SIr*, 26(2) (1997), 249; Babayan, ibid., 114f; Isfahani, 164; Munshi, 2: 1322–3; Matthee, *The Politics*, 129f.

14 For differing interpretations of these coups, see Babayan, 'The Waning', 95–6, 114–22; Floor, 'The Rise', 246–50, 263f; Babayan, *Mystics*, 401n91. The analysis of the former is also on offer in Babaie, et al., *Slaves of the Shah*, 20–48. Floor (ibid., 264) also notes Röhrborn's analysis (50f) that at the end of Safi's reign *ghulams* governed but three of eleven key provinces. See also Matthee, 'Administrative Change and Stability in Late 17th c. Iran: The Case of Shaykh Ali Khan Zanganah (1669–89)', *IJMES*, 26 (1994), 78.

   The careers of the Saru Taqi and the *ghulam* Rustam Bek illustrate yet again how loyalty to the person of the shah and ability promised advancement. On Saru Taqi, who had, in fact, been castrated as a punishment by Abbas I, see Floor, 'The Rise', 249; Babayan, 'The Waning', 114f; idem, *Mystics*, 383; Isfahani, 164; Munshi, 2: 1322–3; Matthee, *The Politics*, 129f. On Rustam Bek, see the sources cited in n12 above, and also Babayan, 'The Waning', 102; Floor, 'Judicial', 22; idem, *Safavid Government*, 18, 21, 185.

15 Isfahani, 49–54; Floor, 'The Rise', 249, 246. Isfahani (50) notes that the rebels targeted Rasht's merchants, broke into royal warehouses and seized and sold off the silk therein, forcing a drop in prices – suggesting an economic aspect to the rising. See also Matthee, *The Politics*, 122; Floor, 'The Dutch', 351–3. On Gilan, see Röhrborn, 90–1, 178. See also Roemer, 6: 283–6.

16 Isfahani, 117–21; Babayan, 'The Waning', 103–4, 148f. Isfahani notes (121) the 'strange sciences (*ulum ghariba*)' by which were produced luxurious goods seen in the Darvish's house. Babayan's figure of seventy-five killed in the final clash with Safavid forces is based on Yusuf Valhi's *Khuld-i Barin*, itself completed in 1667.

17 Matthee, 'Coffee', 25–6, citing contemporary travellers' accounts. See also n35. The association between Sufi discourse and the bazaar continued strong: in 1634–5 a prominent local fruit merchant funded repairs to the tomb of Baba Qasim in Isfahan (Blake, 170; Hunarfar, 302–11). About the same time a local dyer built and donated a number of shops as *vaqf* to a small mosque in the city

(Hunarfar, 541–3). At his death in 1640 Mir Findiriski, on whom see above, was buried near the tomb of Baba Rukn al-Din, a popular local site of pilgrimage built by Abbas (Blake, 170; Hunarfar, 543–6). On such Sufi tendencies in such provincial cities as Kashan, see Naraqi, 196–7, 335–6, 347–8; Zarrabi, 505.

18 Soon after his accession, Safi visited Qum and the Iraqi shrine cities, where he distributed funds among local religious officials, and Hilla. In 1631 major improvements were ordered to the Najaf shrine. See Isfahani, 64, 111f, 129–130, 149, 158, 164; Saru Taqi's association with the latter project contributed to his subsequent rise to prominence. In Isfahan, substantial sums were earmarked for religious teaching (Tabrizi, *Faraid*, 297) and work continued on the Shah Mosque, which was completed in 1630–1 (Hunarfar, 450–2; Godard, 107f.). The Aqa Nur mosque, in which a 1629 inscription referred to Safi in Persian as 'the just shah (*shah-i adil*)', was completed in these years (Hunarfar, 501–4; Canby, 121). The Imamzada of Ismail, the grandson of the second Imam, begun by Abbas, was also completed now; a 1631 inscription therein described Safi as the 'propagator of the faith of the Infallibles . . . the Husaynid . . . the Musavid'. See Blake, 47, 171; Hunarfar, 521–40; Godard, 131–42. The Abdallah Shushtari school is usually dated to the reign of Abbas I. Cf. Canby, 121, citing Hillenbrand, 6: 796. Safi's court retainer Isfahani refers to Safi as the 'shadow of Allah' (37, 110, 208, 269, 297–9).

Outside the capital, however, Safi was not consistently ascribed such titles. A 1637–8 *firman* in Yazd referred to Safi only as 'the Husaynid'. See I. Afshar, 'Similar Farmans from the reign of Shah Safi', in Melville, ed., *Safavid Persia*, 293. For a 1637–8 *firman* in Kashan, where Abbas I was buried, see Naraqi, 222–3, and for a 1634–5 *firman* in Isfahan itself, see Hunarfar, 541–3. Compare Khatunabadi, 508.

Upon his accession Safi also dropped the ban on tobacco instituted by his grandfather but is known to have reinstituted it several times. See Isfahani, 39; Jafariyan, *Ilal bar Uftadan-i Safaviyyan* (Tehran, 1373), 355, dating a *firman* against tobacco to 1628–9. On similar Ottoman and Mughal bans, see Matthee, 'Tutun' *EI²*, 10: 755; idem, 'Tobacco in Iran', 66. See also Floor, *The Economy*, 259.

19 Mir Damad participated in Safi's accession, led the Friday prayer in Isfahan thereafter and accompanied Safi on his trip to Iraq, during which he died. Isfahani (96, 111) calls Mir Damad 'the seal of the *mujtahids*', a title previously ascribed to Mir Damad's ancestor Ali Karaki and the latter's daughter's son Sayyid Husayn Karaki. See also Tehrani, 1: 407. Safi also invited Fayz Kashani, student of Shaykh Bahai and Mulla Sadra and the latter's son-in-law, to the capital, though Fayz declined (see ad n30 and n43, both in the following chapter). Sometime before 1634–5 Safi asked Mulla Sadra himself to translate portions of the *Ihya* of Ghazali (d. 1111) into Persian and also made overtures to Mir Findiriski, the close associate of Bahai and Mir Damad well known for his interest in Indian faiths and for his lower-class Sufi connections. Before Safi's accession Shaykh Bahai's student Taqi Majlisi himself apparently approached Safi with details of a dream portending Abbas' death and Safi's accession. See Babayan, 'The Waning', 279–80. On Safi and Fayz, see our 'Fayz', 41.

20 Matthee, *The Politics*, 120–1; McCabe, 146. See also Keyvani, 159. Though such contemporary Europeans as Olearius, on whom see below, Tavernier, and Chardin held that Safi introduced the *khassa* system of direct central ownership of land (see Minorsky, *Tadhkirat*, 26; Röhrborn, 173) the first major accrual of

land to the crown during Safi's reign, that of Fars, occurred after the 1632 murder of governor Imam Quli Khan and his family. The only other area made *khassa* land during Safi's reign was Lar, in 1636. See Röhrborn, 177–8; Savory, *Iran Under*, 228–9.

21   Herzig, 'The Volume', 64, 69; Floor, *The Economy*, 173. The 60% profit on Iranian silk sold in Holland in 1629 spurred the Dutch to renegotiate their trade agreements to expand silk purchases. The court, no doubt itself also aware of the profit differentials between the overland and Gulf routes, sent minor officials to conduct these discussions. These latter were happy to receive bribes which, as will be noted in Chapter 8, were in effect a salary, while ignoring Dutch entreaties. When, needing cash, the court levied a surcharge on all privately purchased silk, the VOC turned to the Armenians only to find them also well attuned to the shifting profit margins between selling to the VOC and shipping via the Levant route: the Armenians insisted on payment in advance. Matthee, *The Politics*, 124f, 243. On the Armenians' prosperity in these years, see McCabe, 148–51; Ghougassian, 59. The large sum of money was found with Yusuf Aqa, then supervisor of Isfahan's Armenian community, at his execution in 1632 (n10), further underlines this prosperity, even at the outset of Safi's reign. See Matthee, *The Politics*, 120–1.

22   This overture was, however, not only rebuffed but, in 1638 Ottoman clerics issued a legal ruling (*fatva*) against the Shi'a. See Jafariyan, *Safaviyya dar Arsa-yi Din*, 1:83.

23   Floor, *A Fiscal*, 227; idem, 'The Rise', 248–51; Matthee, *The Politics*, 130; Ghougassian, 59, citing Olearius. Qandahar was lost in when the local governor, disaffected with Saru Taqi's withdrawal of certain subsidies, placed himself under the jurisdiction of the Mughal Shah Jahan (reg. 1628–58). Isfahani, 251, 254–5.

24   On four *firman*s issued in 1636 and inscribed at provincial sites granting concessions, respectively, to Hindus, Kabulis, certain local tribes and numerous guilds and classes of the poor, see Afshar, 'Similar *Farmans*', 285–304.

25   In 1635, during negotiations with the VOC on a new treaty, the *vizier* requested 8,000 *tumans* loan from the Dutch to pay Safavid troops. In 1637, with a German silk mission also present in the country, Saru Taqi drove the Dutch a hard bargain on silk. In 1638 the court limited all private silk purchases to amass cheaper-grade silk itself for sale to the Europeans, though Iran continued to send Armenian merchants to Europe to sell silk directly. The VOC was forced to agree to buy most of the court's silk. See Matthee, *The Politics*, 131–3.

26   Floor, 'The Dutch', 351–3. On the companies' preference to sell their goods for cash, see also Floor, *The Economy*, 117–18.

27   The English depended more than the VOC on selling products in the Iranian market to finance their silk purchases. English cloth being both unsuitable for the Iranian market, and often of poor quality, the EIC had to pay cash for its silk. Economics therefore dictated an end to EIC silk export, and the company exported its last bales of silk in 1641, just as Indian and Chinese silk was becoming available. Unsurprisingly the court treated the EIC with increasingly greater disregard than the Dutch. On the EIC's position in Iran over the period, see Matthee, *The Politics*, 133f, 145, 243; Floor, *The Economy*, 148–9, 173–4; Ferrier, 'The Terms', 65f.

On the companies' silk exports, and consequently the court's attention thereto, as incidental to the overall volume of Iran's silk trade over this entire period, see Floor, 'The Dutch', 352; Herzig, 'The Volume', esp. 63–71, 74; idem, 'The Rise', 317–18. Floor suggests (*The Economy*, 173–5) that the Gulf-based trading companies obtained at best 25% of the market in 1628, 1630, 1640. Thereafter VOC averaged only 400 bales per year and after 1654 200 bales, out of approximately 4,000 bales produced per year. If these are not absolutely accurate figures, as Herzig ('The Volume', 79) acknowledges, they do give a reasonable, relative, picture of the period's trading activity and the relative significance of the Gulf silk trade. See also Matthee, *The Politics*, 133f, 145, 123, 128, 243. On Zuhab itself, see Matthee, 'Iran's Ottoman Diplomacy During the Reign of Shah Sulayman I (1077–1105/1666–94)', in K. Eslami, ed., *Iran and Iranian Studies, Essays in Honor of Iraj Afshar* (Princeton, 1998), 148–9. Coffee imports briefly promised potential profits to the foreign companies but were throttled by competition from private European and local merchant elements. See Matthee, 'Coffee', 7–13.

28 McCabe, 150–1. Armenian wealth in the period was such that by 1634 there were more than twenty active churches in Isfahan. See Ghougassian, 59, 94, 101, 182.

29 Bespeaking the centre's partiality for Armenian over foreign interests in particular, the court consistently sided with the complaints of Armenian church officials against the activities of foreign missionaries. See Ghougassian, 137. In this, the anti-missionary polemics of Mir Damad's son-in-law Sayyid Ahmad Alavi (d. between 1644 and 1650) during the reign of both Abbas and Safi, suited court interests. On Alavi see also further below. See also Matthee, 'Between', 237; A. H. Hairi, 'Reflections on the Shi'i Responses to Missionary Thought and Activities in the Safavid Period', in Calmard, ed., *Études*, 151–64, esp. 155–7; F. Richard, 'L'apport de Missionaires Européens à la Connaissance de l'Iran en Europe et de l'Europe en Iran', in Calmard, ed., *Études*, 251–66; Richard, 'Capuchin', 787. On Sayyid Ahmad, see H. Corbin, 'Ahmad b. Zayn al-Abedin Alavi Ameli Esfahani, Sayyed', *EIr*, 1: 644–6; Abisaab, *Converting Persia*, 79–81.

30 See Floor, *The Economy*, 199f, 245. Floor (ibid., 173) notes the Banyans were sending out silk via the overland route to India. The Indian trade included rice, sugar, spices, steel for weapons, indigo, cotton goods and wool. Cotton was imported despite the centre's best efforts. See Floor, ibid., 125, 126f, 133f, 136f, 147f, 149f, 156f. Keyvani (130) notes trade and manufacture specialisation in various cities in this period. See also Floor, *The Economy*, 247–301.

31 Babayan, 'The Waning', 314–5; Floor, '*sadr*', 482.

32 Sayyid Ahmad penned his own anti-Sufi diatribe in 1633. In 1634 Kamrai composed an essay criticising Safi's request to Mulla Sadra translate Ghazali into Persian. An opponent of Friday prayer during the occultation, Kamrai also declared the present age devoid of any *mujtahid*; that this was not an Akhbari-style criticism, see Stewart, *The Genesis*, 187. See our 'Clerical Perceptions of Sufi Practices in Late Seventeenth-Century Persia: Arguments Over the Permissibility of Singing (*Ghina*)', in L. Lewisohn and D. Morgan, eds, *The Heritage of Sufism, Vol. III: Late Classical Persianate Sufism: the Safavid and Mughal Period (1501–1750)*, (Oxford, 1999), 135–64; Babayan, 'The Waning' 135–6, 141n, 195f, 326–8, 342; idem, *Mystics*, 250f. R. Jafariyan has published a number of these anti-Abu Muslim essays in *Miras-i Islami-yi Iran*, 2 (Qum, 1374), 247–302. Taqi Majlisi's apparent disclaimer of interest in the Dhahabi Sufi order in this period (C. Turner, *Islam Without Allah? The Rise of Religious Externalism in*

Safavid Iran, Richmond, 2000, 153) was likely an effort to defend himself from association with resurgent popular interest in Abu Muslim in the face of such polemics.

Coincident with these events Shaykh Ali Amili, a direct descendant of Shaykh Zayn al-Din Amili and a relative of Ali Karaki on his mother's side, relocated to Iran from the West. Shaykh Ali was a fierce opponent of both Muhammad Amin Astarabadi and the Akhbari school and of philosophical inquiry, Sufism, and Friday prayer. See the following chapter.

33 Melville, 'Shah Abbas', 218; Afshar, 'Similar Farmans', 285; Isfahani, 144, 168–9, 195, 234–5, 238.

34 Absolution involved a ritual beating with a stick called *chub-i tariq*. Morton, 'The *Chub-i Tariq*', 227–9, 231, 233, 233n29, 234–5. Morton (ibid., 243) suggests that the continuation of the ceremony throughout the later Safavid period points to the continued prominence of the Qizilbash in the period, their existence being required to balance 'the new forces he (Abbas I) had created at their expense'. Compare Savory, 'The Office of "Khalifat al-Khulafa" ', 501–2. On the ritual beatings performed by the *Khalifa* during Tahmasp's reign, see Membré (42–3). See also Floor, 'Khalifeh', 73.

35 Olearius, perhaps unwittingly observing dissident spiritual traditions at work, noted the presence of the traditional story-tellers who would recite the stories of the martyrdom of Husayn and other Shi'i historical figures during these festivals. Calmard notes these story-tellers based their recitations at least partly on the works of Muhtasham, the poet ordered by Tahmasp to produce more 'religious' poetry. Calmard includes a 1641 letter on the Ashura festival composed by the lay companion of the Carmelite bishop of Baghdad. Calmard, 'Shi'i Rituals and Power II', 146–7, 148, 152, 154, 155–6, 162, 164; Morton, 'The Ardabil Shrine', (1975), 54–5. See also Babayan (*Mystics*, 219f) on travellers' accounts of these ceremonies. On Olearius' claim to have seen the tomb of Abbas I in Ardabil, see n64 of Chapter 4.

Although Matthee (*The Politics*, 139, 142–5) blames the failure of the Russian trade route on Safi's 'diminished interest in the outside world', the resistance of local Russian merchants, the continuing Cossack raids into Gilan in the early 1630s and the greater profits to be made from and the reliability of the Levant route, especially after Zuhab, were certainly factors as well. See also Canby, 124.

36 In 1640 Safi issued a *firman* confirming the holdings of the Marashi family as custodians of the Qazvin shrine. Mudarrisi, *Bargi*, 31, 169–72. See also Jafariyan, 'Munasibat', 17–18, on several prominent Arab sayyids who visited Isfahan in the late 1630s.

37 Blake, 151, 153; Godard, 146–7; Hunarfar, 547–52. See also S. Babaie, 'Building for the Shah: the Role of Mirza Muhammad Taqi (Saru Taqi) in Safavid Royal Patronage of Architecture', in S. Canby, ed., *Safavid Art and Architecture*, 20–6; Babaie, et al., *Slaves of the Shah*, 101f.

38 The *darugha*'s Tajik assistant in the city built a mansion next to that of the *vizier*. Blake, 89; Hunarfar, 549–52.

39 Blake, 89. Rustam Khan later spearheaded the capture of Tiflis and died in office. See Babayan, 'The Waning', 114.

40 Blake, 94, 90.

41 Canby, 103, 122–4, 134f; Munshi, 2: 1260. The flower paintings, dated to 1640, in the Abdallah Shushtari school suggest his interest in European sources and

may have been produced to be supplied to weavers as the basis for textile designs. The 'Portuguese' carpets, so-called for their serrated, central medallion containing blossoms, partridges and hoopoes and corners, with ships manned by figures dressed in European, apparently Portuguese, clothes, also attest to European influence and an interface between Riza Abbasi's paintings and textile patterns, as do a series of textiles sent with the 1639 Iranian mission to Duke Frederich III. Kirman continued to be a carpet centre where carpets using vase-style techniques were still being produced. See Canby, *The Golden Age*, 124–6; Walker, 'Carpets', 873–4. On Riza Abbasi and his European influences, see Canby, *Reformer*, 172, 175, 167, 193, 195; Matthee, 'Between Aloofness and Fascination: Safavid Views of the West', *IS*, 31(2) (Spring 1998), 231–2. On Dutch painters and jewellers in Iran in this period, see Floor, 'Dutch-Persian Relations'; n77 of the previous chapter.

42   Canby, *The Golden Age*, 61, 78, 111–12, 116–17, 124–7; Floor, *The Economy*, 323–4, 321.

43   Canby, *The Golden Age*, 122. On father and son, see Munshi, 2: 1260, 1316. The career of Qarachaqay Khan and his son in respect of Khurasan thus parallels that of Allahvirdi Khan and his son Imam Quli Khan as successive governors of Fars. Adamova's reference to a *Farhad and Shirin* copied in 1635 whose miniatures were done by Muhammad Qasim, another student of Sadiqi Bek, for Qarachaqay Khan perhaps refers to his son, as Qarachaqay Khan had died some ten years before. See Adamova, 'Muhammad Qasim', in Newman, 209. If Muhammad Qasim was producing for Safi prior to his accession (ibid., 207) he was not averse to seeking out other patrons.

44   Savory discusses the reigns of the last four shahs in his last chapter, which he entitled 'Decline and Fall of the Safavids'. The chapter opens with the quote from Chardin (226), itself cited by Lockhart (*The Fall*, 16), Stevens (441), and in our Introduction. As noted earlier, Chardin arrived in Iran only in 1666, the last year of the reign of Safi's successor, i.e. two decades after Safi's death. See Stevens, 425; J. Emerson, 'Chardin', *EIr*, V(4): 369–77; Lockhart, 'European Contacts', 6: 399–401; H. Winter, 'Persian Science in Safavid Times', in Peter Jackson, ed., 6: 585; Minorsky, *Tadhkirat*, 7, 7n46. Prior to the papers cited in n12 of our Introduction only Stevens (441) had queried the usefulness of a comment made by one so young, twenty-two, when he arrived in Iran more than thirty years after Abbas' death. Savory himself (*Iran Under*, 229) notes that Safi's 'blackened' reputation owes much to the opinions of such European writers as the Jesuit Krusinski and Jonas Hanway who reached Iran only sixty and a hundred years after Safi's death respectively. Chardin's erroneous dating of the development of the *khassa* system to Safi's reign has been noted. But see also Canby, 118; Blake, 10; Matthee, *The Politics*, 124–5, 176, dating to Safi's reign the financial constraints and military weakness which he suggests plagued the polity later in the century; idem, 'Administrative Change', 79, on the growth of *khassa* land as a sign of Safavid weakness.

45   Although *ghulam*s held but three of eleven governorships, versus eight of fourteen at Abbas' death, among the key officials at the centre the balance of power remained roughly the same over the period. The post of *qurchibashi* remained in tribal hands: in 1638 the Dhul-Qadr *qurchibashi* was replaced by Jani Khan Shamlu who remained in office until 1645. The Georgian Rustam Khan remained *divanbeki* until 1635 when he was replaced by his brother who remained in office until 1642. Rustam Khan himself remained *sipahsalar* until

March 1643. A Shamlu replaced the Shamlu *ishikaqasi* of the Supreme Divan in 1637 and another Evughlu replaced the Evughlu *ishikaqasi* of the haram in 1637–8. Saru Taqi himself remained *vizier*. Karaki remained *sadr*, and Tajiks held other of the centre's important administrative posts. See Isfahani, 139, 141, 147, 197, 222, 242, 310; Babayan, 'The Waning' 315, 316; Floor, *Safavid Government*, 140, 21, 21n125; 37; idem, 'Judicial', 22; idem, 'The Rise', 264. On the continued mixed composition of Safavid military forces in this period, see n8.

6 The Peace Dividend Consolidated: Shah Abbas II (1642–1666)

1 Isfahani, 303f; Valiquli b. Daud Quli Shamlu, *Qisas al-Khaqani*, H. S. Nasiri, ed., 2 vols (Tehran, 1371), 266f. Shamlu (d. after 1674), a historian and poet who had served as comptroller in Sistan, completed his chronicle between 1664 and 1674. He occasionally cites *Abbasnama* (e.g. 405, 415), on which see the following note. See also Nasiri's introduction to the text. Thanks to K. Babayan for her comments on the dating of *Qisas*.

2 Tax concessions were distributed among the provinces, key officials were confirmed in their posts, and official robes of honours were sent to all incumbents. According to Mirza Muhammad Tahir Vahid Qazvini's *Abbasnama*, a tax amnesty was granted to all those whose salaries were in arrears, at a cost estimated at 500,000 *tumans*. *Favaid Safaviyya*, completed in 1796, alleges some 300,000 *tumans* in gifts was spent at Abbas II's accession. The hardly dispassionate Dutch claimed the reception of an Uzbek envoy in late 1642 cost some 100,000 *tumans*. See Muhammad Tahir Vahid Qazvini, *Abbasnama*, I. Dihqan ed. (Arak, 1329), 19–20; Matthee, *The Politics*, 150; idem, 'The Career of Mohammed Bek, Grand Vizier of Shah Abbas II (reg. 1642–66), *IS*, 24(1–4) (1991), 22–3, 25; Floor, *A Fiscal*, 227; n54 below.

   Abbasnama of the Tajik Qazvini (d. 1698) covers Abbas II's reign from 1642 to 1666. Qazvini was an associate of Saru Taqi and an associate of the court during the reigns of Abbas II and his successor Sulayman. See Dihqan's introduction to the text. Abbas II died as his 'corrections' were being added to the latter portions of the work. On *Khuld-i Barin*, the universal history written by Qazvini's brother Muhammad Yusuf Valih, and completed in 1667 – though the dates 1660 and 1689 also have been suggested – see the following chapter.

3 Saru Taqi stayed remained the *vizier*, the *ghulam* Rustam Bek the *sipahsalar* and his brother Ali Quli the *divanbeki*. The *ghulam* Siyavush Bek remained *qullaraqasi*. Jani Khan Shamlu remained *qurchibashi*, and another Shamlu remained *ishikaqasi* of the divan. The Evughlu retained the post of *ishikaqasi* of the haram and Habiballah Karaki remained *sadr*. The capital's *shaykh al-Islam* and other lesser court figures also remained in post. See Babayan, 'The Waning', 315–16, 122–4; Floor, *Safavid Government*, 37, 142, 172; idem, 'Judicial', 22; idem, '*sadr*', 482.

4 Babayan, 'The Waning', 120n291, citing Chardin, who identified Saru Taqi's female ally as Abbas II's mother Anna. Floor ('The Rise', 255–6, 255n108, 260n131) identifies her as Safi's mother, citing Tavernier who, having arrived in Iran in 1632, is the more contemporary. Compare Isfahani, 307–10; Shamlu, 271f. See also Floor, 'Judicial', 22. In true Safavid fashion, the 'sins' of one family member did not necessarily tar his relatives: Rustam Bek's brother would be

sipahsalar, be jailed and, in 1666, be freed at Sulayman's accession, become governor of Azerbaijan and, again, *sipahsalar*. See Babayan, 'The Waning', 317–19.

5 Shamlu, 275f, esp. 282–6; Qazvini, 64–9; Khatunabadi, 515–16. See also Babayan, 'The Waning', 126n308, citing the 1741–2 *Zubdat al-Tavarikh*; Floor, *Safavid Government*, 208; idem, 'The Rise', 257–6, 262, 265, citing contemporary and later sources, the latter including Chardin and Persian sources. Jani Khan's extensive property was confiscated but, with typical Safavid pragmatism, was returned to his heirs under Sulayman and Jani Khan's son became *divanbeki* in 1670–1 (Floor, 'The Rise', 262). For an accessible, if much abridged, version of Chardin's (later) account of Saru Taqi's fall, the detail of which strains credibility, see R. Ferrier, *A Journey to Persia, Jean Chardin's Portrait of a Seventeenth-century Empire* (London, 1996), 49. See also McCabe, 173–4.

6 Abbas II eventually had his own brothers blinded and nephews killed; his two sons were spared. See Roemer, 6: 302.

7 Where the key officials during Saru Taqi's vizieate under Abbas II had included three *ghulam*s, three Tajiks – including the sayyid Mirza Habiballah as *sadr* – and five Qizilbash – mainly Shamlu, Khalifa Sultan's second 'cabinet' comprised two *ghulam*s, four Tajiks and six Qizilbash; the six included Qajars, Shamlus and Chagatais, the latter having been incorporated into the Qizilbash during Abbas I's reign. Abbas II's new Shamlu *qurchibashi* was of the same Bekdilu subclan as Zaynal Khan Shamlu, the *vakil* and *sipahsalar* under Khalifa Sultan at Safi's accession. See Babayan, 'The Waning', 124, 133–4, 315–17; Floor, *Safavid Government*, 142, 172, 185; idem, 'Judicial', ibid.; idem, 'The Rise', 264; idem, 'sadr', 482, where he notes that Mirza Habiballah was *sadr* of the *khassa*, but that the post of *sadr al-mamalik* had been vacant from the dismissal of Mirza Rafi al-Din Muhammad in 1632.

8 Floor, *The Economy*, 80, 173; See also Floor, the Dutch, 352. On Ottoman-Safavid relations in this period, see Matthee, 'Iran's Ottoman Diplomacy', 149–51. On domestic silk weaving, see further below.

9 By the end of Abbas II's reign, the Frenchman de Thévenot, who arrived in Iran in 1664, suggested there were some 15,000 Indian merchants in the capital. Blake (125f, citing Dale's *Indian Merchants Indian Merchants and Eurasian Trade, 1600–1750* (Cambridge, 1974), suggests the Indians occasionally dealt in money lending but were mainly merchants but Keyvani argues for their overt and greater participation in specie export. See also Blake, 135, 125; Floor, *The Economy*, 21–5 on Indian traders in Iran and 181f, esp. 183–96, 327f, 245, on the importance of the trade with India; Matthee', Merchants', 246–9, 255. Matthee (ibid., esp. 254f) reviews the literature on merchants' status in this period. See also n26 of Chapter 7.

10 On Qishm, see Floor's *The First Dutch-Iranian Commercial Conflict*. See also idem, *The Economy*, 173; idem, 'The Dutch', 353; Matthee, *The Politics*, 157. On Saru Taqi's negotiations with the VOC, see Matthee, *The Politics*, 148f; idem, 'Between Venice and Surat', esp. 238, on the 1644 ban. On the VOC's silk and specie export, see Matthee, *The Politics*, 156–7, 244; Floor and Clawson, 348–50; Floor, *The Economy*, 173, 181–96, 327f. The extent to which the *hajj* exacerbated the specie outflow, as suggested by Matthee (*The Politics*, 205), is unclear but see, in Chapter 4, the text ad n87 and n87 itself.

11 At Abbas II's accession, despite a gift to the new monarch, the EIC secured no new concessions, nor was the company able to exploit the disfavour into which

the VOC fell after 1645. See Floor, *The Economy*, 173, 186; Floor in Melville, 353; Matthee, *The Politics*, 158–60. On EIC silk exports, see Floor, *The Economy*, 173, 186; idem, 'The Dutch', 353; Matthee, *The Politics*, 158–60. On the Russian route, see Herzig, 'The Volume', 71–3; Matthee, *The Politics*, 168–71; n35 of Chapter 5 and n84 of Chapter 4. On the EIC's suspension of silk purchases after 1641, see n27 of Chapter 5. For an ultimately unsuccessful effort by the EIC to coopt indigenous Armenian merchants and thereby revive the silk trade in the later 1680s and 1690s, see V. Baladouni and M. Makepeace, eds, *Armenian Merchants of the Seventeenth and Early Eighteenth Centuries: English East India Company Sources* (Philadelphia, 1998).

12 Matthee, 'The Career', 27; idem, 'Coffee', 29–30; Floor, *The Economy*, 17. Keyvani (129) cites Tavernier, who made a number of trips to Iran between 1632 and 1668, that Isfahan's Armenian furriers were only allowed to trade at the Armenian bazaar near the Ali Qapu and, citing Qazvini (72), notes Abbas II's 1645 *firman* forbidding their engagement in this trade altogether. On Khalifa Sultan and the Dutch, see Matthee, *The Politics*, 157–8. See also Jafariyan, *Safaviyya dar Arsa-yi Din*, 1: 389. On the devaluations, see Floor, *The Economy*, 80–1; Matthee, 'The Career', 23; idem, 'Merchants', 244; n16 below. See also McCabe, 154–70. On Jewish merchants, see also Floor, 'Commerce', 70; n26. On Jewish conversions, see Netzer, 'Conversion', 234–6, citing Jewish sources.

13 Foreign sources claimed that although more than 5,000 *tumans'* worth of grain was collected for the campaign Safavid troops were unpaid, poorly equipped and hungry. The following year Qandahar itself was said to have been ravaged and verging on famine. Matthee, *The Politics*, 160–3, 165–6; idem, 'The Career', 23; Floor, *Safavid Government*, 208–9; idem, *A Fiscal*, 228. On Qandahar's commercial importance over the period, see Floor, 'Commerce', 68.

The mixed composition of the Safavid expedition is attested in the contemporary sources. Röhrborn (78–9), citing such sources as Qazvini (94), states that at the start of the Qandahar campaign Abbas called up Beklarbeks, tribal amirs, *qurchis*, *ghulams* and elements of the shah's special guards as well as musketeers, many of whom were *ghulams*, and others of tribal origin based in Azerbaijan and Shirvan, i.e. border provinces. See also Qazvini, 114; Shamlu, 429–30; Floor, *Safavid Government*, 194–5, 209, on the use of Turkish and European mercenaries, not for the first time, in the attack on Qandahar, one of the strongest forts in the Middle East. On the musketeers, see also Minorsky, *Tadhkirat*, 32–3. Chardin, who arrived in Iran late in Abbas II's reign, estimated the army as totalling 112,000 troops. The *ghulam* numbered only 10,000 and with the musketeers, who numbered 12,000, were paid from *khassa* land. The *qurchi*, made up of tribal elements, numbered some 30,000, a figure still larger than the *ghulam* and musketeers combined. With local governors maintaining some 60,000 troops, the overwhelming balance of forces thus lay at the provincial level, hence the call in the Qandahar campaign. Floor, *Safavid Government*, 207–14, lists troops and their dispersal over the period and Röhrborn (73, 80), citing contemporary sources, notes that assembling such a large number of troops took months. See Minorsky, *Tadhkirat*, 32–6. Cf. Floor, *Safavid Government*, 152, 162, 209–10; n90 of Chapter 8.

14 Floor, *The Economy*, 173–4, 187–8, 81; Floor, 'The Dutch', 353; Matthee, *The Politics*, 161, 163, 165. Although the figures for Dutch silk exports for 1652 and 1653, let alone other years, given by Floor (*The Economy*, 173–4) and Matthee (165, 243–5) differ, both suggest decline. Although the EIC had purchased no

Iranian silk since the 1640s, EIC specie export continued. See Matthee, *The Politics*, 158–60, 243. On the limited impact of the French East India Company, granted trading rights in 1665, see A. Kroell, 'East India Company (The French)' *EIr*, 8.

15 On these economic hardships, see Matthee, *The Politics*, 164; idem, 'The Career', 20, 27–9.

16 The campaign also banned prostitution and closed brothels. See Qazvini, 70–2; Matthee, 'Prostitutes', 146; idem, 'Coffee', 27, 29–30; idem, *The Politics*, 323–5. Although the alcohol ban lapsed after the taking of Qandahar, owing to widespread celebrations, it was reinstituted *c.* 1653, when shah felt close to death. The potential drop in 'entertainment' tax revenues to the centre, along with the similar potential fall in revenues resulting from conversions, no doubt contributed to the short-lived nature of these campaigns and probably similar earlier campaigns noted above. On these several bans during Abbas II's reign, including that of 1653, and mention thereof by the poet Saib Tabrizi, see also Jafariyan, *Safaviyya dar Arsa-yi Din*, 1: 383f. See also Floor, *A Fiscal*, 158; Keyvani, 129 and n12 above. On the revenue from tobacco taxes, see n75 of Chapter 8.

17 These groups are also accused of participating in gatherings where there was handclapping, wearing unsuitable clothing, including wool, felt hats and patched frocks (*khirqa*). On these texts, see our 'Clerical Perceptions'. On Sufi dancing see R. Friend, 'Dance, III. Modern Persian Dancing', *EIr*, 6: 644. On Ardabili, see n40 of Chapter 3; n95 of Chapter 2. 'Ardabili' also attacked Mirza Jan Shirazi who had, in fact, studied with the real Ardabili, and on whom see n93 of Chapter 2.

18 The descriptions of the groups in Muhammad Tahir's 'Radd' are more often than not nearly perfect, if often shortened, versions of those in *Hadiqa*. See our 'Sufism and Anti-Sufism in Safavid Iran: The Authorship of the *Hadiqat al-Shi'a* Revisited', *Iran*, XXXVII (1999), 95–108.

19 Mir Lawhi's Persian-language treatise 'Salvat al-Shi'a' dates to 1650. On these individuals, see above as well as our 'Clerical Perspectives', pp. 173–4. On Kamrai, see also Jafariyan, *Din va Siyasat dar Dawrah-yi Safavi* (Qum, 1370/ 1991), 173–4, idem, *Safaviyya dar Arsa-yi Din*, 3: 1165–90; Babayan, 'The Waning', 317.

20 During his exile in Qum, Khalifa Sultan had composed a number of essays in this genre, thus distancing himself from allegations of Sufi sympathies made against his own teachers Mir Damad and Shaykh Bahai. See Tehrani, 4: 490; 6: 41–2, 65, 91–2, 111, 130–1, 206.

21 Khatunabadi, 522–3, 531; Babayan, 'The Waning', 85f, 141, citing Shamlu; Floor, '*sadr*', 482.

22 A Tabrizi, Muhammad Bek had participated in trade negotiations with the Dutch and the 1648 currency devaluation. He himself was head of Isfahan's Armenian community at Abbas II's accession and was then harbour master at Bandar Abbas. In 1651 he was promoted to the powerful post of supervisor of the royal workshops. See Matthee, 'The Career', 20–1. On the post of harbour master over the Safavid period, see Matthee, 'Shahbandar', *EI²*, Suppl, 716–17.

23 Qizilbash elements – including two Qajars, two Chagatais and a Shamlu – held five of fourteen of the realm's key posts, *ghulam* held 5, and Tajiks held three; a number of these, including the Qajar *qurchibashi* and *divanbeki* and the Karaki *sadr*, for example, were holdovers from Khalifa Sultan's vizierate. See Babayan, 'The Waning', 129–30, 318–20; Floor, *Safavid Government*, 21, 37, 142, 172;

Floor, '*sadr*', 482; Floor, 'Judicial', 22. Mirza Muhammad Karaki was sole *sadr* from 1651 to 1661, though Qazvini (338) lists three such *sadr*s. See also ibid., 335f. The *ghulam qullaraqasi* Siyavush Bek died *c.* 1651 and was replaced by an Armenian *ghulam*. See Qazvini, 85, 137, 165, 180, 322; Matthee, Career, 29; Floor, *Safavid Government*, 172.

24   Floor, *The Economy*, 173–5; idem, 'The Dutch', 353–4; Herzig, 'The Volume', 65, 69; Matthee, *The Politics*, 166–7. On the Russian route in this period, see Herzig, ibid., 71–3; Matthee, *The Politics*, 168–71; n11.

25   Qazvini, 219–22. See also Floor, 'Judicial', 22; Keyvani, 156–7, citing Chardin.

26   The enforcement of the ban on specie export until 1661, the year of Muhammad Bek's dismissal, was all the easier as one of the *vizier*'s sons was assayer of the mint and another was Bandar Abbas' harbour master. Soon after the institution of the ban, in March 1657, Jewish merchants, at least, offered a large present to the shah. See Matthee, 'The Career', passim, esp. 23, 27–9; idem, *The Politics*, 164–5. On the Jews in this period, see also Qazvini, 218–19; Keyvani, 129; Floor, *The Economy*, 19–20, citing foreign sources; Matthee, 'Merchants', 242–6; V. Moreen, 'The Problems of Conversion Among Iranian Jews in the Seventeenth and Eighteenth Centuries', *IS*, 19(3–4) (1986), 215–28; idem, 'The *Kitab-i Anusi* of Babai ibn Lutf (Seventeenth Century) and the *Kitab-i Sar Guzasht* of Babai ibn Farhad (Eighteenth Century): a Comparison of Two Judaeo-Persian Chronicles', in Mazzaoui and Moreen, eds, *Intellectual Studies on Islam, Essays Written in Honor of Martin B. Dickson* (Salt Lake City, 1990), 41–8. On reports that Fayz Kashani objected to the campaign to convert Iranian Jews, see n30. On the measures against the Armenians, see also n65.

27   Floor and Clawson, 350. Saru Taqi is credited with greater centralisation of land but although he did interfere with *vaqf* properties (Floor, *A Fiscal*, 119–25), in fact only gradually did more land become *khassa* land over Abbas II's reign. In the main, moreover, these lands comprised territory safe from attack, that is not border provinces. Too, not all these lands remained *khassa*: during Muhammad Bek's vizierate, the lands designated *khassa* included Hamadan and nearby areas, from 1653–4 until the middle years of Abbas II's successor; Ardabil, in 1656–7, Simnan from 1656–7 until 1662–3; and Kirman, from 1658 until *c.* 1694. Chardin's claim that only under Abbas II did Gilan and Mazandaran become *khassa* is not substantiated in the Persian sources. See also Minorsky, *Tadhkirat*, 24f, esp. 26; Lockhart, *The Fall*, 23–4; Matthee, *The Politics*, 164–5, 176–7; idem, 'The Career', 24–7. There is little correspondence between the lists of Olearius and Chardin of the areas made *khassa* land under Safi and Abbas II (Minorsky, ibid., 26) and that of Röhrborn (172–83, esp. 177–8). After 1650 Qizilbash troops were stationed in *khassa* provinces but, while revenues from *khassa* land paid such troops, local revenue also went to paying local troops and local governors had some authority over such forces. See Röhrborn, 166; Floor, *Safavid Government*, 109n11, citing Qazvini (320) and Olearius. See also nn13, 28.

28   Chardin's oft-cited story that *c.* 1660 the shah discovered that the same troops had repeatedly passed by him in review (Minorsky, *Tadhkirat*, 35; Floor, *Safavid Government*, 209), no doubt owes its origins to the costs of calling up troops from their provincial bases; see n13; n90 of Chapter 8. Despite such cost-cutting measures, two special corps were established during Abbas II's reign: the 600-strong Jazairi corps, established in 1654 and permanently on guard at the palace gates, and the shah's life-guards, made up of some 200 'Sufis'. Kaempfer, a

German doctor who lived in Isfahan in 1683–4, claimed the former numbered some 2,000. See Minorsky, 33–4. As against Chardin's suggestion (Minorsky, 33) that at the death of the head of the artillery corp in 1655, no successor was appointed, Roemer (6: 291n1) cites Luft that a new artillery detachment was formed the very same year.

On less successful attempts by the *vizier* to raise money, see Matthee, 'The Career', 25–31; idem, *The Politics*, 163f.

29 Babayan, 'The Waning', 143, citing Qazvini, 255. Fayz Kashani is mentioned as having been involved in this process as well.

30 The *firman* inviting Fayz was dated 1654. The same year Abbas commissioned from Taqi Majlisi a Persian translation of and commentary on *Man la Yahdaruhu al-Faqih*, the *hadith* compilation of the Buwayhid-period Twelver scholar Ibn Babawayh (d. 991–2), on which Majlisi had already written an Arabic language commentary for Abbas in 1653. Abbas also patronised Khalil Qazvini (d. 1678–9), an opponent of 'popular' Sufism but a proponent of philosophical inquiry and an associate of the former *vizier* Khalifa Sultan. In a commentary on *al-Kafi*, the *hadith* compilation of Muhammad b. Yaqub Kulayni (d. 941), commissioned by Abbas II and completed between 1653 and 1657, Qazvini interpreted two *hadith*s from the Prophet as references to Abbas II. Qazvini's known opposition to Friday prayer during the Imam's absence suggests a, successful, effort by the centre to identify with potentially sympathetic elements among such opposition, as Khalifa Sultan had attempted earlier. See Khatunabadi, 520, 530; Newman, 'Fayz', 45, n20. Other 'philosopher-clerics' present at court in this period included Rajab Ali Tabrizi (d. 1669), like Sabzavari a student of Mir Findiriski (d. 1640). See Tehrani, 1: 104–5. Abbas II, as his namesake, also encouraged intermarriage of his family with the Shi'i clergy: one of his sisters married a *sadr*. See Roemer, 6: 302; Ferrier in Hambly, 402; Blake, 89, 191; Ferrier, *A Journey*, 153–4. On reports that Fayz objected to official efforts to convert Iranian Jews, see Netzer, 'Conversion', 235, and on his declining of Safi's invitation, see n43. For an alternative view of Khalil Qazvini based on a later source, see M. Momen, 'Usuli, Akhbari, Shaykhi, Babi: The Tribulations of a Qazvin Family', *IS*, 36(3) (2003), 318.

31 Some of the opposition to Fayz was clearly rooted in the Akhbari rejection of clerical authority over the formulation of doctrine and practice and the exercise of *ijtihad* by the clergy during the Imam's absence. Other opponents supported this doctrine of *niyaba*, and the exercise of *ijtihad* by the senior clerics, but still regarded the performance of Friday prayer during the occultation as illegitimate. See our 'Fayz', 42–3.

32 In his autobiography the obviously unhappy Fayz noted that the severity of the discord caused the shah to attend Friday prayers only rarely and to give himself up to pleasure (Newman, 'Fayz', 42–4). According to the Dutch (Matthee, 'The Career', 33, 26), also unhappy with the court in this period but for their own reasons, Abbas now remained in the haram or went on hunting parties, exhibiting little interest in the wider affairs of the state. By contrast, Roemer (6: 301), citing Kaempfer and Chardin, stresses the 'indefatigable concern [Abbas] personally showed for the affairs of state' even after 1662 as symptoms of what European writers deduced was syphilis began to present and he withdrew to Mazandaran. Khatunabadi (524), certainly much better connected to the court at the time than the two foreigners, dated the onset of Abbas' illness only to 1665, the year before his death.

As for Friday prayer, in a 1666 essay Fayz himself declared it was permissible to abandon the Friday prayer if performing it encouraged division, suggesting its possible discontinuation. See our 'Fayz', n28. A reference in Tehrani (15: 81) to a 1653 essay on Friday prayer written by a cleric who seems to have been the first to perform the prayer in Yazd in this period, suggests the performance of the prayer may not have been widespread.

33 As evidence of the continued strength of the 'popular' spiritual feeling and Taqi Majlisi's identification therewith, his critic Mir Lawhi charged that at his death in 1659 Majlisi's coffin was torn to pieces by the crowd and pieces were worn as amulets (Arjomand, *The Shadow*, 186).

34 Muhammad Bek, as Khalifa Sultan following his 1632 dismissal, was sent to Qum, Floor, *Safavid Government*, 37; idem, 'sadr', 482. Accounts of his dismissal usually overlook the contemporary spiritual crisis. See Matthee, *The Politics*, 167; idem, 'The Career', 31–5. See also Khatunabadi, 519.

35 Babayan, 'The Waning', 318. On the post of *sipahsalar*, however, compare Babayan (318–19) and Floor (*Safavid Government*, 18–19, 21). In *c.* 1657 the Qajar *divanbeki* was replaced by Safi Quli Khan who remained in post until 1663 and who, if he was also 'Safi Quli Bek' (Floor, 'Judicial', 22), had Ustajlu connections (Qazvini, 68, 329). The Armenian *qullaraqasi* died in 1663 and was replaced by Jamshid Khan, whose origins are not clear. See Floor, *Safavid Government*, 172; Qazvini, 328.

36 The Shamlu, Ustajlu and Chagatai held key posts over the period and a brother of Khalifa Sultan served as *sadr* from 1661 until 1664 when the post(s) fell vacant. The *divanbeki* Safi Quli Khan was replaced by a *ghulam* and then an Ustajlu, the latter serving until 1666. See Qazvini, 65, 108, 300; Babayan, 'The Waning', 319; Floor, *Safavid Government*, 172; idem, 'sadr', 482; 'Judicial', 23. Qazvini (335–8) briefly addresses the overall organisational structure of the court and the military, absent the names of the office-holders over the period.

37 Matthee, *The Politics*, 165–74; Floor, *The Economy*, 173–5. On the understandable lack of interest at court in negotiating with the VOC in this period, see Matthee, ibid., 167–8.

38 Some European travellers also alleged over-taxation and poor agricultural management; none of these travellers had any apparent expertise. See Matthee, *The Politics*, 175f. On bankruptcies among Indian merchants in 1666, see Blake, *Half*, 131, citing Chardin who, with the Carmelites and others, lost money and whose opinion of the Indian merchants was, unsurprisingly, hostile. By contrast, see n48 of Chapter 8, that in later years court eunuchs entrusted their funds to Indians.

39 His *Tuhfat al-Akhyar* continued the attack on the Sufis, philosophy and Taqi Majlisi, who had died nearly five years earlier, and described 'the youth' as especially prone to Sufi influence. See also Newman, 'Sufism', n46.

40 Attacks on 'singing' in particular featured prominently in the anti-Sufi essays dating from mid-century. Muhammad b. Hasan, Hurr-i Amili (d. 1693), who also came from the West and passed through Isfahan in the early 1660s, later composed an attack on Sufism and Sufis reminiscent of contemporary mid-century denunciations of Sufi doctrine and practices; indeed he referred to and quoted from *Hadiqat al-Shi'a* and identified its author as Ardabili, as did Shaykh Ali Amili. See our 'Clerical Perceptions', n42; idem, 'Sufism', 102, n55, n56.

41 Chardin noted a certain Mulla Qasim preached against the immoral behaviour, including the wine-drinking and sexual promiscuity allegedly rampant at the

court, and argued that 'another pure branch of the imams', specifically the son of *Shaykh al-Islam*, whose mother was a daughter of Abbas I, should rule instead. Both Calmard and Blake cite Chardin on the *c.* 1664 execution of Mulla Qasim, who is otherwise unknown in the primary sources. Compare A. K. S. Lambton, 'Quis Custodiet Custodes, Some Reflections on the Persian Theory of Government', *Studia Islamica* 5 (1956) 132; Arjomand, *The Shadow*, 200–1; Blake, 182–3; Calmard, 'Shi'i Rituals and Power II', 168. On Mulla Qasim see also Babayan, *Mystics*, 404–6, Abisaab, *Converting Persia*, 97, both citing Chardin. Compare Ferrier (*A Journey*, 55, 77) on the apparent clerical approbation of Mulla Qasim's criticisms. Arjomand and Ferrier accept Chardin's emphasis on the involvement of the *Shaykh al-Islam* – the reference to whom is unclear, as Sabzavari had been appointed to that post after 1650 and remained in post through Abbas II's 1668 succession – and his son; the latter two were said to have begged for mercy and been forgiven. On holders of the post of *Shaykh al-Islam*, see M. B. Kitabi, *Rijal-i Isfahan* (Isfahan, 1375), 57f.

42 In a 1658 essay Muhammad Tahir declared for the *ayni* position on Friday prayer – the same pro-court position advocated by both Majlisi and Fayz, otherwise his opponents – in opposition to the court protégé Khalil Qazvini, to whose position Muhammad Tahir in fact called attention. In his 1664 *Tuhfat al-Akhyar* he wrote 'God willing, the reign of Shah 'Abbas II will be linked to the rule of the Lord of the Age', i.e. the Hidden Imam, a comment little different to that of Khalil Qazvini legitimising Safavid rule. See our 'Fayz' on the political implications of this position. See also Tehrani, 15: 72–3; 3: 452; Babayan, 'The Waning', 287; n30. Muhammad Tahir's Arabic-language *Hikmat al-Arifin* – completed between 1657 and 1664, three years after Muhammad Bek's dismissal and two years before Abbas II's death – was more restrained in its attacks on Sufism and philosophy than his earlier essays. See our 'Sufism', n46.

43 Fayz claimed the presence of such individuals at Safi's court had deterred him from accepting the latter's invitation thereto. See our 'Fayz', 44; Jafariyan, *Din va*, 292–5. Lewisohn ('Sufism and the School of Isfahan: *Tasawwuf* and *'Irfan* in Late Safavid Iran', in Lewisohn and Morgan, eds, 112f, 123f) locates Fayz between 'popular' Sufi inquiry and practice and traditional Islamic mysticism.

44 The always unhappy Dutch claimed both Saru Taqi and his murderer Jani Khan Shamlu had accumulated considerable fortunes at their murders in 1645. Floor, 'The Rise', 263. On Armenian wealth after Zuhab, see above, below and also the previous chapter, esp. ad nn20f.

45 Mudarrissi, *Bargi*, 80; Hunarfar, 453–5; Canby, 133; Hillenbrand, 'The Tomb of Shah Isma'il I', 6. Abbas also corresponded with the authorities in Mecca to facilitate the movement of Iranian pilgrims in this period. The centre's endowment of *vaqf* to the Husaynids in the Hijaz also continued apace. See Jafariyan, 'Munasibat', 4–8, 16, 17.

A floor plan of the shrine of Fatima, featuring the tombs of the four Safavid rulers (Safi, Abbas II, Sulayman and Sultan Husayn) buried there, can be found in M. M. J. Fischer, *Iran, From Religious Dispute to Revolution* (Cambridge, MA London, 1980), 110–11. The tombs of Safi and Abbas II are closest to, and look upon, the tomb of Fatima itself.

46 See Blake, *Half*, 46, 167, 90, 121. An inscription in the larger of Dilaram Khanum's schools, completed by Muhammad Riza Imami, described the shah as a Musavid and a Husaynid and 'propagator of the faith of the twelve imams', while an inscription in the smaller calls him 'possessor of the lands of the Arabs

and the *ajam* [the Persians]', a good example of Safavid 'spin' in light of the territorial losses in Iraq ratified by the Zuhab treaty; see also nn48, 49, and n71 of Chapter 7. See Hunarfar, 553–6. On the *vaqf* documents for these two schools, see N. Ahmadi, 'Chahar *Vaqfnama* az Chahar Madrasa-yi Isfahan dar Dawrah-yi Safavi', in R. Jafariyan, ed., *Miras-i Islami-yi Iran* (Qum, 1375/ 1996), 3: 95–9. On women builders in this period, see also Blake, 'Contributors', 412f.

47 The Kashan mosque's 1646 *vaqf* was in the name of the Tajik sayyid who headed Abbas II's library. See Naraqi, 238–41; Blake, *Half*, 49.

48 The Arabic inscription on the large mosque completed in 1643–4, mentioned in the previous chapter, speaks of Abbas II as the Musavid, the Husaynid and 'the propagator of the faith of the infallible imams'. See Blake, *Half*, 45–6, 123, 151; Hunarfar, 547–52; Roemer, 6: 292; Ferrier, 48–9. Hunarfar (608–10) describes a school built by Saru Taqi dated to 1660, in which Sayyid Nimatallah Jazairi (d. 1701), a student of Baqir Majlisi (d. 1699), on whom see below, would later study. The Arabic inscription describes the shah as the 'holder of the lands of the Arabs and the *ajam* . . . the propagator of the faith of the infallible Imams', the former, like the inscriptions of Abbas I's reign (n93 of Chapter 4), a good example of 'spin' in the years following the acknowledgement of the territorial losses in the Zuhab treaty. See also n49.

49 The mosque features numerous Qur'anic inscriptions, the names of the Imams and an Arabic inscription, by the same Muhammad Riza Imami, which refers to the shah as 'possessor of the lands of the Arabs and the *ajam* and propagator of the faith of the infallible Imams'. Hakim Daud's father and mother were physicians under Abbas I and Safi. Daud succeeded his father at the latter's death but, receiving no further promotion, left for India – an economic migrant – where he treated the daughter of Shah Jahan for a burn and subsequently received a promotion. Hakim Daud sent money from India for the erection of this mosque but died in India in 1662–3. See Hunarfar, 612–30; Godard, 152–4; Blake, *Half*, 152; Canby, 133–4; Haneda, 'Emigration', 136–7.

50 The head of imperial household treasury built a school in 1658–9. Sulayman Bek also built a mosque in this period. See Blake, 168; Hunarfar, 605–7, 611–12 and 619–20 on the work done to the Hajji Yunis mosque in 1664. The inscriptions on these mosques endorsed the Safavid claims to the descent from the Imams and referred to Abbas II as 'the propagator of the faith'.

51 A member of the Khuzani family, one of whom authored *Afzal al-Tavarikh* and others of whom had served earlier shahs, built a school in 1656–7, and dedicated to it the revenues of a sarai and five nearby villages. The inscription, also completed by Muhammad Riza Imami, describes Abbas II as 'the propagator of the faith of his forefathers the pure Imams . . . the Musavid, the Husaynid'. See Blake, 168; Hunarfar, 589–92. An Egyptian merchant also built a mosque *c.* 1650–1, on which see Blake, 153; Hunarfar, 585–8; Godard 152. The inscription was done by the same Muhammad Riza. In Natanz, in 1653, repairs were also undertaken to the eight-century tomb of a local notable (Naraqi, 400; Hunarfar, 878). On a 1660 *vaqf* of an otherwise unknown woman, Gawhar Bekum, for the shrine cities, see Ahmadi, 'Du *Vaqfnama* az Du Zan', in R. Jafariyan, ed., *Miras-i Islami-yi Iran* 6 (Qum, 1376), 342, 355–8.

52 Calmard, 'Shi'i Rituals and Power II', 147, 164, 152, 157f, 161f, 167–8, citing both Chardin and Raphael du Mans, superior of the Capuchin mission in Isfahan who lived in Iran from 1647 until his death in 1696, and composed his

Estat de la Perse en 1660 at the request of Louis XIV's minister Colbert. De Thévenot saw commemorations of Ali's martyrdom in Shiraz in 1664 and also Ashura activities. Richard ('Capuchins', 787) notes that du Mans served as a translator for European commercial interests at court and that the accounts of such later European travellers, including Tavernier, de Thévenot, Chardin, Fryer and Kaempfer, owe much to information supplied by him. That he acted as a translator ought not necessarily to give his reportage any added credibility. See also n77 of Chapter 7; Calmard, ibid., 157–63. See also Richard, ed., *Raphael du Mans: missionaire en Perse au XVII*, 2 vols (Paris, 1995).

53 Blake, 45, 121–2. At the Khurasani sarai, located to the Northwest of Abbas I's *maydan*, were sold animal pelts and plums from Bukhara, felt from Jam and Mashhad and carpets from Khurasan. Chardin described this sarai as one of the city's most beautiful.

54 Blake, 45, 47, 124, 12, 121, 182. Note Abbas II's courteous treatment of Sunni Uzbek officials moving through Iran to perform the pilgrimage as per McChesney, 'The Central Asian', 149–50.

55 Hunarfar, 549; Blake, 46, 123; Floor, 'The Rise', 254–5. On Saru Taqi's various building projects, see also S. Babaie, 'Building for the Shah: the Role of Mirza Muhammad Taqi (Saru Taqi) in Safavid Royal Patronage of Architecture', in S. Canby, ed., *Safavid Art and Architecture* (London, 2002), 20–6.

56 Blake, 119.

57 On the first, also called Khvaja or Shahi bridge, dated to 1651–2, see Hunarfar, 582–5, Blake, 43. On the second, completed in 1657–8, during the vizierate of Muhammad Bek, see Hunarfar, 247n1, 575–6; Blake, 33, 43; Canby, 133.

58 Hunarfar, 422–5; Blake, 64; Babaie, 'Building for the Shah', 22–4.

59 The shah celebrated the Iranian New Year there in 1648, 1658 and 1661. See Hunarfar, 557–74; Blake, 66–7. See also Qazvini, 90–1. On Chihil Sutun, see also Babaie, 'Building for the Shah'; idem, 'Shah Abbas II, the Conquest of Qandahar, Chihil Sutun, and its Wall Paintings', *Muqarnas* 11 (1994), esp. 128–9. See also I. Luschey-Schmeisser, 'Chihil Sotun', *EIr*, 5: 111–15. Thanks to S. Babaie for directing my attention to the latter article which, along with Hunarfar (570f), and Blake (68–9), addresses the fire which struck this palace during the reign of Shah Sultan Husayn, the extent of the damage from which is disputed. See also Lockhart, *The Fall*, 42. On the erotic poses of the women in Chihil Sutun's paintings, see Matthee, 'Prostitutes', 123, citing E. Grube, 'Wall Paintings in the Seventeenth Century Monuments of Isfahan', *IS*, 7 (1974), 516.

60 Inscriptions therein dated to 1651 and 1656 suggest the structure was commenced, if not completed, during the vizierate of Khalifa Sultan, another member of the house who suffered a similar, though less final, fate that same year. See Hunarfar, 593–604; Godard, 129–31.

61 A great mirrored hall, similar to of the already completed Chihil Sutun itself, also featured in this garden. In the nearby two-storey salt-cellar, the lower level featured six life-size murals, including depictions of men and women drinking wine. Hunarfar, 576–80; Blake, 74, 77–9, citing Qazvini, 270.

62 Hunarfar, 547f; Blake, 45, 49, 89, 85; Babaie, 'Building for the Shah'.

63 Blake, 89–90; Haneda, 'Emigration', 135.

64 Blake, 185–90. Cf. Canby, 143. Hunarfar (575f) notes the great expansion of the capital city during Abbas II's reign although, citing Chardin, he also calls attention to the many structures from this period of which only names remain.

65 On the social differentiation within the community see, for example, Ghougassian, 69f, and our discussion in Chapter 4, ad nn72, 73. The repressive measures instituted by Muhammad Bek against the Armenians in 1657 seem to have been inspired by senior Armenian clerics reacting to the anti-clerical message of a darvish-style messianic movement based among Armenian artisnal elements (McCabe, 183–4), much as contemporary urban 'popular' Sufi movements attracted the disapproval of orthodox Shi'i clerics.

66 Ghougassian, 100f. The Church of Mary has an inscription dated to between 1660 and 1667. See Hunarfar, 511, 514f; Blake, 188–90. See also Carswell, *New Julfa*, 30–4, and 55–6 on St Minas church, commenced in 1658–9 and completed in 1662–3. Floor (*The Economy*, 15–18) notes Armenian involvement in both local and long-distance trade. See also Matthee, 'Merchants', 237–42, 255; Ferrier, *A Journey*, 64–5. 'Vank' means cathedral in Armenian. Thanks to E. Herzig for this translation.

67 McCabe, 180–4; Ghougassian, 137f, 214, 278. Babaie ('Shah Abbas II', 128, 139) notes the favourable representations of Iranian Armenians in Chihil Sutun's wall paintings. On the Catholic missionaries, see n80 of chapter four. On frustrated Carmelite efforts among the Armenians in this period, see Richard, 'Carmelites', 833. After the failure of their 1646 attempt, the Jesuits bought a house in Isfahan in 1656 and then moved to New Julfa in 1661. On Fr. Aime Chezaud (d. 1664), who participated in debates at court on the faith and wrote a refutation of Ahmad Alavi's attack on Christianity, see F. Richard, 'Fr. Aime Chezaud – Controversialist', paper presented at 'Iran and the World in the Safavid Age' University of London, September 2002.

68 Canby, 134–9. Adamova, 'Muhammad Qasim', 209. See also Adamova, 'On the Attribution', 19–38; n43 of Chapter 5.

69 Abbas II so admired Shaykh Abbasi's style that he was chosen to render an Indian embassy to Iran in 1663. See Canby, 136–7. Cf. Matthee, 'Between Aloofness', 237–8.

70 Babaie, 'Shah Abbas II', esp. 132.

71 Y. Crowe, *Persia and China, Safavid Blue and White Ceramics in the Victoria and Albert Museum, 1501–1738* (London, 2002), 137–8, 150–2, 162–3. See also Crowe, 'Ceramics. xv. The Islamic Period, 10th–13th/16th–19th Centuries', *EIr*, 5: 327.

72 In her 'Safavid Blue and White Bowls and the Chinese Connection', *Iran* 40 (2002), 257–63, esp. 261–3, Crowe notes the VOC had been importing Chinese ceramics into Iran from early in the century, *c.* 1638 especially, sufficient to encourage the appearance of an indigenous industry by mid-century. On the impact of the fall of the Ming dynasty on the production of ceramics in Iran, see her *Persia and China*, esp. 21, 103–4. In both Crowe cites T. Volker, *Porcelain and the Dutch East India Company . . . 1602–1682* (Leiden, 1954, 1971), who dubbed the period 1652 to 1683, during which the VOC ordered quantities of Persian blue and white pottery as a substitute for the no-longer available Chinese ware – on occasion deceiving Western traders – as 'the Persian interlude' and noted that in the process Iranian potters faced special challenges as they lacked the right materials to produce 'real' porcelain. See also Canby, 142–3. In addition to Kirman, Shiraz, Mashhad and Yazd were centres of ceramics production in this period. See Crowe, 'Ceramics', 327, 329–30. See also J. Rogers, 'Chinese-Iranian Relations, iv. The Safavid Period', *EIr*, 5: 436–8.

73 Canby, *The Golden*, 139. In 1659 the EIC in Surat urged their local agent factor

to purchase annually some 100 'loads' of Kirmani wool. Although once home the wool was seen as of poor quality, such demand did spur a local rise in prices. See Matthee, 'The East India Company Trade in Kirman Wool, 1658–1730', in Calmard, ed., *Études Safavides.*, 343–83, esp. 346–7, 367.

74 Canby, 139–41.

75 Yarshater (6: 990) has noted modern critics' disparagement of this style of poetry which has, no doubt, contributed to the relatively poor study, and understanding, of the movement and its practitioners. The tone of Yarshater's discussion of Safavid poetry contrasts markedly with that of Safa's immediately preceding discussion (6: 948f).

76 See Jafariyan, *Safaviyya dar Arsa-yi Din*, 1: 483–91. See also, especially, the discussion of Saib in the Epilogue. On Saib's praise for Chihil Sutun, see also Hunarfar, 569–70. On Saib, see also Browne, 4: 164–5; Safa, 6: 956, 959; Yarshater, 6: 982, 986, 988, 990. Note Browne's unsubstantiated comment (4: 265), cited by Safa (6: 956n1), that Saib was 'without honour' in his own country.

77 On this chronicle see n2.

78 The remaining sections cover, at greater length, the reign of Abbas II, religious scholars of the period, 101 poets of the period and, lastly, nineteen darvishes of note.

79 Babaie, 'Shah Abbas II', *passim*, esp. 127–9. See also Luschey-Schmeisser, 113–14.

7 Meeting the Challenges: Shah Sulayman (1666/68–1694)

1 The *vizier* Muhammad Karaki, Husayn Quli – probably a reference to the future *qurchibashi* – and the *qullaraqasi* Jamshid Khan certified the shah's death. Khatunabadi, 524–9, esp. 525, 530. Floor, *Safavid Government*, 142, 151, 172, 185. Others party to the news included the court historian, the head of the musketeers, two astrologers and an unnamed cleric who was probably Sabzavari, Khatunabadi's own teacher. The *yuzbashi* was himself probably member of a tribe. On the position, referring a commander of 100 men, usually tribal elements, see Floor, *Safavid Government*, 151, 174, 184, 187, 196.

2 Khatunabadi, 529–30. Of all those others in attendance at these ceremonies, Khatunabadi notes only the cleric Mirza Rafia Naini (d. 1688), a Husayni sayyid and student of both Shaykh Bahai and Taqi Majlisi, on whom see also n31. Khatunabadi also attended the ceremonies. The Cossack raids were instigated by the Tsar in his anger at Abbas II's poor treatment of a Russian trade delegation (Lockhart, *The Fall*, 57–8).

3 Karaki continued as *vizier* until 1669, Jamshid Khan remained *qullaraqasi* until his death afterwards near Qandahar, at which the post seems to have been left unfilled until the 1690s. Both the *qurchibashi* Husayn Quli Khan, a member of a tribe, and the musketeers' chief remained in office until 1668. The *sipahsalar*, appointed by Abbas II in 1666, was from the Kurdish Zangana family and remained in post until 1691; his brother became *vizier* in 1669. A Qajar associate was briefly *divanbeki* until, in 1670–1, the post fell to the son of Abbas II's discredited *qurchibashi* Jani Khan Shamlu, to whom was returned the property confiscated from his father. Tajik sayyids continued to hold the *sadr*-ship. See Floor, *Safavid Government*, 21, 37, 142, 172, 185; Floor, 'Judicial', 23; idem,

'*sadr*', 482; idem, 'The Rise', 262; Matthee, 'Administrative', 80–1; Isfahani, 324.

4 On Ottoman-Safavid relations, see Matthee, 'Iran's Ottoman Diplomacy', esp. 161f; Jafariyan, *Safaviyya*, 348–50. The realm's key officials often conferred on key foreign and domestic matters (Khatunabadi, 542). For such meetings during the reign of Abbas I, see n36 of chapter four.

5 On Sulayman's reign as relatively peaceful, see Roemer, 6: 308–9; Matthee, ibid.; idem, 'Administrative', 77, 82; Jafariyan, ibid.

6 Khatunabadi, 537–8, 543–4; Jafariyan, *Safaviyya dar Arsa-yi Din*, 2: 761f, 777; idem, *Ilal*, 331–2; Matthee, *The Politics*, 177–8; Floor, *A Fiscal*, 229.

Floor (*The Safavid Economy*, 2f) evaluates various foreign estimates of Iran's population, and that of its chief cities, in this period, and suggests a total population of no more than nine million – well short of Chardin's estimate of 40 million (!) – with the urban share of the population varying between 10% and 15%. See also n15 of the Introduction; n88, below, and n71 of the following chapter.

7 On the shah's efforts to control grain prices, see Blake (113) citing Chardin. See also n18. On similar efforts by Ismail I, see our 'Safavids – Religion, Philosophy and Science', 784.

The links between the Zangana and the Qizilbash date to Ismail I's time and during Abbas II's reign they were based around Kirmanshah and Hamadan. Shaykh Ali became head of the tribe at his brother's death and in 1666 was sent in command of a Zangana contingent against the Uzbeks. Returned to Isfahan in 1668 by Sulayman, he was made head of the musketeers. See Minorsky, *Tadhkirat*, 16; cf. Munshi, 1: 227, 2: 1312–13; Matthee, 'Administrative', 85–6. Shaykh Ali's appointment is all the more interesting if, as Kasravi and Togan have suggested, the Safavids were actually Kurdish in origin.

8 Matthee, 'Administrative', 91–2.

9 The government also moved to forestall Iranian pilgrims from taking specie out of the country. Matthee, 'Administrative', 83–7; idem, *The Politics*, 180; see also Floor, *A Fiscal*, 21; idem, *The Economy*, 189–91; Jafariyan, *Safaviyya*, 356–7. In his 'Between Venice and Surat', 238, Matthee dates the imposition of the 5% fee to 1672. See also ibid., 242–3. See also Matthee, 'Mint Consolidation and the Worsening of the Late Safavid Coinage: The Mint of Huwayza', *JESHO* 44(4) (2001), 522, 526, 532.

10 Armenian sources record government confiscation of church funds. See Ghougassian, 158–9. Matthee ('Administrative', 87–8) connects pressures on the polity's minorities with the period's broader economic and other tensions, as he did regarding similar policies undertaken by Khalifa Sultan and Muhammad Bek (idem, 'The Career', 27). See also McCabe, 187–8; n60.

11 Ignoring these crises, contemporary European accounts (Matthee, 'Administrative', 84) weave elaborate explanations for Shaykh Ali's dismissal. See also similar accounts from the, hardly disinterested, Dutch on the 1679–80 beating of the *vizier* and the blinding of the *divanbeki* (ibid., 90) which, if true, not coincidentally occurred during the severe famine of 1678–9.

12 See Floor, *The Economy*, 189 citing Dutch accounts; Matthee, 'Administrative', 91. On the war rumours, Matthee ('Iran's Ottoman', 155–7) notes Sulayman's solicitation of Russian and Polish support, his own movements and those of Safavid troops, in the context of his overwhelming desire to maintain the peace.

13 Matthee, *The Politics*, 175–92; McCabe, 193.

14 In 1668, when the VOC exported 212 bales via the Gulf, some 2,500 bales of

silk, mainly Iranian, reached Livorno/Leghorn, in Italy, where there was an Armenian-Iranian consul. The VOC exported no Iranian silk via the Gulf from 1684 to 1690. See Matthee, *The Politics*, 173, 192f, 200–3; idem, 'Iran's Ottoman Diplomacy', 154f; Floor, *The Economy*, 174; idem, 'The Dutch', 354; Herzig, 'The Volume', 65, 69–73. On trade with India, see Floor and Clawson, 347–8; Floor, *The Economy*, 199–216.

15 The Dutch and Sanson, the latter a French priest in Iran from 1683 to 1691, claimed an increase in revenues. See Matthee, 'Administrative', 91; Floor, *A Fiscal*, 165, 159–60, 164. There is no record of further territory being declared *khassa* by the centre and, indeed, Röhrborn (178) suggests that some lands lost their *khassa* status, including Simnan, during Abbas II's reign, and Hamadan, Kirman *c.* 1694, Lar *c.* 1708–9 and Fars in 1718–19. These reversions may have been calculated to increase revenues, since the real tax burden – in cash or in kind – apparently fell less hard on those peasants serving on crown land. See Floor, *A Fiscal*, 30–1, 114.

16 Dutch sources (Matthee, *The Politics*, 175) suggest a decline in Persian Gulf and Levantine trade in this period, but see Herzig ('The Volume', 65, 70, 73) and Floor (*The Economy*, 174).

17 Floor, *The Economy*, 81–3; Minorsky, *Tadhkirat*, 27, 27n3; Matthee, 'Mint Consolidation and the Worsening of the Late Safavid Coinage: The Mint of Huwayza', *JESHO*, 44(4), 2001, esp. 521f; idem, 'The Safavid Mint of Huvayzeh: The Numismatic Evidence', in Newman, ed., *Society and Culture*, 287–9; Matthee, 'Between Venice and Surat', 238–9.

18 Floor (*A Fiscal*, 229–30) notes the successful opposition to the centre's efforts to change perpetual *tuyul*s into temporary ones aligned with salaries attached to the function of their holders in the realm. Some posts were also left vacant as a means of saving money. See also Minorsky, *Tadhkirat*, 28–9.

19 The centre appears to have experienced little change in composition. Thus, for example, Shaykh Ali's son Shah Quli Khan remained *qurchibashi* through Sulayman's death until 1699. The *sadr* remained in post. There were several *qullaraqasi*s, including one known *ghulam*, later in the period. A Georgian *ghulam* was both *sipahsalar* and *divanbeki*. See Floor, *Safavid Government*, 22, 38, 142, 173; Floor, '*sadr*', 482; idem, 'Judicial', 23; Muhammad Nasiri, *Dastur-i Shahryaran*, (Tehran, 1373), 30. On Nasiri, see n1 of the following chapter.

20 Matthee, *The Politics*, 175–92, 244; Floor, *Safavid Government*, 38n255; Floor, *The Economy*, 174, 189–91, 194; Floor, 'The Dutch', 354. On the brief upsurge in demand for Kirmani wool during Sulayman's reign, and the brief, VOC/EIC struggle over this trade, see Matthee, 'The East India Company Trade', esp. 351–2, 357, 367–78; n73 of the previous chapter. On the Dutchman Johan van Leene's 1690–2 Dutch trade mission to Sulayman, see Matthee, 'Negotiating Across Cultures', esp. 50–63.

21 Blake, 113–14, citing Chardin; Ferrier, *A Journey*, 51f, 57f. Matthee ('Merchants', 249–54) discusses the role of 'Muslim' merchants in the Safavid economy, especially their domination of domestic trade and transport. See also Floor, *The Safavid Economy*, 14–26.

22 The latter included, for example, wholesale fruiterers and sellers of foodstuffs, and the lesser guilds, including, according to Chardin, the lemon and pomegranate juice-makers, charcoal and firewood-sellers and vinegar-distillers. Chardin noted that petty tradesmen did conduct business in front of the Shah Mosque but

on a rotating basis. See Keyvani, 125–6, 142–3, 145; Blake, 113–14; Ferrier, 117–18. See also Jafariyan, *Safaviyya dar Arsa-yi Din*, 2: 780.

23 In the early 1690s the bazaars of Tabriz and Ardabil were well stocked with domestic and foreign luxury items. See Keyvani, 126–7.

24 Blake, 113–14; Keyvani, 125–6.

25 Blake, 113, 181f. See also Haneda, 'The Character'.

26 Blake, ibid. As the old *maydan* declined in importance the presence of Indians, as financiers and merchants, grew, sufficiently so to have been noted by contemporary foreigners. See Blake, 125–31, citing Tavernier, who made six trips in and through Iran between 1632 and 1668, Chardin and the anonymously written 'A List of the Caravansarais of Isfahan' completed in the late 1660s. The latter notes that Indians, especially cloth merchants, dominated several of Isfahan's sarais and sections of the bazaar area, and Chardin (Blake, 121) noted the Indians had replaced the Ottoman merchants at another sarai. Blake (125–7) also discusses the secondary source literature on the role of the Indians, particularly Keyvani and Dale's *Indian Merchants*. See also Matthee, *The Politics*, 3n12, 5n18, 7n25; Minorsky, *Tadhkirat*, 19; Ferrier, *A Journey*, 51–2, 95, 136. In 1674, the Venetian Bembo estimated the number of Indians in the capital as 12,000, 'partly Moslems and partly Gentiles (sic)' (Welch, 'Safavi Iran', 105–6).

27 Chardin (Godard, 63f; Matthee, 'Coffee', 22) also noted the continued popularity of the tomb of Harun-i Vilayat itself as a place of pilgrimage in this period. See also Matthee, 'Coffee', 24–7; idem, 'Tobacco in Iran'.

28 See our earlier references to Mulla Sadra's 1617–18 *Kasr Asnam* and *Hadiqat al-Shi'a*, completed in the late 1640s. *Tadhkira-yi Nasrabadi*, written between 1673–4 and 1679, demonstrates this link for the reign of Shah Sulayman and refers to a merchant building a *takiyya* (hospice) for a darvish in the capital. See Nasrabadi, 141, 382, 51, 31, 44, as cited by Babayan in her 'The Waning', 262n647, 648. Keyvani (143–4, 205–11) discusses the role of the guilds in secular and non-secular buildings – mosques and schools were built by the city's porters, grape juice-makers and potters – and the link between the guilds and darvish orders. On *Tadhkira-yi Nasrabadi*'s social dimensions, see also Jafariyan, *Safaviyya dar Arsa-yi Din*, 2: 761f. In 1693–4, the Tajik sayyid physician Muhammad Ardistani built 'The School of the Potters' off the Harun-i Vilayat square; the inscription speaks of the shah as 'the Husaynid' and 'the Musavid' but also of local 'darvishes', suggesting an effort to balance open associations with 'popular' practices with declarations of loyalty to the throne. In a further declaration of such loyalty, the 1692 *vaqf* document (see n36 in Chapter 8) for the School of the Potters included the name of Baqir Majlisi. See Hunarfar, 652–3; Blake, 167–8; Jafariyan, *Safaviyya*, 363; n50 of Chapter 8. The mosque erected in 1688–9 by 'Muhammad Qasim', ad n71 below, was also clearly built with such interests in mind though its inscriptions carefully acknowledge the authority of Sulayman.

29 Baqir Majlisi's student Sayyid Nimatallah Jazairi (d. 1701), in his 1678 *al-Anvar al-Numaniyya*, condemned the 'popular' Sufi presence in the city and the storytelling in the city's coffee-houses. See Jafariyan, *Ilal*, 323–45; Tehrani, 11: 175, 5: 301; Jafariyan, *Safaviyya dar Arsa-yi Din*, 1: 390, 3: 1141–54, 2: 782; Jafariyan, *Safaviyya*, 353; Matthee, 'Coffee', 24–6, citing travellers' accounts. On the connection between poetry and Sufism, see also McChesney's discussion of a 1688–9 source in his 'The Anthology of Poets: "Muzakkir al-Ashab" as a Source for the History of Seventeenth-Century Central Asia', in Mazzaoui and

Moreen, eds, *Intellectual Studies on Islam, Essays Written in Honor of Martin B. Dickson* (Salt Lake City, 1990), esp. 65, 71–2. On the merchant-poet connection, see Matthee, 'Merchants', 251, citing Nasrabadi, 137; Keyvani, 233. See also Keyvani (197f) on the period's poetry and, especially, the to-date poorly studied urban *shahrashub* literature.

30 On Husayn, see Mirza Abdallah Isbahani Afandi, *Riyaz al-Ulama* (Qum, 1401), 2: 57–60; Yusuf ibn Ahmad Bahrani, *Luluat al-Bahrayn* (Najaf, 1969), 90–2; Muhammad Baqir Khvansari, *Rawzat al-Jannat* (Tehran, 1390/1970), 2: 367f. On Jamal, see Bahrani, ibid.; Afandi, 2: 211f; Khvansari, 1: 114. See also Hunarfar, 657–9; Arjomand, *The Shadow*, 151. Afandi (d. 1717) was a student of Baqir Majlisi. See also n63 below.

31 These included Sabzavari's student Rajab Ali Tabrizi and the above-mentioned Mirza Rafi al-Din Naini, a Husayni sayyid and student of Shaykh Bahai and Taqi Majlisi, who attended Sulayman's accession and, like Husayn Khvansari, received an elaborate mausoleum at his death. In this period the Lutfallah Maysi school was a particular centre for the philosopher clerics of the day, including Husayn Khvansari, Shamsa Gilani (d. 1686) – another student of Mir Damad – Tabrizi and Sayyid Ismail Khatunabadi and his son Muhammad Baqir, on whom see the next chapter. See Tabrizi, *Faraid*, 295–6. On these, Mulla Rafia Gilani (d. 1671–2), a student of Mir Findiriski and Baqir Majlisi, and Qadi Said Qummi (d. 1691), a student of Tabrizi and Fayz, see also our 'Safavids – Religion, Philosophy and Science', *EI²*, 8: 777–87, esp. 781–2. For an anthology of work by such figures as Mir Damad, Mulla Sadra, Rajab Ali, Lahiji, Husayn Khvansari, Shamsa Gilani, Ahmad Alavi and Fayz Kashani, and an introduction thereto, see J. Ashtiyani, ed., *Anthologie des Philosophes Iraniens depuis le XVIIe siècle jusqu'à nos jours. Textes persans et arabes choisis et présentés par Sayyed Jalâloddîn Ashtiyânî. Introduction analytique par Henry Corbin*, 3 vols, (Paris/Tehran, 1972–5).

32 See, for example, Tehrani, 6: 45, 114, 130, 45, 224; 4: 506. The issue of the permissibility of Friday prayer during the absence of the Imam continued to be source of disagreement, even among the clerical associates of the court. See Tehrani, 15: 79–81, 66–7. Jamal Khvansari penned an essay to Shah Sulayman in 1680, the year after Sabzavari's death, opposing Friday prayer. Newman, 'Clerical Perceptions', n42.

33 On Sulayman, Khvansari and the debate on the permissibility of wine, see Jafariyan, *Safaviyya dar Arsa-yi Din*, 1: 390f. The legality of tobacco and coffee was also debated. See Tehrani, 11: 175, 5: 301; Jafariyan, ibid., 3: 1141–53; 2: 782; Floor, 'The Art of Smoking in Iran and Other Uses of Tobacco', *IS*, 35(1–3) (2002), esp. 524; Abisaab, *Converting Persia*, 133–4; Matthee, 'Tobacco in Iran', 66. On revenue from tobacco taxes, see n75 of Chapter 8. On a 1682–3 *firman* against gambling, see Hunarfar, 608–9n1. A 1685 decree banned wine at court and female musicians and dancers were absent from court receptions that year as well (Matthee, 'Prostitutes', 146–7, citing Kaempfer), although there is no evidence that this ban, like many earlier, similar bans, lasted long.

34 See our 'Clerical Perceptions', esp. 154f. On Sabzavari and clerical authority during the occultation, see also N. Calder, 'Legitimacy and Accommodation in Safavid Iran: The Juristic Theory of Muhammad Baqir al-Sabzewari (d. 1090/1679)', *Iran* 25 (1987), 91–105.

35 In 1675 Sulayman's physician, the Tajik sayyid Muhammad Tanukabuni,

penned an essay refuting arguments of Muhammad Tahir and Mir Lawhi. See Tehrani, 3: 325, 402–3.

36 Jafariyan, 'Munasibat', 19, 21f. The interest of the Hijazi Shi'a in Safavid support can only have been heightened by the murder of Shi'i cleric, a descendant of Muhammad Amin Astarabadi, in Mecca in 1677, a massacre of Shi'a in the city the same year and other attacks and indignities suffered by Iranian pilgrims and the Shi'a in general. These certainly contributed to an emphasis on the importance of Iran-based centres of pilgrimage in such works as that of Taqi Majlisi's son Baqir's 1677 *Tuhfat al-Zair*. See Khatunabadi, 532; Jafariyan, *Safaviyya dar Arsa-yi Din*, 2: 825–49; Matthee, 'Between Venice', 242–3. Compare n87 in Chapter 4; n49 of Chapter 8.

37 See the 1675 directive of the *sadr* Mirza Abu Salih b. Mirza Muhammad Muhsin Rizavi Mashhadi (d. 1686) – who had assumed his post at Sulayman's accession and built a school at the Mashhad shrine in 1675 – granting certain concessions to the Marashi guardians of the Qazvin shrine, the 1682 *firman* confirming a *firman* of Abbas II in which certain *suyurghal*s were allotted to the same Marashi elements and a similar 1691 *firman* granting these to another family member in Mudarrissi, *Bargi*, 71, 173–9, 179–81; Floor, '*sadr*', 482.

38 This is the famous *Ross Anonymous* discussed in n14 of Chapter 1. See also Woods, 171; Morton, 'The Date', in Melville, *Pembroke Papers*, passim, esp. 197, 199, 181; McChesney, 'Alam Ara'. The illustration features on the dustjacket of the present volume.

39 In his Persian-language *al-Favaid al-Diniyya*, completed during Sulayman's reign, Muhammad Tahir argued philosophical inquiry was incompatible with the faith. Replete with citations from the Imams – hence later descriptions of him as an Akhbari – the work also attacked Fayz' interests in such inquiry. See Tehrani, 16: 335–6; 15: 72–3, 71; 287; Newman, 'Sufism', n46.

40 Tehrani, 1: 428, 18: 101–2; M. T. Danishpazhuh, ed., *Catalogue Méthodique, Descriptif, et Raisonné des Manuscrits Concernant la Tradition … de la Bibliothèque de l'Université de Teheran (don de M. le Professeur Meshkat)*, (in Persian) 5 (Tehran, 1956), 1211; Arjomand, *The Shadow*, 82, 186; Turner, 212–13. Cf. Babayan, 'The Waning', nn717, 741, 750 and 751.

41 See our 'Clerical Perceptions', nn21, 43. Fayz' own 1672 essay *al-Insaf*, in which he regretted his early interest in 'popular' Sufism, attests to the continuing strength of both the anti-Sufi polemic and that 'popular' expression. Fayz' own son also denounced Sufism in an essay composed in this period. See our 'Fayz', 44; Lewisohn, 'Sufism', esp. 123f.

42 Tehrani, 15: 79–81, 66–7; n32.

43 On the various dates for his death, see, for example, Browne, 4: 120 and most recently, Turner, 165. See also Mahdavi, 1: 84–92; Khatunabadi, 551.

44 On the dating of this appointment, see Turner (163–4), citing Khatunabadi, 540; Babayan ('Sufis, Dervishes', 132n4) giving 1689, but citing no sources. See also Mahdavi, 1: 130f.

45 Baqir Majlisi, born in Isfahan in 1627–8, was the great-grandson of a Lebanese student of both Ali Karaki and Shaykh Zayn al-Din Ali who was said to have been an important Twelver scholar in Isfahan in the previous century. Baqir Majlisi's mother was herself descended from a Lebanese clerical family. It is not clear when, why or from where members of either branch of the family came to Iran. See the sources in the following note.

46 On the family, see H. Nuri Tabrisi, *Fayz-i Qudsi*, J. Nabavi, transl. (Qum, 1374),

173f; A. Bihbihani, *Mirat al-Ahval Jahan-nama*, A. Davani, ed. (Tehran, 1370), 99f; Danishpazhuh, 5: 1613, 1144–5; Turner, 179–81; J. Cole, 'Shi'i Clerics in Iraq and Iran, 1722–1780: The Akhbari-Usuli Conflict Reconsidered', *IS*, 18(1) (Winter, 1985), esp. 6–13; idem, *Sacred Space and Holy War, The Politics, Culture and History of Shi'ite* Islam (London/New York, 2002), esp. 60–6; Mahdavi, 1: 67f, 297f. A sister's marriage with the Tajik sayyid Muhammad Shirvani (d. 1687–8), whom Shah Sulayman had invited to Isfahan from Najaf, brought the family a sayyid connection. See Khatunabadi, 506; Nasrabadi, 155; Arjomand, *The Shadow*, 152. A relative and poet, Ashraf (d. 1704), a student of Saib Tabrizi, later moved to India (Dale, 'A Safavid Poet'). A daughter of Baqir Majlisi married into the Khatunabadi sayyid family, whose origins were in the Hijaz and which achieved prominence at court during the reign of Shah Sultan Husayn and on whom see the following chapter, esp. ad n42.

47   Another of Baqir Majlisi's teachers was related by marriage to the Akhbari Muhammad Amin Astarabadi. Majlisi also studied with Sayyid Ali Khan Madani Shirazi (d. 1707), a descendant of the Tajik sayyid Mansur Dashtaki who served Tahmasp as *sadr*. On his teachers, see the sources cited in the previous note and also Danishpazhuh, 5: 1613; Amin, 10: 119–24; Turner, 158–9. On Sayyid Ali Khan, who lived much of his life in India, see M. Salati, *Il Passaggio in India di Ali Khan al-Shirazi al-Madani (1642–1707)* (Padova, 1999).

48   The best-known of these Persian-language 'primers' were completed between 1662 and 1678, before his appointment as *Shaykh al-Islam*. See Tabrisi (87f) and Bahrani (56f) for lists of Majlisi's Arabic and Persian-language works, the latter including many shorter essays on specific points of doctrine and practice. See also Tehrani, 7: 83; Khatunabadi, 533. Turner (166–8) and Arjomand (*The Shadow*, 157–8, 168–9) both miss out the Persian-language contributions of Taqi Majlisi and his teachers Bahai and Damad, on which see n131 of Chapter 4.

49   Majlisi favoured the pro-court position on Friday prayer and, in the tradition of Ali Karaki, in a 1662 Persian-language work he had upheld the authority and legitimacy of temporal rulers and co-operation with them, even if they were unjust tyrants, in order to preserve and protect the community of believers. As early as 1661, he had interpreted certain *hadith* texts as referring to the appearance of the Safavids. See Tehrani, 15: 66, 79 and the following note.

50   Majlisi did not himself live to see the completion of *Bihar*, an early version of which was finished in 1659, the year of his father's death when he himself was 32, and several volumes of which were completed by 1670. On these dates see Khatunabadi, 535–6; E. Kohlberg, 'Behar al-Anwar', *EIr*, 4: 90–3. *Bihar* itself included two *hadith*s which he had earlier interpreted as referring to the coming of the Safavids. See Danishpazhuh, 5: 1204–5, 1207n1, 1210; Babayan, 'The Waning', 182f. Compare Turner, 210–11.

Where Turner (171, 194), for example, questioned the authenticity of *Bihar*'s *hadith* texts, Chittick ('Two Seventeenth-Century Persian Tracts on Kingship and Rulers', in Arjomand, ed., *Authority*, 284–304) carefully traced the texts cited in extracts he examined to earlier collections of Twelver *hadith*. See also the very careful verdict of Kohlberg (ibid.) on the authenticity of *Bihar*'s texts and our discussion of *Bihar* in the following note. See also a similar discussion in our article on Majlisi cited in n56 below.

51   See the sources cited in n47. Majlisi's Persian-language *Sual va Javab* (question and answer), much cited in the Western sources, in which he denounced Sufism as 'this foul and hellish growth', was itself of a genre of essay in which clerics

offered written responses to submitted questions, suggesting Majlisi had not raised the issue himself. This brief essay was the sole basis of Lockhart's characterisations of Majlisi discussed in our Preface, ad n1. See also Arjomand, *The Shadow*, 157n180; Turner, 173–4n112. In his essay 'al-Itiqadat' (Beliefs) Majlisi listed problematic practices popular among the darvish orders, including singing, denounced various earlier Sufi figures and explained his father's association with Sufis as having stemmed from a desire to convert them to the true faith. Few of these points were not, however, already on offer in the essays of Muhammad Tahir and Shaykh Ali, both of whom had devoted considerably more time and energy to the subject. Indeed, Majlisi wrote this essay in one night as a response to a unnamed questioner. See Turner, 174–5, 176. On Baqir Majlisi and his father, see Arjomand, *The Shadow*, 153n162; Babayan, 'The Waning', n715, citing *Sayr va Suluk* (a minor work written in 1675–6 as reply to questions put to him by Khalil Qazvini), as quoted in post-Safavid sources.

By comparison with the field's fixation with these minor essays, Majlisi's work with the *hadith*, which culminated in both his massive *Bihar al-Anvar* (the 1982–3 Beirut edition of which comprises some 110 volumes) and the 16-volume *Muladh al-Akhyar*, recently published in Qum, both in Arabic, have yet to be the subject of any detailed, comparative examination. See, however, K. H. Pampus, 'Die theologische Enzyklopädie *Bihar al-Anwar* Muhammed Baqir al-Majlisi' (unpublished PhD thesis, Bonn, 1970), and our article on Majlisi cited in n56.

52 Sources speak of the Safavid-period *hadith* compilations of 'the three Muhammads', in reference to Fayz' *Vafi*, completed by 1658, Hurr-i Amili's *Vasail al-Shi'a*, completed between 1655 and 1677, and *Bihar*, all in Arabic. See Danishpazhuh, 5: 1627–40, 1232–4.

53 Some of *Bihar*'s texts, for example, presented the Imams as possessing superhuman, and pre-existential knowledge and miraculous abilities and portrayed the Prophet's immediate companions as grave sinners (Kohlberg, 92–3), tendencies which had been downplayed since the time of al-Kulayni in the tenth century. On the latter see our *The Formative Period*, esp. 134f.

54 On an essay dedicated to Sulayman in which Majlisi predicted the return of the Hidden Imam in sixty-five years, a point also addressed in *Bihar*, see Tehrani, 1: 90; Danishpazhuh, 5: 1203f, 1213; Bahrani, 99. See also Arjomand, *The Shadow*, 182; Babayan, 'The Waning', n739, n749; Turner, 210, 218–30.

55 As during the reign of Abbas I, in this period also the centre sent out its own clerics to preach in the 'popular' quarters. For a 1694 example of pro-Safavid clerical orations in the city's coffee-houses, see Matthee, 'Coffee', 25. Majlisi's involvement with the 1693–4 School of the Potters (nn28, 36, and 50 of Chapter 8) also suggests efforts to associate with and thereby influence 'popular' discourse. See also the previous note.

56 See our 'Baqir al-Majlisi and Islamicate Medicine: Safavid Medical Theory and Practice Re-examined', in Newman, ed., *Society and Culture*, 371–96; n50 of Chapter 8.

In line with the *hadith* Majlisi sanctioned recourse to Christian and Jewish doctors (ibid., 392), suggesting, *pace* Moreen, that his continued reputation as a persecutor of the Jews (Lockhart, *The Fall*, 32–3) is overdue for rejection. See V. Moreen, 'Risala-yi Sawa'iq al-Yahud [The Treatise "Lightning Bolts Against the Jews"] by Muhammad Baqir b. Muhammad Taqi al-Majlisi (d. 1699)', *Die Welt des Islams* 32 (1992), 177–95, and compare the reference to Lockhart cited in n77. See also n140, Chapter 4, and n30 of Chapter 6 on the earlier efforts of

Shaykh Bahai and Fayz Kashani to forestall earlier moves to convert Jews and Bahai's tolerance of social interaction with Christians. On the viability, and court patronage, of both these and various other traditions of illness and wellness over the entire Safavid period, see our 'Safavids – Religion, Philosophy and Science', 783–5.

57 Calmard, 'Shi'i Rituals and Power II', 158–9, 162–3, 165–6; Ferrier, 'Women', 399; Keyvani, 188f, partly based on post-Safavid sources.
58 Blake, *Half*, 170–1; Hunarfar, 531; Jafariyan, *Safaviyya*, 362.
59 Mazzaoui, *The Origins*, 51, citing Shaykh Husayn b. Abdal Zahidi *Nasab Nama-yi Safaviyya*, or *Silsilat al-Nasab-i Safaviyya* (Sarwar, 115). The work was published in Berlin in 1924. *Khuld-i Barin*, completed in 1667 by Muhammad Yusuf Qazvini, the brother of Mirza Muhammad Tahir, the author of *Abbasnama* and *vizier* from 1689, took a similar view of Safavid history. Special, very positive, attention was paid to the Nimatallahi Sufi order, which achieved both a 'working relationship' and enjoyed family ties with the Safavids in the previous century, in such court chronicles as *Alam ara-yi Safavi*, dated to 1675–6, and *Alam ara-yi Shah Tahmasp*, completed after 1675–6 (Quinn, 'Rewriting', 211f, 215f). The latter work (I. Afshar, ed., Tehran, 1991, 22) from the first emphasises Tahmasp's status as head of the Safavid Sufi order. See also Floor, 'Khalifeh', 77.
60 Khatunabadi, 541; Blake, 130; nn26, 56. Majlisi's smashing of idols is often cited as proof of his intolerance (Turner, 164; Matthee, *The Politics*, 206; S. Mahdavi, 'Muhammad Baqir Majlisi, Family Values, and the Safavids', in M. Mazzaoui, ed., *Safavid Iran*, 90), absent reference either to his tolerance of 'People of the Book' or to the broader socio-economic context of this particular event to which attention is drawn in discussions of the anti-minority measures undertaken by Khalifa Sultan and Muhammad Bek (compare Matthee, 'The Career', 12; idem, 'Administrative', 87–8). In her 'A Seventeenth-Century Iranian Rabbi's Polemical Remarks on Jews, Christians, and Muslims', in M. Mazzaoui, ed., *Safavid Iran and Her Neighbors* (Salt Lake City, 2003), 157–68, V. Moreen discusses an essay completed in 1686, the year before Majlisi's appointment as Shaykh al-Islam.
    On Sulayman's request that an Arabic-language anti-Christian work be translated into Persian, see Matthee, 'Between Aloofness', 980–1; Jafariyan, *Safaviyya dar Arsa-yi Din*, 3: 965–1000, esp. 980–1; Mahdavi, 1: 129f; A. Hairi, 'Reflections', 159. This essay was likely a continuation of the anti-missionary discourse adopted earlier in the century on which see n29 of Chapter 5, and nn77, 78.
    The *vizier* also played to the realm's anti-philosophy polemic as well (n61). See also n77.
61 See our 'Sufism', nn55, 56; Tehrani, 15: 79; Danishpazhuh 5: 1488–90. On subsequent criticism of them of both as well as Shaykh Bahai, Mir Damad, Khalil Qazvini and Fayz Kashani, however, see n35 of Chapter 8.
    In a further instance of the centre's identification with such elements, the *vaqfnama* of a school in Hamadan built by the *vizier* himself – dated to 1689, two years after Majlisi's appointment as Isfahan's *Shaykh al-Islam*, and signed by many prominent Isfahani clerics – prohibited the study of philosophy. See Jafariyan, *Safaviyya*, 357–8.
62 Mir Lawhi probably died after 1672, when he would have been more than 83. Muhammad Tahir had died in 1687, the year of Majlisi's appointment. Shaykh

Ali died in 1691–2, and Hurr-i Amili died in 1693 – six years after Majlisi's appointment. Sayyid Ahmad Alavi had died before 1650. We have the names of no students of these figures who carried on their teachers' polemic. See n63.

63 By contrast with the opponents of Sufism (n62), Baqir Majlisi, for example, 'produced' a number of prominent students who carried on his legacy, including Muhammad b. Ali Ardabili, Nimatallah Jazairi and Mirza Abdallah Afandi (d. 1717). The latter, for example, held a position on Friday prayer similar to that of both Majlisis (Tehrani, 15: 74), and, like Jazairi, assisted his teacher in compiling *Bihar* (Kohlberg, 91). On Jazairi, see also D. Stewart, 'The Humour of the Scholars: the Autobiography of Nimat Allah al-Jaza'iri (d. 1112/1701)', *IS*, 22(4) (1989), 47–81. On another prominent student of Majlisi, see n40 of Chapter 8.

64 Minorsky, *Tadhkirat*, 13, 13n3, citing Chardin and Sanson.

65 Canby, 148; Hillenbrand, 6: 805; Jafariyan, *Safaviyya*, 363. On the earthquake see also Jafariyan, 'Munasibat', 24. On work on Isfahan's Darb-i Imam dated to 1671, see P. Varjavand's article in *EIr*, 7(1).

66 Jafariyan, *Safaviyya*, 357–8, 360f, 363; Hunarfar, 638–42; n61. A 1686 inscription in the sarai (Hunarfar, 646–8) notes Sulayman's connection to Imam Musa. On these and other private *vaqf*s, see Sefatgol, 'Safavid Administration of *Avqaf*: Structure, Changes and Functions, 1077–1135/1666–1722', in Newman, ed., *Society and Culture*, 403. On the *vaqf* of Sulayman's daughter, see also Ahmadi, 'Du *Vaqfnama*', 341–54. Floor (*A Fiscal*, 119–25) discusses *vaqf* generally and (ibid., 122–3) notes disagreements between the estimates of *vaqf* incomes given by Chardin, Fryer and Kaempfer. See also n69 of the following chapter.

67 Hunarfar, 531–2.

68 The Ilchi's mosque inscription, dated to 1685, speaks of the reigning shah as 'the propagator of the faith of the infallible Imams' and 'the Musavid' and 'the Husaynid'. Blake, 153–4; Hunarfar, 643–5; Jafariyan, *Safaviyya*, 363; Godard, 154–5.

69 A *ghulam* at Sulayman's court built a two-storey school in the Hasanabad quarter, East of Abbas I's new *maydan*; the 1693–4 *vaqf*, dedicating to the mosque the revenues of a sarai and shops to its upkeep, suggests his involvement in trade. Blake, 167. A eunuch whose support was crucial to Sulayman's accession also built a school in this period. See Khatunabadi, 525; Roemer, 6: 305; Jafariyan, *Safaviyya*, 363.

70 In 1687–8 the daughter of a Qummi merchant and wife of 'Mirza Muhammad Mahdi', built the Mirza Husayn School in a suburb located West of the New Gate of the older walled city, and in 1692–3 she dedicated properties to its upkeep. See Blake, 168, 191; Hunarfar, 649–50; Jafariyan, *Safaviyya*, 362–3. If the reference is to the *vizier* Muhammad Mahdi Karaki, the marriage suggests more than a working relationship between clergy and bazaar (see text ad nn87, 88, of Chapter 2). See also n51 of Chapter 8. On Muslim merchants, see Matthee, 'Merchants', 249f. On private *vaqf*s, including those of two women dated to 1679 and 1692, see Sefatgol, 'Safavid Administration', 403–4; John Fryer, an English physician in Iran in 1677–8, as cited in Canby, 144; Ferrier, in Hambly, 400. Perhaps such continued overt involvement of women gave rise to the polemics discussed by Babayan in 'The "Aqaid al-Nisa" ' and Mahdavi in her 'Muhammad Baqir Majlisi', though analyses offered on the basis of a single text can be problematic. On attitudes toward women generally, see also Blake, 'Contributors', 414–15, citing Chardin. See also n88.

71 The mosque's 1688 inscription called the shah 'the shadow of Allah on the Earth' and 'the Musavid' and referred also to the shah as ruling over the 'Arabs and the *ajam*', on which title see nn46, 48, 49 of Chapter 6. See Hunarfar, 472–4, 389–91, 651–2; Blake, *Half*, 152. On the clerical/ merchant alliance, see also the previous note.

72 Blake, *Half*, 153–4; Hunarfar, 626–30; Jafariyan, *Safaviyya*, 362.

73 Canby, 147–8, Blake, *Half*, 71f; Hillenbrand, 6: 804–5; Hunarfar, 622–5. The building was highly praised by the poet Saib Tabrizi, on whom see below. See Jafariyan, *Safaviyya*, 360; Godard, 147–8.

74 Canby, 148; Godard, 162–3; Hunarfar, 580–1; Blake, *Half*, 44, who dates the building to after 1722.

75 Blake, *Half*, 76. The mausolea erected for Naini and Khvansari have been mentioned. The poet Saib Tabrizi, a court associate over the reigns of three shahs, was buried in his own gardens. Hunarfar, 634–8, 657–9; Jafariyan, *Safaviyya*, 362, Tabrizi, *Faraid*, 295.

76 According to Chardin, the *sadr* received the mansion of Ali Quli Khan when the latter died without heir and the property passed to the shah. Blake, *Half*, 89–90, 191; Ferrier, *A Journey*, 153–4.

77 On the consistency with which the court upheld the Armenian side in foreign trade arrangements throughout Shaykh Ali Khan's vizierate and into that of Muhammad Tahir Qazvini, see Matthee, *The Politics*, 192–7, 197–201, 202. On the continued wealth enjoyed by the richest merchants, see also McCabe, 191. McCabe (188–94) links the 1678 persecution of the Armenian, and Jewish, community to that year's 'drought, crop failure and high price of corn' and suggests conversions to Islam in this period were either personal or 'political'. See also Ghougassian, 158. The later conversion to Islam of the very wealthy mayor (*kalantar*) of New Julfa was linked to French Capuchin efforts to convert the Armenians. See also McCabe, 195–8. On Catholic missionary efforts in New Julfa, and court's support for Iranian Armenians, see Ghougassian, 125f, esp. 135f, 145–6, 176. Jafariyan (*Safaviyya*, 353–5) notes Sulayman's visit to an Armenian church and an Armenian priest's dedication to the shah of a book on the faith. Lockhart (*The Fall*, 32) cites Carmelite reports, dated to 1678, of the killing of some Jewish rabbis at the instigation of some hostile clerics, which he attributes, *sans* supporting references, to 'the power and influence' of Baqir Majlisi. See nn56, 60. On Carmelite attitudes toward the centre, see also n16 of the following chapter.

78 St Nerses church was built between 1666–7 and 1670–1 and that of St Nicholas the Patriarch also dates from this period (Carswell, 57, 59). On All Saviour's, see the inscriptions dated to 1667, 1669 and 1670, in Hunarfar, 516. McCabe notes (188–94) that despite the taxes imposed on the community 'the richest were still immensely wealthy' and Chardin (Ferrier, *A Journey*, 65) noted that Julfa contained over 3,500 houses, the most lavish of which were located along the river. Carswell discusses two of the community's finer houses (65f) and offers foreign accounts of New Julfa (73f). In arguing for New Julfa's subsequent apparent 'decline', McCabe (353–5) notes both pressures for conversion and, mainly, 'community infighting' as its causes. In tandem with conventional discussions of Safavid 'decline', she dates the onset of this process to the 1650s even though she also notes that the community's key role in international trade continued until *c.* 1750.

79 In his 'The Tarikh-i Jahanara in the Chester Beatty Library: An Illustrated

Manuscript of the "Anonymous Histories of Shah Ismail" ', *IS*, 37(1) (2004), 89–107, esp. 93f, B. Wood notes a 1683 copy of this text which featured 'old norms' rendered in a European style. Canby (151) refers to other illustrated manuscripts of the same text which do not feature European stylisation. See also Morton, 'The Date'.

80 Muhammad Zaman's recourse to European styles may be seen especially in his additions to earlier works such as the 1539–43 *Khamsa* or the *Shahnama* made for Abbas I. Canby, 148f.

81 Shafi Abbasi, Muhammad Zaman and Ali Quli Jabbadar produced such items; Muhammad Zaman may well have first attracted Shah Sulayman's attention as a lacquer painter. Canby, 15f1.

82 Canby, 151, 154–6, 159. See especially 152, fig. 143 where the rose and butterfly design itself may derive from a European pattern book, reflecting both a cosmopolitan taste and an ability to pay for such a fine fabric and design patterns.

83 Canby, 156.

84 Canby, 159.

85 Crowe, *Persia and China*, 169–70, 174, 176, 187, 197, 205, 226, 240. Crowe calls attention to Dutch shipments in 1670, 1675 and 1678, which attest to ongoing foreign demand for such items.

86 Canby, 157–9.

87 Jafariyan, *Safaviyya*, 347.

88 Browne, 4: 112–13, citing Krusinski and Chardin; Lockhart, *The Fall*, 29–30, citing Fryer, in Iran from 1677–8, Sanson, in Iran from 1683 to 1691 and Muhammad Muhsin's *Zubdat al-Tavarikh*, composed for Nadir Shah in 1741–2, 50 years after Sulayman's death; Roemer, 6: 304–7, 310, citing, among others, Kaempfer, in Iran from 1683–4, on whom see n70 of the following chapter; Savory, *Iran Under*, 238–9, citing Chardin. On the rising influence of the haram from the reign of Abbas II, see also Matthee, 'Administrative', 81; idem, 'Iran's Ottoman Diplomacy', 151–2, citing Chardin, Sanson, Krusinski, and Kaempfer, among other foreign sources. Ferrier (*A Journey*, 69–75) summarises Chardin's remarks on the palace and the haram, direct news of which, as both were not public venues, might usefully be treated with considerable care. See also Carmelite accounts of Sulayman's drinking (Floor, *A Fiscal*, 230). On womens' involvement in society, see also n70.

89 Ferrier, *A Journey*, 44–5. Blake (*Half*, 139–40) suggests that Chardin's figure of 162 mosques within the city and another twenty-eight outwith ignored many smaller neighbourhood mosques and those built by various notables in conjunction with the establishment of such other buildings as sarais, mansions and bathhouses. On the city's various quarters and suburbs generally, see Blake, 181–91; Haneda, 'The Character'. Hunarfar (725–8) citing later sources, notes that over the Safavid period the city grew to some forty quarters from six. See also n64 of the previous chapter. On Chardin's estimate of Isfahan's population as 500,000, see n71 of the following chapter but on his estimate of Iran's total population as 40 million, see n6.

8 Denouement or Defeat: The Reign of Shah Sultan Husayn (1694–1722)

1 Khatunabadi, 549–50, 558, where he notes that in 1708–9 robes were also distributed to religious figures. See also the preface to Nasiri, *Dastur*, 28, and the text itself, 24.

Nasiri (d. *c.* 1714), a descendant both of Nasir al-Din Tusi and more recent, Safavid-period, figures at court, including Abbas I's *vizier* Hatim Bek Urdubadi, was a court historian (preface, 45f; n7). Of his chronicle, only entries for the years 1692–1700, the first six years of Shah Sultan Husayn's twenty-eight-year reign, are extant. See also Lockhart, *The Fall*, 35, citing European sources. As noted in *Dastur*'s preface (27–8), Maryam Bekum is usually identified as the shah's aunt. See also Lockhart, ibid., 36, 39, 48n1; Tabrisi, 245; Jafariyan, *Ilal*, 302; Mirza Rafia Ansari, *Dastur al-Muluk*, M. Danishpazhuh, ed., in *Majallah-yi Danishkadah-i Adabiyat va 'Ulum-i Insani-yi Danishgah-i Tehran*, 15: 501, where she is identified as Safi's daughter and the builder of builder of the school. In a 1703–4 inscription on that school (Hunarfar, 662) she refers to herself as Safi's daughter.

C. Marcinkowski has recently completed a translation of Ansari's text, as *Mirza Rafia's Dastur al-Muluk. A Manual of Later Safavid Administration. English Translation, Comments on the Offices and Services, and Facsimile of the Unique Persian Manuscript* (Kuala Lumpur, 2002). I. Afshar is scheduled to produce a new version of this text based on the recent discovery of the remainder of the manuscript and Marcinkowski has indicated he will produce a new translation thereof. There is little known of the author, except that he was likely a member of the capital's well-known Jabari family (see also n8) which had served the court from Ismail's reign. The text is dedicated to Sultan Husayn and the last date cited in the text is 1712. See Danishpazhuh's prefatory remarks in ibid., 15: 484.

2 Nasiri, preface, 28; Lockhart, *The Fall*, 50–68, based on non-Persian sources. On the treaty with Russia, see Lockhart, 103–8.
3 Nasiri, 70f; 277–8; Lockhart, *The Fall*, 46–7, 50.
4 These manuals include *Dastur al-Muluk*, on which see n1; *Tadhkirat al-Muluk*, written sometime after the assassination of Isfahan's conqueror Shah Mahmud in 1725, for Shah Mahmud's nephew and successor Ashraf (1725–9), although Lockhart (*The Fall*, 513–14) dates it to 1726; and *Alqab va Mavajib-i Dawrah-i Salatin Safaviyya*, of Mirza Ali Naqi Nasiri (Y. Rahimlu, ed., Mashhad, 1372), completed during the reign of Tahmasp II – the son of Shah Sultan Husayn, who proclaimed himself shah in Qazvin following the fall of Isfahan.

Scholars have yet to consider the 'agendas' of these texts, as Quinn has done for earlier court chronicles. The ascription of such a high degree of formality to Safavid administrative structures described in the two post-1722 texts is particularly problematic. *Tadhkirat* is noticeably structured along the lines of *Dastur*. For an overview of the court, based mainly on *Tadhkirat* and foreign, including later, sources, see Savory, 'Courts and Courtiers vi. In the Safavid Period', *EIr*, 6: 371–5. On the role of the eunuchs, especially as attested by these later sources, see K. Babayan, 'Eunuchs in the Safavid Period', *EIr*, 9. Chardin, however, had estimated that 1,000 *ghulam* served the shah and 3,000 eunuchs resided at the court. See S. Babaie, *Slaves of the Shah*, 15. On Chardin's reliability, see n44 of Chapter 5, and n12 of our Introduction. See also n48.
5 Floor, *Safavid Government*, 38, 22, 173; Matthee, 'Between Aloofness', 226n35; Lockhart, *The Fall*, 106, 114, 126, 138; Matthee, 'Administrative Change', 92–3, where he dates Muhammad Tahir's appointment as *vizier* to March, 1691; Khatunabadi, 550. Fath Ali Khan had been *qullaraqasi* and the Bekdilu Shamlu Muhammad Quli Khan, made *vizier* in 1721, had been *qurchibashi* and fought against the Afghans at Gulnabad in 1722; he was dismissed following the

Afghans' subsequent capture of Isfahan. There was no *vakil* in this period (Floor, *Safavid Government*, 13). See also Floor, *Safavid Government*, 142–3, 172–3; idem, 'sadr', 482; Lockhart, *The Fall*, 98–9, 138. The origins of the *divanbekis* of the period are hard to identify, but at least one, Livan Mirza, was Georgian (Floor, 'Judicial', 23–4; Lockhart, 46) and another, Safi Quli Khan, who served 1712–15, was of tribal origin (Lockhart, 98–9). On Fath Ali Khan, see also R. Matthee's recent 'Blinded by Power: The Rise and Fall of Fath Ali Khan Daghestani, Grand Vizier Under Shah Sultan Husayn (1127/1715–1133/1720)', *SIr*, 33 (2004), 179–220.

6 The Dhul-Qadr retained the position of sealkeeper (Floor, *Safavid Government*, 72) and the Shamlu held the post of *ishikaqasibashi* of the Supreme Divan (Nasiri, 19, 33, 196, 258, 272). See also the sources cited in the previous note.

7 On sayyids dominating the posts of court scribe, including Nasiri, author of *Dastur* and descendant of the Urdubadi *vizier*s of the reigns of Abbas I and Safi, and other Nasiris, and other key posts, see Floor, *Safavid Government*, 57, 43, 53; n1. The chief doctor was a sayyid (Khatunabadi, 553). Floor (*Safavid Government*, 40) notes the centre's domination over the period by Qizilbash, *ghulam*, and Tajik elements.

8 Floor ('Judicial', 48) offers a partial list of Isfahan's *kalantar*s, in effect an elected mayor; during Husayn's reign all were drawn from the prominent Jabari family of sayyids, which also provided the comptroller during Abbas II's reign. See also Floor, *Safavid Government*, 43. On those holding posts at court and in the provinces, see Khatunabadi, 551–1, 559, 560, 564. The provincial religious bureaucracy was also dominated by Tajik sayyids. Thus, while the first-generation Lebanese immigrant Hurr-i Amili was Mashhad's *Shaykh al-Islam*, local sayyid families dominated the city's other religious posts, including those connected with Imam Riza's shrine (Khatunabadi, 515, 522–3, 529, 532, 536, 539) one of whom was the centre's *sadr khassa* from 1666 to 1687 (Khatunabadi, 546, 550; Floor, 'sadr', 482) and another married Sulayman's daughter. See also Khatunabadi, 541; Floor, 'sadr', 484f. In Isfahan, the thoroughly Persianised Karaki family retained its influence over this period, with the son of the former *vizier* Muhammad Mahdi Karaki serving as the city's *qadi* (Khatunabadi, 555). The post of *Shaykh al-Islam* of Isfahan and the capital's Friday prayer leader remained in the Majlisi family, now also sayyids, through the fall of Isfahan. See Kitabi, 57–8. Absent, at both the provincial and central administrative levels, are any large number of Arab immigrants. Jurdi ('Migration', 422) lists only eight Amili scholars as holding any 'position' at all during the period 1680–1736; four were sayyids, suggesting their assimilation, like the Karakis and Majlisis, by this period. Compare her 'Converting Persia', 155, where she lists ten.

9 An Ustajlu chief was sent to expel the Abdalis and Ghalzai Afghans from Herat of which the governor was a Shamlu (Lockhart, 96, 97). Sultan Husayn's son Tahmasp appointed a Qajar governor of Simnan, who later turned against him, and sent a Shamlu envoy to Istanbul (Lockhart, 280–1, 344). In Nasiri's *Dastur*, see also mention of the Kurd Rustam Khan Zangana as governor of Jam (213, 269), and other prominent Zanganas (214, 225–6; 58; Matthee, 'Administrative Change', 92), the Sadlu governor of Simnan (114; on the Sadlu, see Woods, *The Aqquyunlu* 108, 196, 199), the Afshar governor of Urmiyya (96), prominent Qajars (166, 219, 222, 233–4; 56–7; 29; 96), including a governor of Simnan (273), prominent Shamlu (19, 33, 106, 196, 258, 272) and the Inallu (61, 70, 193–4).

10 See Floor, *Safavid Government*, 80–123, for a discussion of provincial government over the period, esp. 102. Nasiri, in his *Alqab*, devotes special attention to provincial affairs.

11 Röhrborn (86) cites Sanson's disagreement with Chardin on the degree of local autonomy.

12 Röhrborn, 69, 86, 103, 107, 165–6, 171. See also Khatunabadi, 551–2, 555, 559, 560, 564.

13 See Nasiri, *Dastur*, 30, 71, 85, 104–5, 121, 122, 131, 157–8, 160, 181, 195, 200–1, 206, 225, 234, 237, 246, 258. See also Floor, *A Fiscal*, 200, citing a listing of tribes who supplied both mounted and foot soldiers; idem, *Safavid Government*, 214–15. Although the list probably dates to the Zand or Qajar period, the many references to the Qizilbash in Nasiri's contemporary text (cited above), in both 'political' and military contexts, suggest the continued importance of tribal elements in, and to, the polity. See also n90.

14 Lockhart, *The Fall*, 138–9, citing, as he acknowledges, conflicting sources. On the Kuhgilu see Minorsky, *Tadhkirat*, 163, 173, 193. As noted below, Qajar forces based in Astarabad, and their commander, a former governor of Mashhad, were sent against and defeated by Sistani rebels in 1719–20. See Lockhart, 122–3, 280–1, citing the later *Tarikh-i Nadiri*, on which see n26.

15 See, for example, the text ad n60 of Chapter 7, and our discussions of the anti-minority policies of Khalifa Sultan and Muhammad Bek. See also Ghougassian, 159–61, citing Armenian sources.

16 On the Sunni *vizier* Fath Ali Khan's 1716 refusal of Peter the Great's request to order the Armenians to redirect the silk trade via Russia and, on the eve of the Afghan invasion, the Shamlu *vizier*'s refusal of an Ottoman request to order merchants to redirect all land and maritime silk export via their territory, see Matthee, *The Politics*, 225, 220–1. See also Floor, *The Economy*, 209–10; idem, *A Fiscal*, 181. See also Ghougassian, 145–56, 220–3, 225–6, 280, 284 and 286, the latter including Sultan Husayn's 1712 *firman* forbidding Catholic missionary efforts among the Armenians. In 1694, the Carmelites were expelled from Isfahan, although they were allowed to return in 1697. See Richard, 'Carmelites', 833. The court's, at least passing, interest in anti-Christian polemics, as exhibited by the attacks on Christianity of a European convert to Islam, Ali Quli Jadid al-Islam, and the shah's encouragement of his translation of one such work into Persian, was no doubt rooted in the suspicion of 'foreign' Christians, as Sayyid Ahmad Alavi's hostility to the foreign missionaries had been earlier in the century. On Jadid al-Islam, see Hairi, 'Reflections', 160–3; Jafariyan, *Safaviyya dar Arsa-yi Din*, 3: 965–1000, 1001–42; n18.

17 A 1716 *firman* freed Armenians from the transporting of the bodies of executed criminals and from the cereal tax. See Ghougassian, 160; McCabe, 360–1.

18 Ghougassian, 160. Baqir Khatunabadi's 1696–7 translation of the gospels at the shah's command, on which see n42, suggests a more profound interest in Christianity, especially the indigenous variety, than that exhibited in the polemics of Jadid al-Islam. See also Thomas, 'Chronology', 204; Thomas and Vahman, 'Persian Translations', 211.

19 Ghougassian, 197; Hunarfar, 508–10, 517. See also E. Herzig's forthcoming research.

20 See Floor, *The Economy*, 191–3, 84; Floor and Clawson, 350–1, 361–2; Matthee, 'Between Venice', 239–40, 251–3, citing mainly company sources. The *vizier* Shah Quli Khan Zangana, the son of Shaykh Ali who, as Sulayman's *vizier*, had

tried to stem the specie outflow, played a role in the issuance of the 1713 *firman* (Matthee, *The Politics*, 213–14). The specie drain in this period was perhaps aggravated by the demands of Iranian pilgrims to Mecca. See Matthee, 'Between Venice', 251, citing Khatunabadi, 553 and Dutch reports; Matthee, *The Politics*, 213; Floor, *The Economy*, 192, and on the popularity of the *hajj* in this period, see also ad n49.

21 European demand for Iran's silk rose in 1693 owing to the 1689–97 European wars but fell in 1696 owing to the trade in Chinese silk. See Herzig, 'The Volume', 65; Floor, *The Economy*, 173–5, 191, 225–6; Matthee, *The Politics*, 206f, 210–18, 223–5, 244–5.

22 Lockhart (49–50) citing a contemporary Georgian source, who also claimed rioters demanded the shah's younger brother replace him on the throne. Khatunabadi (556) refers to the shah's visit to Mashhad in 1707–8 but does not mention any disorders in the capital.

23 Lockhart, *The Fall*, 50, and Matthee, *The Politics*, 212, both citing foreign sources.

24 Lockhart, ibid. Apparently no harm befell the shah's younger brother afterwards. The Georgian commander was made governor of the city.

25 Khatunabadi, 558–60. See also 565–6 on the replacement of officials in the provinces in 1712, some owing to military failures.

26 Lockhart, *The Fall*, 83–92, citing foreign accounts, including an Armenian interpreter attached to the French embassy in Istanbul in Iran from 1718 to *c.* 1723, Krusinski and such post-1722 sources as *Zubdat al-Tavarikh, Majma al-Tavarikh* and *Tarikh-i Nadiri*. The latter, composed by Mirza Muhammad Mahdi Kawkabi Astarabadi, dates to *c.* eleven years after Nadir Shah's 1747 assassination. Lockhart (512–13, 92n2, 504f) acknowledged problems with both Astarabadi and the Armenian source. The reliability of Krusinski (d. 1756), the Polish Procurator of Jesuit mission in Iran, in Iran for some twenty years until 1729, and well received by the Afghans after the capture of Isfahan, must be reconsidered, not the least given the centre's consistent support for local Armenian interests against the activities of Catholic missionaries in Iran in this period, on which see also n16. See also Lockhart, 516–25, esp. 517. On Krusinski, see also nn33, 81, 92.

27 Khatunabadi, 567–9; Floor, *A Fiscal*, 230. Matthee cites additional detail on this unrest from Dutch sources. See his 'Blinded by Power', 187–9.

28 Matthee, *The Politics*, 212n46, 216; Floor, *The Afghan Invasion of Safavid Persia, 1721–29* (Paris, 1998), 29–31; Lockhart, *The Fall*, 107, 107n2, 108, all citing foreign sources. Lockhart did not subject the Dutch records to the sort of systematic, critical examination merited given the VOC's position in the country; concerning the Afghans' 1722 siege of Isfahan (144–70, 408–11), for example, the VOC's *Dagregister*, or *Isfahan Diary*, which ends in August of 1722, is, at best, underutilised. For his *The Afghan Invasion* Floor not only translated the bulk of the *Isfahan Diary*, but also included previously unknown Dutch eyewitness accounts of events in Kirman in 1719–21, Lar in 1721 and Shiraz in 1724.

29 Floor, *Safavid Government*, 173. Matthee, 214, citing Dutch sources, says Fath Ali Khan was also *qurchibashi*, but cf. Floor, ibid., 143.

30 Courtiers' salaries were cut, for example, but as these comprised a mixture of payments, in cash and kind, as discussed below, the impact was likely, and possibly purposely, limited. Minorsky, *Tadhkirat*, 152f. The Dutch (Matthee,

'Blinded by Power', 187–9) implicated Fath Ali Khan and Muhammad Baqir Khatunabadi in the earlier food unrest. See n33.

31 *Matthee, The Politics*, 214–15. On Fath Ali Khan's measures see also Matthee, 'Blinded by Power', 189–93. Foreign sources, variously unhappy with the court for a variety of reasons, were, perhaps unsurprisingly, uniformly critical of the centre's responses. The French, upset with court measures taken against Catholic missionaries, charged the *vizier* with pocketing the revenues raised from these measures (Matthee, *The Politics*, 215n63). On the French, see also Matthee, 'Blinded by Power', 197; nn26, 72. On the similarly critical Dutch view, see Floor, *The Afghan*, 26f; Matthee, *The Politics*, 212; idem, 'Blinded by Power', 198–9; nn30, 33. On the Russian view, see Lockhart, *The Fall*, 106–7; n33.

32 Matthee, 'Between Venice', 252, citing contemporary foreign sources and the later *Zubdat*; Floor, *The Afghan*, 29–30; idem, *A Fiscal*, ibid. The *Abbasi* was revalued and in 1717 the minting of gold coins on a large scale was resumed for the first time since 1587. In 1717 also a new trade agreement VOC was reached which prohibited the free export of bullion; local traders' complaints, *c*. 1719, that they could not engage in specie export unless they reported their activities to the authorities suggests some compliance. See Floor, *The Economy*, 191–3, 84, 116–17; Floor and Clawson, 350–1, 361–2; Matthee, 'Between Venice', 239–40, 251–3, citing mainly company sources.

33 Herzig, 'The Volume', 65; Floor, *The Economy*, 173–4, 191, 225–6, 116–17; Floor, 'The Dutch', 355; Matthee, *The Politics*, 206f, 210–18, 223–5; idem, 'Blinded by Power', 191f. On the Levant route and consistent Ottoman efforts to assure the safe passage of Iranian silk through their territory, see Matthee, *The Politics*, 224–5, 216, 222; Herzig, ibid, 65, 71, 75, for *c*. 1720, 79; Floor, *The Economy*, 226. On Russia's limited successes in attracting Armenian interest in the 'Northern' route, see Herzig, ibid, 71–2; Matthee, *The Politics*, 219–20, 227; Ghougassian, 161–2; McCabe, 278f; n16. The continued success of the overland trade, in silk and specie, and the constant movement of Iranian pilgrims to the Hijaz over the period belie frequent suggestions as to the inherent insecurity of travel within the realm, at least to 1715. See Savory, *Iran Under*, 241; Matthee, *The Politics*, 204; idem, 'Between Venice', 243, 245, 247, Floor, *The Economy*, 209–10. For contemporary Dutch 'analysis' of their failure to achieve their desired trade goals, on the 1702 treaty for example, see Matthee, *The Politics*, 214. On Dutch dissatisfaction with the amount of the gift they were expected to give the new *vizier*, see idem, 'Blinded by Power', 191.

Such foreign discontent with the centre cannot but have produced skewed reporting and analysis of domestic developments, as per nn30, 31. Foreign reports of events at court, to which they enjoyed at best extremely limited access, are therefore usefully treated with some caution. See, for example, the reports of the Dutch, (cited by Matthee, 'Blinded by Power', 201n78) or the reports of Krusinski (ibid., 213). On the latter's 'agenda', see nn26, 81, 92.

34 See references to an essay by Fayz's son and other essays dating to this time period in Tehrani, 8: 56; 10: 206; n42 of Chapter 7. For an essay by a minor scholar associated with Maryam Bekum, Safi's daughter and Sultan's Husayn's aunt, see Tehrani, 6: 446, 12: 157.

Seeking spiritual explanations for Afghan successes, post-1722 accounts by proponents of philosophical inquiry and Sufi doctrine and practice perhaps naturally focus on clerical hostility to Sufism and *irfan*. See the references by the Shirazi Qutb al-Din Nayrizi (d. 1759), the well-known Dhahabi Shaykh, in his post-1722 *Fasl al-Khittab*, portions of which appear in Jafariyan, ed., *Ilal*, 259f, and idem, *Safaviyya dar Arsa-yi Din*, 3: 1355–81; n59. See also Nayrizi's post-1729 *Tibb al-Mamalik*, which appears in Jafariyan, ed., *Ilal*, 215–34, and idem, *Safaviyya dar Arsa-yi Din*, 3: 1324–37, and *Mukafatnama* (on which see nn37, 58, 89), written by an imprisoned court retainer between two and five years after the fall of Isfahan. See also Jafariyan's accompanying discussion of these texts in *Ilal* and *Safaviyya dar Arsa-yi Din*.

35 Among the non-living targets of this latter polemic were Shaykh Bahai, Mir Damad, Khalil Qazvini and Fayz Kashani. Even Muhammad Tahir and Hurr-i Amili, also both deceased, were attacked on these grounds; both had accepted court appointments, and both, including Muhammad Tahir who was a critic of philosophy and Sufi inquiry, had permitted the *faqih* to lead Friday prayer during the Imam's absence. See Newman, 'The Nature', 1992, esp. 256f. On Hurr-i Amili and the prayer, see Tehrani, 15: 79.

36 The *firman*, engraved on mosques and other prominent locations, also closed brothels, banned cock-fighting, ram-fights, and bull-fights and enjoined women to behave more modestly. Nasiri, *Dastur*, preface, 29–30; text, page 19, 44f, 29. See also ibid., 35–52; Jafariyan, *Safaviyya dar Arsa-yi Din*, 1: 394f, 406f, citing Nasiri, on a second, harsher, version of the *firman* subsequently signed by eight prominent clerics. See also Lockhart, *The Fall*, 38–40, 72, cited in turn by Arjomand (*The Shadow*, 190) and Turner (164). Floor (*A Fiscal*, 158) and Matthee ('Prostitutes', 147–8) note copies of the *firman* in Amul and Tabriz. Naraqi (230–3) notes a 1694 text of this *firman* in a Kashan mosque.

Interestingly, Nasiri (e.g. 19, 35) and a 1692 *vaqf* document for the School of the Potters (n50) describe Majlisi as 'the *mujtahid* of the age (*mujtahid al-zaman*)', but not 'seal of the *mujtahid*s', a title given Mir Damad, Mir Damad's ancestor Ali Karaki and the latter's daughter's son Sayyid Husayn (n19 of Chapter 5). Khatunabadi (e.g. 551) reserves this term for Muhammad Baqir Khatunabadi, on whom see below. On Majlisi's *khutba*, see also n55.

37 See, for example, Matthee ('Prostitutes', 147–8), citing Cornelius de Bruyn, the Dutch painter who was in Iran, and Isfahan, in 1703, 1704/5 and 1706/7 (Lockhart, *The Fall*, 48, 476; Floor, 'De Bruin (or de Bruyn), Cornelis', *EIr*, 7/(2); Stevens, 426–7, 432), that dancing women were no longer common at official ceremonies, and John Bell, briefly in Isfahan in 1717 as surgeon to a Russian mission (Lockhart, *The Fall*, 105), that women were no longer offered to guests but rather *shirbat*. Canby notes a painting with a more sombre depiction of the shah in 1721, in contrast with that of an audience of Shah Sulayman, complete with music, food, drink and tobacco. See Canby, *The Golden Age*, 167, 153. Cf. Babayan, 'The "Aqaid al-Nisa" ', 358, 373; n36. For different, and conflicting accounts as to the failure of the restrictions, see, for example, Lockhart, *The Fall*, 47, citing de Bruyn; Matthee, *The Politics*, 204–5, citing the post-1722 *Mukafatnama* and the much later *Majma. The* pre-1722 account of Abu Talib Mir Findiriski, *Tuhfat al-Alam*, lauds Sultan Husayn's efforts at military reform and his moral piety. On the author, see Nasiri, *Dastur*, Introduction, 28; Matthee, 'Prostitutes', 147n117.

38 Hunarfar, 662–7; Blake, 90, 167; Sefatgol, 'Safavid Administration', 406.

39 Canby, 163-f; Blake, *Half*, 159–65; idem, 'Contributions', 685–723; Hillenbrand, 6: 808–11. The Chahar Bagh school contained 150 student rooms (Khatunabadi, 557), several times more than the total provided for in the two schools in the Royal or Shah Mosque, now called the Imam Mosque.

40 Sultan Husayn also convened a gathering marking Imam Ali's birthday, attended
    by the realm's key clerics. Students began arriving the same year. Khatunabadi,
    559–62. On the dates of the building of the school, known also as Sultani school
    and the Chahar Bagh School, see Khatunabadi, 556; Tabrizi, *Faraid*, 290–1;
    Blake, *Half*, 159–3. Tabrizi, author of *Faraid*, was a student of Baqir Majlisi,
    Jamal Khvansari and Muhammad Salih Khatunabadi. See also Sefatgol, 'Safavid
    Administration', 404–5.
41 Sefatgol, 'Safavid Administration', 404–5. See also Blake, *Half*, 167. See also a
    similar ban at the Hamadan school established in 1689 by the *vizier* Shaykh Ali
    Khan ad n61 of Chapter 7.
42 Khatunabadi, 551–71, esp. 552, 554–7, 559, 569–71, 585–98; Kitabi, 52f;
    Jafariyan's introduction to Baqir Khatunabadi's 1696–7 translation of the
    gospels, *Tarjuma-yi Anajil-i Arba'a*, R. Jafariyan, ed. (Tehran, 1373), 44f.
    Muhammad Salih Khatunabadi (d. 1704), who had also studied with the Tajik
    sayyid Muhammad Shirvani, Majlisi's brother-in-law (n46 of Chapter 7), was
    Shaykh al-Islam in Isfahan after his father-in-law's death and his sons were the
    capital's Friday prayer leader and *Shaykh al-Islam*. See Tabrisi, 148, 243f;
    Kitabi, 61–2; Jafariyan, *Ilal*, 298–302. Kitabi (57f) lists the holders of the post of
    Shaykh al-Islam in the city. One Muhammad Jafar appears briefly to have been
    Shaykh al-Islam after Majlisi (Khatunabadi, 551; n58).
43 Khatunabadi, 563–4, 566; Jafariyan, *Ilal*, 298–9.
        Minorsky (*Tadhkirat*, 110–11, 41–2) had identified Baqir Majlisi as the first
    mullabashi, an 'analysis' echoed by Lockhart (72). Although Arjomand, in his
    'The Office of *Mulla-bashi* in Shi'ite Iran', *Studia Islamica*, 57 (1983), 135–46,
    showed *Tadhkirat*'s 'Muhammad Baqir' referred to Baqir Khatunabadi, both he
    (*The Shadow*, 155) and, more recently, Turner (165) argue that Baqir Majlisi
    had accumulated so much authority in the realm that he was 'in effect' *mul-
    labashi* before the post was created, some fourteen years after his death. See also
    Mahdavi, 'Muhammad Baqir Majlisi', 90; Floor, '*sadr*', 477. The primary
    sources, textual and otherwise, do not confirm that Majlisi enjoyed such author-
    ity or personal closeness to the shah; in fact, the sources do not even agree on the
    honorifics accorded Majlisi (see n36). By contrast, based on the close association
    between Baqir Khatunabadi and Sultan Husayn, Blake (*Half*, 161–3) suggests
    the Shah in fact built the Chahar Bagh school for the sayyid. Further attesting to
    his prominence, the author Khatunabadi (567, 569) reports that rioters attrib-
    uted to Muhammad Baqir the statement that people who could afford tobacco
    could afford bread, and subsequently torched his house. The Dutch blamed
    Khatunabadi for causing the grain crisis (Matthee, 'Blinded by Power', 187–9;
    n30). See also Blake, 162. At his death in 1715, a son was named teacher at
    the Chahar Bagh school in his father's place, and another was named chief
    teacher at the Royal Mosque. The post of *mullabashi* went to a non-sayyid who
    served through the fall of Isfahan and whom Lockhart (72) erroneously styled
    Baqir Majlisi's grandson and, citing no sources, attributed to him the same
    fanaticism as his 'grandfather' (72n4). See also Roemer (6: 322–3); Jafariyan,
    Ilal, 298–301.
44 The school's great size required extensive *vaqf*. By 1716, according to Sefatgol,
    the income of 11 villages, 33 gardens, 48 farms, 35 *qanats*, 2 baths, 1 caravan-
    sarai, 1 market, 11 tracts of land, 1 coffee shop, 3 mills, 8 walnut trees, 862
    other kinds of trees and 1 castle were given to the custodian, teachers, students
    and other members of the school. See Sefatgol, 'Safavid Administration', 404–5;

Tabrizi, ibid.; Khatunabadi, 563; Blake, *Half*, 163–6. Blake (159–61) suggests that the school's *vaqf* being almost completely in cash reflected the greater monetarisation of the realm since the establishment of the Shah Mosque. Jafariyan (*Safaviyya dar Arsa-yi Din*, 2: 744f) discusses the library associated with the school and cites the text of the 1708–9 *vaqf*.

45 On continued royal patronage of the Qazvin shrine, and its administrators the Marashi sayyids in this period, as evidenced by *firman*s dated from 1694 to 1717, see Mudarrisi, *Bargi*, 181–92, 195–7. On repair work sponsored in the Iraqi shrine cities, under Ottoman control since 1638, see Khatunabadi, 553.

46 Khatunabadi, 558, 565, 563; Nasiri, 218; Jafariyan, *Safaviyya dar Arsa-yi Din*, 3: 1254n4, on descendants of this marriage. See also Floor, *Safavid Government*, 45; n51. See also ad n6 of the following chapter.

47 Blake, *Half*, 167.

48 Hunarfar, 694–5, 711, 803–4; Jafariyan, *Safaviyya dar Arsa-yi Din*, 2: 913–47, esp. 915–16; Khatunabadi, 557; n51; Jafariyan, ed., 'Vaqfnama-i Madrasa-yi Sultan Husayniyya Maruf bi Madrasa-yi Aqa Kamal', *Miras-i Islami Iran*, Jafariyan, ed. 1 (Qum, 1994), 259–90; Babaie, et. al., *Slaves of the Shah*, 17.

    In 1709–10 another eunuch who served the court during the reigns of both Sulayman and Sultan Husayn built a bathhouse, bazaar and sarai to support a mosque. See Blake, 154; Hunarfar, 682–3. On eunuchs, see also n69 of the previous chapter.

    Other *vaqf* documents attest to further co-operation between clerics and eunuchs and show that the eunuchs, who owed something of their wealth to land and farms, entrusted their funds to the city's Indian merchants for safekeeping, thus linking all these groups together. See Jafariyan, *Safaviyya dar Arsa-yi Din*, 2: 879f; n38 of Chapter 6.

49 The *hajj* process was certainly facilitated by continuing peace with the Ottomans but made more difficult by the not-infrequent attacks on, and various indignities suffered by, Shi'i residents of and pilgrims to the Hijaz. See, for example, Khatunabadi, 552–3, 557, 566; Jafariyan, *Safaviyya dar Arsa-yi Din*, 2: 844–5; Matthee, *The Politics*, 213; idem, 'Between Venice', 242–3. See also Jafariyan, 2: 825–49. See also nn20, 33; n36 of Chapter 7.

50 In 1705–6 the Tajik sayyid Ardistani, who built the School of the Potters in 1693–4, and his wife built a school known as the Nim Avard School, located in the Nim Avard quarter of the city, between the old and new *maydan*s, the base of a number of the period's prominent clerics. Both dedicated revenues from their own lands around Ardistan to support these schools. See Blake, 168; Hunarfar, 652–66, 679–82; Ahmadi, 'Chahar Vaqfnama', 3: 99–100, 114f; n28 of Chapter 7. In the Ahmadabad area another medical practitioner, Muhammad Hakim, built a school with the inscription dated to 1702–3. See Hunarfar, 660–2; n55.

    The reference in the *vaqf* document for the School of the Potters to Baqir Majlisi and in that of the Nim Avard to Jamal Khvansari (Ahmadi, 118, 128) suggest continued efforts by both, Majlisi especially, to associate with, and thereby influence, 'popular' discourse in this period.

51 The daughter of a prominent Qummi merchant and sayyid who had married one Mirza Muhammad Mahdi, perhaps a reference to the Karaki *vizier* of that name, dedicated further properties to the Mirza Husayn School she had built in 1687–8, during Sulayman's reign. See Blake, *Half*, 168; Hunarfar, 649–50; n70 of the previous chapter. In 1713–14, another merchant built a small school in the Shamsabad quarter of the city. See Hunarfar, 684. One Hajj Mirza Asadallah

dedicated revenues from two shops to the Dhul-Fiqar mosque in 1697–8 in Blake, 153; Hunarfar, 385.

52 In 1705–6 a high-ranking (*ustad*) tailor made an endowment to the Sufrachi mosque, itself dating to Abbas I's reign. See Blake, *Half*, 152; Hunarfar, 476–7.

53 See the water basin built at the Sufrachi mosque in Blake, *Half*, 152; Hunarfar, 476–7. On the 1712 repair work done at the pre-Safavid Khan Mosque, see Hunarfar, 608n1.

54 See Jafariyan (*Safaviyya dar Arsa-yi Din*, 2: 903) and Sefatgol, 'Safavid Adminis-tration', 408. Sefatgol notes the importance of *vaqf* which 'at a time when no governmental budget existed for the maintenance of schools, mosques and other popular institutions, . . . was fundamental to the cultural, economic and social life of Iran.' On the centre's attention to the provision of health 'services' over the period, see our 'Safavids – Religion, Philosophy and Science', 784–5.

55 The first is found in both an 1696–7 inscription at the Aqa Kamal school and at the school built by the medical practitioner Muhammad Hakim, in an inscrip-tion dated to 1702–3 (nn 48, 50). The second is found in a 1710–11 inscription in the Chahar Bagh complex. See also those of the Darb-i Imam and Imamzada Ismail, cited above. See Hunarfar, 684, 524–5, 539–40, 651–2, 660, 718; Godard, 131–41. For inscriptions dated to 1699–1700, see Hunarfar, 526–31, 682–3. By contrast, Majlisi's *khutba* for the new shah (Nasiri, *Dastur*, 21f) noticeably lacks the distinctly messianic references to the new ruler evident, for example, in these inscriptions and Majlisi's own, earlier writings, on which see ad nn49, 50 of the previous chapter.

56 Astarabadi, *Tarikh-i Sultani*, esp. 13. The intended division of the work – itself based on recourse to, and citing, many well-known earlier chronicles – into three parts, traced the prophets from Adam to Muhammad, the fourteen immaculates, their descendants, and the first three caliphs; the rulers of the world prior to the Prophet's *hijra*; and the Safavid house to the reign of Shah Safi. This almost perfectly mirrors the tripartite arrangement in Qazvini's *Nusakh* and, if slightly less neatly, *Lubb*'s four sections (Quinn, *Historical*, 17). In the published version of the text, which comprises only the third of the three above divisions, the author commences with a genealogy tracing Sultan Husayn himself back to Imam Musa and refers to Timur meeting the early Safavids (22–4), as had Abbas I-period chronicles.

57 Newman, 'Baqir al-Majlisi and Islamicate Medicine'; Tehrani, 2: 186; 5: 83; 13: 64, 376. Jamal Khvansari also authored 'Aqaid al- Niswan' (Tehrani, 18: 112), on which see Babayan, 'The "Aqaid al-Nisa" ', and references ad n37 above and ad n70 in the previous chapter.

58 Arjomand (*The Shadow*, 158) cites Shaykh Ali Hazin's autobiography on the extensive interest in philosophy and *irfan* among the literati of the period. The expulsion of Ardistani is cited from a much later source. The unknown court retainer who, from jail just a few years after the capital's fall, penned *Mukafat-nama* was likewise interested in philosophy. See the text in Jafariyan, *Ilal*, 63–169; Jafariyan, *Safaviyya dar Arsa-yi Din*, 3: 1191–297. In 1709 Tabrizi, the author of *Faraid* and a student of Jamal Khvansari, Baqir Majlisi and Majlisi's son-in-law Muhammad Salih Khatunabadi, penned a critique of Shaykh Ali Ami-li's harsh opinions on philosophy and Sufism and translated into Persian Fayz' 1623 *Khulasat al-Azkar*, a collection of Sufi prayers. See Kanturi, 206; Tabrizi, *Faraid*, esp. 14–19, 297–9; Jafariyan, *Safaviyya dar Arsa-yi Din*, 3: 1113. On Muhammad Jafar, see n42, Khatunabadi, 551; Arjomand, *The Shadow*, 151.

59 S. H. Nasr, 'Shiism and Sufism: Their Relationship in Essence and in History', *Religious Studies*, 6 (1970), 241. Prior to its capture by the Afghans, Qutb al-Din Nayrizi studied both philosophy and theology and studied Sufism with Dhahabi scholars in Isfahan. In his post-1722 *Fasl al-Khitab* (n34) he blames Afghan successes on conflict between clerics and Sufis. See also Floor, 'Khalifeh', 80–1.

60 On the 1702–3 repairs ordered by the shah to the Imamzada Ismail, begun by Abbas I and completed by Safi in 1631–2, see Blake, *Half*, 171; Hunarfar, 524–5, Godard, 131–42. On the 1703 exemption granting the Imamzada's inhabitants from certain Ashura expenses, see Hunarfar, 535–7. On work done at the Imamzada Ahmad, see Blake, 171; Hunarfar, 670–2. On the 1715 repairs ordered to the Imamzada Darb-i Imam, a Qaraquyunlu-period structure now crowded with the tombs of many prominent figures, including that of Tahmasp, and the construction of a new door in 1717 by the shah's order, see Blake, *Half*, 171; Hunarfar, 341–53, esp. 344–5; Godard, 47–54; Varjavand.

61 Blake, 170–1, citing Khatunabadi, 555–6.

62 See Hunarfar, 528–9, 540; Blake, 171. This may have been the figure mentioned by Nasiri (*Dastur*, 84), on whom see also further below.

63 Morton ('*Chub*', 243n59) notes the shah's visits to the *tawhidkhana* (on which see 234, citing Nasiri, *Dastur*, 56; Hunarfar, 422), the issuance of no less than half a dozen *shajara*s, deeds of appointment of the Safavid Sufi *khalifa*, during Husayn's reign and the continued practice of the Safavid Sufi ritual beating ceremony over this period (241–2, 243n59, 231–3). The many spiritual-political references to the Qizilbash by Nasiri (*Dastur*, 30, 71, 85, 104–5) suggest their continued role at that level, commensurate with their continued military import, discussed above. See also Mahdavi, 1: 190–1. On the *taj* in this period, see Morton, 241. In his contemporary *Tarikh-i Sultani* (n56) the Tajik sayyid Astarabadi stresses the '*ghazi* Sufi' bases of the early house (25, 29), associates the famous twelve-pleated *taj* and the term 'qizilbash' with Sultan Haydar (26), and numbers as seven those accompanying the young Ismail from Lahijan, though these individuals are not identified (33). Floor ('Khalifeh', 80–1) cites contemporary primary sources on the shah's wearing of the *taj* and the continued popularity of the shrine at Ardabil in this period.

64 Calmard, 'Shi'i Rituals and Power II', 160, 166, 169–70, 180–1, citing accounts from 1695, 1704, 1705 and 1714. Claims that Sultan Husayn's early *firman* banning wine, issued at Majlisi's behest, coincided with a stringent crackdown on the capital's Sufis are based on post-Safavid sources, chiefly Tanukabuni's nineteenth-century Persian-language clerical biography *Qisas al-Ulama*. See Browne, 4: 404; Lockhart, *The Fall*, 38; Savory, *Iran Under*, 238, citing only Browne; Arjomand, *The Shadow*, 191, 191n33; Turner, 164–5. Compare Morton, '*Chub*', 243, and, esp. 243n59. Sufis were also said to have been massacred and the convent of Fayz Kashani destroyed by order of Sultan Husayn. See Lockhart, *The Fall*, 38, citing only Sanson, who was, in fact, in Iran from 1683 to 1691; Arjomand, *The Shadow*, 154, and Röhrborn, 57, citing a mid-nineteenth- and a late eighteenth-century source respectively. On the latter, written in India, see also Morton, '*Chub*', 243n59. Mahdavi (1: 104f, 185–6 and, esp. 128–9) notes that the Nimatallahi shaykh Zayn al-Abidin Shirvani (d. 1853), who argued for Majlisi's antipathy to Sufism, did not mention his involvement in killings or expulsions. Mahdavi also queried why none of Majlisi's legal writings contain rulings ordering, or approving of, the killing of Sufis. Floor ('Khalifeh', 79–80) argues there is no proof for such allegations against Majlisi.

65   Hunarfar, 722–5; Blake, *Half*, 79–81; Khatunabadi, 562–3; Matthee, *The Politics*, 212, citing Dutch sources. Blake (79) notes later Western sources date the garden to 1700. Muhammad Baqir Khatunabadi erected a house nearby. Perhaps unsurprisingly, given his interest in such matters (see n66), Muhammad Hashim Asaf, in his *Rustam al-Tavarikh* (Tehran, 1929–30), completed in 1831, notes that the site's haram complex contained rooms for 1,000 women (Blake, 81, citing Asaf, 71–2).

66   On the Chihil Sutun repairs, *c.* 1706–7, see Blake, *Half*, 68–9. Reports of the shah's excessive behaviour at the garden complex (Blake, 73) are also from Asaf's *Rustam*.

67   Hunarfar, 662–7; Sefatgol, 'Safavid Administration', 404; Blake, *Half*, 90, 167. On the chief merchant, see Blake, 111, citing the later Asaf.

68   See, for example, Matthee, *The Politics*, 212; Canby, *The Golden*, 163, 160. On Chahar Bagh, see also Hillenbrand, 6: 809.

69   Floor (*A Fiscal*, 35) maintains the impossibility of estimating Iran's budget, though contemporary foreigners did offer estimates. See also idem, 'Commerce', 68. But see Matthee, 'Prostitutes', 134; idem, 'The Career', 22n20, 23, 25; idem, 'Between Venice', 229n20. See also Floor, *A Fiscal*, 114; Afshar, '*Maktub* and *Majmua*: Essential Sources for Safavid Research', in Newman, ed., *Society and Culture*, 61. Indeed, the sources do not even permit agreement on Dutch exports of silk and specie over the century: see n14 of Chapter 6 and, on gold exports during Sultan Husayn's reign, compare Floor and Clawson, 351, with Matthee, 'Between Venice', 241. See also Floor, 'Commerce', 68, citing conflicting VOC accounts of gold exports in this period.

70   Floor (*A Fiscal*, 30–1, 129–213) has attempted to gather as much information on the period's system of taxation. All these taxes discussed herein were distinct from the religious taxes (Floor, ibid., 127–8).
     Chardin suggested that Iranian peasants were better off than their European counterparts (Minorsky, *Tadhkirat*, 21–3, esp. 23; cf. Floor, *A Fiscal*, 233, also citing Chardin). On Chardin's political sympathies, however, see also McCabe's 'Beyond the *Lettres Persanes*'. S. Brakensiek notes that Kaempfer derived most of his information from Olearius, du Mans and, especially, Chardin and that his political assessments derived from prevailing European political philosophical trends. See his 'Political Judgement between Empirical Experience and Scholarly Tradition – Engelbert Kaempfer's Report on Persia (1684/5)', paper presented at the 'Fourth International Round Table on Safavid Studies', Bamberg, July 2003.
     Floor reviews the more important domestic trade and production, often overlooked in the concern with foreign trade, in his 'Commerce', 69. See also his *The Economy*, 247–301, wherein he suggests (301) that 'agriculture, and its ancillary activities, was the most important sector of the economy in Safavid Persia employing about 80% of the population.' See also ibid., 125f, 160f, 197f.

71   Chardin estimated the population of Isfahan, Iran's largest city, as 500,000, a figure also given by the Englishman John Ogilby, who visited the city in the same time period; the Dutch cited the figure of 550,000 for 1710, or about 6% of the total population of nine million. The other major cities of Tabriz, Kashan and Yazd were important centres of production and commerce; Tabriz, a key city on the many local and long-distance trade routes, was likely the only other city with more than 100,000 inhabitants in this period. Mashhad and Qum were primarily important religious centres. Together the urban share of the population varied between 10% and 15% of the total. See Blake, 134, 37–41, 74–7; Keyvani,

157–8; Floor, *The Economy*, 2–5; Lockhart, *The Fall*, 473–85, esp. 477; Ferrier, *A Journey*, esp. 44–65. On Chardin's estimate of the population of all of Iran in this period as 40 million (!), where Floor (ibid., 2f) suggests no more than nine million, see n6 of Chapter 7.

72 Keyvani, 47, 49–52, Ferrier, *A Journey*, 154, 167f. In 1674 the Venetian Bembo met French goldsmiths and watchmakers working for the shah. See Welch, 'Safavi Iran', 105.

73 Keyvani, 52–6; Matthee, 'Coffee', 30. On the guild of prostitutes, see Matthee, 'Prostitutes', 125–7.

74 Keyvani, 71–4, who notes that the position, which also existed in smaller, pro-vincial towns, does not appear in the *Tadhkirat al-Muluk*. Chardin included Isfahan's *malik al-tujjar* among the many 'rich and highly ranked people' who lived in the city's Abbasabad suburb. See Blake, 111; Ferrier, *A Journey*, 60–1, 62–3. On Armenian guilds, for example, see Keyvani and also L. Hunarfar, 'Mashaghil-i Aramanah-yi Julfa', *Majallah-yi Vahid* (1964), 68–73, as cited in Babayan, *Mystics*, 193n41. For examples of merchants being organised in the manner discussed above, see ad n53 of Chapter 6.

75 A tobacco tax also generated substantial revenue, according to Chardin and Tavernier. See Floor, *A Fiscal*, 149f, 163, 170–4; Matthee, 'Tobacco in Iran', 66. On the corvee, see also Matthee, 'Unwalled Cities', 400.
　　Lest some of these taxes seem 'odd' in the twenty-first century, note that in July 1695 in England a tax was introduced on glass windows.

76 Keyvani, 63f, 83f, 115, 117–21, 137–8. See ibid., 113, 117–18, 137–8 on the centre's responses to economic problems during the reigns of Safi and Abbas II and Sulayman's efforts to control inflation during 1666–7. Provincial cities also had price control regimes. Floor, *The Economy*, 189–90, 230.

77 Under Abbas I and II, there is evidence that censuses were periodically carried out. See Floor, *A Fiscal*, 177–89. See also ad n12 of the previous chapter, attest-ing that Zoroastrians paid the Islamic poll tax even though they were not formally 'People of the Book'.

78 Floor, *A Fiscal*, 37, 189f, 126f, 137–8.

79 Floor, *A Fiscal*, 37f. These included such devices as the *tuyul, hamahsala*, and the *suyurghal*. See also Floor, 'Concessions i. In the Safavid Period', *EIr*, 6: 119–20.

80 Farmers had to feed, house, and provide transport to various tiers of officials as well as travellers and ambassadors and provide men for the military and/or defray of the costs of the upkeep thereof on a regular, and irregular, basis. See Floor, *A Fiscal*, 189f. A centrally appointed local water official, like others, acquired his own salary through 'gifts'. See Floor, *A Fiscal*, 126f, 137–8, 177f, 190f.

81 Minorsky, *Tadhkirat*, 29, citing Krusinski, in Iran between 1704 and 1729, on whom see n26. The court also maintained factories outside the capital which produced items for the court and for sale by the court. Keyvani, 171–3, 48–9. Locals were often required to deliver key raw materials to royal workshops as part of their regular gift-giving to the centre (Floor, *A Fiscal*, 210). The court is known to have supplied materials to rural weavers for carpet production; instead of pay, these weavers received tenure of crown lands. On carpet production, see also Walker, 'Carpets', 870f. On gifts generally, see Matthee, 'Negotiating Across Cultures', 37–41; A. K. S. Lambton, '*Pishkash*: present or tribute?', *BSOAS* 57(1) (1994), 148–58. See also n106 of Chapter 4.

82 Minorsky, *Tadhkirat*, 181–2, citing de Bruyn. Matthee (*The Politics*, 212) cites

Dutch sources that funds for construction of Farahabad were 'extorted' from 'courtiers and domestic merchants'.

83 Canby, 'The Pen or the Brush: An Inquiry into the Technique of Late Safawid Drawings', in R. Hillenbrand, ed. *Persian Painting from the Mongols to the Qajars* (London, 2000), 75–82.

84 Canby, *The Golden*, 164f.

85 Canby, ibid., 171, citing J. Allan, 'Silver Door Facings of the Safavid Period', *Iran*, 33 (1995), 123–38, pl. xxib.

86 Canby, 173.

87 Canby, *The Golden*, 168, 165, citing a 1694–5 Muhammad Zaman painting of the Sunni Kurdish *vizier* Shah Quli Khan Zangana.

88 Canby, 173. Crowe, *Persia and China*, 225–6, 234, 170, 226, noting continuing foreign demand for Iranian ceramics through 1730, in spite of competition from genuine Chinese porcelain and Japanese substitutes, and (246, 252, 259, 263, 268, 272) the continued sensitivity of Iranian producers to local and foreign tastes and styles. A 1712 astrolabe (Canby, 171) suggests the continued presence of a production infrastructure sufficient for such complex undertakings. See also Allan, *Persian Steel*, 274f on standards, many bearing very distinctly Twelver Shi'i inscriptions, dating from mid-century into Sultan Husayn's reign. For other steel products also dating to this period, see ibid., 291, 298, 300–1, 311, 419, 426, 446–7, 468–70.

89 See, for example, Lockhart (*The Fall*, 35, 47), citing de Bruyn; Matthee, *The Politics*, 204–5, citing the post-1722 anonymously written *Mukafatnama* and Marashi's much later *Majma al-Tavarikh*.

90 Sanson estimated the number of troops available to the centre in this period as 150,000 (Röhrborn, 171) where Kaempfer estimated 90,000 (Minorsky, *Tadhkirat*, 35). On the latter's reliability, see Floor, *Safavid Government*, 236n1021. Floor (ibid., 211–16; esp. 211–12; n13) cites the post-Safavid estimate of 180,000. Floor (213), also citing the usually conflicting foreign assessments of Safavid military capabilities, quotes Nasiri's *Dastur* (104) that up to six months were needed to mobilise these troops from their bases in the provinces, but adds that the centre was nevertheless able to mount effective responses to 'local incursions'. For a partial listing of the locations of Safavid troops, see Floor, *Safavid Government*, 214, citing Minorsky, *Tadhkirat*, 161. See also n13 of Chapter 6.

91 Floor, *The Afghan*, 43–62; Matthee, 'Unwalled Cities', 407.

92 Foreign sources (Lockhart, *The Fall*, 121n1) attribute Fath Ali Khan's fall to conspiracies at court. See also Floor, *The Afghan*, 134. Savory (*Iran Under*, 246–8) and Roemer (6: 317–24) base their accounts thereof on Lockhart. On Russian and Turkish reports, see Lockhart, *The Fall*, 106, 125–6. For 'analyses' of these events by the Dutch, Krusinski, the much later Mar'ashi and a contemporary Italian source in the service of the Russians, see Matthee, 'Blinded by Power', 201–13. A Bekdilu Shamlu (see n5) replaced Fath Ali Khan only to be dismissed following the Afghan capture of Isfahan.

93 Lockhart, *The Fall*, 130–43. Lockhart, 136n1, notes that three Persian and eight foreign sources, not all contemporary, estimate Iranian forces as numbering between 30,000 and 80,000 and Afghan forces as between 8,000 and 40,000. On the complex composition of the Persian forces, see ad nn14, 94.

94 According to the Dutch the tribal elements which entered the city or at least fought the Afghans during the siege included the Qajar (Floor, *The Afghan*, 130,

147), Kuhgilu (113, 123, 127, 131; Lockhart, *The Fall*, 205) and the Bakhtiyari (125, 144–5, 149, 153, 160, 162, 170; Lockhart, *The Fall*, 207). 'Arab' troops are also mentioned (88, 96, 122, 127, 153) as are other unnamed forces (84, 113, 120, 127, 156, 162), Georgian officials and levies (123, 132, 142, 156) and 'Astarabadi' forces (127, 129, 139). The Dutch hired Georgian and Armenian troops to protect themselves (56). On the shah's own efforts to rally the city, see, for example, Floor, *The Afghan*, 135. Roemer (6: 323) criticises the shah's decision to remain in the capital. See also Lockhart, *The Fall*, 145.

95 On discontent in Isfahan see Floor, *The Afghan*, 110–1, 115, 119, 143, 152, and in Tabriz and Kirman and among some elements of the military itself, see Floor, 35, 225, 229, 133, 147. On Dutch reports of Afghan brutality, see Floor, 50–1, 61, 123, 141, 179, 192, 237, 246, 313. On 'popular' resistance in Isfahan, see Floor, 171; Lockhart, *The Fall*, 165, 165n2. On the Armenians in New Julfa, see McCabe, 362–3. On the Zoroastrians in this period, see Lockhart, *The Fall*, 72–3.

96 On the Afghans' preparations and final attack and the battle of Gulnabad, see especially Lockhart, *The Fall*, 109–29, 130–43, esp. 142n1, in which, however, he relies heavily on foreign sources and such post-Safavid sources as Muhsin's *Zubdat al-Tavarikh, Tarikh-i Nadiri*, composed *c.* 1760, and Marashi's *Majma al-Tavarikh*. On the siege and Mahmud's accession, see Lockhart, *The Fall*, 144–75, using similar sources. For an account of Gulnabad and Isfahan's siege to 31 August 1722 based on the VOC's *Isfahan Diary*, of which Lockhart had used only portions, see Floor, *The Afghan*, 83–172, esp. 115, 119, and, on Mahmud's accession, 173–6.

Epilogue: Poetry and Politics – The Multiplicity of Safavid Discourse

1 R. Jafariyan, *Safaviyya dar Arsa-yi Din*, 1: 483–91, citing Saib's poetry on Safi, Abbas II and Sulayman.

2 Jews were excluded from England from 1290, during the reign of Edward I, until the mid-seventeenth century, under Oliver Cromwell (d. 1658) in whose animosity to Catholicism lie the origins of the present-day 'Irish question'. Jews were expelled from France in 1306 and forced conversions commenced in Spain in 1391. When Spain's remaining Jews were expelled in 1492, they sought refuge among the Muslim Ottomans.

3 See Herzig's reflective 'Safavid Foreign Trade Policy? The Evidence from Persian Sources', paper presented at 'Iran and the World in the Safavid Age', University of London, September 2002.

4 Cf. Matthee, *The Politics*, 233.

5 Lockhart, *The Fall*, 156, 193–5, 151, 153; Floor, *The Afghan*, 184–5, 187, 241, 245. Tribal support for Tahmasp's accession is clear: in addition to the above-mentioned tribal elements, a Qajar served as his *vakil*, as did, in 1730, an Afshar, the future Nadir Shah. See Floor, *Safavid Government*, 16–17.

Perry notes others who appeared after the capital's fall claiming to be the Shah's second son. On the latter and Tahmasp II, see Perry, 'The Last Safavids (1722–73)' *Iran* 9 (1971), 60. Perry's chief sources include Shaykh Ali Hazin, Lockhart, *Tarikh-i Nadiri* and such, much later, Persian sources as Marashi's *Majma al-Tavarikh* and Qazvini's *Favaid al-Safaviyya*. In his 'The Man Who Would Not Be King: Abul-Fath Sultan Muhammad Mirza Safavid in India', *IS*,

32(4) (1999), 513–35 G. Rota utilises the latter, itself completed in India *c.* 1796.

6 Lockhart, 196–211, 300–2; Perry, 60–1; Roemer, 6: 327; Floor, *The Afghan*, 197–203, 263–90 and, on other pretenders, 297, 299, 301. See also n46 of the previous chapter.

7 Roemer, 6: 324f; Lockhart, 233, 259f, 261, 270–2, 286; Floor, *The Economy*, 227.

8 Ashraf was served, briefly, by a Qajar who had turned against Tahmasp II and aligned himself with Mahmud only to return to Tahmasp, be appointed his vizier and suffer execution by Nadir Shah. Lockhart, 123, 281, 304–10, 289. A Turkish envoy received at Chihil Sutun by the Afghan court in 1728 (Lockhart, 293–4) described Ashraf as wearing the shah's crown and sitting on his throne even as he was about to leave the city to attack Tahmasp II. On the distinctly Safavid administrative titles adopted by the Afghans during the decade they held some sway in Iran, see Floor, *The Afghan*, 174–6, 236, 247, 269. *Tadhkirat al-Muluk*, composed for the Afghans in this period, reflected as much the Afghans' interest in the working details of the polity's administration under the Safavids as a desire to legitimise their presence in the country by trading on the Safavid legacy as explained to them thereby.

Like his three immediate predecessors, Sultan Husayn would be buried in the shrine of Fatima in Qum. See n45 of Chapter 6.

9 On Nadir as *qurchibashi* and *vakil*, see Lockhart, 311; Shaykh Ali Hazin, 175; Floor, *Safavid Government*, 13.

10 Lockhart, 292–93, 296, 332–40, 341–45, 348, 423; Floor, *The Afghan*, 258, 260. Lockhart (194–5) cites Persian sources, including Ali Hazin and Muhammad Muhsin's *Zubdat al-Tavarikh* – written at Nadir's command – as deploring the character of Tahmasp and his advisors.

11 Floor, *The Afghan*, 342–3, 336, 355, 358. Lockhart (299–300) quotes Hazin, whose account spans the fall of Isfahan to the murder of Tahmasp II, and who was, in fact, in the company of the Ottomans for some period (*The Life*, 160f), lamenting the state of the realm and, in particular, the lack of leadership.

12 Ali Hazin, 220–2; Lockhart, 311–40; Floor, 260–2. In his memoirs, written in 1742, Shaykh Ali Hazin referred to the Safavid forces as Qizilbash (e.g., 194, 198–9, 203). Thanks to M. Axworthy for his assistance on the marriages of Nadir and his son.

13 Ali Hazin, 272; C. Tucker, 'Nadir Shah and the Jafari *Madhhab*', *IS*, 27 (1994), 163–79.

14 Perry, 62–3, 64–5. On Nadir see also L. Lockhart, *Nadir Shah: A Critical Study Based mainly upon Contemporary Sources* (London, 1938), and M. Axworthy's forthcoming study. Relatives of Nadir included a grandson of Shah Sultan Husayn who extended the Afshar name in Khurasan to 1796 until the coming of the Qajars. The latter, Shah Rukh, was deposed in favour of a grandson of Sulayman who was proclaimed Sulayman II in 1750. At his murder the same year Shah Rukh was returned. See Perry, 65–6; Roemer, 6: 329.

15 Perry, 67–9; Roemer, 6: 330.

16 A general socio-economic, political and 'cultural' overview of the post-Safavid period may be found in P. Avery, et al., eds, *The Cambridge History of Iran*, 7, *From Nadir Shah to the Islamic Republic* (Cambridge, 1991), but see also, in particular, the works listed below.

17 Floor, *A Fiscal*, 233f; Canby, *The Golden Age*, 176; Crowe, *Persia and China*,

225–6. On the economic legacy, see also T. Ricks, 'Politics and Trade in Southern Iraq and the Gulf', unpublished PhD thesis, Indiana University, 1975.

18 On Usuli discourse in particular, see Cole's 'Shiʻi Clerics in Iraq and Iran, 1722–1780', and the revised version of this essay in Cole's *Sacred Space and Holy War, The Politics, Culture and History of Shiʻite Islam* (London/New York, 2002), 58–77. See also idem, 'Imami Jurisprudence and the Role of the Ulama: Mortaza Ansari on Emulating the Supreme Exemplar', in N. Keddie, ed., *Religion and Politics in Iran* (New Haven, 1983), 33–46; J. Calmard, 'Mardja-i Taklid', *EI²*, 6: 548–56. See also R. Gleave, 'Akhbari Shiʻi *Usul al-Fiqh* and the Juristic Theory of Yusuf b. Ahmad al-Bahrani', in Gleave, ed., *Islamic Law, Theory and Practice* (London: 1997), 24–47; idem, *Inevitable Doubt, Two Theories of Shiʻi Jurisprudence* (Leiden, 2000); the essays in L. Walbridge, ed. *The Most Learned of the Shiʻa* (New York, 2001); the essays in *Religion and Society in Qajar Iran*, R. Gleave, ed. (London, 2004), including our own 'Anti-Akhbari Sentiments among the Qajar *Ulama*: The Case of Muhammad Baqir al-Khwansari (d. 1313/1895)', 155–73, and Momen, 'Usuli, Akhbari, Shaykhi, Babi'. See also Cole's 'Ideology', in the following note.

19 Volume 7 of the *Cambridge History of Iran* does not cover developments in this realm of activity well. A basic, if dated, introduction to some of the key figures of post-Safavid philosophical discourse is found in *History of Islamic Philosophy* (London, 1993) of Henry Corbin (d. 1978), 348f, translated from the French *Histoire de la philosophie islamique* (Paris, 1964). See also the latter volumes of Ashtiyani's *Anthologie* and, on Hadi Sabzavari (d. 1872), T. Izutsu, *The Fundamental Structure of Sabzawari's Metaphysics* (in English) (Tehran, 1968). More recent works include, for example, Cole, 'Ideology, Ethics and Philosophical Discourse in Eighteenth Century Iran', *IS*, 22(1) (1989), 7–34. The dissertation of the late John Cooper, had it been completed, would have shed considerable additional light on post-Safavid trends in Shiʻi philosophical thought.

20 Garthwaite, *The Persians*, 2, 86, 97, 114, 117.

21 M. G. S. Hodgson, *The Venture of Islam, III. The Gunpowder Empires and Modern Times* (Chicago/London, 1974), esp. 46f, 49. Hodgson's understanding of the Safavid period, in respect of which he used the term, proved to be conventional.

22 See, for example, J. K. Choksy, *Conflict and Cooperation, Zoroastrian Subalterns and Muslim Elites in Medieval Iranian Society* (New York, 1997).

Select Bibliography

Western-language sources

Abisaab, R. J., *Converting Persia, Religion and Power in the Safavid Empire*, London, 2004.

Abisaab, R., 'The Ulama of Jabal Amil in Safavid Iran, 1501–1736: Marginality, Migration and Social Change', *Iranian Studies (IS)*, 27(1–4) (1994), 103–22.

Abrahams, S., 'A Historiographical Study and Annotated Translation of Volume 2 of the *Ahsan al-Tavarikh* by Fazli Khuzani al-Isfahani', unpublished PhD dissertation, University of Edinburgh, 1999.

Adamova, A., 'Muhammad Qasim and the Isfahan School of Painting', in Newman, ed., *Society and Culture*, 193–212.

Adamova, A., 'On the Attribution of Persian Paintings and Drawings of the Time of Shah Abbas I', in R. Hillenbrand, ed., *Persian Painting from the Mongols to the Qajars*, London, 2000, 19–38.

Adamova, A., 'Persian Portraits of the Russian Ambassadors', in S. Canby, ed., *Safavid Art*, 49–53.

Afshar, I., 'Similar Farmans from the Reign of Shah Safi', in Melville, ed., *Safavid Persia*, 285–304.

Afshar, I., '*Maktub* and *Majmua*: Essential Sources for Safavid Research', in Newman, ed., *Society and Culture*, 51–61.

Ahmad, A., 'Safawid Poets and India', *Iran*, 14 (1976), 117–32.

Al-i Davud, 'Ali, 'Coffeehouse', *EIr*, 6 (1993), 1–4.

Algar, H., et al., 'Emamzadeh', *EIr*, 8 (1998).

Algar, H., 'Naqshbandis and Safavids: A Contribution to the Religious History of Iran and Her Neighbors', in M. Mazzaoui, ed., *Safavid Iran and Her Neighbors*, Salt Lake City, 2003, 7–48.

Allan, J., 'Abbas, Hajji', *EIr*, 1 (1985), 76–7.

Allan, J. and B. Gilmour, *Persian Steel, The Tanavoli Collection*, Oxford, 2000.

Allan, J., 'Safavid Loss, Ottoman Gain – Metalworking Across the Two Empires', paper presented at 'Iran and the World in the Safavid Age', University of London, September 2002.

Allouche, A., *The Origins and Development of the Ottoman–Safavid conflict (906–962/1500–1555)* Berlin, 1983.

Alonso Vanes, Fr. Carlos, 'The Hormuz Convent and the Augustinians (1572–1621)', paper presented at 'Iran and the World in the Safavid Age', University of London, September 2002.

Amanat, A., 'The Nuqtawi Movement of Mahmud Pisikhani and his Persian Cycle of Mystical-materialism' in F. Daftary ed., *Medieval Ismaili History and Thought*, Cambridge, 1996, 281–97.

Amir-Moezzi, M. A. *The Divine Guide in Early Shi'ism, The Sources of Esotericism in Islam*, David Streight, transl., Albany, 1994.

Amoretti, B. S., 'Religion in the Timurid and Safavid Periods', in Peter Jackson, et al., eds, *The Cambridge History of Iran*, 6: 610–55.

Arjomand, S., ed., *Authority and Political Culture in Shi'ism*, Albany, 1988.

Arjomand, A., 'The Office of *Mulla-bashi* in Shi'ite Iran', *Studia Islamica*, 57, (1983), 135–46.

Arjomand, S., *The Shadow of God and the Hidden Imam, Religion, Political Order, and Societal Change in Shi'ite Iran from the Beginning to 1890*, Chicago, 1984.

Arjomand, S., 'Two Decrees of Shah Tahmasp Concerning Statecraft and the Authority of Shaykh Ali al-Karaki', in Arjomand, ed., *Authority and Political Culture*, 250–262.

Aubin, J., 'L'Avenèment des Safavides Reconsidérè (*Études Safavides*. III)', Moyen Orient et Ocean Indien, 5 (1988), 1–130.

Aubin, J., 'La Politique Religieuse des Safavides', in T. Fahd, ed. *Le Shi'isme Imamite*, Paris, 1970, 235–44.

Aubin, J., 'Revolution Chiite et Conservatisme, Les soufis de Lahejan, 1500–1514' (*Études Safavides*. II.)', *Moyen Orient et Océan Indien*, I, 1984, 1–40.

Aubin, J., '*Études Safavides*. I. Shah Ismail and les Notables de l'Iraq Persan', *Journal of the Economic and Social History of the Orient (JESHO)*, 2 (1959), 37–81.

Babaie, S., 'Building for the Shah: the Role of Mirza Muhammad Taqi (Saru Taqi) in Safavid Royal Patronage of Architecture', in S. Canby, ed., *Safavid Art* 20–6.

Babaie, S., 'The Mosque of Ganj Ali Khan in Kirman: *Shahsevani* Loyalty and the Index of Belonging', paper presented at the Fourth International Round Table on Safavid Studies', Bamberg, July 2003.

Babaie, S., 'Shah Abbas II, the Conquest of Qandahar, Chihil Sutun, and its Wall Paintings', *Muqarnas*, 11 (1994), 125–42.

Babaie, S., K. Babayan, I. Baghdiantz-McCabe and M. Farhad, *Slaves of the Shah, New Elites of Safavid Iran*, London, 2004.

Babayan, K., 'The "Aqaid al-Nisa": A Glimpse at Safavid Women in Local Isfahani Culture', in G. Hambly, ed., *Women in the Medieval Islamic World, Power, Patronage and Piety*, London, 1998, 349–81.

Babayan, K., 'Eunuchs in the Safavid Period', *EIr*, 9 (1998).

Babayan, K., *Mystics, Monarchs, and Messiahs: Cultural Landscapes of Early Modern Iran*, Cambridge, MA, 2002.

Babayan, K., 'The Safavid Synthesis: From Qizilbash Islam to Imamite Shi'ism', *IS*, 27(1–4) (1994), 135–61.

Babayan, K., 'Sufis, Dervishes and Mullas: The Controversy over the Spiritual and Temporal Dominion in Seventeenth-century Iran', in Melville, ed., *Safavid Persia*, 117–38.

Babayan, K., 'The Waning of the Qizilbash: The Spiritual and the Temporal in Seventeenth Century Iran', unpublished PhD dissertation, Princeton University, June 1993.

Bacqué-Grammont, J.-L., 'Études Turco-Safavides, I. Notes sur le Blocus du Commerce Iranien par Selim Ier', *Turcica*, 6 (1975), 68–88.

Bacqué-Grammont, J.-L., 'Une liste d'émirs ostaju révoltés en 1526', *Studia Iranica (SIr)*, 5 (1) (1976), 91–114.

Bacqué-Grammont, J.-L., 'Un document ottoman sur la révolte des Ostajlu', *SIr*, 6(2) (1977), 169–84.

Bacqué-Grammont, J.-L., *Les Ottomans, les Safavides, et leurs Voisins*, Istanbul, 1987.

Bahari, E., *Bihzad, Master of Persian Painting*, London, 1996.

Bahari, E., 'The Sixteenth Century School of Bukhara Painting and the Arts of the Book', in Newman, ed., *Society and Culture*, 251–64.

Baldick, J., *Mystical Islam*, London, 1989.

Bashir, S., 'Enshrining Divinity: The Death and Memoralisation of Fazlallah Astara-badi in Hurufi Thought', *The Muslim World*, 90 (Fall 2000), 289–308.

Bashir, S., 'The Imam's Return: Messianic Leadership in Late Medieval Shi'ism', in L. Walbridge, ed., *The Most Learned of the Shi'a*, New York, 2001, 21–33.

Bashir, S., 'Sacred Power and Human Embodiment in Fifteenth Century Iranian Religion', paper presented at the Fourth International Round Table on Safavid Studies, Bamberg, July 2003.

Beeson, C. J., 'The Origins of Conflict in the Safavi Religious Institution', unpublished PhD thesis, Princeton University, 1982.

Bernardini, M., 'Hatifi's Timurnama and Qasimi's Shahnameh-yi Ismail: Consider-ations for a Double Critical Edition', in Newman, ed., *Society and Culture*, 3–18.

Birge, J., *The Bektashi Order of Dervishes*, London, 1937.

Blair, S., 'The Ardabil Carpets in Context', in Newman, ed., *Society and Culture*, 125–43.

Blake, S., *Half the World: The Social Architecture of Safavid Isfahan, 1590–1722*, Costa Mesa, CA, 1999.

Blake, S., 'Contributors to the Urban Landscape: Women Builders in Safavid Isfahan and Mughal Shahjahanabad', in G. Hambly, ed., *Women in the Medieval Islamic World, Power, Patronage and Piety*, London, 1998, 407–28.

Bloom, J., 'Epic Images Revisited: An Ilkhanid Legacy in Early Safavid Painting', in Newman, ed., *Society and Culture*, 237–48.

Bosworth, C. E., 'Ardabil', *EIr*, 2 (1987), 357–60,

Bosworth, C. E., 'Tashmasp II', *EI²*, 10: 110.

Brakensiek, S., 'Political Judgement between Empirical Experience and Scholarly Tradition – Engelbert Kaempfer's Report on Persia (1684/5)', paper presented at the Fourth International Round Table on Safavid Studies, Bamberg, July 2003.

Brend, B., '*Jamal va Jalal*: A Link Between Epochs', in S. Canby, ed., *Safavid Art*, 32–6.

Browne, E., *A Literary History of Persia*, 4, Cambridge, 1953.

F. Cagman and Z. Tanindi, 'Manuscript Production at the Kazeruni Orders in Safavid Shiraz', in S. Canby, ed., *Safavid Art*, 43–8.

Calder, N., '*Khums* in Imami Shii Jurisprudence, from the Tenth to the Sixteenth Century, AD', *BSOAS*, 45(1) (1982), 39–47.

Calder, N., 'Legitimacy and Accommodation in Safavid Iran: The Juristic Theory of Muhammad Baqir al-Sabzewari (d. 1090/1679)', *Iran*, 25 (1987), 91–105.

Calder, N., '*Zakat* in Imami Shii Jurisprudence, from the Tenth to the Sixteenth Century, AD', *BSOAS*, 44(3) (1981), 468–80.

Calmard, J., 'Le Chiisme Imamite sous Les Ilkhans', in D. Aigle, ed., *L'Iran Face à La Domination Mongole*, Tehran, 1997, 261–92.

Calmard, J., ed., *Études Safavides, sous la direction de Jean Calmard*, Paris/Teheran, 1993.

Calmard, J., 'Marashis', *EI²*, 6: 510–18.

Calmard, J., 'Muharram Ceremonies and Diplomacy (a Preliminary Study)', in C. E. Bosworth and C. Hillenbrand, eds, *Qajar Iran*, Costa Mesa, CA, 1992, 213–28.

Calmard, J., 'Popular Literature Under the Safavids', in Newman, ed. *Society and Culture*, 315–39.

Calmard, J., 'Les rituels shiites et le pouvoir. L'imposition du shiisme safavide: eulogies et malédictions canoniques', in Calmard, ed., *Études Safavides.*, 109–50.

Calmard, J., et al., 'Sadr', *EI²*, 8: 748–51.

Calmard, J., 'Shiʿi Rituals and Power II. The Consolidation of Safavid Shiʿism: Folklore and Popular Religion', in Melville, ed., *Safavid Persia*, 139–90.

Canby, S., *The Golden Age of Persian Art, 1501–1722*, London, 1999.

Canby, S., 'The Pen or the Brush: An Inquiry into the Technique of Late Safawid Drawings', in R. Hillenbrand, ed. *Persian Painting from the Mongols to the Qajars* (London, 2000), 75–82.

Canby, S., *The Rebellious Reformer. The Drawings and Paintings of Riza-yi Abbasi of Isfahan.* London, 1996.

Canby, S., ed., *Safavid Art and Architecture*, London, 2002.

Carswell, J., *New Julfa, The Armenian Churches and Other Buildings*, Oxford, 1968.

Chittick, W., 'Two Seventeenth-Century Persian Tracts on Kingship and Rulers', in Arjomand, ed., *Authority and Political Culture*, 267–304.

Cole, J., 'Ideology, Ethics and Philosophical Discourse in Eighteenth Century Iran', IS, 22(1) (1989), 7–34.

Cole, J., *Sacred Space and Holy War, The Politics, Culture and History of Shi'ite Islam*, London/New York, 2002.

Cole, J., 'Shiʿi Clerics in Iraq and Iran, 1722–1780: The Akhbari-Usuli Conflict Reconsidered', *IS*, 18(1) (Winter 1985), 3–34.

Cooper, J., 'Some Observations on the Religious Intellectual Milieu of Safawid Persia', in F. Daftary ed., *Intellectual Traditions in Islam*, London, 2000, 146–59.

Cooper, J., ed. and transl., 'The Muqaddas al-Ardabili on *taqlid*', in Arjomand, ed., *Authority and Political Culture*, 263–66.

Cooper, J., 'From al-Tusi to the School of Isfahan', in *History of Islamic Philosophy*, S. H. Nasr and H. Dabashi, eds, New York/London, 1996, 585–96.

Corbin, H., 'Ahmad b. Zayn al-Abedin Alawi Ameli Isfahani, Sayyed', *EIr*, 1 (1985), 644–6.

Crossley, P., 'The Rulerships of China', *The American Historical Review*, 97 (December 1992), 1468–83.

Crossley, P., *A Translucent Mirror, History and Identity in Qinj Imperial Ideology*, Berkeley/London, 1999.

Crowe, Y., 'Ceramics. xv. The Islamic Period, 10th–13th/16th–19th Centuries', *EIr*, 5 (1992), 327–31.

Crowe, Y., *Persia and China, Safavid Blue and White Ceramics in the Victoria and Albert Museum, 1501–1738*, London, 2002.

Crowe, Y., 'Safavid Blue and White Bowls and the Chinese Connection', *Iran*, 40 (2002), 257–63.

Dabashi, H., 'Mir Damad and the Founding of the "School of Isfahan" ', in S. H. Nasr and H. Dabashi, eds, *History of Islamic Philosophy*, New York/London, 1996, 597–634.

Dadvar, A., *Iranians in Mughal Politics and Society, 1606–1658*, New Delhi, 2000.

Daftary, F., 'Ismaili–Sufi Relations in Early Post-Alamut and Safavid Persia', in Lewisohn and Morgan, eds, *Late Classical . . .*, 275–89.

Dale, S. F., 'A Safavid Poet in the Heart of Darkness: The Indian Poems of Ashraf Mazandarani', *IS*, 36(2) (2003), 197–212.

de Bruijn, J. T. P., 'Safawids. III. Literature', *EI²*, 8: 774–7.

Dickson, M., 'Shah Tahmasb and the Uzbeks (The Duel for Khurasan with 'Ubayd Khan: 930–946/1524–1540)', unpublished PhD dissertation, Princeton University, 1958.

Emerson, J., 'Chardin', *EIr*, 5(4), (1991), 369–77.

Ferrier, R., 'Anglo-Iranian Relations, i. From the Safavids to the Zands', *EIr*, 2 (1987), 41–4.

Ferrier, R., 'East India Company (The British)', *EIr*, 8 (1998).

Ferrier, R., *A Journey to Persia, Jean Chardin's Portrait of a Seventeenth-century Empire*, London, 1996.

Ferrier, R., 'The Terms and Conditions under which English Trade was Transacted with Safavid Persia', *BSOAS* 49(1) (1986), 48–72.

Ferrier, R., 'Trade from the Mid–14th Century to the End of the Safavid Period' in Jackson, ed., 6: 412–90.

Ferrier, R., 'Women in Safavid Iran: The Evidence of European Travellers', in G. Hambly, ed., *Women in the Medieval Islamic World, Power, Patronage and Piety*, London, 1998, 383–405.

Fischer, M. M. J., *Iran, From Religious Dispute to Revolution*, Cambridge, MA/ London, 1980.

Floor, W., *The Afghan Invasion of Safavid Persia, 1721–29*, Paris, 1998.

Floor, W., 'The Art of Smoking in Iran and Other Uses of Tobacco', *IS*, 35(1–3) (2002), 47–85.

Floor, W., 'Commerce, vi. From the Safavid Through the Qajar Period', *EIr*, 6 (1993), 67–71.

Floor, W., 'Concessions i. In the Safavid Period', *EIr*, 6 (1993), 119–20.

Floor, W., 'De Bruin (or de Bruyn), Cornelis', *EIr*, 7(2) (1996).

Floor, W., 'The Dutch and the Persian Silk Trade', in Melville, ed., *Safavid Persia*, 323–68.

Floor, 'Dutch-Persian Relations', *EIr*, 7 (1996).

Floor, W., *The Economy of Safavid Persia*, Wiesbaden, 2000.

Floor, W., A *Fiscal History of Iran in the Safavid and Qajar Periods, 1500–1925*, New York, 1998.

Floor, W., 'The *Khalifa al-Kholafa* of the Safavid Sufi Order', *Zeitschrift der deutschen morgenländischen Gesellschaft (ZDMG)*, 153(1) (2003), 51–86.

Floor, W., 'The Rise and Fall of Mirza Taqi, The Eunuch Grand Vizier (1043–55/ 1633–45), *Makhdum al-Omara va Khadem al-Foqara*', *SIr*, 26(2) (1997), 237–66.

Floor, W., 'The *sadr* or Head of the Safavid Religious Administration, Judiciary and Endowments and other Members of the Religious Institution', *ZDMG*, 150 (2000), 461–500.

Floor, W., *Safavid Government Institutions*, Costa Mesa, CA, 2001.

Floor, W., and P. Clawson, 'Safavid Iran's Search for Silver and Gold', *International Journal of Middle Eastern Studies (IJMES)*, 32 (2000), 345–68.

Floor, W., 'The Secular Judicial System in Safavid Persian', *SIr*, 29(1) (2000), 9–60.

Fragner, B., 'Social and Internal Economic Affairs', in Jackson, ed., 6: 491–565.

Garthwaite, G. R., 'An Outsider's View of Safavid History: Shah Ismail Reconsidered', paper presented at the Third International Round Table on Safavid Persia, Edinburgh, August, 1998.

Garthwaite, G. R., *The Persians*, Oxford, 2005.

Gelashvili, N., 'Iranian Georgian Relations During the Reign of Rostam (1632–1658)', paper presented at 'Iran and the World in the Safavid Age', University of London, September 2002.

Ghazvinian, J., 'British Travellers to Iran, 1580–1645', paper presented at 'Iran and the World in the Safavid Age', London, September 2002.

Gholsorkhi, S., 'Pari Khan Khanum: A Masterful Safavid Princess', *IS*, 28(3–4) (1995), 143–56.

Gholsorkhi, S., 'Ismail II and Mirza Makhdum Sharifi: an Interlude in Safavid History', *IJMES*, 26 (1994), 477–88.

Ghougassian, V., *The Emergence of the Armenian Diocese of New Julfa in the Seventeenth Century*, Atlanta, 1998.

Godard, A., 'Isfahan', in *Athar-i Iran, Annales du Service Archéologique de l'Iran*, Paris, 1937.

Golombek, L., 'Riza Abbasi's Wine Pot and Other Problems of Safavid Ceramics', in Canby, *Safavid Art*, 95–100.

Graham, T., 'Shah Ni'matullah Wali, Founder of the Ni'matullahi Sufi Order in Lewisohn, ed., *The Legacy of Medieval Persian Sufism*, 173–90.

Gran, P., 'Modern Trends in Egyptian Historiography', *IJMES*, 9 (1978), 367–71.

Gray, B., 'The Arts in the Safavid Period', in Jackson, ed., 6: 877–912.

Gurney, J., 'Pietro Della Valle: the Limits of Perception', *Bulletin of the School of Oriental and African Studies (BSOAS)*, 49(1) (1986), 103–16.

Gurney, J., 'Della Valle, Pietro', *EIr*, 7 (1996).

Hairi, Abdul Hadi, 'Reflections on the Shi'i Responses to Missionary Thought and Activities in the Safavid Period', in Calmard, ed., *Etudes*, 151–64.

Haneda, M., *Le Chah et les Qizilbash, Le Systeme militaire safavide*, Berlin, 1987.

Haneda, M., 'The Character of the Urbanisation of Isfahan in the Later Safavid Period', in Melville, ed., *Safavid Persia*, 369–87.

Haneda, M. 'Emigration of Iranian Elites to India During the 16th–18th Centuries', in M. Szuppe, ed., *L'Héritage Timouride. Iran-Asie Centrale-Inde XVe-XVIIIe siècles*, ed. Maria Szuppe, Tashkent /Aix-en-Provence, 1997, 129–43.

Haneda, M., 'La Famille Khuzani Isfahani (15–17 siecles)', *SIr*, 18 (1989), 77–92.

Hazin, Shaykh Ali, *The Life of Sheikh Mohammed Ali Hazin*, F. C. Belfour, transl., London, 1830.

Herzig, E., 'The Deportation of the Armenians in 1604–05 and Europe's Myth of Shah Abbas I', in Melville, ed., *Pembroke Papers*, 59–71.

Herzig, E., 'The Rise of the Julfa Merchants in the Late Sixteenth Century', in Melville, ed., *Safavid Persia*, 305–23.

Herzig, E., 'The Volume of Iranian Raw Silk Exports in the Safavid Period', *IS*, 25(1–2) (1992), 61–79.

Herzig, E., 'Safavid Foreign Trade Policy? The Evidence from Persian Sources', paper presented at 'Iran and the World in the Safavid Age', University of London, September 2002.

Hillenbrand, R., 'The Iconography of the *Shah-nama-yi Shahi*', in Melville, ed., *Safavid Persia*, 53–78.

Hillenbrand, R., 'Safavid Architecture', in Jackson, ed., 6: 759–842.

Hillenbrand, R., 'The Tomb of Shah Ismail I at Ardabil', in S. Canby, ed., *Safavid Art*, 3–8.

Hoffmann, B., 'A Nineteenth Century Glimpse of Safavid Persia', paper presented at the Fourth International Round Table on Safavid Studies', Bamberg, July 2003.

Ishraqi, I., 'Le *Dar al-Saltana* Qazvin, deuxième capital des Safavides', in Melville, ed., *Safavid Persia*, 105–17.

Ishraqi, I., ' "*Noqtaviyya*" à l'époque Safavides', in Newman, ed., *Society and Culture*, 341–9.

Jackson, P., et al., eds, *The Cambridge History of Iran 6, The Timurid and Safavid Periods*, Cambridge, 1986.

Jacobs, Adam, 'Sunni and Shi'i Perceptions, Boundaries and Affiliations in Late Timurid and Early Safawid Persia: an Examination of Historical and Quasi-Historical Narratives', unpublished PhD dissertation, School of Oriental and African Studies, University of London, 1999.

Jafariyan, R., 'The Immigrant Manuscripts: A Study of the Migration of Shi'i Works From Arab Regions to Iran in the Early Safavid Era', in Newman, ed., *Society and Culture*, 351–69.

Jamali, M. K., *The Life and Personality of Shah Ismail I (907–930/1489–1524)*, Isfahan, 1998.

Johnson, R. S., 'Sunni Survival in Safavid Iran: Anti-Sunni Activities during the Reign of Tahmasp I', *IS*, 27(1–4) (1994), 123–34.

Jurdi, R. A., 'Migration and Social Change: The Ulama of Ottoman Jabal Amil in Safavid Iran, 1501–1736', unpublished PhD dissertation, Yale University, 1998.

Kadoi, Y., 'Aspects of Iranian Art under the Mongols: Chinoiserie Reappraised', unpublished PhD dissertation, University of Edinburgh, 2005.

Karamustafa, A., 'Esma'il I. His Poetry', *EIr*, 8 (1998).

Kemp, P. M., transl. and ed., *Russian Travellers to India and Persia, 1624–1798: Kotov, Yefremov, Danibegov*, Delhi, [1959].

Keyvani, M., *Artisans and Guild Life in the later Safavid Period*, Berlin, 1992.

Al-Khamis, U., 'Khusraw Paris as Champion of Shi'ism? A Closer Look at an Early Safavid Miniature Painting in the Royal Museum of Edinburgh', in B. O'Kane, ed., *The Iconography of Islamic Art, Studies in Honour of Robert Hillenbrand*, Edinburgh, 2005, 201–9.

Kiani, M.-Y. and W. Kleiss, 'Caravansary', *EIr*, 4 (1990), 798–802.

Kleiss, W., 'Chehel Sotun, Qazvin', *EIr*, 6 (1993), 116–17.

Kleiss, W., 'Safavid Caravanserais', in S. Canby, ed., *Safavid Art*, 27–31.

Khunji-Isfahani, Fadlallah b. Ruzbihan, *Tarikh-i Alam-Ara-yi Amini*, with the abridged English translation by V. Minorsky, edited, revised and augmented by J. Woods, London, 1992.

Kohlberg, E., 'Behar al-Anwar', *EIr*, 4 (1990), 90–3.

Kohlberg, 'al-Shahid al-Thani', *EI²*, 10: 209–10.

Kondo, N., 'Qizilbash Afterwards: The Afshars in Urmiya from the Seventeenth to the Nineteenth Century', *IS*, 32(4) (1999), 537–56.

Lambourn, E., 'Of Jewels and Horses: the Career and Patronage of an Iranian Merchant under Shah Jahan', *IS*, 36(2) (2003), 213–58.

Lambton, A. K. S., '*Pishkash*: present or tribute ?', *BSOAS* 57(1) (1994), 148–58.

Lambton, A. K. S. 'Quis Custodiet Custodes, Some Reflections on the Persian Theory of Government', *Studia Islamica*, 5, 1956, 125–46.

Lambton, A. K. S., *State and Government in Medieval Islam; an Introduction to the Study of Islamic Political Theory; The Jurists*, London, 1981.

Lewisohn, L., ed., *The Legacy of Medieval Persian Sufism*, London, 1992.

Lewisohn, L. and D. Morgan, eds, *Late Classical Persianate Sufism (1501–1750), The Safavid and Mughal Period*, Oxford, 1999.

Lewisohn, L., 'Sufism and the School of Isfahan: *Tasawwuf* and *'Irfan* in Late Safavid Iran', in Lewisohn and Morgan, eds, *Late Classical . . .*, 63–134.

Lockhart, L., *The Fall of the Safavi Dynasty and the Afghan Occupation of Persia*, Cambridge, 1958.

Lockhart, L., 'European Contacts with Persia, 1350–1736', in Jackson ed., 6: 373–411.

Loloi, P., 'The Image of the Safavids in English and French Literature of the Sixteenth to Eighteenth Century', paper presented at 'Iran and the World in the Safavid Age', London, September 2002.

Losensky, P., *Welcoming Fighani, Imitation and Poetic Individuality in the Safavid-Mughal Ghazal*, Costa Mesa, MA, 1998.

Luschey-Schmeisser, I., 'Chihil Sotun', *EIr*, 5 (1992), 111–15.

Maeda, H., 'On the Ethno-Social Backgrounds of the Four *ghulam* Families from Georgia in Safavid Iran', *SIr*, 32(2) (2003), 243–78.

Maeda, H., 'Shah's Slave or Georgian Noble? Unknown History of Georgian ghulams', paper presented at the Fourth International Round Table on Safavid Studies, Bamberg, July 2003.

Mahdavi, S., 'Muhammad Baqir Majlisi, Family Values, and the Safavids', in M. Mazzaoui, ed., *Safavid Iran*, 81–89.

Marlow, L., 'The Peck Shahnameh: Manuscript Production in Late Sixteenth-Century Shiraz', in Mazzaoui and Moreen, eds, *Intellectual Studies*, 229–43.

Martin, B. G., 'A Short History of the Khalwati Order of Dervishes', in N. Keddie, eds, *Scholars, Saints, and Sufis*, Berkeley/London, 1978, 275–305.

Matthee, R., 'Administrative Change and Stability in Late 17th c. Iran: The Case of Shaykh Ali Khan Zanganah (1669–89)', *IJMES*, 26 (1994), 77–98.

Matthee, R., 'Anti-Ottoman Concerns and Caucasian Interests: Diplomatic Relations Between Iran and Russia, 1587–1639', in M. Mazzaoui, ed., *Safavid Iran and Her Neighbors*, Salt Lake City, 2003, 101–28.

Matthee, R., 'Anti-Ottoman Politics and Transit Rights, the Seventeenth Century Trade in Silk Between Safavid Iran and Muscovy', *Cahiers du Monde russe*, 35(4) (Oct.–Dec., 1994), 739–62.

Matthee, R., 'Between Aloofness and Fascination: Safavid Views of the West', *IS*, 31(2) (Spring 1998), 219–46 (revised edition).

Matthee, R., 'Between Venice and Surat: The Trade in Gold in Late Safavid Iran', *Modern Asian Studies* 34(1) (2000), 223–55.

Matthee, R., 'Blinded by Power: The Rise and Fall of Fath Ali Khan Daghestani, Grand Vizier Under Shah Sultan Husayn (1127/1715–1133/1720)', *SIr*, 33 (2004), 179–220.

Matthee, R., 'The Career of Mohammed Beg, Grand Vizier of Shah Abbas II (r. 1642–1666)', *IS*, 24(1–4) (1991), 17–36.

Matthee, R., 'Coffee in Safavid Iran: Commerce and Consumption', *JESHO*, 37 (1994), 1–32.

Matthee, R., 'The East India Company Trade in Kerman Wool, 1658–1730', in Calmard, ed., *Études Safavids*, 343–83.

Matthee, R., 'Iran's Ottoman Diplomacy During the Reign of Shah Sulayman I (1077–1105/1666–94)', in K. Eslami, ed., *Iran and Iranian Studies, Essays in Honor of Iraj Afshar*, Princeton, 1998, 148–77.

Matthee, R., 'Merchants in Safavid Iran: Participants and Perceptions', *Journal of Early Modern History* 4(3–4) (2000), 233–68.

Matthee, R., 'Mint Consolidation and the Worsening of the Late Safavid Coinage: The Mint of Huwayza', *JESHO*, 44(4), 2001, 505–39.

Matthee, R., 'Negotiating Across Cultures: The Dutch Van Leene Mission to the Iranian Court of Shah Sulayman (1689–1692)', *Eurasian Studies* 3(1) (2004), 35–63.

Matthee, R., *The Politics of Trade in Safavid Iran, Silk for Silver 1600–1730*, Cambridge, 1999.

Matthee, R., 'Prostitutes, Courtesans, and Dancing Girls: Women Entertainers in Safavid Iran', in Matthee and B. Baron, eds, *Iran and Beyond, Essays in Middle Eastern History in Honor of Nikki R. Keddie*, Costa Mesa, CA, 2000, 121–50.

Matthee, R., 'The Safavid Mint of Huvayzeh: The Numismatic Evidence', in Newman, ed., *Society and Culture*, 265–91.

Matthee, R., 'Shahbandar', *EI²*, Suppl, 716–17.

Matthee, R., 'Tobacco in Iran', in S. L. Gilman and Z. Xun, eds, *Smoke, A Global History of Smoking* London, 2004, 58–67.

Matthee, R., 'Tutun', *EI²*, 10: 753–6.

Matthee, R., 'Unwalled Cities and Restless Nomads: Firearms and Artillery in Safavid Iran', in Melville, ed., 389–416.

Mazzaoui, M. and V. B. Moreen, eds, *Intellectual Studies on Islam, Essays Written in Honor of Martin B. Dickson*, Salt Lake City, 1990.

Mazzaoui, M., *The Origins of the Safawids, Shi'ism, Sufism, and the Ghulat*, Freiburger Islamstudien, Vol. 3, Wiesbaden, 1972.

Mazzaoui, M., 'From Tabriz to Qazvin to Isfahan: Three Phases of Safavid History', *ZDMG*. Supp. III, 1. XIX. *Deutscher Orientalistentag*, Wiesbaden, 1977, 514–22.

Mazzaoui, M., 'The Religious Policy of Safavid Shah Ismail II', in Mazzaoui and Moreen, eds, *Intellectual Studies*, 49–56.

McCabe, I., 'Beyond the *Lettres Persanes*: Safavid Iran in the Political Discourse of the French Enlightenment', paper presented at 'Iran and the World in the Safavid Age', London, September 2002

McCabe, I., *The Shah's Silk for Europe's Silver: The Eurasian Trade of the Julfa Armenians in Safavid Iran and India (1530–1750)*, Atlanta, 1999.

McChesney, R., 'Alam Ara-yi Shah Ismail', *EIr*, 1 (1985), 796–7.

McChesney, R., 'Four Sources on Shah 'Abbas's Building of Isfahan', *Muqarnas*, 5 (1988), 103–34.

McChesney, R., 'A Note on Iskandar Beg's Chronology', *Journal of Near Eastern Studies (JNES)*, 39(1) (1980), 53–63.

McChesney, R., 'The Anthology of Poets: Muzakkir al-Ashab As a Source for the History of Seventeenth-Century Central Asia', in Mazzaoui and Moreen, eds, *Intellectual Studies*, 57–84.

McChesney, R., 'The Central Asian Hajj-Pilgrimmage in the Time of the Early Modern Empires', in M. Mazzaoui, ed., *Safavid Iran and Her Neighbors*, Salt Lake City, 2003, 129–56.

McChesney, R., 'Waqf and Public Policy: The Waqfs of Shah Abbas, 1011–1023/ 1602–1614', *Asian and African Studies*, 15 (1981), 165–90.

Medley, M., 'Ardabil Collection of Chinese Porcelain', *EIr*, 2 (1987), 364–5.

Melville, C., 'From Qars to Qandahar: The Itineraries of Shah Abbas I', in Calmard, ed., *Études Safavides.*, 195–224.

Melville, C., 'A Lost Source for the Reign of Shah Abbas: The *Afzal al-tawarikh* of Fazli Khuzani Isfahani', *IS*, 31(2) (1998), 263–5.

Melville, C., 'New Light on the Reign of Shah 'Abbas: Volume III of the *Afzal al-Tavarikh*', in Newman, ed. *Society and Culture*, 63–96.

Melville, C., ed., *Pembroke Papers I*, Cambridge, 1990.

Melville, C., ed., *Safavid Persia, The History and Politics of an Islamic Society*, London/New York, 1996.

Melville, C., 'Shah Abbas and the Pilgrimage to Mashhad', in Melville, ed., *Safavid Persia*, 191–229.

Membré, M., *Mission to the Lord Sophy of Persia (1539–1542)*, translated with Introduction and Notes by A. H. Morton, London, 1993.

Minorsky, V., 'Ak-koyunlu', *EI²*, 1: 311–12.

Minorsky, V., 'The Poetry of Shah Ismail I', *BSOAS*, 10 (1942), 1006a–53a.

Minorsky, V., ed. and transl., *Tadhkirat al-Muluk, A Manual of Safavid Administration, (c. 1137/1725)*, London, 1943.

Minorsky, V., ed., and transl., *Calligraphers and Painters, A Treatise by Qazi Ahmad, son of Mir Munshi (c. AH 1015/AD 1606)*, Washington, 1959.

Minorsky, V., ed., *Persia in AD 1478–1490, An Abridged Edition of Fadlallah b. Ruzbihan Khunji's Tarikh-i Alam Ara-yi Amini*, London, 1957.

Minorsky, V., 'Jihan Shah Qaraquyunlu and his Poetry', *BSOAS*, 16(2), (1954), 271–97.

Minorsky, V., 'Lahidjan', *EI²*, 5: 602–4.

Minorsky, V., [C. E. Bosworth], 'Tabriz', *EI²*, 10: 41–9.

Minorsky, V., [C. E. Bosworth], 'Uzun Hasan', *EI²*, 10: 963–7.

Mirjafari, H., 'The Haydari-Nimati Conflicts in Iran', *IS*, 12(3–4) (1979), 135–62.

Momen, M., 'Usuli, Akhbari, Shaykhi, Babi: The Tribulations of a Qazvin Family', *IS*, 36(3) (2003), 317–37.

Moreen, V., 'A Seventeenth-Century Iranian Rabbi's Polemical Remarks on Jews, Christians, and Muslims', in M. Mazzaoui, ed., *Safavid Iran and Her Neighbors*, Salt Lake City, 2003, 157–68.

Moreen, V., 'The *Kitab-i Anusi* of Babai ibn Lutf (Seventeenth Century) and the *Kitab-i Sar Guzasht* of Babai ibn Farhad (Eighteenth Century): A Comparison of Two Judaeo-Persian Chronicles', in Mazzaoui and Moreen, eds, *Intellectual Studies*, 41–8.

Moreen, V., 'The Problems of Conversion Among Iranian Jews in the Seventeenth and Eighteenth Centuries', *IS*, 19(3–4) (1986), 215–28.

Moreen, V., 'Risala-yi Sawaiq al-Yahud [The Treatise Lightning Bolts Against the Jews] by Muhammad Baqir b. Muhammad Taqi al-Majlisi (d. 1699)', *Die Welts des Islams* 32 (1992), 177–95.

Morton, A., 'The Ardabil Shrine in Reign of Shah Tahmasp I', *Iran*, 12 (1974), 31–64; 13 (1975), 39–58.

Morton, A. The *Chub-i Tariq* and Qizilbash Ritual in Safavid Persia', in Calmard, ed., *Études Safavides.*, Paris Tehran, 1993, 225–45.

Morton, A., 'The Date and Attribution of the *Ross Anonymous*. Notes on a Persian History of Shah Ismail I', in C. Melville, ed., *Pembroke Papers I*, Cambridge, 1990, 179–212.

Morton, A., 'The Early Years of Shah Ismail in the *Afzal al-Tavarikh* and Elsewhere', in Melville, ed., *Safavid Persia*, 27–51.

Morton, A., 'An Introductory Note on a Safawid *Munshi*'s Manual in the Library of the School of Oriental and African Studies', *BSOAS*, 33(2) (1970), 352–8.

Morton, A. 'Maulana Ahmad Pakaraji and the Origins of Anti-Safavid Polemic', paper presented at 'Iran and the World in the Safavid Age', University of London, September 2002.

Munshi, Iskandar Beg, *History of Shah Abbas the Great*, 3 vols., R. M. Savory, transl., Boulder, CO, 1978–86.

Nasr, S. H., 'The School of Ispahan', in M. M. Sharif, ed., *A History of Muslim Philosophy*, Wiesbaden, 1966, 2: 932–61.

Nasr, S. H., 'Shiism and Sufism: Their Relationship in Essence and in History', *Religious Studies*, 6 (1970), 229–42.

Netton, I., 'Suhrawardi's Heir? The Ishraqi Philosophy of Mir Damad', in Lewisohn and Morgan, eds, *Late Classical . . .* 225–46.

Netzer, A., 'Conversion, iv. Of Persian Jews to Other Religions', *EIr*, 6 (1993), 234–6.

Newman, A., 'Baqir al-Majlisi and Islamicate Medicine: Safavid Medical Theory and Practice Re-examined', in Newman, ed., *Society and Culture*, 371–96.

Newman, A., 'Clerical Perceptions of Sufi Practices in Late Seventeenth-Century Persia: Arguments Over the Permissibility of Singing (Ghina)', in L. Lewisohn and D. Morgan, eds, *The Heritage of Sufism, Vol. III: Late Classical Persianate Sufism: The Safavid and Mughal Period (1501–1750)*, Oxford, 1999, 135–64.

Newman, A., 'Fayz al-Kashani and the Rejection of the Clergy/State Alliance: Friday Prayer as Politics in the Safavid Period', in L. Walbridge, ed., *The Most Learned of the Shi'a*, New York, 2001, 34–52.

Newman, A., *The Formative Period of Period of Shi'i Law: Hadith as Discourse Between Qum and Baghdad*, Richmond, 2000.

Newman, A., 'Ghiyas-al-Din Dashtaki', *EIr*, 7 (1996), 100–2.

Newman, A., 'Jalal al-Din Davani', *EIr*, 7 (1996), 132–3.

Newman, A., 'Mir Damad', *EIr*, 6 (1993), 623–6.

Newman, A., 'The Myth of the Clerical Migration to Safawid Iran: Arab Shi'ite Opposition to Ali al-Karaki and Safawid Shi'ism', *Die Welt des Islams*, 33 (1993), 66–112.

Newman, A., 'The Nature of the Akhbari/Usuli Dispute in Late-Safawid Iran. Part One: Abdallah al-Samahiji's "Munyat al-Mumarisin" ', *BSOAS*, 55(1) (1992), 22–51.

Newman, A., 'The Nature of the Akhbari/Usuli Dispute in Late-Safawid Iran. Part Two: The Conflict Reassessed', *BSOAS*, 55(2) (1992), 250–61.

Newman, A., 'Safavids – Religion, Philosophy and Science', *EI²*, 7: 777–87.

Newman, A., ed., *Society and Culture in the Early Modern Middle East: Studies on Iran in the Safavid Period*, Leiden, 2003.

Newman, A., 'Sufism and Anti-Sufism in Safavid Iran: The Authorship of the *Hadiqat al-Shi'a* Revisited', *Iran* 37 (1999), 95–108.

Newman, A., 'Towards a Reconsideration of the Isfahan School of Philosophy: Shaykh Bahai and the Role of the Safawid Ulama', *SIr*, 15(2) (1986), 165–99.

Norris, H. T., 'The Hurufi Legacy of Fadlallah of Astarabad', in Lewisohn, ed., *The Legacy*, 87–97.

Oberling, P., 'Dhul-Qadr', *EIr*, 7 (1996).

Papazian, H., 'Armenia and Iran. vi. Armeno-Iranian Relations in the Islamic Period', *EIr*, 2 (1987), 467–78.

Perry, J., 'The Last Safavids (1722–73)', *Iran*, 9 (1971), 59–71.

Perry, J., 'Toward a Theory of Iranian Urban Moieties: The Haydariyyah and Ni'matiyyah Revisited', *IS*, 32(1) (1999), 51–70.

Petrushevsky, I. P., *Islam in Iran*, H. Evans, transl., London, 1985.

Pinder-Wilson, R., 'Timurid Architecture', in Jackson, ed., 6: 728–58.

Quinn, S., 'The Dreams of Shaykh Safi al-Din and Safavid Historical Writing', *IS*, 29(1–2) (1996), 127–47.

Quinn, S., 'The Historiography of Safavid Prefaces', in Melville, ed., *Safavid Persia*, 1–25.

Quinn, S., *Historical Writing during the Reign of Shah Abbas*, Salt Lake City, 2000.

Quinn, S., 'Notes on Timurid Legitimacy in Three Safavid Chronicles', *IS*, 31 (1998), 149–58.

Quinn, S., 'Rewriting Nimatallahi History in Safavid Chronicles', in L. Lewisohn and D. Morgan, eds, *The Heritage of Sufism, Volume III: Late Classical Persianate Sufism (1501–1750)* Oxford, 1999, 201–22.

Quinn, S., 'The Timurid Historiographical Legacy: A Comparative Study of Persianate Historical Writing', in Newman, ed., *Society and Culture*, 19–31.

Rabino, H., 'Coins of the Shahs of Persia', *Numismatic Chronicle*, 4th series, 1908, 357–73.

Rabino, H., *Coins, Medals and Seals of the Shahs of Iran, 1500–1941*, Dallas, TX, 1973.

Rahimi, B., 'The Rebound Theatre State: The Politics of the Safavid Camel Sacrifice, 1598–1695 C. E.', *IS*, 37(3) (2004), 451–78.

Rahman, F., 'al-Asfar al-Arba'a', *EIr*, 2 (1987), 744–7.

Richard, F., 'L'apport de Missionaires Européens à la Connaissance de l'Iran en Europe et de l'Europe en Iran', in J. Calmard, ed., *Etudes*, 251–66.

Richard, F., 'Capuchins in Persia', *EIr*, 4 (1990), 786–8.

Richard, F., 'Carmelites in Persia', *EIr*, 4 (1990), 832–4.

Richard, F., 'Fr. Aimé Chezaud – Controversialist', paper presented at Iran and the World in the Safavid Age, University of London, September 2002.

Ridgeon, L., *Crescents on the Cross, Islamic Visions of Christianity*, Oxford, 1999.

Rizvi, K., 'The Imperial Setting: Shah Abbas at the Safavid Shrine of Shaykh Safi at Ardabil', in S. Canby., ed., *Safavid Art*, 9–15.

Rizvi, S., 'Reconsidering the Life of Mulla Sadra Shirazi: Notes towards an Intellectual Biography', *Iran*, 40 (2002), 181–201.

Robinson, B. W., 'Ismail II's copy of the Shahnama', *Iran*, 14 (1976), 1–8.

Roemer, H. R., 'The Safavid Period', in Jackson, ed., 6: 189–350.

Roemer, H. R., 'The Türkman Dynasties', in Jackson, ed., 6: 147–88.

Rogers, J., 'Chinese-Iranian Relations, iv. The Safavid Period', *EIr*, 5 (1992), 436–8.

Röhrborn, K.-M., *Provinzen und Zentralgewalt Persiens im 16. und 17. Jahrhundert*, Berlin, 1966, translated by K. Djahandari as *Nizam Iyalat dar Dawrah-yi Safaviyya*, Tehran, 1978.

Rota, G., 'The Man who would not be King: Abul-Fath Sultan Muhammad Mirza Safavid in India', *IS*, 32(4) (1999), 513–35.

Roxburgh, D. J., 'Bahram Mirza and His Collections', in S. Canby, ed., *Safavid Art*, London, 2002, 37–42.

Rumlu, Hasan, *A Chronicle of the Early Safawis, being the Ahsan al-Tawarikh of Hasan-i Rumlu*, C. N.. Seddon, transl., Baroda, 1934.

Safa, Z., 'Persian Literature in the Timurid and Türkman Periods', in Jackson, ed., 6: 913–28.

Safa, Z., 'Persian Literature in the Safavid Period', in Jackson, ed., 6: 948–64.

Salati, M., *Il Passaggio in India di Ali Khan al-Shirazi al-Madani (1642–1707)*, Padova, 1999.

Salati, M., 'Toleration, Persecution and Local Realities: Observations on the Shiism in the Holy Places and the Bilad al-Sham (16th–17th centuries)', *Convegno sul Tema La Shī'a Nell' Impero Ottomano*, Roma, 1993, 121–48.

Sarwar, G., *History of Shah Ismail*, Aligarh, 1939.

Savory, R., 'Abbas I', *EIr*, 1 (1985), 71–5.

Savory, R., 'Abbas II', *EIr*, 1 (1985), 76.

Savory, R., 'Abbas III', *EIr*, 1 (1985), 76.

Savory, R., 'Courts and Courtiers vi. In the Safavid Period', *EIr*, 6 (1993), 371–5.

Savory, R., 'A Curious Episode of Safavid History', in C. Bosworth, ed., *Iran and Islam*, Edinburgh, 1971, 461–73.

Savory, R., 'Esma'il I', *EIr*, 8 (1998).

Savory, R., *Iran Under the Safavids*, Cambridge, 1980.

Savory, R., 'Ismail I', *EI²*, 4: 186–7.

Savory, R., 'Ismail II', *EI²*, 4: 188.

Savory, R., 'The Office of Khalifat al-Khulafa under the Safavids', *Journal of the American Oriental Society (JAOS)*, 85 (1965), 497–502.

Savory, R., 'The Principal Offices of the Safavid State During the Reign of Ismail I (907–30/1501–24)', *BSOAS*, 23, Part 1 (1960), 91–105.

Savory, R., 'The Principal Offices of the Safawid State during the Reign of Tahmasp I (930–984/1524–1576)', *BSOAS*, 24, Part 1 (1961), 65–85.

Savory, R., 'The Safavid Administrative System' in Jackson, ed., 6: 351–72.

Savory, R., 'Safawids: Dynastic, Political and Military History', *EI²*, 8: 765–71.

Savory, R., *Studies on the History of Safawid Iran*, London, 1987.

Savory, R., 'Tahmasp', *EI²*, 10: 109–10.

Savory, R., 'Takkalu', *EI²*, 10: 136–7.

Scarcia, G., 'Al-Hurr al-Amili', *EI²*, 3: 588–9.

Sefatgol, M., 'Safavid Administration of *Avqaf*: Structure, Changes and Functions, 1077–1135/1666–1722', in Newman, ed., *Society and Culture*, 397–408.

Sims, E., 'A Dispersed Late-Safavid Copy of the *Tarikh-i Jahangusha-yi Khaqan Sahibqiran*', in S. Canby, ed., *Safavid Art*, 54–7.

Sims, E., 'Two 17th Century Firdausi Manuscripts: The Windsor and the Rashida *Shahnamas*', paper presented at 'Shahnama: The Visual Language of the Persian Book of Kings', Royal Museum of Scotland, Edinburgh, March 2001.

Soucek, P., 'Abd al-Baqi Yazdi', *EIr*, 1 (1985), 105–6.

Soudavar, A., 'The Early Safavids and Their Cultural Interactions with Surrounding States', in N. Keddie and R. Matthee, eds, *Iran and the Surrounding World* (Seattle/London, 2002), 89–120.

Stanfield, R., 'Mirza Makhdum Sharifi: A 16th Century Sunni sadr at the Safavid Court', unpublished PhD thesis, New York University, 1993.

Stanfield-Johnson, R., 'The *Tabarraiyan* and the Early Safawids', *IS*, 37(1) (2004), 47–71.

Stevens, R., 'European Visitors to the Safavid Court', *IS*, 7(3–4) (1974), 421–57.

Stewart, D., 'A Biographical Note on Baha al-Din al-Amili (d. 1030/1621)', *JAOS*, 111(3) (1991), 563–71.

Stewart, D., 'The First Shaykh al-Islam of the Safavid Capital Qazvin', *JAOS*, 116(3) (1996), 387–405.

Stewart, D., 'The Genesis of the Akhbari Revival', in M. Mazzaoui, ed., *Safavid Iran and Her Neighbors*, Salt Lake City, 2003, 169–93.

Stewart, D., 'The Humor of the Scholars: The Autobiography of Nimat Allah al-Jazairi (d. 1112/1701)', *IS*, 22(4) (1989), 47–81.

Stewart, D., 'Husayn b. Abd al-Samad al-Amili's Treatise for Sultan Suleiman and the Shi'i Shafii Legal Tradition', *Islamic Law and Society*, 4(2) (1997), 156–99.

Stewart, D., 'The Lost Biography of Baha al-Din al-Amili and the Historiography of Safavid Shah Ismail II's Reign', *IS*, 31(2) (1998), 177–205.

Stewart, D., 'Notes on the Migration of Amili Scholars to Safavid Iran', *JNES*, 55(2) (1996), 81–103.

Stewart, D., 'Taqiyyeh as Performance: The Travels of Baha al-Din al-Amili in the Ottoman Empire (991–93/1583–85', *Princeton Papers*, Spring 1996, Vol. IV, 1–70.

Sümer, F., 'Kara-koyunlu', *EI²*, 4: 584–8.

Szuppe, M., 'The "Jewels of Wonder": Learned Ladies and Princess Politicians in the Provinces of Early Safavid Iran', in G. Hambly, ed., *Women in the Medieval Islamic World, Power, Patronage and Piety*, London, 1998, 325–47.

Szuppe, M., 'Kinship Ties Between the Safavids and the Qizilbash Amirs in the Late-Sixteenth Century: A Case Study of the Political Career of Members of the Sharaf al-Din Ogli Tekelu Family', in Melville, ed., *Safavid Persia*, 79–104.

Szuppe, M., 'La participation des Femmes de la Famille Royale à l'Exercice du Pouvoir en Iran Safavide au XVIe Siècle (première partie)', *SIr*, 23(2) (1994), 211–58.

Szuppe, M., 'La participation des Femmes de la Famille Royale à l'Exercice du Pouvoir en Iran Safavide au XVIe Siècle (seconde partie)', *SIr*, 24(1) (1995), 61–122.

Szuppe, M., 'Status, Knowledge and Politics: Women in Sixteenth-Century Safavid Iran', in G. Nashat and L. Beck, eds, *Women in Iran from the Rise of Islam to 1800*, Urbana/Chicago, 2003, 141–69.

Thackston, W., 'The *Diwan* of Khata'i: Pictures for the Poetry of Shah Ismail', *Asian Art* 1(4) (Fall 1988), 37–63.

Thomas, K., 'Chronology of Translations of the Bible', *EIr*, 4, 203–6.

Thomas, K. and F. Vahman, 'Persian Translations of the Bible', *EIr*, 4, 209–13.

Togan, Z. V., 'Sur L'Origine des Safavides', *Mélanges Louis Massignon*, 3 (Damas, 1957), 345–57.

Tucker, C., 'Nadir Shah and the Jafari *Madhhab*', *IS*, 27 (1994), 163–79.

Turner, C., *Islam Without Allah? The Rise of Religious Externalism in Safavid Iran*, Richmond, 2000.

Varjavand, P., 'Darb-i Imam', *EIr*, 7(1).

Varjavand, P., 'Emamzadeh', *EIr*, 8.

Walker, D., 'Carpets IX. Safavid Period', *EIr*, 4: 866–75.

Welch, A., 'Art in Iran ix. Safavid to Qajar', *EIr*, 2: 620–7.

Welch, A., 'Painting and Patronage under Shah Abbas I', *IS*, 7(3–4) (1974), 458–507.

Welch, A., 'Safavi Iran Seen through Venetian Eyes', in Newman, ed., *Society and Culture*, 97–121.

Winter, H., 'Persian Science in Safavid Times', in Jackson, ed., 6: 581–609.

Wood, B., 'Shah Ismail and the Shahnama', paper presented the Second Edinburgh Shahnama Conference, Royal Museum of Scotland, Edinburgh, March, 2003.

Wood, B., 'The Tarikh-i Jahanara in the Chester Beatty Library: An Illustrated Manuscript of the "Anonymous Histories of Shah Ismail" ', *IS*, 37(1) (2004), 89–107.

Woods, J., *The Aqquyunlu: Clan, Confederation, Empire*, rev. ed., Salt Lake City, 1999.

Woods, J., 'Timur's Genealogy', in Mazzaoui and Moreen, eds, *Intellectual* 85–125.

Yarshater, E., 'Persian Poetry in the Timurid and Safavid Periods,' in Jackson, ed., 6: 965–94.

Yarshater, E., 'Safavid Literature: Progress or Decline', *IS*, 7(3–4) (1974), 217–70.

Zarinebaf-Shahr, F., 'Economic Activities of Safavid Women in the Shrine-City of Ardabil', *IS*, 31(2) (Spring 1998), 247–61.

Primary-language sources

Afandi, Mirza Abdallah Isbahani, *Riyaz al-Ulama*, 5 vols., Qum, 1401.

Ahmadi, N., 'Du *Vaqfnama* az du zan', in R. Jafariyan, ed., *Miras-i Islami-yi Iran*, 6, Qum, 1376, 341–54.

Ahmadi, N., 'Chahar *Vaqfnama* az Chahar Madrasah-yi Isfahan dar Dawrah-yi Safavi', in R. Jafariyan, ed., *Miras-i Islami-yi Iran*, Qum, 1375/1996, 3: 95–129.

Anonymous, *Alam ara-yi Safavi*, Y. A. Shukri, ed., Tehran, 1350/1971.

Anonymous, *Alam ara-yi Shah Ismail*, A. M. Sahib, ed., Tehran, 1349/1970.

Anonymous, *Alam ara-yi Shah Tahmasp*, I. Afshar, ed., Tehran, 1370/1991.

Anonymous, *Mukafatnama*, in Jafariyan, ed., *Ilal*, 63–169; idem, ed., *Safaviyya dar Arsa-yi Din*, 3: 1191–297.

Ansari, Mirza Rafia, *Dastur al-Muluk*, M. Danishpazhuh, ed., in *Majallah-yi Danishkadah-i Adabiyat va Ulum-i Insani-yi Danishgah-i Tehran*, 15 (1347/1968): 475–504; 16 (1347–8/1968): 62–93, 298–322, 416–20, 540–64.

Asaf, Muhammad Hashim, *Rustam al-Tavarikh*, Tehran, 1352.

Ashtiyani, J., ed., *Anthologie des Philosophes Iraniens depuis le XVIIe siècle jusqu'à nos jours. Textes persans et arabes choisis et présentés par Sayyed Jalâloddîn Ashtiyânî. Introduction analytique par Henry Corbin*, 4 vols., Paris and Tehran, 1972–5.

Astarabadi, Sayyid Hasan, *Tarikh-i Sultani*, I. Ishraqi, ed., 2nd ed. Tehran, 1366.

Bahrani, Yusuf ibn Ahmad, *Luluat al-Bahrayn*, Najaf, 1969.

Bidlisi, Sharaf Khan, *Sharafnama*, 2 vols., Cairo, nd.

Bihbihani, A., *Mirat al-Ahval Jahan-nama*, A. Davani, ed., Tehran, 1370.

Danishpazhuh, M. T., ed., *Catalogue Méthodique, Descriptif, et Raisonné des Manuscrits Concernant la Tradition . . . de la Bibliothèque de l'Université de Teheran (don de M. le Professeur Meshkat)*, (in Persian) 5 vols., Tehran, 1951–1956.

Falsafi, Nasrallah, *Zindigani-yi Shah Abbas-i Avval*, 5 vols., Tehran, 1352–3.

Hazin, Muhammad Ali, *The Life of Sheikh Mohammed Ali Hazin*, F. C. Belfour, ed., London, 1830.

Hunarfar, L., *Ganjinah-i Asar-i Tarikhi-i Isfahan*, Isfahan, 1344.

Isfahani, Muhammad Masum, *Khulasat al-Siyar*, I. Afshar, ed., Tehran, 1368/1989.

Isfahani, Muhammad Yusuf Valih, *Khuld-i Barin*, M. H. Muhaddath, ed., Tehran, 1372.

Jafariyan, R., *Din va Siyasat dar Dawrah-yi Safavi*, Qum, 1370/1991.

Jafariyan, R., *Ilal bar Uftadan-i Safaviyyan*, Tehran, 1373.

Jafariyan, R., 'Munasibat-i Isfahan va Hijaz dar Dawrah-yi Safavi', paper presented at 'Isfahan and the Safavids', Isfahan, February 2002.

Jafariyan, R., 'Nufuz-i Davistsalih-yi Khandan-i Muhaqqiq-i Karaki dar Dawlat-i Safaviyya', paper presented at the Fourth International Round Table on Safavid Persia, Bamberg, July 2003.

Jafariyan, R., *Safaviyya, Az Zuhur ta Zaval*, Tehran, 1378.

Jafariyan, R., *Safaviyya dar Arsa-yi Din, Farhang, va Siyasat*, 3 vols. Qum, 1379/2000.

Jafariyan, R., ed., '*Vaqfnama*-yi Madrasa-yi Sultan Husayn Maruf be Madrasa-yi Aqa Kamal', *Miras-i Islami Iran*, R. Jafariyan, ed., Qum, 1994, 1: 259–90.

Jazairi, N, *al-Anvar al-Numaniyya*, Tabriz, nd.

Junabadi, Mirza Hasan, *Rawzat al-Safaviyya*, G. R. Tabatabai Majd, ed., Tehran, 1378/1999.

Kanturi, Ijaz Husayn, *Kashf al-Hujub*, Calcutta, 1914.

Khatunabadi, Abd al-Husayn al-Husayni, *Vaqai al-Sinin val-Avvam*, M. Bihbudi, ed., Tehran, 1352/1973.

Khvandamir, Amir Mahmud, *Tarikh-i Shah Ismail va Shah Tahmasp Safavi*, M. A. Jarrahi, ed., Tehran, 1991.

Khvandamir, Ghiyas al-Din, *Tarikh-i Habib al-Siyar*, J. Humai, ed., 4 vols., 3rd ed., [Tehran], 1362.

Khvansari, Muhammad Baqir, *Rawzat al-Jannat*, 8 vols., Tehran, 1390/1970.

Kitabi, S. Muhammad Baqir, *Rijal-i Isfahan*, Isfahan, 1375.

Mahdavi, S. M., *Zindiginama-yi Allama-yi Majlisi*, 2 vols, Tehran, 1378.

Marashi, Mirza Muhammad Khalil, *Majma al-Tavarikh*, A. Iqbal, ed., Tehran, 1362.

Mudarrissi Tabatabai, H., *Bargi az Tarikh-i Qazvin*, Qum, 1361.

Mudarrissi Tabatabai, H., *Misalha-yi Sudur-e Safavi*, Qum, 1353/1974.

Muhsin, Muhammad, *Zubdat al-Tavarikh*, I. Afshar, ed., Tehran, 1375.

Naraqi, H., *Athar-i Tarikhi-yi Shahristanha-yi Kashan va Natanz*, Tehran, 1348/1969.

Nasiri, Mirza Ali Naqi, *Alqab va Mavajib-i Dawreh-i Salatin Safaviyya*, Y. Rahimlu, ed., Mashhad, 1372.

Nasiri, Muhammad Ibrahim, M. N. Nasiri, ed., *Dastur-i Shahryaran*, Tehran 1373.

Nasrabadi, Muhammad Tahir, *Tadhkirah-yi Nasrabadi*, V. Dastgirdi, ed., Tehran, 1982.

Natanzi, Mahmud b. Hedayatallah Afushta, *Nuqavat al-Asar fi zikr al-akhyar*, I. Ishraqi, ed., 2nd ed., Tehran, 1373.

Nayrizi, Qutb al-Din, *Tibb al-Mamalik*, in R. Jafariyan, ed., *Ilal*, 215–35; idem, ed., *Safaviyya dar Arsa-yi Din*, 3: 1324–37.

Pashazada, Muhammad Arif, *Inqilab-i Islam bayn al-Khavvas val-Avvam*, R. Jafariyan, ed., Qum, 1379.

Qazvini, Abul-Hasan Qazvini, *Favaid al-Safaviyya*, M. Mir Ahmadi, ed., Tehran, 1990.

Qazvini, Budaq, *Javahir al-Akhbar*, M. Bahramnizhad, ed., Tehran, 1378.

Qazvini, Muhammad Tahir Vahid, *Abbasnama*, I. Dihqan, ed., Arak, 1329.

Qummi, Qazi Ahmad, *Khulasat al-Tavarikh*, I. Ishraqi, ed., 1, Tehran, 1359; 2, Tehran, 1363.

Rumlu, Hasan, *Ahsan al-Tavarikh*, Tehran, 1357.

Savaqib, J., *Tarikhnigari-i Asr-i Safavi va shinakht-i manabi va maakhiz*, Shiraz, 2001.

Shamlu, Valiquli b. Daud Quli, *Qisas al-Khaqani*, H. S. Nasiri, ed., 2 vols., Tehran, 1371.

Shirazi, Abdi Beg, *Takmilat al-Akhbar*, A. Navai, ed., Tehran, 1369.

Shirazi, Sadr al-Din Muhammad, *Kasr Asnam al-Jahiliyyih*, M. T. Danishpazhuh, ed., Tehran, 1340/1962.

Shubbar, J. H., *Tarikh al-Mushashaiyin va Tarajim Alaihim*, Najaf, 1385/1965.

Shushtari, Nurallah, *Majalis al-Muminin*, 2 vols., Tehran, 1354.

Tabrisi, H. Nuri, *Fayz-i Qudsi*, J. Nabavi, transl., Qum, 1374.

Tabrizi, M. Z., *Faraid al-Favaid Dar Ahval-i Madaris va Masajid*, R. Jafariyan ed., Tehran, 1994.

Tahmasp, Safavi, *Tadhkira-yi Shah Tahmasp*, A. Safari, ed., 2nd ed., Tehran, 1363.

Tanukabuni, Muhammad, *Qisas al-Ulama*, Tehran, nd.

Tehrani, Aqa Buzurg Muhammad Muhsin, *al-Dharia ila Tasanif al-Shi'a*, Tehran and Najaf, 1353–98.

Al-Yasin, Shaykh Muhammad Al-Hasan, *Tarikh al-Mashhad al-Kazimi*, Baghdad, 1387/1967.

Yazdi, Mulla Jalal al-Din Munajjim, *Tarikh-i Abbasi ya Ruznama-yi Mulla Jalal*, S. Vahid Niya, ed., Tehran, 1366/1987.

Zarrabi, A. Kalantar (Suhayl Kashani), *Tarikh-i Kashan*, I. Afshar, ed., Tehran, 2536.

Index

Husayn, Imam 16, 36, 151, 189, 207
Husayn b. Abd al-Samad Amili 38, 58,
    174–75, 178, 189, 200, 203
Husayn Bayqara, Sultan (Timurid) 12,
    18, 19, 20, 30, 33, 153, 156, 158,
    166, 170, 186, 246
Husayn Bek Shamlu 17, 20
Husayn Khan Shamlu 153, 164
Husayn Khvansari 97, 98, 100, 111, 224
Husayn Karaki, Sayyid 38, 58, 77, 178,
    180, 201, 203, 237
Husayni/d 23, 30, 32, 46, 48, 57, 64,
    66–67, 151, 166, 177–78, 195, 204,
    216–17, 220, 223–24, 229

Iberian 61
Ibn al-Arabi 70
Ibn Babawayh 214
Ibn Bazzaz 136
Ibn Sina 108
Ibrahim b. Bahram 29, 42, 47–8,
    165–66, 168, 170, 172
Ibrahim b. Malik 180
Ibrahim Amini, Sultan 156, 166
Ibrahim Aqa 112
idols 120
ijtihad 199, 214
Ilchi Mosque 100, 229
Ilkhanids 11, 148, 170
illuminated manuscripts 18, 34, 48, 66,
    102
illustration 171, 173
Imadi mosque 63, 168
Imam/s 2, 13–4, 19, 23, 30, 35, 37, 57,
    59, 68, 71, 98, 99, 110, 111, 129,
    160, 204, 151–52, 155, 158, 161,
    169, 179, 216–17, 225, 227, 229, 238
Imam Juma 84
Imam Quli (son of Abbas I) 74, 101
Imam Quli Khan 65, 76, 185, 202, 205,
    208
Imamzada Ahmad 241
Imamzada Ismail 100, 111, 112, 204,
    240–4
Imamzada Shah Zayd 47
imamzadas 99, 161, 194
Imperial Canal 79
Imanlu 184
Inallu 233
India, Indian 1, 20, 61, 63, 66–7, 76, 77,
    79, 82–3, 88–9, 90–1, 95, 102, 104,
    113, 120, 126, 131, 134, 137, 139,
    146, 149, 155–56, 160, 166, 167,
    171, 173, 180, 182, 183, 185, 186,
    191, 193, 194, 197, 198, 204–05,

210, 215, 217, 219, 223, 226, 228,
    239, 241
Indian Ocean 128
Indian style (poetry) 158
indigo 63, 206
Indus 1
inflation 83, 85, 94, 132, 243
Inju 181, 187
inscription/s 5, 10, 19, 23, 30, 32, 47,
    57, 64, 65, 90, 110, 111, 151,
    157–59, 167, 180–81, 195, 216–19,
    223, 229–30, 232, 240
inspector general 177
iqta 28
Iram gardens 34
Iranshahr 128
Iranzamin 128
Iraq 20, 24, 57, 80, 87, 177, 195, 202,
    204
irfan (gnosis) 69–70, 111, 236, 240
Irish question 245
Irivan 52, 78, 125, 245
irrigation 112, 113
Irzinjan 11, 21, 159
Irzirum 28, 165
Isa Khan Safavi 54, 74–5, 89, 184,
    186–87, 200–02
Isfahan xi, 2, 3, 6, 16, 19, 20, 22, 23, 27,
    28, 30, 32, 36, 44, 47, 51, 52, 54–5,
    58, 60, 62, 68, 70–2 75–6, 87, 91,
    94–5, 98, 103, 105, 107, 110, 116,
    119, 120–21, 124–25, 127, 130–33,
    139, 147, 153, 155, 157, 158, 159,
    165, 168, 172, 177, 178, 182–83,
    187, 191, 193, 194, 196, 201, 204,
    211, 219, 221, 232, 233–34, 237,
    238, 242, 244–46
Isfahan Diary 235
Isfahan's congregational mosque 161,
    181
ishikaqasi 200, 203
ishikaqasi of the divan 209
ishikaqasi of the haram 209
ishikaqasi of the Supreme Divan 209
ishikaqasibashi 81, 185–86, 200,
    203
ishikaqasibashi of the Supreme Divan
    233
Ismail I xi, 2–3, 9, 11, 13, 15–6, 22, 26,
    30–34, 36–37, 40, 43, 46, 51, 58, 61,
    62, 64, 72. 75, 81, 92, 97, 104,
    117–18, 120, 122–24, 129, 136, 150,
    153, 157, 163–64, 166–69, 170–4,
    177–78, 180, 182, 192, 197, 221, 241
Ismail II 29, 33, 39, 41, 43, 46, 47, 50,

Made in the USA
Las Vegas, NV
29 June 2022

50855081R00164